PETERSON'S

MASTER THE

GRE

13th Edition

PETERSON'S

A **nelnet.** COMPANY

PETERSON'S

A **nelnet** COMPANY

An ARCO Book

ARCO is a registered trademark of Peterson's, and is used herein under license by Peterson's.

About Peterson's, a Nelnet company

Peterson's (www.petersons.com) is a leading provider of education information and advice, with books and online resources focusing on education search, test preparation, and financial aid. Its Web site offers searchable databases and interactive tools for contacting educational institutions, online practice tests and instruction, and planning tools for securing financial aid. Peterson's serves 110 million education consumers annually.

For more information, contact Peterson's, 2000 Lenox Drive, Lawrenceville, NJ 08648;
800-338-3282; or find us on the World Wide Web at: www.petersons.com/about.

© 2006 Peterson's, a Nelnet company

Previous editions published as *Case Worker Exam* © 1980, 1985, 1989, 1995, 1997, 1998, 1999, 2000, 2001

Editor: Bernadette Webster; Production Editor: Teresina Jonkoski; Manufacturing Manager: Ivona Skibicki; Composition Manager: Michele Able

ISBN-13: 978-0-7689-2232-5
ISBN-10: 0-7689-2232-1

Printed in the United States of America

10 9 8 7 6 5 4 3 2   09 08 07

Thirteenth Edition

Contents

PART IV: FIVE PRACTICE TESTS

APPENDIX

Before You Begin

HOW THIS BOOK IS ORGANIZED

You want to pass this test. That's why you bought this book. Used correctly, this self-tutor will show you what to expect and provide you with the most effective review of the subjects you can expect to see on the actual exam. *ARCO Master the Case Worker Exam* will provide you with the necessary tools to make the most of the study time you have, including:

- **"Top 10 Ways to Raise Your Score"** gives you a preview of some of the test-taking strategies you'll learn in the book.

- **Part I** provides career information about case workers, eligibility specialists, and social investigators, along with information about the application and examination processes.

- **Part II** is a full-length Diagnostic Test, which is your first chance to work with samples of every question type. It can show you where your skills are strong and where they need some shoring up.

- **Part III** includes five full-length practice tests followed by detailed answer explanations.

- The **Glossary** contains a complete list of definitions you'll need to know during your career.

SPECIAL STUDY FEATURES

ARCO Master the Case Worker Exam is designed to be as user-friendly as it is complete. To this end, it includes several features to make your preparation much more efficient.

Overview

Each chapter begins with a bulleted overview listing the topics to be covered in the chapter. This will allow you to quickly target the areas in which you are most interested.

Summing It Up

Each chapter ends with a point-by-point summary that captures the most important points contained in the chapter. They are a convenient way to review key points.

As you work your way through the book, keep your eye on the margins to find bonus information and advice. Information can be found in the following forms:

Note

Notes highlight critical information about a career as a case worker, eligibility specialist, or social investigator, as well as the written exam.

Tip

Tips provide valuable advice for effectively handling the job-search process.

Alert!

Alerts do just what they say—alert you to common pitfalls or misconceptions.

YOU'RE WELL ON YOUR WAY TO SUCCESS

You have made the decision to pursue a career as a case worker. *ARCO Master the Case Worker Exam* will prepare you for the steps you'll need to take to achieve your goal—from understanding the nuances of the job to scoring high on the Case Worker Exam. Good luck!

Top 10 Ways to Raise Your Score

1. **Get to the test center early.** Make sure you give yourself plenty of extra time to get there, park your car, if necessary, and even grab a cup of coffee before the test.

2. **Listen to the test monitors and follow their instructions carefully.**

3. **Read every word of the instructions. Read every word of every question.**

4. **Mark your answers by completely darkening the answer space of your choice.**

5. **Mark only ONE answer for each question, even if you think that more than one answer is correct.** You must choose only one. If you mark more than one answer, the scoring machine will consider you wrong.

6. **If you change your mind, erase completely.** Leave no doubt as to which answer you mean.

7. **Check often to be sure that the question number matches the answer space, that you have not skipped a space by mistake.**

8. **Stay alert.** Be careful not to mark a wrong answer just because you were not concentrating.

9. **Do not panic.** If you cannot finish any part before time is up, do not worry. If you are accurate, you can do well even without finishing. It is even possible to earn a scaled score of 100 without entirely finishing an exam part if you are very accurate. At any rate, do not let your performance on any one part affect your performance on any other part.

10. **Check and recheck, time permitting.** If you finish any part before time is up, use the remaining time to check that each question is answered in the right space and that there is only one answer for each question. Return to the difficult questions and rethink them.

PART I

ALL ABOUT A CAREER AS A CASE WORKER

CHAPTER 1   Getting Started

Getting Started

OVERVIEW

- A career as a case worker
- The exam
- Test–taking techniques
- Summing it up

A CAREER AS A CASE WORKER

The goals of case workers, eligibility specialists, and social investigators are based on the central theme of helping individuals solve problems (financial or other) and improving their functioning as it relates to society. Case workers may focus on individual work, community organization, family centered programs, or case management. They may be employed in agencies, hospitals, or other social welfare businesses.

Career Information Resources

Finding a job is very often a matter of luck. However, we'd like to take some of the luck out of it and make it more directive. Below are a variety of sources you can contact in your search for employment.

The Private Sector

Most jobs in the private sector can be found in two ways: employment agencies or newspaper classified advertisements. Wherever you live, there is certainly a local employment agency. Call to make an appointment and bring your resume. Keep in mind that this will be the first interview that you will have in the line for employment, so you should dress appropriately, be informed about the types of job in which you are interested, and know where you'd like to work. Then review the classified section of the newspaper from the town or city in which you'd like to work. Usually, you will find classified ads in the "Health Care Professionals" section. In many cases, you will be directed toward an employment agency to apply for a job. In others, you may be asked to call the agency, company, or hospital directly; write a letter; or send you resume. Remember that just like an interview, your telephone call, letter, and/or resume is the first impression someone has of you.

You might also contact the hospitals in your area, or, if you don't mind relocating, you can choose almost any place in the country that might use someone with your experience as a case worker.

USEFUL WEB SITES

- **Hospital Jobs USA (www.hospitaljobsusa.com/list.html):** One of the better Web sites for hospital employment, this site has a list of fifty individual state sites with jobs listed in all categories of private hospital employment.

- **Case Management Jobs (www.casemanagementjobs.com):** On this site, you can post your resume, look for specific jobs with specific companies or agencies, and get information about salaries.

- **America's Job Bank (www.jobsearch.org):** This site allows you to post your resume online, as well as search for jobs on a state-by-date basis.

Federal Jobs

The Department of Veterans Affairs hires 250 to 300 social workers every year as well as case workers, eligibility specialists, and investigators. Jobs are available in both inpatient facilities (172 nationwide) and outpatient clinics. To obtain application forms, log on to the Department of Veterans Affairs Web site at www.va.gov/jobs.

The Office of Personnel Management (OPM) is another excellent resource. It has a list of job openings that is updated daily. In addition, it also publishes the Federal Exam Announcement every quarter. Although OPM is not responsible for hiring for jobs, it does provide access to the hiring agencies that have specific details about each available job. OPM can be contacted via telephone at (202) 606-1800.

The Office of Personnel Management can also be found on the Web at www.opm.gov. Here you will find a complete application for federal employment along with instructions on how to fill it out. At this site, you can find explanations of federal job categories and specific job descriptions. You can then search geographically and alphabetically to find out which jobs have current openings and exactly where the openings are located. The listings, in turn, refer you to full vacancy announcements, including qualifications, requirements, and application procedures and deadlines. With adequate equipment, you can download the announcement, or you can take notes from the information on your screen. Likewise, you can download application forms or even apply electronically using your computer. You can also follow instructions for getting the proper forms by telephone or mail.

Another excellent source is the Federal Jobs Digest, a biweekly newspaper that lists thousands of government jobs, both in the United States and in foreign countries. The Digest also has a Web site that features thousands of job listings. You can visit the Web site at www.jobsfed.com or contact the Federal Jobs Digest by e-mail at webmaster@jobsfed.com or by telephone at 610-965-5825.

TIP

You can try other general job search sites, such as www.monster.com, www.hotjobs.com, and www.careerbuilder.com.

Finally, after you have exhausted the resources previously listed, consider looking under the heading "U.S. Government" in the blue pages of your telephone directory for a listing for the Office of Personnel Management or Federal Job Information Center. A telephone call to this number may give you automated information pertinent to your own area or may direct you to a location at which you can pick up printed materials or conduct a search on a computer touch screen.

USEFUL WEB SITES

- **Career City (www.careercity.com):** A guide to federal and local government employment.

- **Employment Index (www.employmentindex.com/govjob.html):** Links to Web sites of government agencies throughout the United States. Site lists both public- and private-sector jobs.

- **Federal Job Search (www.federaljobsearch.com):** Listings for 40,000 U.S. jobs in the United States

- **FedWorld (www.fedworld.gov):** Provides searchable abstracts of federal government jobs.

- **Government and Law Enforcement Jobs (http://jobsearch.tqn.com/msubgov.htm):** An annotated list of Web sites that list jobs with federal, state, and local governments, and law enforcement agencies.

- **HRS Federal Job Search (www.hrsjobs.com):** A subscription job search and e-mail delivery service.

- **The Internet Job Source (www.statejobs.com):** The federal jobs section of this site links users to job listings at a variety of federal agencies and also to online newspapers listing federal job opportunities.

- **Public Services Employees Network (www.pse-net.com):** A guide to government employment, including job listings.

- *USAJOBS* **(www.usajobs.opm.gov):** The official site for federal employment listings from the U.S. Office of Personnel Management.

APPLICATIONS AND OTHER FORMS

- **Electronic forms (www.opm.gov/forms):** All forms and applications relating to federal employment from the Office of Personnel Management.

- **The Federal Job Search and Application Form (www.usajobs.opm.gov/forms):** A description of the federal job search as a three-step process, including three downloadable versions of the OF-612 application.

State Employment

Almost every state has its own Web site. The following is a list of the latest URLs for the state sites. Be aware, however, that this list may change from time to time.

Alabama: www.state.al.us

Alaska: www.state.ak.us

Arizona: http://az.gov/webapp/portal

Arkansas: www.state.ar.us

California: www.state.ca.us

Colorado: www.colorado.gov

Connecticut: www.ct.gov

Delaware: www.delaware.gov

District of Columbia: www.dchomepage.net

Florida: www.myflorida.com

Georgia: www.georgia.gov

Hawaii: www.hawaii.gov/portal

Idaho: www.state.id.us

Illinois: www.illinois.gov

Indiana: www.state.in.us

Iowa: www.state.ia.us

Kansas: www.state.ks.us

Kentucky: http://kentucky.gov

Louisiana: www.louisiana.gov/wps/portal

Maine: www.state.me.us/

Maryland: www.maryland.gov

Massachusetts: www.mass.gov

Michigan: www.michigan.gov

Minnesota: www.state.mn.us

Mississippi: www.state.ms.us/index.jsp

Missouri: www.state.mo.us

Montana: www.mt.gov

Nebraska: www.nebraska.gov/index.phtml

Nevada: www.nv.gov

New Hampshire: www.state.nh.us

New Jersey: www.state.nj.us

New Mexico: www.state.nm.us

New York: www.state.ny.us

North Carolina: www.state.nc.us

North Dakota: www.nd.gov

Ohio: http://ohio.gov

Oklahoma: www.state.ok.us

Oregon: www.oregon.gov

Pennsylvania: www.state.pa.us

Rhode Island: www.state.ri.us

South Carolina: www.myscgov.com

South Dakota: www.state.sd.us

Tennessee: www.state.tn.us

Texas: www.state.tx.us

Utah: www.utah.gov

Vermont: http://vermont.gov

Virginia: www.virginia.gov/cmsportal

Washington: http://access.wa.gov

West Virginia: www.wv.gov

Wisconsin: www.wisconsin.gov

Wyoming: http://wyoming.gov

Local Employment

In many instances, city or county employment information can be found on your state's Web site. However, if you live in a large city, it is likely that the city has its own site. Use some of the popular search vehicles such as yahoo.com, ask.com, or google.com, to locate other job-related sites. Use search terms such as "health care," "case worker jobs," "employment," "labor," and "business." You might type in "Where can I find a job as a case worker in Washington, D.C.?" You may get more "hits" if you ask about working as a "social worker" since it's a more generic term. Within the listings that are returned to you, you'll most likely find several in the subcategory of case worker. You also might enter into the search box something like "case worker+Miami." The plus sign (+) indicates that you want both Miami and case worker to appear in the same suggested sites. You should also investigate to see if there is a local (large) city civil service publication that lists upcoming job announcements. You will also find information about state and federal jobs in the newspaper.

How to Land a Job as a Case Worker

Now that you know where to look for a job, you need to understand the procedure. The procedure that you must follow to get a government job varies little from job to job and from one level of government to another. There are variations in details, of course, but certain steps are common to all.

NOTE

Once you have found a Notice of Examination (it may be called an announcement), read it very carefully. If you can, get a copy for yourself. If not, then take the time to write notes. Make sure you have written down all of the details.

The Notice of Examination or Announcement

The Notice of Examination will give a brief job description. It will tell the title of the job and describe some of the job duties and responsibilities. On the basis of the job description, you will decide whether or not you want to apply for this job. If the job appeals to you, you must concentrate on the following.

- **Education and experience requirements**. If you cannot meet these requirements, do not bother to apply. Government service can be very competitive. The government has more than enough applicants from which to choose. It will not waive its requirements for you.

- **Age requirements.** Discrimination on the basis of age is illegal, but a number of jobs demand so much sustained physical effort that they require retirement at an early age. For these positions, there is an entry age limit. If you are already beyond that age, do not apply. If you are still too young, inquire about the time lag until hiring. It may be that you will reach the minimum age by the time the position is to be filled.

- **Citizenship requirements.** Many jobs are open to all people who are eligible to work in the United States, but all law enforcement jobs and most federal jobs are limited to U.S. citizens. If you are well along the way toward citizenship and expect to be naturalized soon, inquire as to your exact status with respect to the job.

- **Residency requirements.** If there is a residency requirement, you must live within the prescribed limits or be willing to move. If you are not willing to live in the area, do not waste time applying.

- **Required forms.** The announcement of the position for which you are applying will specify the form of application requested. For most federal jobs, you may submit either the Optional Application for Federal Employment (OF 612) or a resume that fulfills the requirements set forth in the pamphlet "Applying for a Federal Job" (OF 510). For other than federal jobs, the Notice of Examination may tell you where you must go or write to to get the necessary form or forms. Be sure you secure them all. The application might be a simple form asking nothing more than name, address, citizenship, and social security number, or it may be a complex Experience Paper. An Experience Paper, as its title implies, asks a great deal about education, job training, job experience, and life experience. Typically, the Experience Paper permits no identification by name, sex, or race; the only identifying mark is your social security number. The purpose of this procedure is to avoid permitting bias of any sort to enter into the weighting of responses. The Experience Paper generally follows a short form of application that does include a name. When the rating process is completed, the forms are coordinated by means of the social security number.

- **Filing date, place, and fee.** There is great variation in this area. For some positions, you can file your application at any time. Others have a first day and last day for filing. If you file too early or too late, your application will not be considered. Sometimes, it is sufficient to have your application postmarked by the last day for filing. More often, your application must be received by the last date. If you are mailing your application, allow five full business days for it to get there on time. Place of filing will be stated right on the notice. Most applications may be filed by mail, but occasionally in-person filing is specified. Make sure you follow all directions. Federal and postal positions require no filing fee. Most other government jobs do charge a fee for processing your application. The fee is not always the same. Be sure to check this out. If the notice specifies "money order only," plan to purchase a money order. If you send or present a personal check, your application will be rejected without consideration. Of course, you should never mail cash; but if the announcement specifies "money order only," you cannot submit cash, even in person.

- **How to qualify.** This portion of the notice will tell you the basis on which the candidate will be chosen. Some positions only weigh education and experience factors. This type of examination is called an "unassembled exam," because you do not have to go to one place to take the exam; instead, whether you are qualified or not is based upon your responses on the application and supplementary forms. Obviously, these must be complete for you to get full credit for all you have learned and accomplished. The notice may tell you of a qualifying exam—an exam that you must pass in addition to scoring high on an unassembled, written, or performance test. In addition, the notice may tell you of a written, performance, or combined competitive exam. The competitive exam may be described in very general terms or may be described in detail. It is even possible that a few sample questions will be attached. If the date of the exam has been set, that date will appear on the notice. Write it down.

When you have the application forms in hand, photocopy them. Fill out the photocopies first. This way you can correct mistakes or make changes before transferring the information to the original application. Work at fitting what you have to say into the space allowed. Do not exaggerate, but be sure to give yourself credit for responsibilities that you took on, for cost-saving ideas that you gave your prior employer, or for any accomplishments. Be clear and thorough in communicating what you have learned and what you can do.

When you are satisfied with your draft, copy the application onto the original form(s). Be sure to include any backup material that is requested; by the same token, do not send more "evidence" than is truly needed to support your claims of qualification. Your application must be complete according to the requirements of the announcement, but should not be overwhelming. You want to command hiring attention by exactly conforming to requirements. Check over all forms for neatness and completeness. Sign wherever indicated. Attach the fee, if required. Then mail or personally file the application on time.

When the civil service commission or personnel office to which you submitted your application receives it, the office will date, stamp, log, and open your file. The office may acknowledge receipt with more forms, with sample exam questions, or with a simple receipt slip. You may not hear anything from the office for months.

Eventually, you will receive a testing date or an interview appointment. Write these on your calendar so that you don't let the dates slip by. If you receive an admission ticket for an exam, be sure to put it in a safe place, but keep it in sight so that you will not forget to take it with you to the exam. Begin to study and prepare right away, if you have not already done so.

If you are called for an exam, arrive promptly and dress appropriately. Neatness is always appropriate; however, you do not need to "dress up" for a performance exam or a written exam. If you will do manual work for your performance exam, wear clean work clothes. For a written exam, neat, casual clothing is fine.

THE INTERVIEW

If there is no exam and you are called directly to an interview, what you wear is more important. Take special care to look businesslike and professional. A neat dress, slacks and blouse, or skirted suit is fine for women; men should wear a suit or slacks, a jacket, shirt, and tie.

If you are called for an interview, you are most likely under serious consideration. There may still be competition for the job—someone else may be more suited than you—but you are qualified, and your skills and background have appealed to someone in the hiring office. The interview may be aimed at getting information about the following.

- **Your knowledge.** The interviewer wants to know what you know about the area in which you will work. You may also be asked questions probing your knowledge of the agency for which you are interviewing. Do you care enough to have educated yourself about the functions and role of the agency?

- **Your judgment.** You may be faced with hypothetical situations—job-related or interpersonal—and be asked questions like "What would you do if . . . ." Think carefully before answering. Be decisive and diplomatic. There are no "right answers." The interviewer is aware that you are being put on the spot. How well you can handle this type of question is an indication of your flexibility and maturity.

- **Your personality.** You will have to be trained and supervised. You will have to work with others. What is your attitude? How will you fit in? The interviewer will make judgments in these areas on the basis of general conversation with you and from your responses to specific lines of questioning. Be pleasant, polite, and open with your answers, but do not volunteer a great deal of extra information. Stick to the subjects introduced by the interviewer. Answer fully, but resist the temptation to ramble on.

- **Your attitude toward work conditions.** These are practical concerns. If the job will require frequent travel for extended periods, how do you feel about it? What is your family's attitude? If you will be very unhappy about the travel, you may leave the job and your training will have been a waste of the taxpayers' money. The interviewer also wants to know how you will react to overtime or irregular shifts.

MEDICAL EXAMINATION

A medical exam is self-explanatory. Passing or failing this exam does not necessarily have any bearing upon your passing or failing other exams. However, if there are eyesight and/or hearing requirements for the specific position, these must be checked against agency standards. If the job requires standing, lifting, or running, the applicant must be medically able to withstand the rigors. Because many case workers are employed in a hospital setting, it's important to be in excellent health, especially since at times a case worker may be exposed to contagious illnesses. Furthermore, since all government employers and most hospitals provide some sort of health coverage, there must be assurance of the general health of the employee or at least full awareness of current or potential problems. Drug testing may be included, depending upon the hospital or agency. Drug testing is legal if applied routinely and equally to all applicants and if notice of it is given beforehand.

PHYSICAL EXAMINATION

Physical performance testing is limited to applicants for physically demanding jobs. Police officers, firefighters, and correction officers, for example, must be able to run, climb, and carry, often under stress of personal danger as well as under the pressures of the immediate situation; normally, a case worker's responsibilities are less physically stressful. However, hospitals may require a physical examination if they believe that it's an important part of performing your duty as a case worker. Usually, the physical performance test is a qualifying test—either you can do it or you can't.

PSYCHOLOGICAL INTERVIEW

Finally, there may be a psychological interview. It is not a prerequisite for passing the exams, but instead may be used to determine your suitability for a specific job. This interview differs from the general information interview or the final hiring and placement interview in that it tries to assess your behavior under stress.

Reading all the applications and weeding out the unqualified ones takes time. Weighing education and experience factors, administering and scoring exams, conducting interviews, medical exams, and physical performance tests, and verifying references also take time. Finally, the vacancies must be available, and the hiring agency must have the funds to fill the vacancies.

The examination and job announcements on the following pages will give you a good idea of what will be required of you on the job, whether you are a case worker, a social investigator, or an eligibility specialist. Also included is information for social workers, social worker program specialists, and psychiatric social workers to give you a more complete overview of the field.

NOTE

Like the medical examination, passing or failing this test may have little bearing upon passing the exams—only your suitability for a specific job.

ALERT!

Don't be surprised if the hiring process takes several weeks, if not months.

Sample City Notices of Examination

Notice of Examination: Case Worker

The City of New York is an Equal Opportunity Employer.

Test Date

Candidates are notified by mail when to report for the written test.

List Establishment

Eligible lists will be established in groups periodically as needed. Each list will be terminated one year from the date it is established unless extended by the City Personnel Director.

Salary and Vacancies

The appointment rate is per annum. Vacancies exist in the Human Resources Administration/Department of Social Services and the Department of Juvenile Justice.

Minimum Requirements

The minimum requirements must be met by the date of appointment.

A baccalaureate degree from an accredited college is required.

Candidates who were educated in countries other than the United States must file form DP-404 for evaluation of education outside the U.S. with their experience paper. Education outside the U.S. is evaluated by the Department of Personnel to determine its comparability to education received in domestic-accredited institutions.

Section 424a of the New York Social Services Law requires an authorized agency to inquire whether a candidate for employment with child-caring responsibilities is or has been the subject of a child abuse and maltreatment report. The agency has the discretion to assign a candidate who has been the subject of a child abuse and maltreatment report to a position with no child-caring responsibilities.

At the time of interview for appointment, all candidates for positions in Special Services for Children and Crisis Intervention Services will be required to complete a satisfactory writing sample in English.

Duties and Responsibilities

Under supervision, with considerable latitude for independent action individually or as a team member, the case worker identifies, develops, and implements social service plans for disadvantaged clients, including recipients of public and medical assistance and child welfare services, adults/children receiving or needing institutional care, and homeless adults/families. The case worker may also determine eligibility for these services, may perform counseling and investigative activities, and performs related work.

Special Working Conditions

Eligible candidates appointed to this position may be required to work shifts, including nights, Saturdays, Sundays, and holidays.

Tests

Written, weight 100, 70 percent required. The written test is multiple choice and may include questions on techniques of gathering, organizing, and assessing information; interpretation of agency rules, regulations, and procedures; interpretation of federal, state, and city social service laws and guidelines; preparation of narrative reports, letters, and case records; forms completion; record keeping; basic arithmetic; and other related areas.

Accommodations are available for certified disabled applicants. Applications for accommodations must be submitted as early as possible and in no event later than fifteen working days before the test or part of a test for which accommodation is requested. Consult the General Examination Regulations for further requirements.

The Department of Personnel makes provisions for candidates who claim an inability to participate in an examination when originally scheduled because of the candidates' religious beliefs. Such candidates should consult the City Personnel Director's Rule 4.4.6 for applicable procedures in requesting a special examination.

Selective Certification

The eligible list resulting from this examination may be selectively certified to fill vacancies in the title of Case Worker that require six months of case work experience in child welfare, shelter care for the homeless, or protective services for adults. This requirement must be met by the last date for filing.

Candidates who wish to be selectively certified in any or all of the above fields must complete Experience Paper Form A, including all of the required information in the boxes provided and describing their duties clearly.

Candidates who do not wish to be considered for selective certification should complete the education section of Experience Paper Form A only.

Qualifying Language Oral Test for Selective Certification

The eligible list resulting from this examination may be selectively certified to fill case worker vacancies that require a working knowledge of both English and another language. Those who pass the written test and are placed on the eligible list may be permitted to take a qualifying language oral test to determine ability to speak and understand other languages as needed. Candidates wishing to take such a qualifying test must so indicate at the time of the written test the language for which they wish to be tested. Only those who pass the qualifying oral test are eligible for such selective certification.

Notice of Examination: Eligibility Specialist

The City of New York is an Equal Opportunity Employer.

In conjunction with the holding of this examination, a promotion examination will be held. The names appearing on the promotion list receive prior consideration in filling vacancies. However, it is expected that there are sufficient vacancies so that the open competitive list will be used as well.

The Department of Personnel makes provisions for candidates claiming inability to participate in an examination when originally scheduled because of the candidate's religious beliefs.

Selective Certification

The eligible list resulting from this examination may be selectively certified to fill vacancies in the title of Eligibility Specialist that require a working knowledge of both English and another language.

Salary and Vacancies

The appointment rate for this position is ____ per annum. There are three assignment levels for this position: for Level I, the appointment rate is ____; for Level II, ____; and for Level III, ____. After the original appointment, appointees may be assigned to any of these levels as the needs of the service require. Vacancies exist in the Human Resources Administration/Department of Social Services.

Promotion Opportunities

Employees in the title of Eligibility Specialist are accorded promotion opportunities, when eligible, to the title of Principal Administrative Associate.

Minimum Requirements

1. An associate degree from an accredited college or completion of two years of study (60 credits) at an accredited college; or

2. A four-year high school diploma or its equivalent, and two years of full-time experience in the following areas: interviewing for the determination of eligibility for public assistance or unemployment, health, or other insurance benefits; book-keeping; preparation of statistical reports; validation of vouchers, warrants, invoices; or

3. Education and/or experience equivalent to 1 or 2 above. However, all candidates must have a high school diploma or its equivalent.

Candidates who were educated in countries other than the United States must file form DP-404. Education outside of the U.S. is evaluated by the Department of Personnel to determine comparability to education received in domestic accredited educational institutions.

The Experience Paper must be filled out completely and in detail and filed with your application.

At the time of appointment and at the time of investigation, candidates must present all the official documents and proof required to qualify, as stated in the Notice of Examination. Failure to present required documents, including proof of education and experience requirements, will result in disqualification for appointment.

The minimum requirements must be met by the last date for the receipt of applications.

Applicants may be summoned for the written test prior to the determination of whether they meet the minimum requirements.

Residency Requirements

A person who enters city service on or after September 1, 2001, shall be a resident of the city on the date that he or she enters city service or shall establish city residence within 90 days after such date, and shall thereafter maintain city residence as a condition of employment. Failure to establish or maintain city residence as required shall constitute a forfeiture of employment. This requirement does not apply to some city agencies.

Duties and Responsibilities

This position encompasses the performance of tasks, under supervision, with some latitude for independent action or decision. This work is performed under well-defined procedures of the Human Resources Administration/Department of Social Services in Income Maintenance, Food Stamps, Medical Assistance, and Crisis Intervention Services; determining and verifying initial and continuing eligibility for Public Assistance, Medicaid, and Food Stamps through the use of agency procedures, automated systems, and/or based on face-to-face client interviews. There are three assignment levels within this class of positions. All personnel perform related work.

There is a two- to four-week training program prior to assignment. Candidates who do not successfully complete this training may be terminated from employment with the Human Resources Administration/Department of Social Services.

Tests

Written weight 100, 70 percent required. The written test is multiple choice and may include questions on reading comprehension, including the interpretation and application of appropriate rules and regulations; the ability to obtain pertinent data from documents, printouts, files, and coding; the ability to communicate effectively both orally and in writing with clients and others; the knowledge and application of interviewing techniques in face-to-face client contact or by telephone; the ability to follow instructions and to complete forms accurately; the knowledge of clerical functions, general office procedures, and filing systems; the ability to perform basic mathematical computations; and the ability to prepare statistical and activity reports, as required.

There is a two- to four-week training program prior to assignment. Candidates who do not successfully complete this training may be terminated from employment with the Human Resources Administration/Department of Social Services.

Qualifying Language Oral Test for Selective Certification

The competitive written test is in English. Those who pass the written test and who meet the minimum requirements and are placed on the eligible list may be permitted to take a qualifying language oral test to determine ability to speak and understand another language. Candidates wishing to take this qualifying test must so indicate at the time the written test is given. Candidates who do not so indicate at the time the written test is given are not permitted to take the qualifying language oral test. Only those who pass this qualifying test are eligible for selective certification to fill vacancies that require a working knowledge of both English and another language. Eligible candidates will be called for the qualifying language oral test in groups as the needs of the service require.

Sample State Announcement

Social Worker I

Social Worker II

Psychiatric Social Worker I

Psychiatric Social Worker II

As a Social Worker I, you would perform a wide variety of social services depending upon the facility you join and the specific unit and/or department in which you work. For example, you may be working in an inpatient or outpatient setting, or in a Social Services or Community Services Department.

In whichever setting you work, your tasks would be likely to include a case work load, therapy work (individual and/or group), and work with community resources and services. In addition, you would most likely be working as a member of an intradisciplinary or interdisciplinary team helping to make referrals and organize and participate in various interdisciplinary activities as a part of a team.

As a Social Worker II, your tasks, in principle, would be similar to those of the Social Worker I. The difference lies in the degree of development displayed. As a Social Worker II, you would be expected to handle complex work assignments with less supervision and with an expertise honed by two years of experience. At times, a part of the job may be creating, organizing, and/or supervising special projects and programs.

As a Psychiatric Social Worker I, you would perform a wide variety of social services depending upon the facility that you join and the specific unit and/or department in which you work. For example, you may be working in an inpatient or outpatient setting, or in a Social Services or Community Services Department.

In whichever setting you work, your tasks would be likely to include a case work load, therapy work (individual and/or group), and work with community resources and services. You would most likely be working as a member of an intradisciplinary or interdisciplinary team helping to make referrals and helping to organize and participate in various interdisciplinary activities as a part of a team.

As a Psychiatric Social Worker II, your tasks, in principle, would be similar to those of the Psychiatric Social Worker I. The difference lies in the degree of development displayed. As a Psychiatric Social Worker II, you would be expected to handle complex work assignments with less supervision and with an expertise honed by two years of experience. At times, a part of the job may be creating, organizing, and/or supervising special projects and programs.

Minimum Qualifications

On or before the date of filing your application, you must have a master's degree in social work from a regionally accredited college or university, or one recognized by the State Education Department as following acceptable educational practices.

Applicants for Social Worker II must have, in addition, two years of social work experience, one year of which must be professionally supervised post-master's degree experience.

If eligible, you may compete in both Social Worker I and Social Worker II examinations by filing one application, listing both examination numbers and titles.

If you are an applicant for Psychiatric Social Worker II, you must have, in addition, two years of social work experience. One year of this experience must be professionally supervised post-master's degree experience, and one year must be in the field of mental health.

If eligible, you may compete in both Psychiatric Social Worker I and Psychiatric Social Worker II examinations by filing one application, listing both examination numbers and titles.

Selection

There are no written or oral tests for these positions. The examinations consist of an evaluation of your training and experience in relation to the duties and requirements of the position(s). Final scores are based on the ratings given in this evaluation.

You are urged to give complete and accurate information on your application. Vagueness and omissions will not be decided in your favor. For example, include a full description of duties and the percentages of time spent working on each aspect of the job and indicate the specific setting(s) in which you have worked, whether you have engaged in team work, whether you have worked with behavior modification and/or token economy programs, and whether you have experience with community resources and agencies. Describe your continuing education, such as graduate courses taken beyond the master's degree; attendance at seminars; conferences and workshops; and professional papers written.

Some of these positions require the ability to understand and speak a second language fluently. Positions are so designated because of the nature of the client group served. Fluency must be demonstrated prior to appointment.

Although promotion examinations are also being announced for Social Worker II and Psychiatric Social Worker II, it is expected that appointments will also be made as a result of these open-competitive examinations. Candidates eligible for the promotion examinations are not admitted to the open-competitive examinations.

Sample Federal Government Announcements

Announcements like this one are used to fill all professional Social Worker positions nationwide at grades GS-9 through GS-12. Government social workers work in a kaleidoscopic range of settings: from remote Native American reservations to crowded inner-city facilities in 1-person offices to involvement with a team of medical specialists. Of more than 2,400 social workers and social work program specialists who work in the federal government, only 10 percent work in Washington, D.C. Of those who work outside the capital area, 85 percent work in Veterans Administration hospitals, outpatient clinics, and special settings—such as mental hygiene clinics, day treatment centers, and restoration centers—and with veterans in community care and outreach programs. Other major employers include the Department of Health and Human Services, Department of Justice (Bureau of Prisons), Department of the Interior (Bureau of Indian Affairs), and the Army. In Washington, D.C., the government of the District of Columbia is also a major employer.

Social Worker—Veterans Administration

Note: Most VA social workers are originally hired at GS-9 and GS-11.

Education

Completion of all requirements for a master's degree in social work that includes field practice assignments from a school of social work accredited by the Council of Social Work Education.

Training and Experience

Experience gained prior to the completion of all requirements for the master's degree does not meet the criteria for qualifying.

GS-9: No additional experience or training is required.

GS-11: In addition to the basic education requirements, you must have a minimum of one year of professional social work experience, under qualified social work supervision, which demonstrates the potential to perform advanced assignments independently. To qualify, the experience must have been obtained in the social work program of a hospital, clinic, or other voluntary or public social or health agency.

GS-12: In addition to the GS-11 requirements, you must have a minimum of one additional year of professional social work experience, which demonstrates broad knowledge of social work and superior skill and judgment in professional practice. For research and education positions, this additional year must be in social work education (class or field instruction) or social work research, as appropriate.

For all positions except social work research, one year of the total qualifying experience must have been in professional social work in a clinical setting. A clinical setting is a medical or psychiatric hospital or clinic, a residential treatment center, or any other type of facility where social work is involved in collaborative treatment and is identified with the medical profession.

For social work research positions, applicants must have knowledge of research methods and have demonstrated potential or observed skill in planning, developing, and carrying through studies of social work practice or processes.

For positions with social work educational responsibilities, the required experience must have included planning or conducting a staff development program for graduate social workers or extensive field instruction of social work students or teaching in an accredited school of social work.

Substitution of Additional Education

For specialized staff or research positions at GS-12, you may substitute successful completion of the advanced curriculum beyond a master's degree in an accredited school of social work on a year-for-year basis in your specialization for a maximum credit of two years.

SOCIAL WORKER

SOCIAL WORK PROGRAM SPECIALIST

For agencies other than the Veterans Administration.

Education

Successful completion of all requirements for a master's degree in social work from a school of social work accredited by the Council on Social Work Education.

Training and Experience

Experience gained before completion of all requirements for the master's degree does not meet the criteria for qualifying.

GS-9: No additional experience is required if your education has included field practice assignments in professional social work. Otherwise, one year of professional social work experience under professional supervision is required.

GS-11: In addition to meeting the requirements for GS-9, you must have a minimum of one year of professional social work experience under professional supervision, which demonstrates the ability to perform advanced assignments independently.

GS-12: In addition to meeting the requirements for GS-11, you must have a minimum of one additional year of professional social work experience, which demonstrates a broad knowledge of social work and superior skills and professional judgment.

For Social Work Program Specialist positions, your experience must have included one—or in some cases a combination of two or more—functions, such as program planning, program development, program evaluation, consultation, and cooperative community relationships in an agency providing social work service to families, children, or adults; or supervisory, administrative, or consultative work in a welfare or health agency (public or voluntary) with an organized social work program. In this experience, you must have demonstrated the ability to analyze, evaluate, and advise on overall aspects of social work programs, plans, and operations and to work effectively with representatives of other agencies and groups in developing program standards and requirements.

For positions with staff development responsibilities, the required experience must have included experience in planning or conducting social work education or staff development programs in a health or welfare agency, or teaching in an accredited school of social work.

How You Are Rated?

There is no written test. You are rated on your professional experience, education, and training as described in your application, along with any additional information that may be obtained. If you meet the qualifications, your name is placed on a list with names of other qualified applicants and may be referred to federal agencies as vacancies occur. For specialized jobs, only names of applicants whose qualifications meet the special needs of the job are referred.

Describe Your Experience Fully

Be sure to provide sufficient information on your background and accomplishments so that you can be evaluated fairly. Formal job titles, official position descriptions, and elaborate terminology describing positions held are not accepted as establishing the quality of value of your experience. Describe your duties and responsibilities in your own words.

For field practice assignments during your graduate study, please provide the dates and a brief statement of your duties and responsibilities. If the assignments involved working with drug addicts and/or alcoholics, indicate this as well.

Part-Time or Unpaid Experience

Pertinent part-time or unpaid experience is evaluated on the same basis as paid experience. If you have experience that is relevant to the kind of job you are applying for, you should describe it on your application in detail, showing the actual number of hours per week in the activity.

Graduate Students

Applications are accepted from candidates for graduate social work degrees who expect to complete all requirements for the degree, including acceptance of the thesis, within nine months of the date of filing. Applications should be accompanied by a list of courses, including a full description of field practice assignments and semester hours, which will be completed within the nine-month period.

If you qualify on the basis of an anticipated degree, you may not start work until all educational requirements have been successfully completed.

Eligibility

If you are qualified, you are eligible for job consideration for twelve months from the date that appears on your notice of rating. If you want to extend your eligibility, you must submit an updated application after ten but no more than twelve months from that date.

How to Apply

Send the following to the address indicated on the vacancy announcement:

- a completed Personal Qualifications Statement, SF 171, clearly indicating the locations where you are available to work; or
- Optional Application for Federal Employment, OF 612; or
- a resume fulfilling the requirements set forth in the pamphlet, Applying for a Federal Job, OF 510, which you may order by calling (912) 757-3000; and
- supporting documents as requested by the vacancy announcement

Obtain vacancy announcements, application forms, and additional information on government employment by visiting www.usajobs.opm.gov on the Web. You may also find information by calling the OPM Federal Job Information Center listed in the blue (government) pages of your local phone directory.

THE EXAM

The written exam is a key component of the case worker screening process. Following is a breakdown of the topics you can expect to encounter when taking the case worker exam.

Social Work Vocabulary

These questions are designed to test your knowledge of words that may be important to you in your daily work with clients, preparation of reports, and discussions of cases with your colleagues. This section of the exam includes concept questions, vocabulary questions, and word-definition problems.

Reading Interpretation

There is rarely an instance in any profession, in any job, at any level, where you are not required to read and interpret some type of information. Reading interpretation questions present you with extended passages and ask that you read them, understand them, and then find the best possible answer based ONLY on the material that you have just read. Unlike other types of questions, you cannot bring in other outside information to answer the questions. The questions cover a wide range of topics relevant to any of the occupations covered in this book.

Eligibility for Public Assistance and Housing

One of the more important aspects of client contact is determining one's eligibility for assistance. Eligibility for public assistance and housing questions are designed to test your knowledge about making these determinations, including reporting, interviewing, and making client visits.

Housing and Social Welfare

These question types deal with low-income housing that often affects the lives of the people that will be seen by case workers. You will be required to have some understanding of the nature of clients' living conditions in order to determine courses of treatment for them or to help determine eligibility for assistance from you and your agency.

Judgment

Whether you are determining your client's course of treatment, assessing his or her eligibility for assistance, or planning the scope of your intervention, the actions you take relies on your judgment. The decisions you make may be based on specific guidelines or your professional instinct. The following questions cover a range of situations and ask you to determine the appropriate courses of action.

Public Health

Even if you don't plan to work in a hospital or other medical setting, you should understand the concepts of medical social work. Although specific medical treatment is performed by physicians or nurses, you may be responsible for directing the client so that he or she receives appropriate attention, both before and after treatment. Public health questions are designed to test your knowledge of health issues that may affect your clients.

Procedures and Records

There is no more important aspect in the field of social work than procedures and records. Procedures help guide professionals through all aspects of developing a relationship with a client, from original intake procedures to tracking progress during the case worker's interaction with the client. Further, proper record keeping is the key to assuring continuity with your client, for you and your staff, and others within your agency. In addition to interoffice requirements, there are usually also a variety of governmental requirements, and thus, it's important to follow accurate procedures and record keeping.

Interpretation of Social Work Problems

Interpretation of social work questions cover a wide range of topics, normally the types of information for which, in a real-life situation, you would be responsible for understanding. These questions require a bit of thinking, logic, and the ability to interpret information given and select the best possible answer.

Case Work Techniques

What is the ultimate effect of good case work? How do you determine what type of assistance a client will need? What happens if illness strikes a family member on welfare? These questions cover some of the basic aspects of being an effective case worker. Essentially, you are being asked to determine what you know about doing case work.

Social Work with Children

Whether you are employed in a hospital facility or a private agency, you are likely to encounter situations that require you to deal with children or handle some situation that will have an effect on the children of your client. These questions test your knowledge of dealing with some of these situations in a variety of settings.

General Review

From health to economics, general review questions test your knowledge of a wide range of material. Your role as a case worker, eligibility specialist, or social investigator requires you to have a very broad understanding of many areas that affect the individuals with whom you will be working. You will deal with the sick and infirm. You will encounter welfare clients and "deadbeats." You will counsel clients on all areas of their lives.

TEST-TAKING TECHNIQUES

Multiple-Choice Questions

Almost all of the tests given on civil service exams are in a multiple-choice format. This means that you have four or five answer choices from which to select the correct answer. It's not something that should be overwhelming. There is a basic technique to answering these types of questions. Once you've understood this technique, it will make your test-taking far less stressful.

First, there should only be one correct answer. Since these tests have been given time and again, and the test-developers have a sense of which questions work and which questions don't work, it is rare that your choices will be ambiguous. They may be complex and somewhat confusing, but there will still be only one right answer.

The first step is to look at the question, without looking at the answer choices. Now select the correct answer. That may sound somewhat simplistic, but it's usually the case that your first choice is the correct one. If you go back and change it, redo it again and again, it's more likely that you'll end up with the wrong answer. Thus, follow your instinct. Once you have come up with the answer, look at the answer choices. If your answer is one of the choices, you're probably correct. It's not 100 percent infallible, but it's a strong possibility that you've selected the right answer.

But suppose you don't know the correct answer. You then use the "process of elimination." It's a time-honored technique for test-takers. There is always one correct answer. There is usually one answer choice that is totally incorrect—a "distracter." If you look at that choice and it seems highly unlikely, then eliminate it. Depending on the number of choices (four or five), you've just cut down the number of choices to make. Now weigh the other choices. They may seem incorrect, or they may be correct. If they seem incorrect, eliminate them. You've now increased your odds at getting the correct answer.

In the end, you may be left with only two choices. At that point, it's just a matter of guessing. But with only two choices left, you now have a 50 percent chance of getting it right. With four choices, you only have a 25 percent chance, and with five choices, only a 20 percent chance at guessing correctly. That's why the process of elimination is important.

"Testwiseness"

Many factors enter into a test score. The most important factor should be the ability to answer the questions, which in turn indicates the ability to learn and perform the duties of the job. Assuming that you have this ability, knowing what to expect on the exam and familiarity with techniques of effective test taking should give you the confidence you need to do your best on the exam.

There is no quick substitute for long-term study and development of your skills and abilities to prepare you for doing well on tests. However, there are some steps you can take to help you do the very best that you are prepared to do. Some of these steps are done before the test, and some are followed when you are taking the test. Knowing these steps is often called being "test-wise." Following these steps may help you feel more confident as you take the actual test.

"Testwiseness" is a general term that simply means being familiar with some good procedures to follow when getting ready for and taking a test. The procedures fall into four major areas: (1) being prepared, (2) avoiding careless errors, (3) managing your time, and (4) guessing.

Being Prepared

Don't make the test harder than it has to be by not preparing yourself. You are taking a very important step in preparation by reading this book and taking the sample tests that are included. This will help you to become familiar with the tests and the kinds of questions you will have to answer.

As you use this book, read the sample questions and directions for taking the test carefully. Then, when you take the sample tests, time yourself as you will be timed in the real test.

As you are working on the sample questions, don't look at the correct answers before you try to answer them on your own. This can fool you into thinking you understand a question when you really don't. Try it on your own first, and then compare your answer with the one given. Remember, in a sample test, you are your own grader; you don't gain anything by pretending to understand something you really don't.

On the examination day assigned to you, allow the test itself to be the main attraction of the day. Do not squeeze it in between other activities. Be sure to bring your admission card, identification, and pencils, as instructed. Prepare these the night before so that you are not flustered by a last-minute search. Arrive rested, relaxed, and on time. In fact, plan to arrive a little bit early. Leave plenty of time for traffic tie-ups or other complications that might upset you and interfere with your test performance.

In the test room, the examiner will hand out forms for you to fill out. He or she will give you the instructions that you must follow in taking the examination. The examiner will tell you how to fill in the grids on the forms. Time limits and timing signals will be explained. If you do not understand any of the examiner's instructions, ASK QUESTIONS. It would be ridiculous to score less than your best because of poor communication.

At the examination, you must follow instructions exactly. Fill in the grids on the forms carefully and accurately. Misgridding may lead to loss of veteran's credits to which you may be entitled or misaddressing of your test results. Do not begin until you are told to begin. Stop as soon as the examiner tells you to stop. Do not turn pages until you are told to do so. Do not go back to parts you have already completed. Any infraction of the rules is considered cheating. If you cheat, your test paper will not be scored, and you will not be eligible for appointment.

The answer sheet for most multiple-choice exams is machine scored. You cannot give any explanations to the machine, so you must fill out the answer sheet clearly and correctly.

Marking Your Answer Sheet

1 **Blacken your answer space firmly and completely.**

2 **Mark only one answer for each question.** If you mark more than one answer, it will be considered wrong, even if one of the answers is correct.

3 **If you change your mind, you must erase your mark.** Attempting to cross out an incorrect answer will not work. You must erase any incorrect answer completely. An incomplete erasure might be read as a second answer.

4 **All of your answering should be in the form of blackened spaces.** The machine cannot read English. Do not write any notes in the margins.

5 **Answer each question in the right place.** Question 1 must be answered in space 1; question 52 in space 52. If you should skip an answer space and mark a series of answers in the wrong places, you must erase all those answers and do the questions over, marking your answers in the proper places. You cannot afford to use the limited time in this way. Therefore, as you answer each question, look at its number and check that you are marking your answer in the space with the same number.

Avoiding Careless Errors

Don't reduce your score by making careless mistakes. Always read the instructions for each test section carefully, even when you think you already know what the directions are. It's why we stress throughout this book that it's important to fully understand the directions for these different question-types before you go into the actual exam. It will not only reduce errors, but it will save you time—time you will need for the questions.

What if you don't understand the directions? You will have risked getting the answers wrong for a whole test section. As an example, vocabulary questions can sometimes test synonyms (words with similar meanings), and sometimes test antonyms (words with opposite meanings). You can easily see how a mistake in understanding in this case could make a whole set of answers incorrect.

If you have time, reread any complicated instructions after you do the first few questions to check that you really do understand them. Of course, whenever you are allowed to, ask the examiner to clarify anything you don't understand.

Other careless mistakes affect only the response to particular questions. This often happens with arithmetic questions, but can happen with other questions as well. This type of error, called a "response error," usually stems from a momentary lapse of concentration.

A common error in reading interpretation questions is bringing your own information into the subject. For example, you may encounter a passage that discusses a subject you know something about. While this can make the passage easier to read, it can also tempt you to rely on your own knowledge about the subject. You must rely on information within the passage for your answers—in fact, sometimes the "wrong answer" for the questions are based on true information about the subject not given in the passage. Since the test-makers are testing your reading ability, rather than your general knowledge of the subject, an answer based on information not contained in the passage is considered incorrect.

Managing Your Time

Before you begin, take a moment to plan your progress through the test. Although you are usually not expected to finish all of the questions given on a test, you should at least get an idea of how much time you should spend on each question in order to answer them all. For example, if there are 60 questions to answer and you have 30 minutes, you will have about one-half minute to spend on each question.

Keep track of the time on your watch or the room clock, but do not fixate on the time remaining. Your task is to answer questions. Do not spend too much time on any one question. If you find yourself stuck, do not take the puzzler as a personal challenge. Either guess and mark the question in the question booklet or skip the question entirely, marking the question as a skip and taking care to skip the answer space on the answer sheet. If there is time at the end of the exam or exam part, you can return and give marked questions another try.

Guessing

You may be wondering whether or not it is wise to guess when you are not sure of an answer (even if you've reduced the odds to 50 percent) or whether it is better to skip the question when you are not certain. The wisdom of guessing depends on the scoring method for the particular examination part. If the scoring is "rights only," that is, one point for each correct answer and no subtraction for wrong answers, then by all means you should guess. Read the question and all of the answer choices carefully. Eliminate those answer choices that you are certain are wrong. Then guess from among the remaining choices. You cannot gain a point if you leave the answer space blank; you may gain a point with an educated guess or even with a lucky guess. In fact, it is foolish to leave any spaces blank on a test that counts "rights only." If it appears that you are about to run out of time before completing such an exam, mark all the remaining blanks with the same letter. According to the law of averages, you should get some portion of those questions right.

If the scoring method is rights minus wrongs, DO NOT GUESS. A wrong answer counts heavily against you. On this type of test, do not rush to fill answer spaces randomly at the end. Work as quickly as possible while concentrating on accuracy. Keep working carefully until time is called. Then stop and leave the remaining answer spaces blank.

In guessing the answers to multiple-choice questions, take a second to eliminate those answers that are obviously wrong, then quickly consider and guess from the remaining choices. The fewer choices from which you guess, the better the odds of guessing correctly. Once you have decided to make a guess, be it an educated guess or a wild stab, do it right away and move on; don't keep thinking about it and wasting time. You should always mark the test questions at which you guess so that you can return later.

For those questions that are scored by subtracting a fraction of a point for each wrong answer, the decision as to whether or not to guess is really up to you.

A correct answer gives you one point; a skipped space gives you nothing at all, but costs you nothing except the chance of getting the answer right; a wrong answer costs you $\frac{1}{4}$ point. If you are really uncomfortable with guessing, you may skip a question, BUT you must then remember to skip its answer space as well. The risk of losing your place if you skip questions is so great that we advise you to guess even if you are not sure of the answer. Our suggestion is that you answer every question in order, even if you have to guess. It is better to lose a few $\frac{1}{4}$ points for wrong guesses than to lose valuable seconds figuring where you started marking answers in the wrong place, erasing, and re-marking answers. On the other hand, do not mark random answers at the end. Work steadily until time is up.

One of the questions you should ask in the testing room is what scoring method will be used on your particular exam. You can then guide your guessing procedure accordingly.

Scoring

If your exam is a short-answer exam such as those often used by companies in the private sector, your answers will be graded by a personnel officer trained in grading test questions. If you blackened spaces on the separate answer sheet accompanying a multiple-choice exam, your answer sheet will be machine scanned or will be hand scored using a punched card stencil. Then a raw score will be calculated using the scoring formula that applies to that test or test portion—rights only, rights minus wrongs, or rights minus a fraction of wrongs. Raw scores on test parts are then added together for a total raw score.

A raw score is not a final score. The raw score is not the score that finds its way onto an eligibility list. The civil service testing authority converts raw scores to a scaled score according to an unpublicized formula of its own. The scaling formula allows for slight differences in difficulty of questions from one form of the exam to another and allows for equating the scores of all candidates. Regardless of the number of questions and possible different weights of different parts of the exam, most civil service clerical test scores are reported on a scale of 1 to 10. The entire process of conversion from raw to scaled score is confidential information. The score you receive is not your number right, is not your raw score, and, despite being on a scale of 1 to 100, is not a percentage. It is a scaled score. If you are entitled to veterans' service points, these are added to your passing scaled score to boost your rank on the eligibility list. Veterans' points are added only to passing scores. A failing score cannot be brought to passing level by adding veterans' points. The score earned plus veterans' service points, if any, is the score that finds its place on the rank order eligibility list.

SUMMING IT UP

- When you have your application forms in hand, photocopy them and complete the photocopies first. This way you can correct mistakes or make changes before transferring the information to the original application.

- Job announcements are designed to give you a good idea of what will be required of you on the job, whether you are a case worker, a social investigator, or an eligibility specialist.

- The written exam is a key component of the case worker screening process and tests a variety of subject areas, including:

    1. Social Work Vocabulary

    2. Reading Interpretation

    3. Eligibility for Public Assistance and Housing

    4. Housing and Social Welfare

    5. Judgment

    6. Public Health

    7. Procedures and Records

    8. Interpretation of Social Work Problems

    9. Case Work Techniques

    10. Social Work with Children

    11. General Review

PART II

DIAGNOSING STRENGTHS AND WEAKNESSES

CHAPTER 2   Practice Test 1: Diagnostic

Practice Test 1: Diagnostic

PREPARING TO TAKE THE DIAGNOSTIC TEST

An examination is an evaluation tool. Therefore, you should evaluate yourself to identify areas of strength and weakness. Taking the Diagnostic Test in this chapter will help you determine your strengths and weaknesses and apportion your study time.

The following questions will test your knowledge about various areas of social work, and more specifically, those of a case worker, eligibility specialist, and social investigator. Although most of these types of questions may appear on your exams, it is also important that you understand this material for whatever you plan to do in these areas of employment. As you go through each section and check your answers, keep in mind that this is a learning process. Not only will you be learning how to answer these types of questions—an important skill for doing well on any exam—but you will also be gaining additional knowledge about these specific subjects.

ANSWER SHEET PRACTICE TEST 1: DIAGNOSTIC

Vocabulary

1. (A) (B) (C) (D) 7. (A) (B) (C) (D) 13. (A) (B) (C) (D) 19. (A) (B) (C) (D) 25. (A) (B) (C) (D)

2. (A) (B) (C) (D) 8. (A) (B) (C) (D) 14. (A) (B) (C) (D) 20. (A) (B) (C) (D) 26. (A) (B) (C) (D)

3. (A) (B) (C) (D) 9. (A) (B) (C) (D) 15. (A) (B) (C) (D) 21. (A) (B) (C) (D) 27. (A) (B) (C) (D)

4. (A) (B) (C) (D) 10. (A) (B) (C) (D) 16. (A) (B) (C) (D) 22. (A) (B) (C) (D) 28. (A) (B) (C) (D)

5. (A) (B) (C) (D) 11. (A) (B) (C) (D) 17. (A) (B) (C) (D) 23. (A) (B) (C) (D) 29. (A) (B) (C) (D)

6. (A) (B) (C) (D) 12. (A) (B) (C) (D) 18. (A) (B) (C) (D) 24. (A) (B) (C) (D) 30. (A) (B) (C) (D)

Reading Interpretation

1. (A) (B) (C) (D) 6. (A) (B) (C) (D) 11. (A) (B) (C) (D) 16. (A) (B) (C) (D) 21. (A) (B) (C) (D)

2. (A) (B) (C) (D) 7. (A) (B) (C) (D) 12. (A) (B) (C) (D) 17. (A) (B) (C) (D) 22. (A) (B) (C) (D)

3. (A) (B) (C) (D) 8. (A) (B) (C) (D) 13. (A) (B) (C) (D) 18. (A) (B) (C) (D) 23. (A) (B) (C) (D)

4. (A) (B) (C) (D) 9. (A) (B) (C) (D) 14. (A) (B) (C) (D) 19. (A) (B) (C) (D) 24. (A) (B) (C) (D)

5. (A) (B) (C) (D) 10. (A) (B) (C) (D) 15. (A) (B) (C) (D) 20. (A) (B) (C) (D) 25. (A) (B) (C) (D)

Eligibility for Public Assistance and Housing

1. (A) (B) (C) (D) 15. (A) (B) (C) (D) 29. (A) (B) (C) (D) 43. (A) (B) (C) (D) 57. (A) (B) (C) (D)

2. (A) (B) (C) (D) 16. (A) (B) (C) (D) 30. (A) (B) (C) (D) 44. (A) (B) (C) (D) 58. (A) (B) (C) (D)

3. (A) (B) (C) (D) 17. (A) (B) (C) (D) 31. (A) (B) (C) (D) 45. (A) (B) (C) (D) 59. (A) (B) (C) (D)

4. (A) (B) (C) (D) 18. (A) (B) (C) (D) 32. (A) (B) (C) (D) 46. (A) (B) (C) (D) 60. (A) (B) (C) (D)

5. (A) (B) (C) (D) 19. (A) (B) (C) (D) 33. (A) (B) (C) (D) 47. (A) (B) (C) (D) 61. (A) (B) (C) (D)

6. (A) (B) (C) (D) 20. (A) (B) (C) (D) 34. (A) (B) (C) (D) 48. (A) (B) (C) (D) 62. (A) (B) (C) (D)

7. (A) (B) (C) (D) 21. (A) (B) (C) (D) 35. (A) (B) (C) (D) 49. (A) (B) (C) (D) 63. (A) (B) (C) (D)

8. (A) (B) (C) (D) 22. (A) (B) (C) (D) 36. (A) (B) (C) (D) 50. (A) (B) (C) (D) 64. (A) (B) (C) (D)

9. (A) (B) (C) (D) 23. (A) (B) (C) (D) 37. (A) (B) (C) (D) 51. (A) (B) (C) (D) 65. (A) (B) (C) (D)

10. (A) (B) (C) (D) 24. (A) (B) (C) (D) 38. (A) (B) (C) (D) 52. (A) (B) (C) (D) 66. (A) (B) (C) (D)

11. (A) (B) (C) (D) 25. (A) (B) (C) (D) 39. (A) (B) (C) (D) 53. (A) (B) (C) (D) 67. (A) (B) (C) (D)

12. (A) (B) (C) (D) 26. (A) (B) (C) (D) 40. (A) (B) (C) (D) 54. (A) (B) (C) (D) 68. (A) (B) (C) (D)

13. (A) (B) (C) (D) 27. (A) (B) (C) (D) 41. (A) (B) (C) (D) 55. (A) (B) (C) (D) 69. (A) (B) (C) (D)

14. (A) (B) (C) (D) 28. (A) (B) (C) (D) 42. (A) (B) (C) (D) 56. (A) (B) (C) (D) 70. (A) (B) (C) (D)

Housing and Social Welfare

1. Ⓐ Ⓑ Ⓒ Ⓓ	8. Ⓐ Ⓑ Ⓒ Ⓓ	15. Ⓐ Ⓑ Ⓒ Ⓓ	22. Ⓐ Ⓑ Ⓒ Ⓓ	29. Ⓐ Ⓑ Ⓒ Ⓓ
2. Ⓐ Ⓑ Ⓒ Ⓓ	9. Ⓐ Ⓑ Ⓒ Ⓓ	16. Ⓐ Ⓑ Ⓒ Ⓓ	23. Ⓐ Ⓑ Ⓒ Ⓓ	30. Ⓐ Ⓑ Ⓒ Ⓓ
3. Ⓐ Ⓑ Ⓒ Ⓓ	10. Ⓐ Ⓑ Ⓒ Ⓓ	17. Ⓐ Ⓑ Ⓒ Ⓓ	24. Ⓐ Ⓑ Ⓒ Ⓓ	31. Ⓐ Ⓑ Ⓒ Ⓓ
4. Ⓐ Ⓑ Ⓒ Ⓓ	11. Ⓐ Ⓑ Ⓒ Ⓓ	18. Ⓐ Ⓑ Ⓒ Ⓓ	25. Ⓐ Ⓑ Ⓒ Ⓓ	32. Ⓐ Ⓑ Ⓒ Ⓓ
5. Ⓐ Ⓑ Ⓒ Ⓓ	12. Ⓐ Ⓑ Ⓒ Ⓓ	19. Ⓐ Ⓑ Ⓒ Ⓓ	26. Ⓐ Ⓑ Ⓒ Ⓓ	33. Ⓐ Ⓑ Ⓒ Ⓓ
6. Ⓐ Ⓑ Ⓒ Ⓓ	13. Ⓐ Ⓑ Ⓒ Ⓓ	20. Ⓐ Ⓑ Ⓒ Ⓓ	27. Ⓐ Ⓑ Ⓒ Ⓓ	34. Ⓐ Ⓑ Ⓒ Ⓓ
7. Ⓐ Ⓑ Ⓒ Ⓓ	14. Ⓐ Ⓑ Ⓒ Ⓓ	21. Ⓐ Ⓑ Ⓒ Ⓓ	28. Ⓐ Ⓑ Ⓒ Ⓓ	35. Ⓐ Ⓑ Ⓒ Ⓓ

Judgment

1. Ⓐ Ⓑ Ⓒ Ⓓ	9. Ⓐ Ⓑ Ⓒ Ⓓ	17. Ⓐ Ⓑ Ⓒ Ⓓ	25. Ⓐ Ⓑ Ⓒ Ⓓ	33. Ⓐ Ⓑ Ⓒ Ⓓ
2. Ⓐ Ⓑ Ⓒ Ⓓ	10. Ⓐ Ⓑ Ⓒ Ⓓ	18. Ⓐ Ⓑ Ⓒ Ⓓ	26. Ⓐ Ⓑ Ⓒ Ⓓ	34. Ⓐ Ⓑ Ⓒ Ⓓ
3. Ⓐ Ⓑ Ⓒ Ⓓ	11. Ⓐ Ⓑ Ⓒ Ⓓ	19. Ⓐ Ⓑ Ⓒ Ⓓ	27. Ⓐ Ⓑ Ⓒ Ⓓ	35. Ⓐ Ⓑ Ⓒ Ⓓ
4. Ⓐ Ⓑ Ⓒ Ⓓ	12. Ⓐ Ⓑ Ⓒ Ⓓ	20. Ⓐ Ⓑ Ⓒ Ⓓ	28. Ⓐ Ⓑ Ⓒ Ⓓ	36. Ⓐ Ⓑ Ⓒ Ⓓ
5. Ⓐ Ⓑ Ⓒ Ⓓ	13. Ⓐ Ⓑ Ⓒ Ⓓ	21. Ⓐ Ⓑ Ⓒ Ⓓ	29. Ⓐ Ⓑ Ⓒ Ⓓ	37. Ⓐ Ⓑ Ⓒ Ⓓ
6. Ⓐ Ⓑ Ⓒ Ⓓ	14. Ⓐ Ⓑ Ⓒ Ⓓ	22. Ⓐ Ⓑ Ⓒ Ⓓ	30. Ⓐ Ⓑ Ⓒ Ⓓ	38. Ⓐ Ⓑ Ⓒ Ⓓ
7. Ⓐ Ⓑ Ⓒ Ⓓ	15. Ⓐ Ⓑ Ⓒ Ⓓ	23. Ⓐ Ⓑ Ⓒ Ⓓ	31. Ⓐ Ⓑ Ⓒ Ⓓ	39. Ⓐ Ⓑ Ⓒ Ⓓ
8. Ⓐ Ⓑ Ⓒ Ⓓ	16. Ⓐ Ⓑ Ⓒ Ⓓ	24. Ⓐ Ⓑ Ⓒ Ⓓ	32. Ⓐ Ⓑ Ⓒ Ⓓ	40. Ⓐ Ⓑ Ⓒ Ⓓ

Public Health

1. Ⓐ Ⓑ Ⓒ Ⓓ	5. Ⓐ Ⓑ Ⓒ Ⓓ	9. Ⓐ Ⓑ Ⓒ Ⓓ	13. Ⓐ Ⓑ Ⓒ Ⓓ	17. Ⓐ Ⓑ Ⓒ Ⓓ
2. Ⓐ Ⓑ Ⓒ Ⓓ	6. Ⓐ Ⓑ Ⓒ Ⓓ	10. Ⓐ Ⓑ Ⓒ Ⓓ	14. Ⓐ Ⓑ Ⓒ Ⓓ	18. Ⓐ Ⓑ Ⓒ Ⓓ
3. Ⓐ Ⓑ Ⓒ Ⓓ	7. Ⓐ Ⓑ Ⓒ Ⓓ	11. Ⓐ Ⓑ Ⓒ Ⓓ	15. Ⓐ Ⓑ Ⓒ Ⓓ	19. Ⓐ Ⓑ Ⓒ Ⓓ
4. Ⓐ Ⓑ Ⓒ Ⓓ	8. Ⓐ Ⓑ Ⓒ Ⓓ	12. Ⓐ Ⓑ Ⓒ Ⓓ	16. Ⓐ Ⓑ Ⓒ Ⓓ	20. Ⓐ Ⓑ Ⓒ Ⓓ

Procedures and Records

1. Ⓐ Ⓑ Ⓒ Ⓓ	4. Ⓐ Ⓑ Ⓒ Ⓓ	7. Ⓐ Ⓑ Ⓒ Ⓓ	10. Ⓐ Ⓑ Ⓒ Ⓓ	13. Ⓐ Ⓑ Ⓒ Ⓓ
2. Ⓐ Ⓑ Ⓒ Ⓓ	5. Ⓐ Ⓑ Ⓒ Ⓓ	8. Ⓐ Ⓑ Ⓒ Ⓓ	11. Ⓐ Ⓑ Ⓒ Ⓓ	14. Ⓐ Ⓑ Ⓒ Ⓓ
3. Ⓐ Ⓑ Ⓒ Ⓓ	6. Ⓐ Ⓑ Ⓒ Ⓓ	9. Ⓐ Ⓑ Ⓒ Ⓓ	12. Ⓐ Ⓑ Ⓒ Ⓓ	15. Ⓐ Ⓑ Ⓒ Ⓓ

Interpretation of Social Work Problems

1. Ⓐ Ⓑ Ⓒ Ⓓ   9. Ⓐ Ⓑ Ⓒ Ⓓ   17. Ⓐ Ⓑ Ⓒ Ⓓ   25. Ⓐ Ⓑ Ⓒ Ⓓ   33. Ⓐ Ⓑ Ⓒ Ⓓ
2. Ⓐ Ⓑ Ⓒ Ⓓ   10. Ⓐ Ⓑ Ⓒ Ⓓ   18. Ⓐ Ⓑ Ⓒ Ⓓ   26. Ⓐ Ⓑ Ⓒ Ⓓ   34. Ⓐ Ⓑ Ⓒ Ⓓ
3. Ⓐ Ⓑ Ⓒ Ⓓ   11. Ⓐ Ⓑ Ⓒ Ⓓ   19. Ⓐ Ⓑ Ⓒ Ⓓ   27. Ⓐ Ⓑ Ⓒ Ⓓ   35. Ⓐ Ⓑ Ⓒ Ⓓ
4. Ⓐ Ⓑ Ⓒ Ⓓ   12. Ⓐ Ⓑ Ⓒ Ⓓ   20. Ⓐ Ⓑ Ⓒ Ⓓ   28. Ⓐ Ⓑ Ⓒ Ⓓ   36. _____
5. Ⓐ Ⓑ Ⓒ Ⓓ   13. Ⓐ Ⓑ Ⓒ Ⓓ   21. Ⓐ Ⓑ Ⓒ Ⓓ   29. Ⓐ Ⓑ Ⓒ Ⓓ   37. _____
6. Ⓐ Ⓑ Ⓒ Ⓓ   14. Ⓐ Ⓑ Ⓒ Ⓓ   22. Ⓐ Ⓑ Ⓒ Ⓓ   30. Ⓐ Ⓑ Ⓒ Ⓓ   38. _____
7. Ⓐ Ⓑ Ⓒ Ⓓ   15. Ⓐ Ⓑ Ⓒ Ⓓ   23. Ⓐ Ⓑ Ⓒ Ⓓ   31. Ⓐ Ⓑ Ⓒ Ⓓ   39. _____
8. Ⓐ Ⓑ Ⓒ Ⓓ   16. Ⓐ Ⓑ Ⓒ Ⓓ   24. Ⓐ Ⓑ Ⓒ Ⓓ   32. Ⓐ Ⓑ Ⓒ Ⓓ   40. _____

Case Worker Techniques

1. Ⓐ Ⓑ Ⓒ Ⓓ   6. Ⓐ Ⓑ Ⓒ Ⓓ   11. Ⓐ Ⓑ Ⓒ Ⓓ   16. Ⓐ Ⓑ Ⓒ Ⓓ   21. Ⓐ Ⓑ Ⓒ Ⓓ
2. Ⓐ Ⓑ Ⓒ Ⓓ   7. Ⓐ Ⓑ Ⓒ Ⓓ   12. Ⓐ Ⓑ Ⓒ Ⓓ   17. Ⓐ Ⓑ Ⓒ Ⓓ   22. Ⓐ Ⓑ Ⓒ Ⓓ
3. Ⓐ Ⓑ Ⓒ Ⓓ   8. Ⓐ Ⓑ Ⓒ Ⓓ   13. Ⓐ Ⓑ Ⓒ Ⓓ   18. Ⓐ Ⓑ Ⓒ Ⓓ   23. Ⓐ Ⓑ Ⓒ Ⓓ
4. Ⓐ Ⓑ Ⓒ Ⓓ   9. Ⓐ Ⓑ Ⓒ Ⓓ   14. Ⓐ Ⓑ Ⓒ Ⓓ   19. Ⓐ Ⓑ Ⓒ Ⓓ   24. Ⓐ Ⓑ Ⓒ Ⓓ
5. Ⓐ Ⓑ Ⓒ Ⓓ   10. Ⓐ Ⓑ Ⓒ Ⓓ   15. Ⓐ Ⓑ Ⓒ Ⓓ   20. Ⓐ Ⓑ Ⓒ Ⓓ   25. Ⓐ Ⓑ Ⓒ Ⓓ

Social Work with Children

1. Ⓐ Ⓑ Ⓒ Ⓓ   5. Ⓐ Ⓑ Ⓒ Ⓓ   9. Ⓐ Ⓑ Ⓒ Ⓓ   13. Ⓐ Ⓑ Ⓒ Ⓓ
2. Ⓐ Ⓑ Ⓒ Ⓓ   6. Ⓐ Ⓑ Ⓒ Ⓓ   10. Ⓐ Ⓑ Ⓒ Ⓓ   14. Ⓐ Ⓑ Ⓒ Ⓓ
3. Ⓐ Ⓑ Ⓒ Ⓓ   7. Ⓐ Ⓑ Ⓒ Ⓓ   11. Ⓐ Ⓑ Ⓒ Ⓓ   15. Ⓐ Ⓑ Ⓒ Ⓓ
4. Ⓐ Ⓑ Ⓒ Ⓓ   8. Ⓐ Ⓑ Ⓒ Ⓓ   12. Ⓐ Ⓑ Ⓒ Ⓓ   16. Ⓐ Ⓑ Ⓒ Ⓓ

General Review

1. Ⓐ Ⓑ Ⓒ Ⓓ   7. Ⓐ Ⓑ Ⓒ Ⓓ   13. Ⓐ Ⓑ Ⓒ Ⓓ   19. Ⓐ Ⓑ Ⓒ Ⓓ   25. Ⓐ Ⓑ Ⓒ Ⓓ
2. Ⓐ Ⓑ Ⓒ Ⓓ   8. Ⓐ Ⓑ Ⓒ Ⓓ   14. Ⓐ Ⓑ Ⓒ Ⓓ   20. Ⓐ Ⓑ Ⓒ Ⓓ   26. Ⓐ Ⓑ Ⓒ Ⓓ
3. Ⓐ Ⓑ Ⓒ Ⓓ   9. Ⓐ Ⓑ Ⓒ Ⓓ   15. Ⓐ Ⓑ Ⓒ Ⓓ   21. Ⓐ Ⓑ Ⓒ Ⓓ   27. Ⓐ Ⓑ Ⓒ Ⓓ
4. Ⓐ Ⓑ Ⓒ Ⓓ   10. Ⓐ Ⓑ Ⓒ Ⓓ   16. Ⓐ Ⓑ Ⓒ Ⓓ   22. Ⓐ Ⓑ Ⓒ Ⓓ   28. Ⓐ Ⓑ Ⓒ Ⓓ
5. Ⓐ Ⓑ Ⓒ Ⓓ   11. Ⓐ Ⓑ Ⓒ Ⓓ   17. Ⓐ Ⓑ Ⓒ Ⓓ   23. Ⓐ Ⓑ Ⓒ Ⓓ   29. Ⓐ Ⓑ Ⓒ Ⓓ
6. Ⓐ Ⓑ Ⓒ Ⓓ   12. Ⓐ Ⓑ Ⓒ Ⓓ   18. Ⓐ Ⓑ Ⓒ Ⓓ   24. Ⓐ Ⓑ Ⓒ Ⓓ   30. Ⓐ Ⓑ Ⓒ Ⓓ

answer sheet

VOCABULARY

Directions: Each question has four possible answers. Choose the letter that best answers the question and mark your answer on the answer sheet.

1. Clinics are now seeing many people who complain of seriously disturbed feelings and other symptoms relating to <u>traumatic</u> war experiences. The underlined word in the preceding sentence means most nearly

   (A) recent.
   (B) worldwide.
   (C) prodigious.
   (D) shocking.

2. There should be no <u>opprobrium</u> attached to the term "second-hand housing" since every house is second-hand after the first occupancy. The underlined word in the preceding sentence means most nearly

   (A) stigma.
   (B) honor.
   (C) rank.
   (D) credit.

3. The Community Chest movement seems to have been <u>indigenous</u> to the North American continent. The underlined word in the preceding sentence means most nearly

   (A) important.
   (B) essential.
   (C) native.
   (D) homogeneous.

4. Which pair of terms below are most similar in meaning?

   (A) feebleminded and mentally deficient
   (B) illiterate and unintelligent
   (C) client and investigator
   (D) rehabilitation and remuneration

5. The legal proceedings by which a municipality may take private property for public use is known as

   (A) search and seizure.
   (B) elective franchise.
   (C) habeas corpus.
   (D) condemnation proceedings.

6. The Alcoholics Anonymous Program, which in essence amounts to a <u>therapeutic</u> procedure, is codified into twelve steps. The underlined word in the preceding sentence means most nearly

   (A) compensatory.
   (B) curative.
   (C) sequential.
   (D) volitional.

7. When people <u>vicariously</u> live out their own problems in novels and plays, they are engaging in an experience that is, in terms of the underlined word in this sentence,

   (A) dynamic.
   (B) monastic.
   (C) substituted.
   (D) dignified.

8. Local responsibility for the relief of economic need long having been recognized as inadequate, the state and federal governments have established plans of <u>categorical</u> assistance and social insurance. In the preceding sentence, the underlined word means most nearly

   (A) conditional.
   (B) economic.
   (C) pecuniary.
   (D) classified.

9. If the interests of a social welfare agency are concerned with bringing opportunities for self-help to underprivileged eth‐nic groups, its activities involve most nearly, in terms of the underlined word in this sentence,

   (A) racial factors.

   (B) minority units.

   (C) religious affiliation.

   (D) economic conditions.

10. Increased facilities for medical care (though interrupted to some extent by the exigen‐cies of wartime) will safeguard the health of many children who in previous genera‐tions would have been doomed to an early death or to physical disability. In the fore‐going sentence, the most nearly correct equivalent of the underlined word is

    (A) obstacles.

    (B) occurrences.

    (C) extenuations.

    (D) exactions.

11. The written authority for one person to act for another in legal matters is called

    (A) a deposition.

    (B) a power of attorney.

    (C) an endorsement.

    (D) legal tender.

FOR QUESTIONS 12–25, CHOOSE THE WORD OR PHRASE THAT HAS THE SAME OR NEARLY THE SAME MEANING AS THE WORD IN ITALICS.

12. *Postulate*

    (A) Protest

    (B) Dxpostulation

    (C) Hypothesis

    (D) Prognathism

13. *Domination*

    (A) Denomination

    (B) Denial

    (C) Manifesto

    (D) Control

14. *Reprisal*

    (A) Reward

    (B) Retaliation

    (C) Embezzlement

    (D) Reappraisal

15. *Parity*

    (A) Similarity

    (B) Equivalence

    (C) Supremacy

    (D) Agreement

16. *Hegemony*

    (A) Dictatorship

    (B) Homogeneity

    (C) Leadership

    (D) Inheritance

17. *Amortization*

    (A) Liquidation

    (B) Improvement

    (C) Interest

    (D) Principal

18. *Rapport*

    (A) Mutual service

    (B) Controversial issue

    (C) Emotional dependency

    (D) Harmonious relationship

19. *Prognosis*

    (A) Progenitor

    (B) Prediction

    (C) Causal relationship

    (D) Prophetic vision

20. *Sibling*

    (A) Relative by marriage

    (B) Relative by adoption

    (C) Blood relative

    (D) Legally responsible relative

21. *Congenital*

    (A) A trait always transmitted in the germ plasma

    (B) A condition dating from birth

    (C) A characteristic acquired in adolescence

    (D) An inherited physical characteristic

22. *Psychosis*

    (A) Mental disease

    (B) Compulsive neurosis

    (C) Mental deficiency

    (D) Psychometrics

23. *Coercion*

    (A) Immersion

    (B) Restraint

    (C) Persuasion

    (D) Inclusion

24. *Adoption*

    (A) Legal custody of a child

    (B) Legal guardianship of a child

    (C) Power of attorney of a child

    (D) Provision of foster parents

25. *Occupational therapy*

    (A) Curative handicraft

    (B) Job analysis

    (C) Ciatherm treatment

    (D) Vocational guidance

26. The nature of the *pathology* underlying the compulsion is obscure. In the preceding sentence, the italicized word means most nearly

    (A) drive.

    (B) disease.

    (C) deterioration.

    (D) development.

27. *Mandated* means most nearly

    (A) required assignment.

    (B) involuntary participant.

    (C) crucial member.

    (D) intellectually challenged

28. A *hospice* is

    (A) a mobile hospital.

    (B) the training needed to work with cancer patients.

    (C) the training needed to work in hospital setting.

    (D) a place that cares for the terminally ill.

29. *Advocacy* means most nearly

    (A) political lobbying.

    (B) making decisions for the mentally handicapped.

    (C) acting on behalf on a client.

    (D) training in effectively leading a group.

30. *Ambivalent* means most nearly

    (A) established forces.

    (B) dependent.

    (C) stressed.

    (D) undecided.

READING INTERPRETATION

> **Directions:** Read the following passages, then chose the best answer to each question based solely on the information contained in the passage.

1. "Expansion, succession, and mobility have played a part in determining the social characteristics of the slum. The immigrant populations that have poured into the transitional zones of American cities have not sought the slum, have not created slums, but have been forced by their low economic status to live in the low rental dwellings created in these zones by the city's expansion. The variety of cultural backgrounds immigrant groups have brought with them have contributed to the cultured confusion of the slum."

On the basis of this quotation, which of the following statements is the least accurate?

(A) As the population of a city expands and moves out of certain areas, these areas tend to change in character.

(B) Slums have been created by the variety of immigrant cultured backgrounds.

(C) The low earnings of immigrants have forced them into housing left behind in the expansion process.

(D) The cultured confusion of the slum existed before the influx of immigration.

2. "A general area in which unsanitary or substandard housing conditions exist may include land, either improved or unimproved, and buildings or improvements not in themselves unsanitary or substandard. Demolition or rehabilitation of the latter may be necessary for effective replanning or reconstruction of the entire area."

On the basis of this quotation, it would be most accurate to state that

(A) an area may be considered substandard from the housing viewpoint even though it contains some acceptable housing.

(B) in replanning an entire area, little if any consideration needs to be given to buildings or improvements not in themselves unsanitary or substandard.

(C) it is not easy to determine the exact boundaries of slum areas.

(D) under existing law, only substandard dwelling quarters may actually be demolished.

3. "The slum is not only a grimy mass of brick and mortar that can be torn down and demolished; it is also a way of living— a whole series of habits, attitudes, and sentiments."

On the basis of this quotation, it would be most correct to state that

(A) demolition of substandard housing in slum areas will provide the basis for a new way of living.

(B) desirable urban community life is menaced by the existence of a social class forced into inferior housing and living standards.

(C) substandard housing and inferior living conditions constitute social problems of the first magnitude.

(D) the slum is imprinted in the lives of the people that occupy it—both adults and children.

4. "There is urgent need to proceed as rapidly as possible with the revision of existing zoning regulations, especially with regard to so-called 'unrestricted' districts. These districts, in which much current private building activity is going on, are to all intents and purposes unzoned."

If the revision referred to in this quotation were to be placed in effect, an immediate result would probably be that

(A) blighted areas would be saved and prevented from becoming slums.

(B) new industrial and business construction would have to conform to whatever regulations are set up.

(C) slums would be eliminated.

(D) the unsightly and uneconomic mixture of land uses found in many neighborhoods would disappear.

5. "The housing problem itself clearly is a consequence of the lack of proper distribution of income and wealth, unemployment, and other economic factors."

On the basis of this quotation, it would be most correct to state that

(A) eradication of unemployment is the key to the housing problem.

(B) good housing generally could be available for all if every family had adequate income.

(C) proper distribution of housing is a basic factor in solving the housing problem.

(D) slums are a direct result of the unavailability of acceptable housing.

6. "Human society in a slum area is extremely mixed. A majority of the adults are self-respecting, law-abiding working men and women in low-paid or irregular occupations who want to bring their children up right and have them get ahead in the world. A smaller group has been pushed down from a higher income level by illness, accident, or incompetence."

On the basis of the above quotation, it would be most accurate to state that

(A) adults earning good salaries should not live in slum areas.

(B) children who are raised in a slum area are more likely to present problems of juvenile delinquency.

(C) residents of slum areas include adults who formerly had a higher income level.

(D) self-respecting, law-abiding working men and women in low-paid occupations are as likely to be found in slum areas as anywhere else.

7. "A considerable body of substandard housing can be made acceptable by repairs and modernization. For this reason and others, the volume of substandard housing is much greater than the volume reasonably recommended for demolition. On the other hand, any slum clearance scheme will involve the demolition of some houses, which, if located elsewhere, would not need to be demolished. No locality large enough for neighborhood development is made up completely of housing unfit for use."

On the basis of the quotation, it would be most correct to say that

(A) a combination of unsanitary conditions exists only in slum areas that need to be redeveloped.

(B) clearing slums always involves demolition of some acceptable housing.

(C) localities that need to be redeveloped contain substandard housing only.

(D) repairs and modernization are an acceptable substitute for redevelopment of a slum area.

8. "Zoning ordinances have generally served a highly useful purpose in preserving neighborhoods unspoiled for the greatest good of the greatest number. Zoning has been a boon to families of moderate means. The wealthy could always protect themselves by living in restricted districts or owning large estates. Working people well enough off to live in new sections have been helped too, those in older sections very little, those in slums not at all."

On the basis of this quotation, it may properly be assumed that

(A) adequate zoning laws will, over a long period, rehabilitate slum areas.

(B) business districts do not benefit from zoning laws.

(C) homeowners need the protection afforded by zoning laws.

(D) new homes for families of moderate income can change the character of a decadent area.

9. "Complete absence of policy hampered the World War II housing program from the start. Operations were again centralized in federal government. As further appropriations were authorized, a dozen uncoordinated federal agencies began to scramble for a share of the purse. They competed for sites and personnel and sometimes outbid one another. In one city, one agency actually blocked off another's street."

On the basis of this quotation, it would be most correct to assume that

(A) appropriations for war housing reflected wartime rush and confusion.

(B) centralization of federal war-housing operations would have resulted in a more coordinated program.

(C) centralized authority can bring order out of chaos.

(D) overlapping functions and operations of different bureaus led to inefficiency.

10. "Tearing down slums may be esthetically satisfying and emotionally soothing but it does not, of itself, improve the housing conditions of low income families. Slum clearance tends to impose additional hardships on tenants and does nothing to remedy the underlying condition."

On the basis of the above quotation, it would be most correct to state that

(A) healthful decent housing for low-income families implies the demolition of slums.

(B) healthful decent housing within the means of low-income families must be provided before slums can be torn down.

(C) low-income families are forced to live in slum areas.

(D) slum clearance is a necessary preliminary to improving housing conditions of low-income families.

11. "More damage has been done to the health of children of the United States by a sense of chronic inferiority due to consciousness of life in substandard dwellings than by all the defective plumbing those dwellings may contain."

Of the following, the most reasonable conclusion that may be drawn from this statement is that

(A) esthetic satisfaction in the home and its surroundings has some bearing on the physical well-being of children.

(B) normal physical and mental development is not possible when children are conscious of the substandard nature of their homes.

(C) psychiatric treatment is a necessary component of the adjustment of the children of slum families after transfer to public housing projects.

(D) the physical aspects of good housing are far less important in the healthful development of children than the provision of adequate play facilities.

12. "Across the years, our social sense has decreed that every position of social leadership, every place of influence, every concentration of social power in the hands of an individual, and every instrument or agency that has aggregated to itself the power to affect the common welfare has become by that very fact a social trust that must be administered for the common good. In our moral world, the social obligations of power are real and inescapable."

On the basis of this quotation, it would be most correct to state that

(A) an individual engaged in private enterprise does not have the social responsibility of one who holds public office.

(B) social leadership carries with it the obligation to administer for the public good.

(C) in our moral world, the abuse of power is real and inescapable.

(D) social leadership depends upon the aggregation of power in the hands of an individual or in an agency that wields concentrated influence.

13. "Personnel selection has been a critical problem for local housing authorities. The pool of qualified workers trained in housing procedures is small and the colleges and universities have failed to grasp the opportunity for enlarging it. While real estate experience makes a good background for management of a housing project, many real estate people are deplorably lacking in understanding of social and governmental problems. Social workers, on the other hand, are likely to be deficient in business judgment."

On the basis of this quotation, it would be most accurate to state that

(A) colleges and universities have failed to train qualified workers for proficiency in housing procedures.

(B) social workers are deficient in business judgment as related to the management of a housing project.

(C) real estate experience makes a person a good manager of a housing project.

(D) local housing authorities have been critical of present methods of personnel selection.

14. "The financing of housing represents two distinct forms of costs. One is the actual capital invested and the other is the interest rate that is charged for the use of capital. In fixing rents, the interest rate that capital is expected to yield plays a very important part."

On the basis of this quotation, it would be most correct to state that

(A) the financing of housing represents two distinct forms of capital investment.

(B) reducing the interest rate charged for the use of capital is not as important as economies in construction in achieving lower rentals.

(C) in fixing rents, the interest rate is expected to yield capital gains justifying the investment.

(D) the actual capital invested and the interest rate charged for the use of this capital are factors in determining housing costs.

15. "The housing authority faces every problem of the private developer and it must also assume responsibilities of which private buildings are free. The authority must account to the community; it must conform to federal regulations; it must provide durable buildings of good standard at low cost; it must overcome the prejudices against public operations of contractors, bankers, and prospective tenants. These authorities are being watched by anti-housing enthusiasts for the first error of judgment or the first evidence of high costs, to be torn to bits before a congressional committee."

On the basis of this quotation, it would be most correct to state that

(A) private builders do not have the opposition of contractors, bankers, and prospective tenants.

(B) congressional committees impede the progress of public housing by petty investigations.

(C) a housing authority must deal with all the difficulties encountered by the private builder.

(D) housing authorities are no more immune from errors in judgment than private developers.

16. "Another factor that has considerably added to the city's housing crisis has been the great influx of low-income workers and their families seeking better employment opportunities during wartime and defense boom periods. There was one such influx during World War II, and another coincided with the Korean War and defense buildup. The circumstances of these families forced them to crowd into the worst kind of housing and produced on a renewed scale the conditions from which slums flourish and grow."

On the basis of this quotation, one would be justified in stating that

(A) the great influx of low-income workers has aggravated the slum problem.

(B) New York City has better employment opportunities than other sections of the country.

(C) the high wages paid by our defense industries have made many families ineligible for tenancy in public housing.

(D) the families who settled in the city during World War II, the Korean War, and the defense buildup brought with them language and social customs conducive to the growth of slums.

17. "Much of the city felt the effects of the general postwar increase of vandalism and street crime, and the greatly expanded public housing program was no exception. Projects built in congested slum areas with a high incidence of delinquency and crime were particularly subjected to the depredations of neighborhood gangs. The civil service watchmen who patrolled the projects, unarmed and neither trained nor expected to perform police duties, were unable to cope with the situation."

On the basis of this quotation, the most accurate of the following statements is that

(A) neighborhood gangs were particularly responsible for the high incidence of delinquency and crime in congested slum areas having public housing programs.

(B) civil service watchmen who patrolled housing projects failed to carry out their assigned police duties.

(C) housing projects were not spared the effects of the general postwar increase of vandalism and street crime.

(D) delinquency and crime affected housing projects in slum areas to a greater extent than other dwellings in the same area.

18. "Another peculiar characteristic of real estate is the absence of liquidity. Each parcel is a discrete unit as to size, location, rental, physical condition, and financing arrangements. Each property requires investigation, comparison of rents with other properties, and individualized haggling on price and terms."

On the basis of this quotation, the least accurate of the following statements is that

(A) although the size, location, and rent of parcels vary, comparison with rents of other properties affords an indication of the value of a particular parcel.

(B) bargaining skill is the essential factor in determining the value of a parcel of real estate.

(C) each parcel of real estate has individual peculiarities distinguishing it from any other parcel.

(D) investigation of each property is necessary in relation to rent and price.

19. "In part, at least, the charges of sameness, monotony, and institutionalism directed at public housing projects result from the degree in which they differ from the city's normal housing pattern. They seem alike because their very difference from the usual makes them stand apart. In many respects, there is considerably more variety between public housing projects than there is between different streets of apartment houses or tenements throughout the city."

On the basis of this quotation, it would be least accurate to state that

(A) there is considerably more variety between different streets of tenements throughout the city.

(B) public housing projects differ from the city's normal housing pattern to the degree that sameness, monotony, and institutionalism are characteristic of public buildings.

(C) public housing projects seem alike because their deviation from the usual dwellings draws attention to them.

(D) the variety in structure between public housing projects and other public buildings is related to the period in which they were built.

20. "The amount of debt that can be charged against New York City for public housing is limited by law. Part of the city's restricted housing means goes for cash subsidies, so that it may be required to contribute to state-aided projects. Under the provisions of the state law, the city must match the state's contributions in subsidies, and while the value of the partial tax exemption granted by the city is counted for this purpose, it is not always sufficient."

On the basis of this quotation, it would be most accurate to state that

(A) the amount of money New York City may spend for public housing is limited by annual tax revenues.

(B) the value of tax exemptions granted by the city to educational, religious, and charitable institutions may be added to its subsidy contributions to public housing projects.

(C) the subsidy contributions for state-aided public housing projects are shared equally by the state and the city under the provisions of the state law.

(D) the tax revenues of the city, unless implemented by state aid, are insufficient to finance public housing projects.

21. "Maintenance costs can be minimized and the useful life of houses can be extended by building with the best and most permanent materials available. The best and most permanent materials in many cases are, however, much more expensive than materials that require more maintenance. The most economical procedure in home building has been to compromise between the capital costs of high quality and enduring materials and the maintenance costs of less desirable materials."

On the basis of this quotation, one would be justified in stating that

(A) savings in maintenance costs make the use of less durable and less expensive building materials preferable to high-quality materials that would prolong the useful life of houses constructed from them.

(B) financial advantage can be secured by the home builder if he or she judiciously combines costly but enduring building materials with less desirable materials that, however, require more maintenance.

(C) compromise between the capital costs of high-quality materials and the maintenance costs of less desirable materials makes it easier for a home builder to estimate construction expenditures.

(D) the most economical procedure in home building is to balance the capital costs of the most permanent materials against the costs of less expensive materials that are cheaper to maintain.

22. "The shift from public to private facilities for those who need institutional care can be seen in most areas of services. Care for the infirmed and aged, dependent children, youthful offenders, people who are physically disabled, and people with mental illness has moved from public to private resources. Some observers of social policy, as noted, refer to the shift as the privatization of services."

A reason for the privatization of services would be due to

(A) public policy making many shifts throughout history.

(B) governmental involvement in constructing facilities and staffing development very often increases expenses due to tremendous fiscal obligations that would continue indefinitely.

(C) private care being much more humane.

(D) public agencies having more control than private ones.

23. "A variety of efforts first developed under the Economic Opportunity Act of 1965 continue to help clients with basic needs. Although these are not typically income-maintenance organizations or programs, they often assist with helping low-income people keep their dwellings warm during the winter months, maintain food and clothing emergency supplies for people who need them, and operate advocacy and information programs for people who need economic assistance of one kind or another."

Based on this reading, the most accurate of the statements below is that

(A) the Economic Opportunity Act of 1965 offered generous and costly social programs to the community at large.

(B) housing development was greatly neglected by the Economic Opportunity Act of 1965.

(C) the Economic Opportunity Act of 1965 provides individuals with many basic services, to help those in need to cope with various aspects of poverty.

(D) the Economic Opportunity Act of 1965 was widely discouraged and seen as a form of handouts to the community.

24. "Community mental health programs provide for mental health counseling, hospitalization in community hospitals for people who require it for short periods of time, employment referral, and training and community education about mental health problems. Today's community mental health centers typically provide screening for those who appear to need mental hospitalization. The effort is to prevent commitment to an institution and to serve the patient in the community instead."

On the basis of the above quotation, it would be most precise to say that

(A) community mental health programs offer a wide scope of services that are focused on continuity of care.

(B) community mental health programs avoid institutionalizing individuals who may be in desperate need of such services.

(C) community mental health programs are sadly lacking in a clear understanding of really mental health problems in the areas serving the poor.

(D) community mental health programs are greatly lacking in resources to provide adequate services in slum areas.

25. "Part of the competence of a professional is systematic knowledge of one's roles and the reason for one's work. In human services, simply following rules and regulations that implement social policy minimizes the professional's role. One should know why the policy is being applied, the social values the policy reflects, the alternative ways in which the policy might be applied, alternative policies, the source of funding and financing alternatives, and the effectiveness of the policy."

This reading is best captured in which of the following statements?

(A) The competence of a professional is based on attitude toward his or her work.

(B) The competence of a professional is based on many factors, which include a thorough knowledge of one's field as well as a broad scope of the various components of his or her work.

(C) The competence of a professional is rarely affected by policy decisions.

(D) The competence of a professional's knowledge of his or her role is completely intuitive.

ELIGIBILITY FOR PUBLIC ASSISTANCE AND HOUSING

Directions: Each question has four possible answers. Choose the letter that best answers the question and mark your answer on the answer sheet.

1. In attempting to discover whether an applicant for aid to dependent children has had any previous experience as an aid recipient through other social service agencies in the community, the case worker should

   (A) check the application for such aid with the social service exchange.

   (B) send the fingerprints of the applicant to the police department.

   (C) consult the latest records of the Department of Social Services.

   (D) ask the applicant to submit a notarized statement to the effect that such aid has not been received from any other source.

FOR QUESTIONS 2–11, SELECT THE BEST REASON FOR ASKING CLIENTS THE QUESTIONS LISTED BELOW.

   (A) Identification
   (B) Eligibility aside from income
   (C) Income or financial resources
   (D) Debts and obligations

2. Maiden name of wife

3. Address and name of landlord

4. Equity in the home

5. Service in the armed forces

6. Mortgages on home

7. Duration of previous employment

8. Amounts of premiums on insurance

9. Adult children employed away from home

10. Prior occupation

11. Apartment number and floor

12. Official information with regard to the naturalization of a client is most properly obtained from the

    (A) Department of Commerce.

    (B) U.S. Department of Labor.

    (C) State Department of Labor.

    (D) U.S. Department of Justice.

13. Interviewing skills are an essential element of case work. Which of the following reasons is proper training for these skills needed?

    (A) To determine the clarity with which an applicant speaks

    (B) To determine the level of truthfulness of an applicant

    (C) To acquire the most through knowledge about the clients' problems

    (D) To develop a case worker's skills in becoming impartial

14. A new case worker can best utilize a case record to increase the value of services that a client receives by

    (A) sharing the record with the client and explaining to him or her the various examples of prejudice that have been found.

    (B) increasing their knowledge about the client and the history of his or her situation as it is detailed in the record.

    (C) reviewing all the recommendations that have been attempted in the past.

    (D) increasing the confidence of the case worker's actions by learning what was done by his or her predecessors.

15. Of the following, the least reliable form of proof showing continuous residence are

    (A) rent receipts.

    (B) leases.

    (C) school records.

    (D) dispossess and eviction notices.

16. Mr. Ritter asks the Department of Social Services to place his son, age 5, in a foster home. In a subsequent interview, Mr. Ritter refuses to divulge what sources of income are at his disposal. As the case worker trying to obtain this information, you should explain to Mr. Ritter that

    (A) you want to know whether he is seeking placement for his son because he does not want to provide for him financially.

    (B) part of the placement procedure involves determining the extent of financial responsibility parents can continue to assume.

    (C) if he makes no payment, his parental rights will be affected.

    (D) the frequency of his visits will depend on the amount of support he continues to furnish.

17. The best way to ensure that you have accurate employment information from a client would be to

    (A) have the client write out a resume of his or her work experience.

    (B) personally confer with the client's previous employer.

    (C) send letters in writing to the client's previous employers.

    (D) have a relative of the client's come in to support the information.

18. All of the following are desirable aspects of the social investigator EXCEPT

    (A) notifying the client that any misinterpretations on his or her part will result in arrest.

    (B) assisting the family in obtaining dental care.

    (C) seeking out employment opportunities for the families.

    (D) obtaining the confidence of the family.

19. All of the following are desirable aspects of making social investigations EXCEPT

    (A) familiarizing the family with the process of budgeting the assistance that they will be receiving.

    (B) calculating the minimum needs of a family according to their budget.

    (C) informing the family that they must maintain a minimum family budget whether or not it is to their liking because they are a public assistance client.

    (D) obtaining knowledge of client's work history form other agencies.

20. The following are practices involved in making social investigations of persons applying for aid. The one that is of the greatest immediate importance is

    (A) discovering the recreational habits of the family.

    (B) discovering any evidence of criminality.

    (C) searching property records to find the exact status of property that the family may have owned in the past.

    (D) discussing economic needs frankly.

21. The chief purpose of social investigation is to

    (A) gather statistical data.

    (B) understand the causes of distress and maladjustment so that suitable legislation may be devised and enacted.

    (C) understand the situation of the client to discover causes and possible treatment of the particular case.

    (D) determine whether the client has previously been a beneficiary of public aid.

22. Suppose an applicant for assistance objects to answering a question regarding his recent employment and asks, "What business is it of yours?" As the case worker conducting the interview, the most constructive course of action for you to take under the circumstances would be to

    (A) tell the applicant you have no intention of prying into his personal affairs and go on to the next question.

    (B) refer the applicant to your supervisor.

    (C) rephrase the question so that only a "yes" or "no" answer is required.

    (D) explain why the question is being asked.

23. In view of the fact that periodic home visits to clients are required by the department, according to good case work practice it is most desirable for the investigator to

    (A) visit without an appointment as this gives him or her a chance to see the person and the house "as they really are" and forestalls changing things to create a different impression.

    (B) write to the client providing him or her with an appointment time, as this saves the investigator from visiting when people are not at home and helps in planning work more efficiently.

    (C) write to the client suggesting an appointment time so that the client may be prepared for the interview and the investigator may use his or her time economically.

    (D) advise all applicants during their first interview that they will be visited periodically but will not be given definite appointments.

24. Under the law, it is always necessary to establish eligibility for public assistance. While the facts that must be established are clearly defined by law and by policy, the case worker has a good deal of freedom in choice of method. Of the methods given below for obtaining desired information from applicants for assistance, the one considered the best interviewing method in social work practice is to

    (A) work from an outline, asking the questions in the order in which they appear and requiring the applicant to give specific answers.

    (B) allow the applicant to describe what he or she has to say in his or her own words first, then ask questions on points not covered.

    (C) tell the applicant all the facts that you will need from him or her, then allow him or her to provide the information in any way he or she chooses.

    (D) verify all such facts as birth date, income, and past employment before seeing the applicant, then asking the applicant to fill in the remaining gaps when he or she is interviewed.

25. Mrs. Smith currently supports her 60-year-old mother and is applying for supplementation of her current benefit. Mrs. Smith's doctor has informed her that she needs to reduce her work schedule to four days a week so that she can receive her medical treatments for her illness. This would reduce her earning schedule by $50 a week, which would hinder her ability to continue to support her mother. Assuming that Mrs. Smith's request has been verified, you should

    (A) grant her supplementary aid because the reduction of work is necessary to maintain her health.

    (B) grant her support because she is caring for and supporting her elderly mother.

    (C) not grant her support because she can still manage to support herself on that income.

    (D) not grant her support because her mother can get assistance for herself.

26. If a client that you are working with fails to call for his relief check or to make further requests, you should

    (A) contact the client's family to find out why they are not contacting you.

    (B) complain to your supervisor.

    (C) close the case.

    (D) report the client and document it, but maintain his assistance because you know he needs it.

27. Since changes in aid need to be made in accordance with financial changes in a family's situation, an eligibility specialist should

    (A) not report changes in the family situation that might affect their income until you can be sure that it will directly affect the family.

    (B) not report changes in the family's situation because the family may not realize that this will change their benefits.

    (C) continue to check in with your client on a periodic basis, but keep your appointments informal because you do not want to make the family members anxious.

    (D) continue mandated contact with assistance recipients.

28. Mr. Cain and his 3 children are struggling despite the maximum level benefit you were able to obtain for them. You should

    (A) tell Mr. Cain that you will apply to have his case reviewed, although he is receiving the maximum level benefit. You believe that there is always more help available.

    (B) tell Mr. Cain that he is doing much better than people in other countries.

    (C) explain to Mr. Cain that he is currently receiving the maximum benefit for his family.

    (D) tell Mr. Cain that his grant is based on a scientific calculation of needs and is actually only a small percentage of what is really needed.

29. Which of the following cases would warrant your recommendation to Mrs. Arrow's allowance to be increased?

    (A) She is too frail to cook on her own and requests an increase in order that she may pay someone to come in and cook for her.

    (B) She is too frail to cook on her own and requests an increase in order that she may eat out in restaurants.

    (C) She is too frail to cook on her own and proposes to cut back on her heat so that she can eat in a restaurant.

    (D) None of the above, because people who are on aid should not be hiring a cook or eating in a restaurant.

30. It is most important for a client to understand what assistance eligibility is

    (A) so that he or she will be able to help others in need of aid.

    (B) because his or her family may be suffering.

    (C) so that he or she can immediately assume his or her share of responsibility by giving the necessary information and helping to verify it.

    (D) because the law requires it.

31. Definitions of need by which to determine eligibility for aid vary. The condition that most nearly approximates the definition of need according to current practice is

(A) the applicant has no income to meet the minimum standards of the department, no liquid resources, and no relatives able to contribute to his or her support.

(B) the applicant has insufficient income to meet the minimum standards set by the department, no insurance, and no relatives able to contribute to his or her support.

(C) the applicant has insufficient income to meet the minimum standards set by the department, no employed relatives, and no more than $2000 worth of insurance.

(D) the applicant has insufficient income to meet the minimum standards set by the department, no relatives able to contribute to his or her support, and no liquid resources.

32. Although the establishment of eligibility for aid must usually be a cooperative process, the ultimate burden of proof rests on

(A) the investigator because it is his or her sole responsibility to verify eligibility.

(B) the client because it is his or her responsibility to provide data concerning eligibility.

(C) the supervisor because he or she authorizes giving of aid.

(D) the resource consultant because he or she is responsible for preventing "chiseling."

33. The Carter family is applying for aid for the first time because of unemployment. They are a young couple with one child. All are in good health. Mr. Carter is a skilled laborer in a seasonal trade. The intake interviewer, in order to recommend emergency aid, must know if Mr. Carter

(A) feels that his needs are emergent.

(B) has siblings who are legally responsible for his support.

(C) is receiving any union benefits or unemployment insurance.

(D) has a $2000 life insurance policy.

34. The Brown family, applicants for aid, live in a fine apartment in a high-rent district. The landlord, a prominent businessman, has carried the family for some time without payment of rent. The family is unaccustomed to hardship. Of the following, the best procedure for the case worker to follow in making a first visit to the family is to

(A) explain to the family that the rules of the agency do not permit a budget large enough to continue that scale of living.

(B) tell the family that no aid can be given them until they get out of this apartment.

(C) tell the family to move out without telling the landlord of their plans to do so.

(D) explain to the family that the landlord will have to worry about the rent while the family meets other obligations.

35. Mrs. Mary Wooster, who has been caring for her 10-year-old orphaned niece, applies for aid to dependent children when her husband's income is reduced. If you are the one assigned to this case, you should tell Mrs. Wooster that her application

    (A) cannot be accepted for investigation because her niece must be removed from her home and placed out by the state.

    (B) can be accepted for investigation because she falls within the group of relatives who are eligible to receive aid to dependent children.

    (C) cannot be accepted for investigation because relatives other than parents are never granted help through aid to dependent children.

    (D) can be accepted for investigation because her niece is her legal responsibility.

36. The primary purpose in discussing with an applicant the steps in determining his or her eligibility and the kind of verification of facts the agency will need is to

    (A) enable the applicant to understand the basis of eligibility and participate in determining it.

    (B) protect the position of the agency so that there will be no comeback if aid is not granted.

    (C) give the applicant an opportunity to modify any statement he or she may have made previously.

    (D) promote public relations for the agency since the applicant will tell others how the agency is operating.

37. One of the following disclosures is made regarding an applicant for old-age assistance and he is accordingly disqualified to receive the grant requested. In the recommendation submitted by the case worker, the applicant would be found ineligible because he

    (A) is not a citizen.

    (B) has $100 in a bank account that he is saving for burial purposes.

    (C) has 3 married children and could probably live with one of them.

    (D) refuses to give information concerning a bank account of $5000 that had been in his name until four months prior to his application.

38. When a man applies for public assistance, he gives a complete and straightforward account of his past employment and earnings, of the inability of his relatives to help, and of his attempts to find work. The way the family has managed in the past indicates excellent planning ability in the use of money and making limited resources go a long way. He says he has exhausted all of his resources before applying and gives a detailed account. The family lived on less than a full allowance while receiving unemployment compensation. They have exhausted their credit at the grocery store. The landlord is threatening eviction because of rent arrears of two months. He explains he went through all this because it is so painful for him to apply for welfare. The man is obviously honest and reliable. Under these circumstances, a conscientious case worker would find that

    (A) it is unnecessary to verify the foregoing information in order to establish eligibility.

    (B) it is necessary to verify the facts given above in order to establish eligibility.

    (C) the interviewer should be free to decide whether any verifications are needed.

    (D) eligibility considerations should be waived and an immediate grant made in order to help the man feel better.

39. Miss Lowe applies for public assistance and is able to account for her work history and her financial expenditures with the exception of three months in 1987. As acting intake interviewer, it would be your responsibility to inform her that

    (A) she will remain ineligible until she accounts for her complete work history.

    (B) her application can be accepted, but that certain verification will have to be made as to her statements regarding lack of resources.

    (C) she is obviously hiding pertinent information and that her application cannot therefore be considered.

    (D) she obviously had some source of help in 1987 and that she should use this source again.

40. The least reliable method of obtaining information about a client would be

    (A) the client's statements and observations.

    (B) the case worker's opinions of the client's pattern of interaction.

    (C) school reports.

    (D) nonverbal cues.

41. Which of the following would be least acceptable as proof of residence at a specific address?

    (A) An automobile driver's license

    (B) A gas and electric bill

    (C) A hospital clinic appointment card

    (D) A life insurance premium receipt

42. The head of a family applying for an apartment in a low-rent housing project is a widow who was born in another country, married a citizen of the United States in 1971, and has lived here since then. At the time of her marriage, she was not a citizen of the United States. Which of the following would be required as proof of her citizenship?

    (A) Proof of naturalization in her own right

    (B) Proof of her marriage, inasmuch as her husband was a citizen

    (C) Proof of her marriage and proof of her husband's citizenship

    (D) Proof of her marriage with proof of continuous residence in this country

43. The development of a fixed pattern for all initial interviews of applicants for public housing is

    (A) desirable, chiefly because it helps to provide a complete record in the least time.

    (B) desirable, chiefly because it permits the development of a uniform procedure and simplifies the training of interviewers.

    (C) undesirable, chiefly because it fails to provide for the varying circumstances of individual applicants.

    (D) undesirable, chiefly because it sacrifices rapport in order to secure uniformity.

44. Of the following methods of beginning an interview with an applicant for an apartment, the most desirable method to use is to

    (A) allow the applicant to discuss his or her housing problem.

    (B) assure the applicant of your interest in his or her need for housing.

    (C) discuss the purpose of the interview.

    (D) discuss some impersonal topic familiar to everyone.

45. In order to attain accurate information when interviewing an applicant for public housing, a housing assistant should not

    (A) allow the applicant to qualify his or her answers.

    (B) anticipate the applicant's answers.

    (C) ask one question at a time.

    (D) ask questions that are easy for the applicant to answer.

46. The time when it is generally considered desirable to add to the record subjective comments concerning an applicant and family is

    (A) during the interview.

    (B) right after the interview has been concluded and the applicant has left.

    (C) right after the interview has been concluded but before the applicant has left.

    (D) at the end of the day, after all interviews have concluded.

47. The interviewer's choice of words may determine the success or failure of the interview. To be successful in this respect, the interviewer should be careful to

    (A) adjust terminology to the language of the applicant.

    (B) employ expressions similar to those of the applicant.

    (C) speak in terms that are easily understood.

    (D) use correct technical terms with explanations when necessary.

48. When conducting a first interview for an apartment with an applicant who speaks English poorly, the skill of the housing assistant is indicated by

(A) asking the applicant to return the following day when a staff member familiar with the applicant's language will be available.

(B) creating a spirit of rapport in spite of the language difficulty.

(C) explaining to the applicant how his or her language skills affect eligibility.

(D) explaining to the applicant that he or she would probably find it difficult to get along with the other tenants because of their prejudice against persons from other countries.

49. A porter employed at your project asks you if a friend of his whose application was processed by you has been approved as eligible for an apartment at the project. Of the following, the most appropriate action to take is to

(A) ascertain the relationship between the porter and the applicant before discussing his status.

(B) discuss the facts of the situation confidentially with the porter to develop a cooperative relationship with him.

(C) inform him of the tenant's status only if you actually know the final decision on this application.

(D) inform the porter that the applicant will be notified shortly of the results of his application.

50. Assume that an applicant for an apartment in a public housing project objects to answering a question concerning whether he has any income other than that which he receives from his regular employment. The best course of action for the housing assistant to take is to

(A) advise the applicant that he is ineligible and terminate the interview.

(B) advise the applicant to reconsider his refusal to answer and then ask the question again.

(C) go on to the next question and return to this one later in the interview when better rapport has been established.

(D) inform the applicant of the reason for asking the question and tell him he must answer.

51. At an interview to determine whether an applicant is eligible for public housing, the applicant provides information different from that which she submitted on her application. The most advisable action to take is to

(A) cross out the old information and enter the new information.

(B) enter the new information on the applicant form and initial the entry.

(C) give the applicant another application form, have her fill it out correctly, and resume the interview.

(D) give the applicant another application form to fill out, and set a later date for another interview.

52. In interviewing, the practice of anticipating an applicant's answer to questions is generally

    (A) desirable because it is effective and economical when it is necessary to interview large numbers of applicants.

    (B) desirable because many applicants have language difficulties.

    (C) undesirable because it is the inalienable right of every person to answer as he or she sees fit.

    (D) undesirable because applicants may tend to agree with the answer proposed by the interviewer even when the answer is not entirely correct.

53. A follow-up interview was arranged for an applicant so that he could furnish certain requested evidence. At this follow-up interview, the applicant still fails to furnish the necessary evidence. It would be most advisable for you to

    (A) advise the applicant that he is now considered ineligible.

    (B) ask the applicant how soon he can get the necessary evidence and set a date for another interview.

    (C) question the applicant carefully and thoroughly to determine if he has misrepresented or falsified any information.

    (D) set a date for another interview and tell the applicant to get the necessary evidence by that time.

54. In reviewing applications of prospective tenants, you notice that an application was approved by a management assistant who is the daughter of the applicant. You should

    (A) reject the application and reprimand the management assistant.

    (B) review the application and notify the group of management assistants to refer to you all applications of friends and relatives.

    (C) approve the application but warn the management assistant of punishment if a similar incident should occur.

    (D) reject the application and make no further reference to the matter.

55. An applicant complains to you that the management assistant who investigated her disqualified her on racial grounds only. You should

    (A) explain to the applicant that racial discrimination is illegal.

    (B) call the management assistant and demand to know why the tenant was disqualified.

    (C) review the report of the management assistant and accept or reject it.

    (D) assign the case to another management assistant for investigation.

56. In checking applications of prospective tenants that have been passed upon by a management assistant, you discover an error that has led to the acceptance for an application that should have been rejected. You should

    (A) approve the application and reprimand the management assistant.

    (B) reject the application and advise the applicant of the error.

    (C) assign the application to another management assistant to be investigated further.

    (D) approve the application and advise the applicant to remove the disqualifying factor.

57. A management assistant under your supervision reports to you that the application of a prospective tenant, which has been assigned to her, is that of a friend. You should

(A) reprimand the management assistant for accepting an application from a friend.

(B) tell the management assistant to supply you with intimate details of the family history of the applicant.

(C) assign the application to another management assistant.

(D) reject the application.

58. Of the following, the most important reason for registration of applicants for low-rent public housing with the Social Service Exchange is to

(A) avoid duplication of services to the family of the applicant.

(B) determine the current economic status of the applicant.

(C) inform other social agencies of the current need of the applicant for low-rent housing.

(D) provide a more complete picture of current and possible future needs of the family.

59. When an initial interview is being conducted, one way of starting is to explain the purpose of the interview to the applicant. The practice of starting the interview with such an explanation is generally

(A) desirable because the applicant can then understand why the interview is necessary and what will be accomplished by it.

(B) desirable because it creates the rapport necessary for successful interviewing.

(C) undesirable because time will be saved by starting off directly with the questions that must be asked.

(D) undesirable because the interviewer should have the choice of starting an interview in any manner he or she prefers.

60. When a housing assistant visits the home of an applicant to obtain necessary eligibility verification she finds the applicant's 8-year-old son present in the room. In order to conduct the interview properly, the most reasonable action that the housing assistant should take with respect to the boy is to

(A) allow the boy to stay, but warn him not to make any comments during the interview.

(B) ask the parent to send the child to another room to emphasize the confidential nature of the visit.

(C) elicit from the child details of his interest, school record, and health to demonstrate to the parent the attitude of management.

(D) greet the child, but direct the interview toward the parent or adult members of the family.

61. After you have secured all the necessary information from an applicant, he shows no intention of leaving and starts to tell you a long personal story. Of the following, the most advisable action for you to take is to

    (A) explain to the applicant why personal stories are out of place in a business office.

    (B) listen carefully to the story for whatever relevant information it may contain.

    (C) interrupt him tactfully, thank him for the information he has already given, and terminate the interview.

    (D) inform your supervisor that the time required for this interview will prevent you from completing the interviews scheduled for the day.

62. The information that the interviewer plans to secure from an individual with whom he or she talks is determined mainly by the

    (A) purpose of the interview and the functions of the agency.

    (B) state assistance laws and the desires of the individual.

    (C) privacy they have while talking and the willingness of the individual to give information.

    (D) emotional feelings of the individual seeking help and the interviewer's reactions to those feelings.

63. Which is the most effective way of dealing with an interviewee who frequently digresses from the subject under discussion or starts to ramble?

    (A) Tell the person that you will have to terminate the interview unless he or she sticks to the point.

    (B) Increase the tempo of the interview.

    (C) Demonstrate that you are a good listener and allow the person to continue.

    (D) Inject questions that relate to the purpose of the interview.

64. "Being a good listener" is an interviewing technique that, if applied properly, is desirable mostly because it

    (A) catches the client more easily in misrepresentations and lies.

    (B) conserves the energies of the investigator.

    (C) encourages the client to talk about personal affairs without restraint.

    (D) encourages the giving of information which is generally more reliable and complete.

65. When questioning applicants for public assistance or public housing, it would be best to ask questions that are

    (A) direct so that the applicant will realize that the interviewer knows what he or she is doing.

    (B) direct so that the information received will be as pertinent as possible.

    (C) indirect so that the applicant will not realize the purpose of the interview.

    (D) indirect so that they can trap the applicant into making admissions that he or she would not otherwise make.

66. The chief reason for a social investigator or a housing assistant to conduct an interview with a new applicant in complete privacy is that the

    (A) interviewer will be better able to record the facts without any other worker reading the case notes.

    (B) applicant will be impressed by the businesslike atmosphere of the agency.

    (C) interviewer will be able to devote more time to questioning the applicant without interruption.

    (D) applicant will be more likely to speak frankly.

67. When interviewing a client for public housing eligibility, which of the following would NOT be a purpose of the initial interview?

    (A) To obtain sufficient data do determine the applicant's mental health status

    (B) To create an atmosphere of mutual confidence

    (C) To obtain data to determine eligibility

    (D) To obtain data to determine an applicant's ability to cope independently in his or her housing situation

68. The eligibility specialist notices that an applicant suddenly shifts topics during an interview. This would indicate which of the following?

    (A) The interview is too long.

    (B) The applicant is afraid of boring the worker.

    (C) The applicant is exhibiting schizophrenia.

    (D) The topic has become too anxiety provoking.

69. In an assessment during which multiple family members will be present, the eligibility specialist will focus on

    (A) the personalities of each family member.

    (B) the interaction of the family members.

    (C) the issues that appear to be challenging points for the family.

    (D) trying to divide the time for everyone to speak.

70. During an assessment, you notice the applicant that you are interviewing is especially receptive to your interventions and he seems positive and responsive to you. This may be due to the fact that the applicant

    (A) wants your approval.

    (B) is experiencing a state of crisis.

    (C) is free of anxiety.

    (D) feels very fortunate to work with such a skilled eligibility specialist.

HOUSING AND SOCIAL WELFARE

Directions: Each question has four possible answers. Choose the letter that best answers the question and mark your answer on the answer sheet.

1. It is generally agreed by those who have closely studied the housing shortage in this country that, of the new housing needed in the next decade to meet the shortage and to raise standards, the greatest part will be required to
   - (A) house families now seeking separate dwellings.
   - (B) house new families formed during the period.
   - (C) maintain a suitable percentage of vacancies.
   - (D) replace substandard dwelling units.

2. The best statement as to where slum dwellings and slum areas are found in the United States is
   - (A) in New York and several other of the largest cities.
   - (B) in nearly all large cities.
   - (C) in nearly all towns and cities of every size.
   - (D) in nearly all towns and cities of every size and in nearly all rural areas.

3. Which of the following is least characteristic of a slum area?
   - (A) High disease rate
   - (B) High incidence of fires
   - (C) High rate of juvenile delinquency
   - (D) High tax rate

4. The most important step in improving the housing conditions of low-income families living in slum dwellings is to
   - (A) demolish slum dwellings in areas where conditions are worst.
   - (B) enforce existing building and tenement regulations more strictly.
   - (C) provide satisfactory housing at rents that they can afford.
   - (D) replan residential and commercial areas more carefully.

5. The statement has been made that "slum dwellers create the slums." This is generally
   - (A) true because slum dwellers are both unsanitary and unhealthful in their habits.
   - (B) true because environment is as strong a force as heredity in molding character.
   - (C) untrue because slum dwellers do not care to keep their dwellings in clean and sanitary condition.
   - (D) untrue because slums are caused by conditions that are not under the control of the slum dweller.

6. The building of some scattered new housing in a slum area is generally
   - (A) undesirable because the need to adhere to new zoning ordinances will make such construction economically unsound.
   - (B) undesirable because it may be unable to maintain itself against the surrounding slum.
   - (C) desirable because it may serve as the focus for an overall improvement of living conditions.
   - (D) desirable because it may provide an incentive for other new construction.

7. The high tax expenditures in slum areas tend to decrease upon the demolition of the slum buildings and rehousing of the population. The expenditures that decrease least rapidly are those for

  (A) delinquency prevention.

  (B) fire alarms.

  (C) garbage collection.

  (D) street cleaning.

8. It has been said that borne ownership is a magnificent ideal and that the greatest good would be attained when every family in the country owned its own home. The chief limitation of this belief is that

  (A) changing economic and labor conditions may cause the loss of much of the homeowner's investment.

  (B) it applies only to ownership of one-family dwellings.

  (C) it would discourage large-scale speculative building activity.

  (D) public housing would then no longer offer serious competition to private construction.

9. Slum areas and bad housing are expensive to a city chiefly because

  (A) crime and delinquency flourish there.

  (B) higher rents are usually charged there than the tenants can afford.

  (C) more city services of all kinds need to be provided.

  (D) such areas generally represent the larger portion of the city.

10. Tenancy in low-rent government housing projects is usually limited to people of low income. Of the following, the principle upon which this limitation is most probably based is that

  (A) government housing activities should be limited to providing housing for those low-income groups for which private industry cannot provide decent housing at a profit.

  (B) the total amount of desirable housing that is available in a community is limited and the first choice of the better housing should be offered to people of low income.

  (C) low-rent housing developments should not pay high taxes.

  (D) people of high income do not usually want to live in government housing projects.

11. Studies of cities have shown that the rate of juvenile delinquency was highest in areas where housing was least adequate. On the basis of this statement, it is most correct to say that

  (A) no relationship can be established at all since bad housing is but one factor among many that may cause delinquent behavior.

  (B) provision of adequate housing is probably the most effective tool in combating juvenile delinquency.

  (C) areas of substandard housing are generally areas of high juvenile delinquency.

  (D) slum areas are less effectively policed than other areas in the cities in which the studies were conducted.

12. Studies on the relation of juvenile delinquency and housing have in general indicated that the

    (A) effect of poor housing operates independently of family relationships, regardless of city size.

    (B) larger the city, the more significant the factor of poor housing in causing juvenile delinquency.

    (C) relationship between poor housing and juvenile delinquency is almost nonexistent, regardless of urban size.

    (D) size of a city has little significance in the relationship between juvenile delinquency and poor housing.

13. The term "site coverage" as it is usually used in reference to housing projects means

    (A) the area occupied by the buildings alone divided by the total area of the project.

    (B) the area occupied by the buildings and recreation areas divided by the total area of the project.

    (C) the area occupied by the buildings and recreation areas divided by the total area of the project excluding streets.

    (D) the area occupied by the present buildings previously on the site.

14. Impairment of desirability and usefulness resulting from changes in the arts or in design, or from internal influences that make a property less desirable for continued use, is most nearly a definition of

    (A) blight.

    (B) depreciation.

    (C) deterioration.

    (D) obsolescence.

15. A collection of legal requirements, the purpose of which is to protect the safety, health, morals, and general welfare of those in and about buildings, is most nearly a definition of the

    (A) Administrative Code.

    (B) Building Code.

    (C) Welfare Code.

    (D) Sanitary Code.

16. An area in which the majority of dwellings are detrimental to safety, health, or morals because of dilapidation, overcrowding, lack of ventilation, and other similar faults is termed a

    (A) blighted area.

    (B) condemned zone.

    (C) slum area.

    (D) tenement district.

17. The theory that the housing needs of the lower-income groups will be met when the higher-income groups move out of their present housing into newly constructed homes and buildings is known as

    (A) concurrent use.

    (B) economic mobility.

    (C) filter down.

    (D) housing fluidity.

18. NORC stands for

    (A) Naturally Occurring Retirement Community.

    (B) Non-Observable Restrictive Condition.

    (C) Noticeably Offensive Reportable Condition.

    (D) Named Outstanding Replacement Commune.

19. In order to access funds to establish a NORC, social service agencies apply for funds through a Request for Proposal (RFP). This is a

    (A) survey study.

    (B) granting process.

    (C) engineer's report.

    (D) socioeconomic study.

20. A disabled person requests to have a ramp built on her city-funded apartment building. Under the Americans with Disabilities Act the building must

    (A) refuse to comply, as it is too costly for a city-funded building's budget.

    (B) comply because it is mandatory for all buildings to have a ramp, regardless of their funding.

    (C) comply because it is mandatory for a building that receives city funding.

    (D) comply because it is the right thing to do.

21. If an emergency condition is verified by the inspector, the last validly registered owner and managing agent of the property will be notified of said emergency condition by letter and/or by phone and instructed to repair the condition. Which of the following is correct?

    (A) There is a $35 fee to file the action; the court may waive the fee if the tenant is unable to pay.

    (B) If the landlord does not correct this condition, a tenant may initiate an action against the landlord in housing court.

    (C) The landlord can bill the tenants for the repairs.

    (D) The court has the authority to order the landlord to correct the condition and can assess serious penalties for failure to comply.

22. The City Housing Maintenance Code and Multiple Dwelling Law requires landlords to

    (A) provide heat and hot water to all tenants.

    (B) provide hot water whenever possible, but at least for a minimum of 300 days a year.

    (C) provide gas and electric to all tenants.

    (D) provide optional cable service if a tenant can afford the monthly access fee.

23. The Department of Housing Preservation and Development provides which of the following?

    (A) High-interest loans for local homeowners and landlords

    (B) New home construction and vacant building renovation with for-profit and not-for-profit partners to produce affordable housing for both renters and homeowners

    (C) Unsupervised and unsafe housing

    (D) Increased taxes in areas of new construction

24. SCRIE stands for

    (A) Safe Cost Renewal Income Exemption.

    (B) Senior Cost Renovation Income Exemption.

    (C) Senior Citizen Rental Fee Increase Exclusion Program.

    (D) Senior Citizen Rent Increase Exemption Program.

25. People who are tenants and/or spouses of tenants who have an impairment resulting from anatomical, physiological, or psychological conditions demonstrable by medically acceptable clinical and laboratory diagnostic techniques that are expected to be permanent and prevent the tenant from engaging in any substantial, gainful employment are protected in all of the situations EXCEPT which of the following?

   (A) If a building is being converted to cooperative or condominium ownership under a legal eviction plan, a tenant who is an eligible disabled person must relocate.

   (B) An owner can evict a disabled tenant from a rent-stabilized apartment outside New York City or a rent-controlled apartment statewide for purposes of owner occupancy.

   (C) A disabled person may not refuse to purchase his or her apartment and remain in occupancy as a fully protected, rent-stabilized tenant with lease-renewal privileges.

   (D) An owner cannot evict a disabled tenant or the spouse of a disabled tenant from a rent-stabilized apartment in New York City for the purpose of owner occupancy unless the owner provides an equivalent or superior apartment at the same or lower rent in an area near the tenant's present apartment.

26. Which of the following laws of learning would be most helpful in securing tenants' compliance with the rules and regulations of a housing project?

   (A) Adults do not learn as rapidly as children do.

   (B) Effective remembrance is based on periodic repetition.

   (C) Emotional acceptance generally precedes understanding and compliance.

   (D) Understanding is the basis of compliance.

27. As the population of cities increases, there is a decrease in the proportion of the developed urban area that is used for

   (A) commercial purposes.

   (B) industrial purposes.

   (C) parks and open areas.

   (D) residential purposes.

28. The statement that building new homes for the upper-income groups will thereby create a supply of older buildings for the lower-income groups is not tenable unless

   (A) the concurrent elimination of slum dwellings takes place.

   (B) the erection of potential new slums is prevented.

   (C) private enterprise has the facilities to build for all families in the upper-income groups.

   (D) the low-income groups are able to afford the buildings thus vacated.

29. Of the following, the most effective way to reduce the monthly cost of home ownership is to secure reductions in

   (A) interest rates.

   (B) maintenance expenses.

   (C) property taxes.

   (D) the capital cost of the house.

30. If valid criteria have been used in tenant selection for public housing projects, the result most likely to be attained is

   (A) homogeneity of tenant characteristics will be assured.

   (B) larger federal subsidies will be required.

   (C) the neediest families will receive the greatest proportion of assistance.

   (D) the underlying conditions of slums will be ameliorated.

31. It has been claimed that "subsidized housing for workers who cannot pay rent high enough to secure good housing on a profit basis is, in effect, subsidizing low wages for the benefit of parsimonious employers." The defect of this argument is that

    (A) it fails to distinguish between money wages and real wages.

    (B) sanitary and decent housing costs more than slums.

    (C) wage and hour legislation would then be unnecessary.

    (D) wages have not been high enough in the past, prior to the time subsidized housing became available, to enable the average worker to secure good housing.

32. The enforcement of existing or procurable legislation regarding public health, safety, and morals would eliminate slums without the use of public funds. An important defect in this statement is that

    (A) compulsory increases in standards mean higher rentals.

    (B) existing acceptable housing is still insufficient to meet housing needs.

    (C) it assumes the continuation of a high level of home building activity by private enterprise.

    (D) legislation regarding public welfare is absolutely necessary for civilized urban life.

33. A study made of residents in a public housing project one year after it was open for occupancy showed that there was less crime, less disease, and fewer divorces than in a group of the same size and average income living in a slum area. This shows that

    (A) slums tend to breed crime, disease, and marital discord.

    (B) public housing projects have a beneficial effect upon the health and morals of the inhabitants.

    (C) the inhabitants of the public housing project are healthier than those of the slum area.

    (D) the data are insufficient to make any of the foregoing conclusions.

34. Because of present housing conditions in New York City, there are families on the public assistance caseload who require some assistance because of payment of high rentals. This group could be helped best by

    (A) providing satisfactory housing at rents they can afford.

    (B) creating a "relief village" on the outskirts of town where they could live at reduced rents.

    (C) providing homemaker services so that the mothers of these families can seek employment.

    (D) urging them to move to less congested areas outside of New York.

35. Which of the following factors is the greatest obstacle in the assimilation of immigrant groups?

    (A) The difference in the customs and patterns of the present and former environments

    (B) Language difficulties

    (C) The difference in the standards of living enjoyed in the old and the new environments

    (D) The contact that the immigrants maintain with friends and relatives who have remained in the immigrants' former environment

JUDGMENT

Directions: Each question has four possible answers. Choose the letter that best answers the question and mark your answer on the answer sheet.

1. When a family asks for the help of the eligibility specialist because they are consistently exceeding their food and clothing allowance, he or she should

   (A) use the services of the home economist for consultation on the management problem that has developed.

   (B) order the family to live within their budget allowance.

   (C) ignore the situation as it is the family's responsibility to make ends meet.

   (D) recommend small increases in the food and clothing allowance for this family.

2. When a client requests that the Department of Social Services take some action because her unemployed husband is indifferent to her and unconcerned about the welfare of their children, the eligibility specialist should

   (A) inform the husband that he will be cut out of the grant if he does not change his attitude.

   (B) advise the woman to separate and try to build a life apart from her husband.

   (C) tell the woman to appeal to the family court to have her husband ordered to spend his evenings at home.

   (D) suggest that the woman discuss this matter with a private family agency.

3. Knowing that a client needs a period of rest and that another agency can arrange this, it would be the responsibility of an eligibility specialist to

   (A) notify the client of this resource and suggest that he apply there if he wishes to.

   (B) try to make all the arrangements for the client, telling the other agency he or she knows all about the client's situation and can supply information on him.

   (C) tell the client that unless he applies to the other agency, he or she will do so for him.

   (D) tell the client he seems insufficiently interested in getting well enough to work and the Department of Social Services may discontinue his assistance.

4. The homemaking center of the Department of Social Services furnishes the services of mother's aides to families to help care for their children because of the mother's temporary incapacity or absence. Mother's aides can assume responsibility for such household duties as feeding infants, preparing meals, cleaning the house, etc. They are mature, responsible women with previous homemaking experience who have passed a literacy test and have undergone a thorough physical examination. According to current thinking in the field, for the eligibility specialist assigned in any case where a mother's aide is furnished, to use the mother's aide as a source of obtaining confidential information for the department would be

   (A) advisable. As a result of contact with the family, the mother's aide will have observed many details concerning their daily activities.

   (B) inadvisable. While the mother's aide will have observed many details concerning the daily activities of the family, she has not been trained to interpret these observations.

   (C) advisable. The mother's aide has been thoroughly examined regarding her ability to perform her duties in the household.

   (D) inadvisable. The mother's aide has a primary obligation to the family rather than to the department.

5. One of your clients finds it necessary to be away from home for two weeks and arranges with her mother to care for her children, for whom she receives an aid-to-dependent-children grant, without notifying your department about this plan. You discover her absence, however, when making a periodic revisit to the client's apartment. In view of these facts, it would be most advisable to

   (A) stop the grant immediately because you are unable to see the client at this time.

   (B) let the grant continue as the temporary planned absence of the client does not affect her eligibility.

   (C) tell the client's mother that a recipient of aid to dependent children may not leave her children even for a temporary period.

   (D) order the client's mother to wire her return within two days or the grant will stop.

6. Assuming that careful interpretation has been given but an applicant for public assistance refuses to consent to the necessary procedures to establish his eligibility for aid, the most preferable of the following courses of action for the eligibility specialist would be to

   (A) do nothing further.

   (B) grant temporary aid in the hope that the applicant will change his mind.

   (C) try to ascertain why the applicant feels as he does but to respect his decision if he refuses to change his mind.

   (D) proceed to check on all the facts possible even though the applicant has not given his permission.

7. The best of the following reasons for which a public assistance agency should not insist on certain standards of cleanliness as a factor in eligibility to receive public assistance is that it is generally acknowledged that

   (A) people have a right to decide how they will live, provided their mode of living does not hurt others.

   (B) standards of cleanliness vary so much among people as to make one standard impracticable.

   (C) a little dirt has never hurt anyone.

   (D) it would take too much of the eligibility specialist's time to maintain a constant check on this factor.

8. Assume that Mr. Sears applied for aid three weeks ago. As he had not yet received any assistance, he comes to see the eligibility specialist, claiming department neglect. A checkup on Mr. Sears' status reveals that his application has been active pending receipt of a reply from a former employer. When informed of this contingency, Mr. Sears offers to expedite matters by getting in touch with the employer himself. The best way to handle this case would be to tell Mr. Sears that

   (A) the determination of his eligibility is the responsibility of the eligibility specialist alone.

   (B) it would help if he could hurry the reply.

   (C) if he discusses this with the employer, the information will be invalidated.

   (D) he should just go home and wait.

9. Before beginning to demolish a slum area, the families concerned should be assisted, when necessary, in moving. The families' social adjustment is more likely to be achieved, according to case work theory, if the families move to

   (A) a neighborhood chosen by the agency because the agency knows what is best for the families.

   (B) a neighborhood chosen by professional social workers because social workers will choose a better neighborhood.

   (C) a neighborhood chosen by the families themselves because people should be permitted to make their own plans.

   (D) a neighborhood chosen because relatives live nearby, since relatives are always helpful.

10. Social workers generally agree that except for the problems presented in individual cases, financial dependency should be treated as a

    (A) symptom of general industrial unrest.

    (B) manifestation of individual inadequacy and personality maladjustment.

    (C) problem in relationships.

    (D) symptom of economic and personal problems.

11. John Smith, a 40-year-old unemployed carpenter, lost a leg in an accident five years ago. This is his first application for public assistance. The least valid assumption for the eligibility specialist to make prior to investigation is that

    (A) he should be classified as permanently unemployable.

    (B) he is receiving workers' compensation.

    (C) although disabled, he may do well in suitable employment.

    (D) his physical handicap may limit his opportunities for reemployment.

12. When conducting a first interview with an international client who is applying for aid, the skill of the eligibility specialist is indicated by

    (A) discussing the situation with the client without any particular consideration of his cultural background.

    (B) explaining to the client that he will probably find it difficult to get work because of the prejudices of English-speaking persons against persons from other countries.

    (C) utilizing his or her familiarity with the cultural background of the client in order to promote the purpose of the interview.

    (D) explaining to the client how his cultural background affects his dependency.

13. It is important for the eligibility specialist to realize that the use of authority is

    (A) natural only to the aggressive person and that any of its manifestations should be avoided.

    (B) indicative of an assumption of power that the eligibility specialist should not hesitate to apply in all instances.

    (C) a necessary technique for the eligibility specialist to make the client conform to the agency policies.

    (D) inherent in the role of the eligibility specialist and he or she should be aware of its potential uses and abuses.

14. Suppose a client whom you are investigating has borrowed $25 in order to purchase an evening gown for one of her children who is graduating from high school. She is planning to repay the loan at the rate of $1 a week and presents verification of this transaction as well as of the purchase. As an eligibility specialist, you would be complying with the best case work principles by

    (A) telling the client her grant will be reduced in view of her ability to manage on $1 less each week.

    (B) telling the client that she must never do this again.

    (C) explaining to the client how her action will make it more difficult for the family to get along on their limited grant.

    (D) suggesting that she return the dress and repay the borrowed money in this way.

15. The best of the following principles to keep in mind in handling persons who come to social agencies is that

    (A) destitution is not the only reason for opening a case.

    (B) families of the same size should be given the same amount of relief regardless of other factors.

    (C) one can usually accomplish more by the use of authority than by suggestion and cooperation.

    (D) persuasion by means of reasoning is always effective.

16. Mr. Durand, a widower with 3 children, has been receiving aid for about two months. The case worker noticed on a visit that the children had new clothing. Mr. Durand explained that the clothing came from an aunt in a distant city. He stated that the aunt could not help regularly and asked that no contact be established with her. Since the aunt was not legally responsible, the case worker consented to this arrangement. About two weeks later, the worker was told by a neighbor that Mr. Durand was working regularly. The neighbor did not know where Mr. Durand was employed. The best of the following procedures to follow is to

    (A) go to Mr. Durand at once and accuse him of concealing assets.

    (B) investigate the matter further before taking action.

    (C) cut the family off assistance without further investigation.

    (D) tell Mr. Durand that the case worker would never again believe anything he said and that other case workers would be informed of Mr. Durand's unreliability.

17. The Drover family consists of a mother and 5 children. The father had disappeared five years before. The oldest boy, 17, unable to find work, is considering leaving home to avoid becoming a burden to the family. The family owns its six-room home, and rents out one room for $60 a month. Mrs. Drover does day work, but does not earn enough to cover expenses. Her health is poor. A partial aid to dependent children allowance is granted. The best practice for the case worker to follow in this case would be to

    (A) encourage the oldest boy in his plan to leave home.

    (B) determine whether the allowance should be increased to permit Mrs. Drover to stay home.

    (C) get in touch with neighbors to determine if Mr. Drover has been seen recently.

    (D) urge the Department of Aid to Dependent Children to grant the full allowance immediately.

18. Mr. Semple was sent to prison in 2003 as a result of conviction for armed robbery. He will not be eligible for parole until 2008. His former employer is giving the family a small weekly allowance. The family owns a home, but has heavy taxes to pay and interest on the mortgage. The family consists of 3 children, none of whom is older than 16. No payments have been made since Mr. Semple left home and there is no income, other than the employer's allowance. Jack, the second-oldest boy, is in the seventh grade in school and wants to go through high school. His IQ is 74. The family has lived in New York City for twenty-five years. The best of the following procedures is to

(A) refer Mrs. Semple to the Division of Aid to Dependent Children.

(B) warn Mrs. Semple that the children may turn out to be like the father.

(C) urge Jack to continue through high school.

(D) use the agency's influence to get Mr. Semple paroled at once.

19. A social services division was helping the family of Jane Jones. Board money from her brother, James, helped to cut down the amount of aid the family received. A hospital dispensary worker informed the investigator that James was receiving regular treatments for syphilis at the dispensary. The disease was in the noninfectious stage, and the dispensary stated that the family was in no danger of contracting the disease. James had asked the medical social worker not to tell his sister of his condition because he feared that it would worry her. The best of the following procedures for the case worker to adopt is to

(A) initiate with the sister a discussion of the danger of syphilitic infection, permitting her to draw her own conclusions.

(B) tell the sister about the brother's condition without telling her the source of the information.

(C) leave the health matters of the man in the hands of the medical social worker.

(D) question the sister about the morals of her brother.

20. The best of the following practices in handling cases in social agencies is to

(A) use indirect questioning sometimes in preference to direct questioning to obtain more complete information from the client.

(B) use general terms in preference to specific terms in writing case records.

(C) give advice and make promises freely in a first interview in order to gain the confidence of the client.

(D) attempt to increase the client's nervous tension so that he or she will be more anxious to find work.

21. Assume that in making your first visit to the home of an applicant for aid to dependent children, you find the bed unmade, the dishes unwashed, and the furniture so dusty that you cannot find a clean place to sit down. The applicant has 4 small children. Under the circumstances described, you should inform the applicant that

    (A) she is ineligible for the grant because she does not give her children the proper physical environment.

    (B) her application will be investigated and her eligibility determined.

    (C) her application will be investigated but if her home in not cleaned up when you visit next week, her application will be rejected.

    (D) if found eligible for aid to dependent children, she must take instruction in housekeeping from the welfare center home economist.

22. A 15-year-old girl calls on you, the eligibility specialist, to say that her mother is negligent and buys clothing for herself and treats her male friends to movie dates with her grant from aid to dependent children. According to the most generally accepted social case work principles, you should tell the girl that

    (A) the grant will be stopped immediately.

    (B) she does not have to put up with that kind of environment and can arrange to leave her mother immediately.

    (C) you will take this matter up with her mother and see her again at some future time.

    (D) she should file a formal complaint against her mother.

23. A case history describes a client as a delinquent, illiterate, and shy individual who hardly ever engages in group activities and never goes to church, the movies, or the theater. She is regarded by others with annoyance or condescension. The case worker would be justified in forming the conclusion that

    (A) the social isolation is responsible for the delinquency.

    (B) the delinquency is responsible for the social isolation.

    (C) both the poverty and isolation are responsible for the delinquency.

    (D) a single case is insufficient for the inference that social isolation is regularly associated with poverty and delinquency.

24. Mr. and Mrs. Nolan appear to be struggling each month to meet their budget; however, they continue to exceed this amount. They applied for an increase, and were denied. You should advise them to

    (A) continue to request small increases in their allowance.

    (B) explain to the family that they must live within their budgeted allowance.

    (C) refer the case to another worker.

    (D) meet with the family to decide on ways that they can better manage their budget and if necessary seek out the assistance of the professional economists on staff to assist you.

25. Mrs. Berry, a client of yours, consults you to discuss her family situation. She is managing on her allowance; however, she has monthly disagreements with her son who steals her money and appears to be abusing drugs. You can best help her by

    (A) referring her to a counseling agency.

    (B) telling her that you have also had some clients with drug problems with whom she may want to talk.

    (C) pointing out to her that this is not an area that you can help her with.

    (D) informing her that you can try and apply for some extra funds for her so that she can help her son.

26. Mr. Dunne has AIDS and is getting by with his assistance, which you have processed for him. He is upset about being financially dependent on the government and being "on the dole." He tells you that he is ashamed and that he wants to withdraw his case and find an alternative way rather than depending on others. You know that he is quite ill and has no other means of support. You should

    (A) ignore what he is saying because you know he is ill and he needs these services.

    (B) close his case and refer him to Division of AIDS Services (DAS).

    (C) take him off of your case list and refer him to another worker.

    (D) be sensitive to his situation, and explain to him that he has an illness that makes him unable to do certain things for himself. Help him understand that his intentions are noble but this grant money is to help him be strong.

27. Mr. Jones has been a paraplegic since he was 14. He was injured in a diving accident. He is not yet 33 and his mother who has supported him has passed away leaving him with no other supports. He will need to apply for public assistance because

    (A) he is unemployable.

    (B) his disability will limit his ability to be employed.

    (C) he can never marry someone who can assist him.

    (D) he was injured at such a young age.

28. In meeting with a client for an interview, the best reason to be knowledgeable about someone's culture is because

    (A) it will help you build a rapport with this individual.

    (B) it will decrease the client's anxiety.

    (C) it will make you look more knowledgeable.

    (D) it will limit the client's predisposition about the U.S.

29. The degree of social intelligence a person possesses can best be determined by the

    (A) extent of success the person has in getting along with people.

    (B) score obtained on a test of social intelligence.

    (C) judgment of a psychologist in an interview with the person.

    (D) person's own judgment of his or her success in dealing with social situations.

30. Which of the following statements best describes the relationship that exists among environment, intelligence, and learning to read and write?

    (A) The proper environment is necessary to make the most of one's intelligence in learning to read and write.

    (B) There is no relationship among environment, intelligence, and the ability to read and write.

    (C) A person with low intelligence cannot learn to read and write, regardless of environment.

    (D) Intelligence develops with reading and writing, regardless of environment.

31. Assume a young, healthy-looking male client who is jobless and on public assistance tells you he feels and thinks he may have AIDS. As his case worker, you should first

    (A) assure him that he is probably all right, not to worry, and to find a job.

    (B) inform him he will be ineligible for public assistance if he has AIDS, but may be able to receive SSI.

    (C) refer him to his doctor or to a health provider who is knowledgeable about AIDS to learn the truth.

    (D) assure him that he will not be cut off public assistance if he has AIDS.

32. Assume that it is Friday and you are planning your schedule for the following week. The final session of a ten-session training class you are required to take is scheduled for 2 p.m. Thursday. It will last all afternoon and will review all of the material that has been covered as well as talks by specialists in certain matters not covered in past sessions. Assume also that your agency requires you to visit the homes of clients on a planned basis. In planning your activities for Thursday, of the following, your most efficient and correct use of time would be to plan to

    (A) skip the training session since it is largely a repeat of information that has already been covered.

    (B) visit one AFDC family near the training center whose previously scheduled visit you had been forced to cancel because of illness.

    (C) visit one family on public assistance that is known to have long-standing problems that should be discussed. The family lives a considerable distance from the training center and you must first check in at your office before going to the field.

    (D) refrain from going to the session and copy a coworker's notes so that you will not miss anything.

33. Assume that a client calls with an emergency problem that appears to require an immediate home visit. You, his case worker, are handling the supervisor's phone messages since she is at an important meeting with the agency's director. Of the following, your best action is to

(A) tell the client you cannot leave the office but that he should come to the office to see you as soon as possible.

(B) send another case worker to visit the client and to handle the emergency.

(C) schedule a visit to the client for the following morning.

(D) request another case worker to handle the phone, leave a note for your supervisor explaining the situation, and visit the client immediately.

34. Assume you are the case worker for an elderly woman not working and living alone. She is constantly visiting the social service office and holding long conversations unrelated to her case with you, your supervisor, your coworkers, and with anyone else who is around. You should understand that this client

(A) may be trying to tell you something of vital importance related to her eligibility.

(B) is trying to ingratiate herself with staff so that she will be given special consideration.

(C) is in need of psychiatric help and should be referred to a clinic for consultation and therapy.

(D) may be lonely and seeking the companionship of other people but not knowledgeable about community programs and activities that might be of interest to her.

35. Assume that a new case worker sits next to you in the public assistance office and is constantly besieging you with questions, only some of which are connected with your agency's work. As a result, you are somewhat behind in your own responsibilities. Of the following, you should initially

(A) report to your supervisor that the new worker needs further training.

(B) request that your desk be moved without giving an explanation.

(C) say nothing to the supervisor or to the new worker but remain after working hours to complete your responsibilities in a timely manner.

(D) explain to the new worker that you will be glad to answer pertinent questions related to her duties but that you must complete your own work on time.

36. A case worker who attempts to impose his or her judgments on clients is most likely to elicit

(A) appreciation.

(B) collaboration.

(C) submission.

(D) resistance.

37. A 16-year-old client in foster care reveals to you that she is involved in many casual and unprotected sexual relationships. She asks you for guidance. You should respond by

(A) notifying the foster parents and explain your concern.

(B) suggesting that she talk to her foster parents about this.

(C) not notifying the foster parents but referring the girl for counseling.

(D) doing nothing.

38. An anxious client of yours involved in mental health treatment is repeatedly being asked for money by his drug-addicted son. Recently, the son has threatened violence and begun calling the father at all hours of the night. How should you advise the father?

(A) Suggest that he has a right to be fearful and that he should consider calling the police if his son does not stop his threats.

(B) Ask the client if you can call his son.

(C) Do nothing.

(D) Suggest that he disconnect the phone or get an answering machine.

39. A client is upset and disappointed about not being called back after a job interview. You should respond by saying

(A) "You have to be patient in a job search."

(B) "I guess you are hurt and angry about not getting the job."

(C) "I would be very angry if I were you."

(D) "Remember, this will take a long time."

40. Which one of these is NOT evidence of discrimination in a job interview or on a job application?

(A) Please send in a photograph with the application.

(B) What is your birth date?

(C) List your last three jobs.

(D) What is your husband's occupation?

PUBLIC HEALTH

Directions: Each question has four possible answers. Choose the letter that best answers the question and mark your answer on the answer sheet.

1. Among people who are blind, the ones who may be expected to display a range of experience most comparable with that of sighted people are those who

    (A) receive no special consideration from others.

    (B) are closely protected by their relatives and friends against the severe limitations imposed by their blindness.

    (C) are urged to greater attainments than would be expected of sighted people in order to compensate for their blindness.

    (D) are urged to understand their potentialities and limitations and are encouraged to make the most of their opportunities.

2. Medical social work is distinguished from other forms of case work by the fact that

    (A) it is always performed by a trained nurse.

    (B) it is always carried on directly under the supervision of a physician.

    (C) it is directed primarily at bringing about conditions suitable for medical treatment and recovery of the patient.

    (D) it relates only to chronic ailments that allow a sufficient length of time for service to make it effective.

3. The nutritive value of foods is determined principally by

    (A) specific gravity.

    (B) shelf life.

    (C) mineral content.

    (D) enzyme components.

4. A knowledge of nutrition is of importance to a case worker chiefly because

    (A) it adds to his or her stock of cultural information.

    (B) it helps him or her understand the client's needs and may assist in formulating a plan for meeting these needs.

    (C) the case worker should be familiar with modern sociological theories and practices.

    (D) the case worker is thus enabled to act as a nutrition expert.

5. The term "vital statistics" is most commonly applied to such data as

    (A) births, deaths, and marriages.

    (B) unemployment rates and cost of living indices.

    (C) the number of people applying for public assistance and costs of public assistance administration.

    (D) costs of health and safety education.

6. An occupational disease is one that arises from

    (A) continued employment in particular types of work.

    (B) an accidental injury sustained by the employee.

    (C) continued unemployment.

    (D) dependence on public assistance.

7. The part of medicine that relates to foods is called

    (A) mastication.

    (B) deglutition.

    (C) pediatrics.

    (D) dietetics.

8. The disease in connection with the Schick Test is best known as
   (A) diphtheria.
   (B) tuberculosis.
   (C) typhoid fever.
   (D) syphilis.

9. A contributing factor to the decline in the death rate in the United States within recent years is generally considered by authorities to be the
   (A) decline in the incidence of heart disease.
   (B) shorter hours of work in industry.
   (C) decline in the incidence of infectious diseases in childhood.
   (D) increase in the number of group medical treatment plans.

10. The population of the United States is said to be "aging"; that is, there are more older people proportionately now than in the past. The most probable reason for this is the
    (A) increasing knowledge of diseases of older age groups.
    (B) constantly declining birth rate and immigration rate.
    (C) increase in public hospital and clinic facilities.
    (D) unemployment and increased leisure among older age groups.

11. The essential purpose of health education is to
    (A) lower the cost of medical service to the public.
    (B) advertise public medical service.
    (C) instruct the public in the value of good medical services.
    (D) give the public information on self-treatment.

12. The most accurate of the following statements about visiting nurses is that they
    (A) may visit families independently of a physician to give instruction in hygiene or minor services such as baths to patients.
    (B) always restrict their work to bedside service to the sick patient and take no responsibility for other members of the family.
    (C) never visit a family except by order of a physician.
    (D) always provide service free of charge.

13. The most certain test of whether the authorities of the public health administration in a large city are doing effective work is seen in the
    (A) decrease in death rates from yellow fever, smallpox, pneumonia, and mumps.
    (B) decrease in death rates from typhoid, diphtheria, and tuberculosis.
    (C) decrease in death rates from diabetes, heart disease, and cancer.
    (D) increase in the birth rate.

14. The best of the following methods of combating communicable diseases is
    (A) fumigating homes in which persons with contagious diseases have been living.
    (B) inoculating against typhoid fever all persons known to have been in contact with a typhoid patient.
    (C) imposing a quarantine period upon all incoming vessels.
    (D) enforcing the law requiring reporting of communicable diseases.

15. Authorities on health education emphasize certain things that all persons should do as a preventive measure. The most important of these is a(n)

    (A) routine X-ray examination of the teeth.

    (B) cold shower every morning.

    (C) annual typhoid inoculation.

    (D) annual medical examination.

16. The best way to stop the spread of infectious diseases is to

    (A) check all expiration dates on foods.

    (B) wear protective garments such as rubber gloves when working with someone who is ill.

    (C) wash your hands.

    (D) not come in contact with individuals who are suffering from any illness.

17. Alcohol offers what type of nutritional value?

    (A) None

    (B) It is the equivalent of a carbohydrate since it is made from barley and similar yeasts.

    (C) Cholesterol

    (D) Protein

18. Abuse can take all of the following forms EXCEPT

    (A) physical.

    (B) nutritional.

    (C) sexual.

    (D) financial.

19. Women who are pregnant are advised to avoid alcohol because

    (A) the baby will have a difficult time adjusting to breast milk after it is born.

    (B) drinking when pregnant increases the baby's weight and causes its development to increase.

    (C) drinking when pregnant increases the chance of a low birth weight and fetal alcohol syndrome.

    (D) alcohol affects the increase of the growing baby and this can hurt the mother.

20. All of the following are attributed to heart disease EXCEPT

    (A) low blood pressure.

    (B) a family history of heart disease.

    (C) smoking or use of smokeless tobacco.

    (D) the inability to handle stress.

PROCEDURES AND RECORDS

> **Directions:** Each question has four possible answers. Choose the letter that best answers the question and mark your answer on the answer sheet.

1. In spite of the need that most of us have of finding rules and procedures to guide us, we must face the difficulty at the outset that there is no such thing as a model case record. Of the following, the best justification for this statement is that

   (A) records should be written to suit the case.

   (B) case recording should be patterned after the best models obtainable.

   (C) rules cannot be applied to social case work because each case requires individual treatment.

   (D) the establishment of routine procedures in social work is an ideal that cannot be realized.

2. Of the following, the best statement with regard to the efficiency of the eligibility specialist in a public assistance agency is that

   (A) clerical efficiency automatically speeds up the satisfaction of clients' needs.

   (B) clerical efficiency automatically increases skill in client relationships.

   (C) clients resent clerical efficiency in social work.

   (D) clerical efficiency automatically meets the client's needs.

3. A woman applying for aid says that her husband is a drunkard, beats her, and mistreats her children. The eligibility specialist, when referring this case to a case worker, should make a notation that this man should be

   (A) committed to an institution for alcoholics.

   (B) taken to court and ordered to keep the peace.

   (C) referred to a psychiatric clinic.

   (D) None of the above

4. The essential purpose of the face sheet of a case record is to present

   (A) identifying data about the particular individuals in the social situation who present a problem to the agency.

   (B) intimate personal facts about the persons concerned in the social situation.

   (C) identifying data about the persons concerned in the social situation.

   (D) a social diagnosis of the family for reference purposes.

5. One of the primary functions of an eligibility specialist is to

   (A) receive and record all complaints.

   (B) interview all applicants for aid.

   (C) take inventories of materials and supplies received.

   (D) receive the commodities to be used by needy persons.

6. Writing a case record in a busy agency involves knowledge of acceptable practices in social case recording. Below are four practices an interviewer might follow in writing up a long first investigation. Choose the best of the four.

   (A) Write verbatim in the presence of the client everything he or she says.

   (B) Omit from the record any mention of agreements or promises made by the case worker.

   (C) Omit any mention of tension observed between members of the family, describing only what has to do with the economic condition of the family.

   (D) Give a picture of the problem as it appears to the family.

7. Which of the following is NOT a good practice in writing up a case?

   (A) Include everything of importance said by the case worker.

   (B) Give a clear account of the client's difficulties.

   (C) Record any line of action the case worker may have agreed to follow.

   (D) Make the case record as lengthy and as detailed as possible.

8. Of the following, the least valid reason for the maintenance of the case record in public assistance administration is to

   (A) furnish reference material for other case workers.

   (B) improve the quality of service to the client.

   (C) show how the public funds are being expended.

   (D) reduce the complexities of the case to manageable proportions.

9. A public assistance agency will lean more on forms than a private agency in the same field of activity because

   (A) forms simplify the recording responsibilities of newly appointed eligibility specialists.

   (B) public welfare records are of the family agency type.

   (C) the government framework requires a greater degree of standardization.

   (D) more interviews and visits are made in connection with public assistance cases.

10. During an interview with a client in which you are to determine his eligibility, he shares confidential information with you and asks you to withhold it from the record. You should

    (A) listen to the client—because that is what is most important—and record the information since you must report all information as part of the case record.

    (B) listen to the client—because that is what is most important—and respect his wishes by keeping the material private and separate from their record.

    (C) provide the client with an open ear—after all, you are aware that he has no one else to share his problems with.

    (D) explain to the client that he should not share any information with you that he will want withheld from his record since you must report all information as part of the case record.

11. A face sheet will include all of the following EXCEPT a client's

    (A) name.

    (B) prior sexual relationships.

    (C) address.

    (D) demographic data.

12. In a case record, you should do which of the following?

    (A) Keep it brief, succinct, and clear.

    (B) Keep it prolonged and repetitious so that you make your point.

    (C) Add your personal observations of the client's personal preferences.

    (D) Describe what you did not like about the person.

13. Which of the following is NOT considered an asset that will be included in someone's budget?

    (A) Wages

    (B) Stocks

    (C) IRA

    (D) Burial fund

14. In a case record, you should include all of the following EXCEPT

    (A) the family history.

    (B) anything the family shares with you.

    (C) the family's perception of each other's problems.

    (D) any occurrence of family problems.

15. It is often good case management procedure for the worker to set up a personal "tickler" file in order to have easy accessibility to the essential matters involving each case responsibility. Of the following, the information least needed to be included on most cases would be the

    (A) client's name, address, and phone number, if any.

    (B) case number for reference to the actual case record.

    (C) medical history of each client.

    (D) dates when required visits are made.

INTERPRETATION OF SOCIAL WORK PROBLEMS

Directions: Use the following table to answer questions 1–6. Do not assume that the facts in the schedule are either actual or current. They were simply devised to test your ability to apply fact in solving the kinds of problems that are part of your work.

SCHEDULE OF MONTHLY ALLOWANCES FOR ASSISTANCE

Item of Expense	Allowance for Recipient		
	Adult	Child 13–18	Child under 13
Food	$17.96	$70.00	$60.00
Clothing	$18.00	$16.80	$15.80
Rent	As paid by the client		
Utilities	$2.40 per person		
Incidentals	$1.40 per person		

1. The Anderson family, consisting of father, mother, and 4 children, ages 4, 10, 15, and 17, is eligible for public assistance. The rent is $160 a month. Public assistance granted on the basis of the above items is given semimonthly. According to the schedule shown, the proper semimonthly grant for this family would be

    (A) $688.75
    (B) $516.14
    (C) $289.96
    (D) $172.29

2. Assuming that all the expenditures except rent were reimbursable under the State Welfare Law to the same extent that reimbursements for assistance are now being made to the city, the annual cost to the city for all the items included in the public assistance budget of the Anderson family would be

    (A) $1,920.67
    (B) $5,039.04
    (C) $8,260.56
    (D) $5,058.02

3. Mrs. Peet is 67 years old and applies for old-age assistance. She lives with her widowed niece who has a family of 3 children. The rent of the apartment is $112 a month. The niece has agreed to pay for the utilities of the whole group and also to give Mrs. Peet some money for personal incidentals, provided that Mrs. Peet can pay one fifth of the rent. On medical advice, a special diet allowance of $15.44 a month is authorized for Mrs. Peet, in addition to the regular food allowance. The proper monthly grant for Mrs. Peet would be

    (A) $96.96
    (B) $112.40
    (C) $73.80
    (D) $161.44

4. Mrs. Scalise applies for aid for herself and her 2 children, ages 2 and 4. Her rent costs $130 a month. She is separated from her husband, who contributes $36 a week by court order. It has also been verified that Mrs. Scalise earns $22.40 a week doing piecework at home. Assuming that for budget computation purposes, the department considers 4.3 weeks as equivalent to one month, the monthly grant in this case would be

   (A) $96.32
   (B) $77.84
   (C) $154.80
   (D) $251.12

5. A 36-year-old sightless widower applies for aid to the blind. His rent and utilities are met by relatives with whom he lives. In aid-to-blind cases, $17.40 per month is allowed for expenses incidental to blindness as substitute for the personal incidentals item in the schedule. Under the circumstances, the proper monthly grant would be computed at

   (A) $89.40
   (B) $53.36
   (C) $78.00
   (D) $128.00

6. John Burke is 52 years old and needs supplementary assistance. He pays $74 a month for his room and earns $84 a month doing odd jobs. Basing your computations on these facts and on the schedule, you can determine that the proper semi-monthly grant for Mr. Burke would be

   (A) $167.80
   (B) $83.80
   (C) $29.76
   (D) $25.28

7. The knowledge and understanding of situations and people attained through social case work may well serve as a basis for sound social action and for effective social welfare planning. The most logical assumption that the social case worker can draw from this statement is that

   (A) since social welfare planning is related to broad social issues and needs, it is unnecessary to consider the individual.

   (B) the individual is the only unit to be considered in planning effective social welfare programs.

   (C) all social planning should be directed primarily toward the individual and his or her needs.

   (D) knowledge of the individual attained through social case work can be effectively utilized in planning a broad social welfare program.

8. The inability of people to obtain employment during a time of economic depression is an example of the principle that

   (A) anyone who really wants a job can get one if he or she tries hard enough.

   (B) the more capable people get jobs when jobs are scarce.

   (C) at certain times employment is not available for many people, irrespective of ability, character, or need.

   (D) full employment is a thing of the past.

9. If the budget allowance, T dollars, granted each child under V years of age, is increased W percent of the base figure every X years, the percentage increase in the budget per child for a family of Y children all under V minus P years of age would, at the end of P years, be

   (A) W times $\dfrac{T}{PX}$.

   (B) V minus $\dfrac{P}{YX}$.

   (C) P times $\dfrac{W}{X}$.

   (D) None of the above

10. The real worth of the family court cannot be estimated in dollars and cents. This statement most nearly means

    (A) that taxpayers should not begrudge the cost of administering this court, no matter how large.

    (B) that the importance of this court to the community is the service that it renders in the preservation of family life.

    (C) that the cost of administering the court must increase from year to year.

    (D) that the value of the court's work in terms of dollars and cents should be ignored by the taxpayers.

11. During the year 2004, N families applied for aid, representing an increase of M families over the number applying in 2002. In 2003, however, the number applying was P less than in 2002. If there were R investigators in each of the three years, the average case load per investigator in 2003 was

    (A) N minus $\dfrac{M}{PR}$.

    (B) N minus M minus $\dfrac{P}{R}$.

    (C) M plus N minus $\dfrac{R}{P}$.

    (D) N plus M plus $\dfrac{P}{R}$.

12. If it is assumed that the study of anthropology has no value for social work, then

    (A) no anthropologist should be interested in social work.

    (B) no primitive cultures have any meaning for social workers.

    (C) people who study anthropology should be interested in social work.

    (D) primitive cultures have meaning for the student of modern society.

13. It has been found by a research study in England that, during the time that social insurance has been in effect, there has been a decrease in the consumption of alcohol. The most valid assumption on the basis of this information is that

    (A) people receiving social insurance tend to spend their money on alcohol.

    (B) social insurance income is so small that people cannot afford to buy alcohol.

    (C) the use of alcohol is a means of escape from an intolerable situation.

    (D) a decrease in the consumption of alcohol may be related to the receipt of social insurance.

FOR QUESTIONS 14–18, READ THE FOLLOWING PASSAGE AND DETERMINE WHETHER EACH STATEMENT THAT FOLLOWS IS (A) ENTIRELY TRUE, (B), ENTIRELY FALSE, (C) PARTLY TRUE AND PARTLY FALSE, OR (D) CANNOT BE ANSWERED BASED ON THE FACTS GIVEN.

The child labor provisions of the Minimum Wage Act prohibit any producer, manufacturer, or dealer to ship or deliver in interstate commerce any goods produced in an establishment that has employed oppressive child labor in the previous thirty days. Oppressive child labor is defined as employment of children under 16 years of age. Exception is made for children of 14 or 15 in kinds of work other than manufacturing or mining in which it has been determined by the Chief of the Children's Bureau, that the work does not interfere with school, health, or well-being. However, employment of children 16 or 17 years of age is prohibited in any occupation found and declared by the Chief of the Children's Bureau to be particularly hazardous or detrimental to health.

14. The Minimum Wage Act sets up minimum wages and hours for children who are legally permitted to work.

15. The Minimum Wage Act makes no provision for children over 16 years of age.

16. The employment of children of any age in a hazardous occupation is considered oppressive child labor.

17. According to the Act, a producer in New York State may not employ oppressive child labor for goods that he intends to ship to New Jersey, but is not affected if he sells the goods within New York State.

18. The Chief of the Children's Bureau may determine what exceptions may be made for children of 14 engaged in farming, and for children of 16 engaged in only manufacturing and mining.

FOR QUESTIONS 19–25, A QUOTATION IS GIVEN IN WHICH ONE WORD OR TWO CONSECUTIVE WORDS ARE INCORRECT. SELECT THE OPTION THAT, IF INSERTED IN THE PLACE OF THE INCORRECT WORD OR WORDS, WILL MAKE THE STATEMENT CORRECT

19. Efforts to deal constructively with the juvenile delinquent have been thwarted by the commonly held beliefs of a decade or two ago that most of them are social failures. The evidence against that today is overwhelming.
    (A) Mentally challenged
    (B) Normal child
    (C) Psychotic adult
    (D) Adult mentality

20. Perhaps startling to some people, although a commonplace to the public assistance workers themselves, is the recently ascertained fact that of those people who became eligible for unemployment compensation, more than 90 percent had notified the assistance offices of the receipt of their agreement with the agency before official notification was received from the unemployment compensation authorities.
    (A) Work assignments
    (B) Benefit checks
    (C) Insurance pensions
    (D) Endowment policies

21. The public aid program must focus on means of training and maintaining the skills of its clients, must play an aggressive leadership role in the placement of its clients in labor camps, and must do this fully aware of the importance of preventing the flooding of the labor market with people forced to accept substandard sweatshop wages.
    (A) Relief categories
    (B) Government projects
    (C) Public institutions
    (D) Private industry

22. The psychoanalysts evolved theories as to the stages of intellectual development through which the personality matures and threw much light on the life situations and mental mechanisms by which this process is thwarted.

(A) Psychological

(B) Abnormal

(C) Emotional

(D) Retrogressive

23. Popular belief in the efficacy of punishment by imprisonment is apparently based on ignorance of the statistics on classification. While the figures supplied by prison officials are as low as 39 percent for some states, they are as high as 78 percent in others, and the general average for the whole country is approximately 64 percent. Some authorities frankly express their opinion that large numbers of prisoners emerge from existing institutions worse than when they entered.

(A) Probation

(B) Recidivism

(C) Health

(D) Perversion

24. When aid standards are discussed, it is often difficult to work out the problem that centers on granting allowances to provide health and decency standards and what the self-supporting family can afford. The subsistence diet procedure in aid administration has been one method used to meet this problem.

(A) Grocery order

(B) Cash grant

(C) Budgetary deficiency

(D) Security wage

25. With the increasing interest in the contribution of group experience to individual growth, there has developed within the past few years, in several communities, considerable cooperation between case work agencies and those agencies in the public welfare field.

(A) Child guidance

(B) Mental hygiene

(C) Community housing

(D) Group work

26. Merely looking at a client is enough to tell an intelligent eligibility specialist

(A) whether the client is lying.

(B) whether the client is actually in need.

(C) whether the client is likely to cooperate.

(D) None of the above

27. A family of 5 has one employed member earning K dollars a month. The family receives a total semimonthly assistance grant of L dollars. If the rent allowance is M dollars, and the amount spent for food is twice that for rent, the amount spent monthly for all items other than food and rent is

(A) K plus 2L minus 3M.

(B) M plus K plus $\frac{L}{5}$.

(C) K plus L minus 2M.

(D) L minus $\frac{2M}{5}$.

28. In a survey of N families on assistance, it was found that P percent consists of 2 persons. Q percent of the N families consist of 1 parent and 1 child. The percent of families on assistance which consists of 2 persons not of the parent-child category is

    (A) larger that W percent but less than P percent.

    (B) P minus $\dfrac{Q}{N}$.

    (C) N.

    (D) P minus Q.

29. In the following instances, cooperative behavior that results from loyalty to the same objective is best exemplified by

    (A) the citizens of a community forming a committee for the purpose of building a school.

    (B) an employer and employee agreeing to a conference for the purpose of arriving at an equitable wage settlement.

    (C) people attending a championship tennis match held for charitable purposes.

    (D) a conquered people accepting aid from their conquerors.

30. It is often held that cooperative activity is difficult to achieve because "individuals are basically selfish" and their alleged selfishness makes it difficult, if not impossible, to subordinate their individual wills to the collective enterprise. The chief factor overlooked in such a conception of the matter is that

    (A) there is no necessary discrepancy or conflict between selfishness and co-operation.

    (B) people do not seek to further their self-interest by competitive activity.

    (C) competition and cooperation are essentially alike.

    (D) most successful people are not selfish.

QUESTIONS 31 AND 32 ARE BASED ON THE FOLLOWING TABLE.

SCHEDULE OF MONTHLY ALLOWANCES FOR ASSISTANCE

Item of Expense	Allowance for Recipient		
	Adult	Child 13–18	Child under 13
Food	$17.96	$70.00	$60.00
Clothing	$18.00	$16.80	$15.80
Rent	As paid by the client		
Utilities	$2.40 per person		
Incidentals	$1.40 per person		

31. Mr. Ross, age 55, receives a monthly food allowance of $12.44 for his special dietary needs. He receives his monthly allowance semimonthly. His rent is $96.50. His allowance would be

    (A) $107.67

    (B) $206.70

    (C) $130.74

    (D) $101.45

32. Mrs. Ages applies for aid for herself and her 3 children, ages 13, 12, and 11. She pays rent of $145.20, which includes utilities. Mrs. Ages' oldest son receives a monthly stipend of $14.40 toward his disability. Her monthly grant would be

    (A) $593.96

    (B) $449.16

    (C) $791.56

    (D) $464.16

33. One of the roles of human service workers is to

(A) identify and bring to public attention the social problems that they encounter in their daily work.

(B) fix social problems.

(C) diagnose and identify budgetary needs.

(D) observe problem areas in society.

34. Economics and finance are such important components of social policy that they are central to much of the work done by the executive and legislative branches every year in the form of budgeting and budget preparation. The budget process begins well before the end of the budget, or fiscal year, which is in the federal government. The most common state fiscal year is

(A) October 1 to September 30.

(B) July 1 to June 30.

(C) September 1 to August 31.

(D) January 1 to December 31.

35. By giving people cash payments in cases of unemployment, old age, and loss of the family breadwinner—some of the leading causes of poverty—it helped prevent destitution and dependency. This was done so in a way that

(A) maintained the country's financial situation.

(B) was additionally a relief to the working class.

(C) created tremendous opposition from the government.

(D) maintained individual freedom and human dignity.

FOR QUESTIONS 36–40, TWELVE POSSIBLE ANSWERS ARE SUGGESTED. FOR EACH QUESTION, WRITE DOWN THE LETTERS OF THE THREE BEST ANSWERS.

36. The problem of rearing children in a modern city is due, in part, to the survival of older attitudes that are in a practical way incompatible with modern urban conditions, and to the absence of definite patterns of guidance in a changing society for parents whose intelligence quotient (IQ) may not be very high. No ethic has yet risen to take the place of the one followed in the Victorian era. The individual no longer has moral problems solved by the family group. The heterogeneity of society and the rapidity of social change make impossible specific formulae that tell one what to do in different situations. Right and wrong have to be figured out by the individual, which calls for a high IQ and some ability to think in an emotional situation.

Which three options best illustrate the implications of this paragraph?

(A) Since modern society has fewer ethics than the Victorian era, attempts should be made to provide patterns of behavior for families.

(B) Parents who do not have high IQs cannot bring up their children properly in a changing society without assistance.

(C) Parents with high IQs can be counted upon to think more clearly in emotional situations than parents with average IQs.

(D) The family can be helped to solve the children's problems if specific formulae, now lacking, are provided.

(E) In our present society, parents are given patterns by which they may gauge their attitudes and behavior toward their children.

(F) Since the family no longer has any influence over its individual members, one should deal directly with each member of the family group as individuals.

(G) Since many parents do not have high IQs, modern patterns of guidance should be provided for them.

(H) Social change, which develops more rapidly than formulae for meeting it, creates problems for the individual as well as for the family.

(I) Since people are not as emotional as they used to be, individuals with high IQs are not apt to need assistance in meeting their problems.

(J) The children in the modern family may not depend upon their families for definitions of right and wrong.

(K) The family is no longer a unit of society because modern urban conditions have broken down parental authority.

(L) Present society has not evolved generally accepted patterns of behavior comparable to those of the Victorian era.

37. The handling of public assistance funds seems very simple to those who have never pondered the power that is concentrated within giving assistance. Unleashed, it can destroy morale and self-respect; harnessed, it can preserve courage and rebuild self-confidence. The key to sound assistance administration is fairness. In other words, everyone who is eligible for assistance under the organization's policies should be able to secure financial help, whether or not he or she is civil or rude. Often township poormasters have a tendency to work off old grudges or present irritations by considering not a family's resources, but their reputation and courtesy. Case work brings a disciplined use of power.

Which three options most clearly illustrate the meaning of the above paragraph?

(A) Civil behavior on the part of applicant is indicative of the extent of the client's need of assistance.

(B) A family's experience with assistance today vitally influences the pattern of its life tomorrow.

(C) The power inherent in the assistance-giving situation has a deleterious effect on clients.

(D) Clients' behavior is not important to the eligibility specialist in his or her function of administering assistance.

(E) The power of the person administering assistance is not inherent in his or her situation.

(F) Case work is a method of disciplining clients.

(G) Fairness on the part of the eligibility specialist does not depend upon determining financial need on the basis of the client's behavior.

(H) Case work is a method of determining assistance needs in accordance with the client's resources and his or her value to society.

(I) A disciplined use of power means that the eligibility specialist only uses his or her power over the client when persuasion fails.

(J) The eligibility specialist can eliminate the power inherent in the assistance-giving situation if he or she is fair to the client.

(K) The client's civility or rudeness may not be an indication of the extent of his or her financial need.

(L) The power inherent in the aid-giving situation builds up morale and self-respect when the eligibility specialist treats all clients in the same way.

38. "Why do you pry into my private life? You have my canceled bankbook. You've seen my dispossess notice. Do you think I'd let things like that happen if I had any way to stop them?" Such questions made the eligibility specialist, often convinced of the client's need, ask "Why investigate?"

Which three explanations best represent accepted social work concepts as to the reason for investigation?

(A) It is a policy of the agency not to grant assistance unless every clue has been investigated.

(B) Need is relative and people with a lower standard of living may be able to get by with less income.

(C) Investigation tends to clear up the client's fears of arbitrary action by defining his or her status and responsibilities in relation to the agency.

(D) It is both administratively sounder and psychologically easier for clients that there should be, in general, basic requirements in any determination of eligibility.

(E) The investigation places an additional responsibility on the client at a time when he or she wants to be dependent, temporarily at least, upon someone else.

(F) The investigation is a method of finding out whether or not the client has a tendency to remain permanently on assistance.

(G) The honest client does not need investigation, but other clients do and it would be difficult to explain why some clients should and other clients should not be investigated.

(H) The client's potential for independence may be discovered or developed during the investigation process.

(I) Investigation must be made in order to complete the necessary case record before assistance can be given.

(J) Assistance without investigation is too easy and will tend to make the client too ready to accept assistance as a means of livelihood.

(K) If the case is so urgent that immediate assistance without investigation is necessary, a private agency should be used.

(L) Investigation leads to an intimate relationship between the investigator and the client.

39. The three major purposes for which professional social work uses publicity today are to

   (A) restrict the social audience to professional workers in its own and allied fields.

   (B) change mental attitudes and behavior patterns in order to assure mental and physical health.

   (C) enlist public assistance in securing or enforcing social legislation.

   (D) secure necessary financial support for social services, whether publicly or privately financed.

   (E) present services and problems that are distinctly isolated from normal community life.

   (F) place responsibility for interpretation exclusively in the province of the specialist.

   (G) enlist public opinion to prevent social, economic, and political changes.

   (H) limit areas of interpretation to those that provide tangible results.

   (I) develop social services as ends in themselves for the protection of the underprivileged groups.

   (J) increase understanding of social needs and social purposes.

   (K) guarantee the continuance of democratic processes by combating subversive propaganda.

   (L) isolate services to avoid confusion with current public health programs.

40. In working with the problems of American-born children of parents born in other countries, modern social workers are concerned with

   (A) helping the children to have a sense of pride in their backgrounds.

   (B) securing estimates of the number of illegal entries of aliens into the United States.

   (C) discovering the continuance of international customs and folk festivals.

   (D) mediating in conflicts of cultural differences between parents and children.

   (E) referring all such problems to group work agencies.

   (F) organizing community forces into compulsory Americanization enterprises.

   (G) assisting the parents to carry out punitive measures consistent with the standard of their background.

   (H) discouraging the formation of international interest groups in community centers.

   (I) knowing the culture and resources of ethnic communities.

   (J) reducing cultural conflicts by helping the children forget their backgrounds.

   (K) encouraging the children to overcome feelings of inferiority by disregarding the influence of the ethnic community.

   (L) assisting the children in their adjustment by defending attitudes contrary to parental opinions.

CASE WORKER TECHNIQUES

Directions: Each question has four possible answers. Choose the letter that best answers the question and mark your answer on the answer sheet.

1. The skill of the eligibility specialist in conducting the first interview with a client in a public assistance agency is important because

    (A) the attitude of the client toward assistance may be observed at this time and his or her future reactions determined.

    (B) after the first interview, the client may compare notes with other clients and change his or her story.

    (C) it may establish a mutual understanding between the client who expresses needs and the worker who interprets the agency.

    (D) if the worker is not skillful, the client may secure information about the agency policies that he or she may use later to his or her own advantage.

2. A significant result of doing a good job is that

    (A) the clients will be grateful and tell others of the good service they have received.

    (B) the functions of the agency will be interpreted to the community.

    (C) the supervisor will give the worker a higher rating because the clients will never complain.

    (D) the newspapers will give publicity to the program only if the work is well done.

3. From the social point of view, the most desirable requisite for a potential eligibility specialist to have at the outset is

    (A) a desire to return full value for the taxpayer's dollar.

    (B) knowledge of eligibility requirements for assistance.

    (C) understanding of the functions of the Department of Social Services.

    (D) a desire to help people work through their problems.

4. Your client and his wife are quarreling continually. This is having a bad effect upon the children and causing friction in the home. The husband has been unemployed for some time. You would

    (A) arrest the client.

    (B) commit the children to institutions.

    (C) determine the underlying cause.

    (D) cut off assistance.

5. An anonymous letter is received by your office stating that one of your clients has several unacknowledged children in good financial circumstances. You would

    (A) cut off assistance immediately.

    (B) attempt to verify the information.

    (C) bring charges for refund.

    (D) trace the writer of the letter.

6. A son of your client secures work. You do not know any of the details. You would

    (A) continue assistance as before.

    (B) cut off assistance immediately.

    (C) ascertain length of employment and wages.

    (D) summon the employer to court.

7. An applicant for assistance moved about a great deal in the city since becoming a resident of New York. His required time of residence is still questionable. You would

   (A) refuse assistance because of nonresidence.

   (B) return him to his birthplace.

   (C) make efforts to verify his residence.

   (D) turn him over to the Transient Bureau.

8. A member of a client's family develops a definite mental condition. His presence in the home jeopardizes the welfare of the family. You would

   (A) call a police officer.

   (B) call an ambulance.

   (C) obtain a mental examination.

   (D) subdue him yourself if necessary.

9. A client obtains work that lasts for two months at wages that are twice as much as his assistance allowance. You would

   (A) continue assistance.

   (B) cut off assistance temporarily.

   (C) cut off assistance permanently.

   (D) require a refund for benefits paid.

10. A husband on assistance has an accident and is taken to the hospital. You would

    (A) discontinue assistance because the hospital is taking care of him.

    (B) increase assistance because of the situation.

    (C) adjust the family budget during his absence in the hospital.

    (D) require married children to support the family.

11. A family applies for assistance. The man was born in Ireland but is a citizen. He is 66 years old and able to work but unemployed. You should

    (A) refer him to the State Department of Labor Employment Division for work.

    (B) grant assistance because of need.

    (C) refer him for old-age assistance.

    (D) deny assistance on grounds that he is able to work.

12. A client brings to his home the family of an unemployed married son from another state. He asks for increased assistance to cover additional needs of the son's family. You would

    (A) discontinue assistance because the client brought the family in without permission.

    (B) increase assistance to take care of additional needs.

    (C) communicate with the legal residence of the son's family for reimbursement of additional assistance.

    (D) bring charges against the son for trying indirectly to get assistance for a nonresident.

13. You find that a client has withheld the information that he and his son own a piece of property jointly. Sale of the property is pending and the client feels that his interests are being endangered. You would

    (A) continue aid during the transaction.

    (B) discontinue aid because of fraudulent statements as to assets on the part of the client.

    (C) help the client protect his interest in the property so that reimbursement of the assistance grant is assured.

    (D) make a claim on the property because of aid granted.

14. You find that an applicant has a war-connected disability for which he never thought he could receive a veteran's pension. He has the necessary papers to prove his war disability. He is in extreme need. You would

    (A) grant immediate assistance because of need.

    (B) transfer him to another center.

    (C) arrange for him to stay at a lodging house until he finds work.

    (D) refer him to the Department of Veteran's Affairs for assistance.

15. A child of one of your clients develops tuberculosis of the lung and is rapidly getting worse. The welfare of the entire family is thus endangered. You would

    (A) increase assistance because of sickness.

    (B) discontinue assistance because of the health menace created.

    (C) arrange hospital care for the child.

    (D) send the child to a summer camp to get well.

16. An applicant has previously been denied assistance because a son in the home was working. The son marries and establishes an independent home. You would

    (A) deny assistance because of the son's marriage.

    (B) grant assistance because of need.

    (C) force the son to support his parents.

    (D) make the parents live in their son's new home.

17. A client whom you inform that assistance will be decreased threatens to kill you the next time he receives his assistance check. You would

    (A) reason with him, pointing out the cause of your action.

    (B) tell him you are not afraid of him and will be ready for him the next time you call, armed with a weapon of protection.

    (C) bring a special officer with you the next time you visit his home.

    (D) discontinue assistance because of his threats.

18. Yon find that a married brother of an applicant is reputed to be wealthy and able to support his brother. You would

    (A) deny assistance because the brother is able to support the applicant.

    (B) interview the brother and attempt to obtain help for the applicant.

    (C) bring action against the wealthy brother because his brother is liable to become a public charge.

    (D) grant assistance immediately because of need.

19. When a client receives assistance, he or she

    (A) gives up the right to manage money in his or her own way.

    (B) is justified in assuming that he or she has proved eligible for assistance and is free to use the money according to his or her best judgment.

    (C) is limited in spending the money only for expenditures itemized in the agency budget.

    (D) is obligated to keep an itemized list of expenditures.

20. A widow with a 17-year-old girl and an 18-year-old boy applies for aid. There are rumors that she has been supported by a boarder living in her home and the moral relationship is questioned. You would

(A) ascertain the facts and grant aid if warranted.

(B) deny assistance because the boarder seems to be able to support the family.

(C) refer the applicant to the Board of Child Welfare for a widow's pension.

(D) bring charges immediately against the mother for jeopardizing the morals of her children.

21. Mary, a client of yours, is a 55-year-old mother who is caring for her 2 children, Alex, a 5-year-old boy, and Shelly, a 10-year-old girl who is wheelchair-bound. You learn that Mary has developed a heart condition that will affect her ability to care for her children. You should

(A) refer her case to Child Protective Services as a case of child neglect.

(B) refer her case to Child Protective Services so the agency can find Mary a homemaker to help her to care for her children in her home.

(C) tell Mary that she should keep this quiet because she could lose her benefits and her children.

(D) refer Mary for counseling to deal with this stressful situation.

22. You learn from Mr. Stuart that he is very stressed and has been abusing his 14-year-old daughter for several months now. You should

(A) anonymously report him to Child Protective Services.

(B) inform him that you are a mandated reporter and explain to him that you will need to report him to Child Protective Services.

(C) help him get counseling.

(D) see if you can increase his financial grant so that his stress level will be reduced.

23. Mr. Carnes is a 45-year-old man who is severely disabled. He is currently receiving public assistance, and you learn during your most recent interview that he has taken on a part-time job that is generating some income. You should

(A) discuss with him that this will affect his case, and tell him that you will need to close his case.

(B) close his case immediately.

(C) discuss his income with him and find out how long he has been receiving this income.

(D) report him to the administration.

24. A client with a disability is receiving disability payments, but you know she is able to work. This client wants to take in 2 foster children, but this means she will have to give up her disability payments. She is aware of this. You should

(A) call the foster-care agency and tell them that she is untrustworthy.

(B) report this immediately to the foster-care agency.

(C) ask her to discuss this matter in further detail and try to determine how she will manage financially.

(D) allow her to make this decision to take in these foster children.

25. You are outside of your office and you see your client out at a local store buying a large amount of clothing in an expensive department store. You should

(A) address this with your client at your next meeting, and ask her how she plans to financially manage such a large purchase.

(B) call your client at home the next day and confront her.

(C) stop the client in the store and question her about her purchases.

(D) ignore the situation.

SOCIAL WORK WITH CHILDREN

Directions: Each question has four possible answers. Choose the letter that best answers the question and mark your answer on the answer sheet.

1. Eight-year-old Johnny, on whose account his mother is receiving aid to dependent children, is a truant from school. Disturbed by the course of events, his mother appears at the center and informs you, her case worker, that her efforts to stop Johnny's truancy have been unavailing. You should tell Johnny's mother that

   (A) the grant will be discontinued since Johnny's truancy is evidence of her failure as a parent.

   (B) she can be referred to a specialized agency in the community.

   (C) you will institute court action to remove Johnny from his home environment.

   (D) you will give her two months to straighten out the problem before taking further action.

2. A woman appears at your center and asks for advice on how she can remain at home with her 3 children, ages 4, 7, and 10. She declares that her husband has been killed and she is unable to manage on her old-age and survivor's insurance. Assuming the facts to be true as stated, the eligibility specialist should advise her

   (A) to apply for Aid to Dependent Children.

   (B) to try to find a job.

   (C) to apply for more money under old-age and survivors insurance.

   (D) that there are no other public financial resources available in her case.

3. From a mental hygiene point of view, good parental attitudes offer a child: (A) emotional security—a feeling of stability, permanence, and safety; (B) acceptance—a feeling of belonging and being welcome for what he or she is and being held only to a child's accountability for actions; (C) freedom for experience—an environment that offers a child opportunities to try out his or her own abilities, interests, ideas, and games; and (D) the right to feel and to express feelings both of affection and aggression.

   According to the ideas expressed in the paragraph,

   (A) a family in which there is economic dependence cannot be good for children.

   (B) emotionally secure children do not have feelings of aggression.

   (C) children should not be held accountable for their actions.

   (D) parental attitudes that are inadequate do not give the child feelings of belonging and freedom for experience.

4. One of the deleterious effects of child labor from the social work point of view is that it inevitably deprives the child of

   (A) valuable discipline.

   (B) opportunities for play.

   (C) a sense of responsibility.

   (D) opportunities for companionship.

5. Aid to Dependent Children is premised upon the assumption that children

    (A) are better off with their mothers under any circumstances.

    (B) should not be removed from their homes because of poverty alone.

    (C) should not be removed from their homes because of behavior problems alone.

    (D) whose mothers work are generally neglected.

6. A child was born out of wedlock to Ms. Smith and has been placed in a private foster home. Ms. Smith is unable to pay anything toward the child's care. She asks about visiting her little girl. The most desirable reply for the case worker to make in this situation would be that Ms. Smith

    (A) cannot visit the child because she would exert an adverse influence over her.

    (B) should not visit since she is not paying for the child's care.

    (C) should not visit because it will be difficult for the child to explain to her friends that her mother is unmarried.

    (D) has the same right as any other mother to visit her child.

7. The best thing to do with a problem child is to

    (A) advise the parents to maintain strict discipline.

    (B) ask the police to watch the child.

    (C) put the child on probation.

    (D) follow an individual plan after analysis of the case.

8. The modern practice in the child-care field recognizes that the boarding care of children is desirable

    (A) at all times.

    (B) under no circumstances.

    (C) provided there is adequate supervision of the boarding home.

    (D) in very few cases.

9. The most widely accepted of the following principles of child welfare work is that

    (A) foster homes in which children are placed should be, so far as practicable, of the same religious persuasion as that of the child.

    (B) no illegitimate child should ever be permitted to stay with her mother.

    (C) it is important that prospective foster parents be far above the average in their social and economic status.

    (D) no child should be placed with foster parents until arrangements have been completed for having the foster parents adopt the child.

10. Anthony, age 8, has had many difficult experiences in his life. His father deserted when Anthony was 2 years old and his whereabouts are unknown. Anthony's mother, whom he loved dearly, died three months ago. Since that time he has been living with his grandmother, who is old and ill, and cannot care for such an active little boy. Together, the grandmother and you, the social case worker, have decided that placement in a foster home is essential for Anthony's well being. You know he will resist any change in his living arrangement. According to acceptable case work practice, the best of the following methods for you to apply in this situation is to

    (A) take the boy to his new home without telling him anything beforehand.

    (B) explain that it is necessary to move him and that he is going to a very nice place where he will be happy and have many things he does not have now.

    (C) tell him you are sorry if he feels bad about it, but grown-ups know best what is good for him and he will have to do what you say.

    (D) give the child a chance to get to know you before he is moved and to express his feelings in relation to the plan being made for him.

11. Suppose you, as a case worker, are considering institutional care for several different types of children for whom removal from present homes is indicated. Of the following, the type least suited for such care would be a

    (A) child needing observation, study, and treatment for a severe crippling condition.

    (B) 5-year-old boy who resents adult authority.

    (C) family of 6 brothers and sisters who are devoted to each other.

    (D) 3-year-old girl without any physical or mental disabilities whose mother is dead and whose father is employed at night.

12. It is generally agreed among psychologists that children need to have certain experiences to develop into healthy, well-integrated adults. Of the following, which is most important to the development of the preadolescent child?

    (A) That he or she lives in a good neighborhood

    (B) That he or she has a room of his or her own

    (C) That he or she has nice clothes

    (D) That he or she has the feeling that he or she is loved and wanted by the parents

13. Ms. Hanson is an 18-year-old client with 2 children. During your next meeting she informs you that she may be pregnant. You should

    (A) discuss safe sex practices with her.

    (B) discuss how she is going to manage her home and plan for this new baby.

    (C) tell her that you will report her to the authorities for neglect.

    (D) do nothing; it is none of your business.

14. Child Welfare Services conduct programs that provide help to children apart from financial assistance and education. This falls into several categories. In every category, it is fundamental that the focus be on the well-being of the child. All of the following are significant people whose best interests are significant for the welfare of the child EXCEPT

    (A) agency personnel and the courts.

    (B) abusive parents.

    (C) adoptive parents.

    (D) biological parents.

15. All of the following are involved in the nutritional assistance to Child Care Facilities EXCEPT

    (A) the U.S. Department of Agriculture.

    (B) purchasers and redistributors of surplus food.

    (C) donors from local restaurants.

    (D) Food and Nutritional Services.

16. The licensing of facilities for children must meet all of the following EXCEPT

    (A) a solid recreational program that addresses each physical need for development.

    (B) public health inspections.

    (C) sufficient staffing.

    (D) fire and safety controls.

GENERAL REVIEW

Directions: Each question has four possible answers. Choose the letter that best answers the question and mark your answer on the answer sheet.

1. Of the types of mental breakdown listed below, the disorder that ordinarily occurs at the most advanced age is
   (A) cerebral arteriosclerosis.
   (B) neurasthenia.
   (C) dementia praecox.
   (D) paresis.

2. The cost of senior assistance is borne
   (A) entirely by the local government.
   (B) entirely by the federal and state governments.
   (C) entirely by the federal government.
   (D) by the federal, state, and local governments.

3. Most senior assistance programs have been limited in general to the financial and physical needs of the aged because
   (A) it is impossible to determine their other needs with any degree of practicality.
   (B) social agencies are unwilling to enlarge their responsibilities for the care of the aged.
   (C) old people are not interested in social participation.
   (D) social service administrators have not been given the means to undertake more augmented programs.

4. During a period of economic adjustment when unemployment is on the rise, the invention of a labor-saving device would, in the long run, be economically and culturally
   (A) unsound because it would stir up unrest among the organized labor groups.
   (B) unsound because it would result in accelerating unemployment.
   (C) sound because the rise of unemployment is a temporary phenomenon, while the labor-saving device would add permanent values.
   (D) sound because it would enable the user to produce more with the small working population still employed.

5. The chief purpose of insurance adjustment is to
   (A) ensure maximum protection to the client at minimum cost.
   (B) reduce the number of persons receiving assistance.
   (C) make sure that insurance companies do not lose money.
   (D) investigate solvency of insurance companies in which clients are concerned.

6. The parole movement of releasing prisoners before the expiration of their sentences is based mostly on the assumption on the part of the taxpaying public that

   (A) prison officials and parole officers can watch the paroled prisoners closely and help them adjust themselves in the community at the same time.

   (B) recidivism is greater for persons serving their full sentence.

   (C) parolees are sent out with an obligation rather than a score to settle.

   (D) total costs for prison administration are materially reduced when a large percentage of the prison population has the terms of incarceration reduced.

7. A small town without a hospital is located near a large city that boasts of its excellent medical facilities. These facilities are extended liberally to nonresidents who come from adjacent centers that do not have hospitals of their own. If it is shown statistically that the death rate of the small town is lower compared to that of the large city, the most logical inference for the alert case worker to make is that

   (A) small-town life is more healthful than living in a big city.

   (B) the statistical data have been improperly manipulated.

   (C) death rates should not be determined by political boundaries.

   (D) the deaths of nonresidents have boosted the death rate of the large city.

8. The greatest limitation on the general effectiveness of marriage courses in college curricula is that

   (A) there is no evidence to prove that such courses result in better matches and happier homes.

   (B) successful completion of such courses is no indication that the knowledge contained in the courses will be successfully applied by the students who have taken them.

   (C) there is no complete agreement as to whether the family, the church, or the school should be responsible for guiding marriage education.

   (D) most of the people who marry are ineligible to enroll in such courses.

9. The least accurate of the following statements regarding intelligence is that

   (A) a person's intelligence is not directly related to biological factors.

   (B) people differ radically in the degree of intelligence they have.

   (C) people cannot learn beyond the limits of their native intelligence, regardless of the amount and kind of effort they expend.

   (D) ill health, isolation, and certain kinds of temperament may seriously limit the proportion of one's intelligence that may actually be able to be put to use.

10. The only educative agency that can be thought of properly as really starting with a "clean slate" in developing a person's behavior is the

    (A) family.

    (B) play group.

    (C) church group.

    (D) elementary school.

11. Councils of social agencies or welfare councils are

    (A) organizations of executives of private social work agencies whose function it is to clear the programs of their respective agencies to avoid duplicating one another's work.

    (B) federations or associations of agencies with formal representation of joint planning of social work in a way so that every agency can contribute its most appropriate service to the whole, avoid duplication, and study gaps.

    (C) federations of social agencies for the sole purpose of joint and more effective financing of their work.

    (D) advisory committees or bodies composed of both board members and executives, who pass on and approve or veto the actual or proposed programs of social agencies.

12. Of the following types of cases, medical social work seems to be the least needed, according to various studies, in cases of

    (A) recurrent and chronic illness.

    (B) physical handicap.

    (C) invalidism.

    (D) acute illness.

13. Adoption is best defined as a

    (A) friendly and informal agreement by which the second husband agrees to provide for the children of his wife by the first husband.

    (B) legal instrument in the form of an affidavit made out before a notary public by which the father legitimizes the child born to his wife before their marriage.

    (C) legal process as described above, but valid only if approved by a children's agency, which for that purpose, and in accordance with the needs of the case, can override the will of the natural parent.

    (D) method through which a person legally assumes full parental responsibility for a child that is not his or her own child, adoption being made by authority of a court having suitable jurisdiction.

14. A "pay as you go policy" is most nearly one in which

    (A) annual expenditure does not exceed annual income.

    (B) money is expended to meet new needs.

    (C) a bond issue is the instrument for raising money.

    (D) the budget is never balanced.

15. Of the following, the most important of the present housing difficulties is

(A) financing bodies refuse to give mortgage money for use in residential construction, reserving their funds for factory, office, and mercantile construction.

(B) people in the slums are so used to their kind of housing that they refuse to go to better places, and if they do, they soon reduce the best housing to slums, depress values, and so make investment in multiple dwellings unprofitable.

(C) the cost of new construction on modern standards does not provide apartments cheap enough for low-income rent and still be profitable for investment.

(D) it is impossible to build low-rent houses profitably from private investment and it is illegal and unsound to use public subsidies.

16. Social Security legislation, as enacted by the federal government, is characterized by the fact that

(A) it makes widows' pensions compulsory throughout the United States.

(B) it is the first comprehensive security law that provides health insurance as well as other forms of social insurance and pensions.

(C) it offers unemployment and old-age benefits only where the states do not already provide these.

(D) it carries into effect a combination of state and federal operation, of employer and employee contribution, and a gradual development of the system over the years.

17. The visiting teacher may be of assistance to the case worker in understanding family problems because the visiting teacher is able to

(A) explain the child's social problems and assist in his or her care by remedial teaching of reading or other subjects.

(B) explain the needs of the family for clothing and provide for these needs.

(C) explain the social and educational maladjustments of school children and assist in meeting their needs.

(D) explain the effects of dependency upon school children and assist in obviating these effects by providing free lunches.

18. Accepted social work practice holds that assistance in-kind is less useful to client and community than assistance in cash because

(A) assistance in-kind is inflexible and tends to develop dependent attitudes in clients.

(B) it is impossible for clients to maintain a balanced diet on grocery orders issued in-kind.

(C) assistance in-kind is economically unsound and keeps less money in circulation.

(D) friction between the agency and the tradespeople is the usual result of assistance issued in-kind.

19. According to current thinking, public welfare agencies should consider private social agencies as

    (A) separate and competing agencies with a different purpose and function.

    (B) cooperating agencies whose advice and support should be sought.

    (C) independent agencies concerned entirely with people who have emotional and behavioral problems.

    (D) part of the public agency with whom cases may be interchanged because they are serving the same purpose.

20. In public assistance administration, the basic determinant of eligibility for assistance is

    (A) need.

    (B) citizenship.

    (C) need through no fault of the applicant.

    (D) settlement.

21. Analysis of migratory agricultural workers indicates that, in general, the most characteristic definition of them is that

    (A) they are not an ill-defined, undifferentiated group unconcerned with a stabilized occupation.

    (B) they are a constantly shifting, undifferentiated group who are not concerned with a stabilized occupation.

    (C) they are not a well-defined, differentiated group concerned with a stabilized occupation.

    (D) they are an ill-defined, constantly shifting group who are jacks-of-all-trades and not concerned with a stabilized occupation.

22. The work of the case worker may be considered a protection to the community because it includes

    (A) recording antisocial attitudes and serious grievances expressed by clients that may be destructive to society.

    (B) recognizing potentially serious health and behavior problems and referring them to the appropriate services for care.

    (C) recording the incidence of disease and promoting community programs for prevention based on the data thus secured.

    (D) recognizing the potential criminal tendencies that are inherent in economic dependents.

23. The most modern point of view among those who offer social treatment to the blind is that

    (A) because of their disability, the blind should be given special privileges such as being allowed to live together so that they may associate on the basis of their common disability, preference in placement of jobs suitable for them, etc.

    (B) as many of the difficulties in which blind persons find themselves come from causes other than their blindness, which serves to heighten their difficulties, treatment should be based upon their total situation rather than their disability.

    (C) blind children should secure their complete education in special schools and colleges provided for them and should not have to go to the regular high schools and colleges where they will be unable to adjust.

    (D) sheltered workshops for the blind and the provision of vending stands in public buildings are an unfortunate means of support for blind persons since they emphasize their disability.

24. The best definition of parole is

    (A) a continuation of the social policy, or social control, instituted by the state when it first places the lawbreaker under apprehension.

    (B) the shortening of the prison term of an offender against the law who is then no longer subjected to the disciplinary control of the state.

    (C) a form of clemency or leniency granted to lawbreakers under apprehension who have established records for good conduct and who cannot be returned to the institution.

    (D) the withholding of punishment of an adult offender due to the clemency of the court in an individual instance warranted by the compliant behavior of the offender.

25. The provision of free hot lunches to needy schoolchildren may have some disadvantages because

    (A) dietitians cannot prepare food of sufficient variety to satisfy the children and at the same time conform to minimum budget requirements.

    (B) fewer children are now in need of free hot lunches because their families are on public assistance and are receiving adequate budgets.

    (C) school principals are not in favor of maintaining lunchrooms in the elementary schools because of the difficulties of providing this service.

    (D) those who cannot afford to buy their lunches are apt to be identified as dependent children.

FOR QUESTIONS 26–30, SELECT THE DESCRIPTION IN COLUMN II TO WHICH THE REFERENCE IN COLUMN I IS MOST APPROPRIATE. YOU MAY USE AN ANSWER IN COLUMN II MORE THAN ONCE.

Column I

26. The area in which a predominantly male resident population would probably be found

27. The area in which a "slum" would be located if it existed in this city

28. The area in which the most prominent citizens of the community would probably be found living

29. The area likely to contain the sparsest resident population

30. The area likely to be inhabited by middle-class families

Column II

(A) retail stores, eating establishments, movie theaters, offices of professional people and business organizations

(B) made-over private dwellings, rooming houses, cheap hotels, pawnbrokers, wholesale business establishments

(C) less crowding than in the area described in (B), more modern houses, fewer children

(D) fashionable suburbs, homes of professional and business leaders, relative cleanliness and modernity

ANSWER KEY AND EXPLANATIONS

Vocabulary

1.	D	7.	C	13.	D	19.	B	25.	A
2.	A	8.	D	14.	B	20.	C	26.	B
3.	C	9.	A	15.	B	21.	B	27.	A
4.	A	10.	B	16.	C	22.	A	28.	D
5.	D	11.	B	17.	A	23.	B	29.	C
6.	B	12.	C	18.	D	24.	A	30.	D

1. **The correct answer is (D).** In this sentence, the word "traumatic" refers to a bodily injury or shock. It also refers to a painful emotional experience or shock, often producing a lasting effect and sometime neurosis.

2. **The correct answer is (A).** "Opprobrium" means disgrace or infamy attached to shame. It ca also be contempt for something thought of as inferior.

3. **The correct answer is (C).** In this question, "indigenous" is defined as existing or growing naturally, belonging to as a native, or inborn. Therefore, choice (C) is the best answer.

4. **The correct answer is (A).** "Feeble-minded" refers to mental retardation and subnormal intelligence; therefore, the most closely related choice would be "mentally deficient."

5. **The correct answer is (D).** "Condemnation proceedings" are the legal proceedings by which a municipality may take private property for public use.

6. **The correct answer is (B).** "Therapeutic" means to heal, to preserve health, or to cure. Therefore, "curative" is the best response.

7. **The correct answer is (C).** "Vicariously" is best defined as living through the experience of another; therefore, "substituted" is the best definition.

8. **The correct answer is (D).** The word "categorical" is best defined as being placed in a category or to classify; therefore, "classified" is the best choice.

9. **The correct answer is (A).** The word "ethnic" is best defined as designating any of the basic groups or divisions of mankind as distinguished by customs, characteristics, history, or language. So, the best selection is "racial factors."

10. **The correct answer is (B).** The word "exigencies" is best defined as calling out for action or attention; therefore, the best choice is "occurrences."

11. **The correct answer is (B).** "Power of attorney" is the written authority for one person to act for another in legal matters.

12. **The correct answer is (C).** To "postulate" is to ask or assume without proof; therefore, "hypothesis" is the best selection.

13. **The correct answer is (D).** "Domination" refers to ruling or controlling; therefore, choice (D) is the best answer.

14. **The correct answer is (B).** "Reprisal" is the forcible seizure of property in retaliation for an injury inflicted by another nation.

15. **The correct answer is (B).** "Parity" is associated with being in the same power or rank; in other words, equivalent.

16. **The correct answer is (C).** "Hegemony" is to lead others or a nation or to go ahead.

17. **The correct answer is (A).** "Amortization" is the act of putting money aside to reduce a debt or the legal process of reducing, transferring, or selling property.

18. **The correct answer is (D).** A "rapport" is a close or sympathetic relationship.

19. **The correct answer is (B).** A "prognosis" is a forecast of the possible cause of a disease and the recovery process.

20. **The correct answer is (C).** "Siblings" are individuals who share the same parent.

21. **The correct answer is (B).** "Congenital" is defined as existing from birth or resulting from one's prenatal environment.

22. **The correct answer is (A).** "Psychosis" is a major mental disorder in which the personality becomes very seriously disorganized.

23. **The correct answer is (B).** "Coercion" means to surround or constrain by force.

24. **The correct answer is (A).** "Adoption" is the process of taking a child into a family by a legal process.

25. **The correct answer is (A).** "Occupational therapy" is therapy used to focus the mind to correct a physical defect relating to the upper extremities.

26. **The correct answer is (B).** "Pathology" is a branch of medicine that deals with the nature of disease.

27. **The correct answer is (A).** "Mandated" is defined as having been assigned by court or legal process.

28. **The correct answer is (D).** A "hospice" is both a facility to care for the terminally ill as well as a form of care at home to treat those who have been diagnosed with a terminal illness.

29. **The correct answer is (C).** "Advocacy" is the process of pleading or speaking on behalf of another's cause.

30. **The correct answer is (D).** To be "ambivalent" is to have conflicted feelings toward another person or object.

answers

Reading Interpretation

1.	B	6.	C	11.	A	16.	A	21.	B
2.	A	7.	B	12.	B	17.	C	22.	B
3.	D	8.	C	13.	A	18.	B	23.	C
4.	B	9.	D	14.	D	19.	B	24.	A
5.	B	10.	B	15.	C	20.	C	25.	B

1. **The correct answer is (B).** Slums have been created by the variety of expansion, succession, and mobility, all of which have played a part in determining the social characteristics of the slum.

2. **The correct answer is (A).** Areas containing acceptable housing may be considered substandard from the housing viewpoint, even though they may contain some acceptable housing. This happens because demolition or rehabilitation of the latter may be necessary for effective replanning or reconstruction of the entire area.

3. **The correct answer is (D).** Within the community of the slum, one can see a culture that exists. This culture has become imprinted in the lives of the people that occupy it—both adults and children.

4. **The correct answer is (B).** The preceding regulations dictate the construction that will be conducted on future industrial and business areas.

5. **The correct answer is (B).** Housing is essentially dependent on the lack of proper distribution of income and wealth, unemployment, and other economic factors.

6. **The correct answer is (C).** Slums are composed of residents from a variety of backgrounds, including those who have been pushed down from a higher income level by illness, accident, or incompetence.

7. **The correct answer is (B).** It appears that localities that need to be redeveloped contain substandard housing since the volume of substandard housing is much greater than the volume reasonably recommended for demolition.

8. **The correct answer is (C).** Zoning laws offer homeowners neighborhood preservation.

9. **The correct answer is (D).** In World War II, overlapping functions and operations of different bureaus led to inefficiency as a result of complete absence of policy.

10. **The correct answer is (B).** The tearing down of slums may not, of itself, improve the housing conditions of low-income families unless tenants are offered healthful decent housing within their means. It is essential that low-income families be provided for before slums can be torn down.

11. **The correct answer is (A).** Quality of life in the home and its surroundings has a direct impact on the physical well being of children. As a result, a sense of chronic inferiority due to consciousness of life in their substandard dwellings has caused damage to the health of children of the United States.

12. **The correct answer is (B).** Leadership, especially social leadership, carries with it the obligation to administer for the benefit of the public and social trust that must be administered for the common good.

13. **The correct answer is (A).** Many real estate professionals are lacking in the understanding of social and governmental problems; training for proficiency in housing procedures by colleges and universities needs to be improved.

14. **The correct answer is (D).** Home financing is represented by two distinct forms of cost: the actual capital invested and the interest rate charged for the use of this capital.

15. **The correct answer is (C).** A housing authority carries multiple responsibilities; therefore, it must deal with all the difficulties encountered by the private builder.

16. **The correct answer is (A).** In addition to the city's housing dilemma, the slum problems have been exacerbated by the great influx of low-income workers.

17. **The correct answer is (C).** The general postwar increase of vandalism and street crime was also experienced within the housing projects.

18. **The correct answer is (B).** Properties require the skill of bargaining through investigation, comparison of rents with other properties, and individualized haggling on price and terms in order to determine the value of a parcel of real estate.

19. **The correct answer is (B).** Although there is considerably more variety between public housing projects than between different streets of apartment houses or tenements throughout the city, public housing projects differ from the city's normal housing pattern to the degree that sameness, monotony, and institutionalism are characteristic of public buildings.

20. **The correct answer is (C).** The subsidy contributions for state-aided public housing projects are shared equally by the state and the city under the provisions of the state law.

21. **The correct answer is (B).** Financial advantage can be secured by the homebuilder if material and building costs are combined; however, these procedures would require more maintenance.

22. **The correct answer is (B).** There has been a shift to privatization of services from the public resources from the government. This directly involves the shift from public to private facilities for those who need institutional care.

23. **The correct answer is (C).** As a means to help clients with their basic needs, the Economic Opportunity Act of 1965 provides individuals with many basic services to help those in need cope with various aspects of poverty. The act assists with helping low-income people keep their dwellings warm during the winter months, maintain food and clothing emergency supplies for people who need them, and operate advocacy and information programs for people who need economic assistance of one kind or another.

24. **The correct answer is (A).** Community mental health programs offer a wide scope of services, such as mental health counseling, hospitalization in community hospitals for people who require it for short periods of time, employment referral and training, and community education about mental health problems.

25. **The correct answer is (B).** One should know why the policy is being applied, the social values the policy reflects, the alternative ways in which the policy might be applied, alternative policies, the source of funding and financing alternatives, and the effectiveness of the policy. The competence of a professional is based on many factors, which include a thorough knowledge of one's field as well as a broad scope of the various components of their work.

Eligibility for Public Assistance and Housing

1.	A	15.	D	29.	B	43.	A	57.	C
2.	A	16.	B	30.	C	44.	C	58.	D
3.	D	17.	B	31.	D	45.	B	59.	A
4.	C	18.	A	32.	B	46.	B	60.	D
5.	B	19.	C	33.	C	47.	C	61.	C
6.	D	20.	D	34.	A	48.	B	62.	A
7.	D	21.	A	35.	B	49.	D	63.	D
8.	D	22.	D	36.	A	50.	D	64.	D
9.	A	23.	C	37.	D	51.	B	65.	B
10.	D	24.	B	38.	A	52.	D	66.	D
11.	A	25.	A	39.	C	53.	B	67.	A
12.	D	26.	C	40.	A	54.	B	68.	D
13.	C	27.	D	41.	C	55.	C	69.	B
14.	B	28.	C	42.	A	56.	B	70.	B

1. **The correct answer is (A).** To discover whether an applicant for aid to dependent children has had any previous experience as an aid recipient, the case worker should check the application for such aid with the social service exchange.

2. **The correct answer is (A).** A person would be asked to give the maiden name of his wife as a means for identification.

3. **The correct answer is (D).** The address of an individual and the name of his or her landlord is a means of identifying debts and obligations.

4. **The correct answer is (C).** The best reason for asking a client about equity in the home would be to determine income or financial resources.

5. **The correct answer is (B).** The best reason for asking a client about his or her military service would be to determine eligibility aside from income.

6. **The correct answer is (D).** The best reason for asking a client about mortgages on his or her home would be to determine debts and obligations.

7. **The correct answer is (D).** The best reason for asking a client about the duration of his or her previous employment would be to gather information on debts and obligations.

8. **The correct answer is (D).** The best reason for asking a client about amounts of premiums on his or her insurance would be to determine debts and obligations.

9. **The correct answer is (A).** The best reason for asking a client about adult children that may be employed away from home would be to determine identification.

10. **The correct answer is (D).** The best reason for asking a client about his or her prior occupation would be to determine debts and obligations.

11. **The correct answer is (A).** The best reason for asking a client about his or her apartment number and floor would be to gather information about his or her identification.

12. **The correct answer is (D).** The United States Department of Justice is the best

place to obtain information on the naturalization of a client.

13. **The correct answer is (C).** Proper training on interviewing skills is an essential element of case work, since interviewing is the method that a case worker uses to acquire the most thorough knowledge about the client's problems.

14. **The correct answer is (B).** A new case worker can best utilize a case record to increase the value of services that a client receives by increasing his or her knowledge about the client and the history of the client's situation as it is detailed in the record.

15. **The correct answer is (D).** Dispossess and eviction notices are the least reliable form of proof showing continuous residence.

16. **The correct answer is (B).** As a case worker, you must point out to Mr. Ritter that part of the foster-care placement procedure involves determining the extent of financial responsibility that parents can continue to assume.

17. **The correct answer is (B).** The best way to ensure that you have accurate employment information from a client would be to personally confer with the client's previous employer.

18. **The correct answer is (A).** Assisting the family in obtaining dental care, seeking out employment opportunities for the families, and obtaining the confidence of the family are all desirable aspects of the social investigator.

19. **The correct answer is (C).** Familiarizing the family with the process of budgeting the assistance that they will be receiving, calculating the minimum needs of a family according to their budget, and obtaining knowledge of client's work history from other agencies are desirable aspects of making social investigations.

20. **The correct answer is (D).** Discovering the recreational habits of the family, finding any evidence of criminality, and searching property records to find the exact status of property that the family may have owned in the past are all practices involved in making social investigations of persons applying for aid. However, the ability to discuss economic needs frankly holds the greatest immediate importance.

21. **The correct answer is (A).** Although it is important for a social investigator to understand the causes of distress and maladjustment, comprehend the situation of the client, and determine whether the client has previously been a beneficiary of public aid, the chief purpose of social investigation is to gather statistical data.

22. **The correct answer is (D).** When an applicant for assistance objects to answering a question regarding his recent employment and questions the actions of the other parties involved, the case worker conducting the interview should explain why the question is being asked.

23. **The correct answer is (C).** A case worker should write to a client to suggest an appointment time to prepare a client for their interview. By doing this, the investigator can use his or her time more efficiently.

24. **The correct answer is (B).** According to the law, it is always necessary to establish eligibility for public assistance. In order for a case worker to obtain desired information from applicants for assistance, the best interviewing method in social work practice is to allow the applicant to describe what he or she has to say in his own words first, then ask questions on points not covered.

25. **The correct answer is (A).** In order to help Mrs. Smith continue to support her mother, you should grant her supple-

mentary aid because the reduction of work is necessary to maintain her health.

26. **The correct answer is (C).** If a client that you are working with fails to call for his relief check or to make further requests, you should close the case.

27. **The correct answer is (D).** With changes in aid needing to be made in accordance with financial changes in the family's situation, an eligibility specialist should continue mandated contact with assistance recipients.

28. **The correct answer is (C).** Unfortunately in your position, you must explain to Mr. Cain that he is currently receiving the maximum benefit for his family.

29. **The correct answer is (B).** Because she is too frail to cook on her own, Mrs. Arrow's allowance should be increased if she requests an increase, so that she may eat out in restaurants.

30. **The correct answer is (C).** It is most important for a client to understand what assistance eligibility is so that he or she can immediately assume his or her share of responsibility by giving the necessary information and helping to verify it.

31. **The correct answer is (D).** The condition that most closely approximates the definition of need is when the applicant has insufficient income to meet the minimum standards set by the department, no relatives able to contribute to his or her support, and no liquid resources.

32. **The correct answer is (B).** Although the establishment of eligibility for aid is a cooperative process, the ultimate burden of proof rests on the client to provide data concerning eligibility.

33. **The correct answer is (C).** In order for an intake interviewer to recommend emergency aid, he or she must first know if Mr. Carter is receiving any union benefits or unemployment insurance.

34. **The correct answer is (A).** A case worker must explain to the Brown family that the rules of the agency do not permit a budget large enough to continue their current standard of living.

35. **The correct answer is (B).** You should tell Mrs. Wooster that her application may be accepted for investigation because she falls within the group of relatives eligible to receive aid to dependent children.

36. **The correct answer is (A).** The primary purpose in discussing the steps in determining an applicant's eligibility and the kind of verification of facts the agency needs is to enable him or her to understand the basis of eligibility and participate in determining it.

37. **The correct answer is (D).** The applicant would be found ineligible because he refuses to give information concerning a bank account of $5000 that had been in his name until four months prior to his application.

38. **The correct answer is (A).** Since the man is obviously honest and reliable, a conscientious case worker would find that it is unnecessary to verify the foregoing information in order to establish eligibility.

39. **The correct answer is (C).** You must explain to Miss Lowe that she is obviously hiding pertinent information and that her application for public assistance cannot be considered.

40. **The correct answer is (A).** The least reliable method of obtaining information about a client is the client's statements and observations.

41. **The correct answer is (C).** A life insurance premium receipt, an automobile driver's license, or a gas and electric bill is sufficient as proof of residence at a specific address. This would not be true for a hospital clinic appointment card.

42. **The correct answer is (A).** As the head of a family applying for an apartment in a low-rent housing project, this woman would be required to provide proof of naturalization in her own right as evidence of her citizenship.

43. **The correct answer is (A).** It is essential to develop a fixed pattern for all initial interviews of applicants for public housing because it helps to provide a complete record in the least amount of time.

44. **The correct answer is (C).** When beginning an interview with an applicant for an apartment, the most desirable method to use is to discuss the purpose of the interview.

45. **The correct answer is (B).** In order to obtain accurate information when interviewing an applicant for public housing, a housing assistant should not anticipate the applicant's answers.

46. **The correct answer is (B).** The time when it is generally considered desirable to add to the record subjective comments concerning an applicant and family is directly after the interview has been concluded and the applicant has left.

47. **The correct answer is (C).** To be successful in an interview, the interviewer should be careful to speak in terms that are easily understood.

48. **The correct answer is (B).** When conducting a first interview with an applicant who speaks English poorly, the housing assistant's skill is demonstrated by creating a rapport in spite of the language difficulty.

49. **The correct answer is (D).** It is important to inform the porter that the applicant will be notified shortly of the results of his application and explain that this information is confidential.

50. **The correct answer is (D).** If an individual objects to answering a question regarding the income he receives, the housing assistant should inform the applicant of the reason for asking the question and tell him he must answer.

51. **The correct answer is (B).** If an applicant provides information different from that which she submitted on her application, the case worker should enter the new information on the applicant form and initial the entry.

52. **The correct answer is (D).** In interviewing, the practice of anticipating an applicant's answer to questions is generally undesirable because the applicant may tend to agree with the answer proposed by the interviewer, even when the answer may not be entirely correct.

53. **The correct answer is (B).** If a follow-up interview was arranged for an applicant so he could furnish certain requested evidence and the applicant still fails to furnish the necessary evidence, it would be most advisable for you to ask the applicant how soon he can get the necessary evidence and set a date for another interview.

54. **The correct answer is (B).** In reviewing applications of these prospective tenants, you should review the application and notify the group of management assistants to refer to you applications of any friends or relatives.

55. **The correct answer is (C).** In reviewing this applicant's report, you should review the report of the management assistant and accept or reject it.

56. **The correct answer is (B).** In checking applications of prospective tenants that have been passed upon by a management assistant, you should reject the application and advise the applicant of the error.

57. **The correct answer is (C).** You should assign the application to another management assistant when the management assistant under your supervision reports to you that she has been assigned an application of a prospective tenant who is a friend of hers.

58. **The correct answer is (D).** The most important reason for registration of applicants for low-rent public housing with the Social Service Exchange is to provide a more complete picture of current and possible future needs of the family.

59. **The correct answer is (A).** When starting the initial interview with a client, an explanation is generally desirable because the applicant can then understand why the interview is necessary and what will be accomplished by it.

60. **The correct answer is (D).** When a housing assistant visits the home of an applicant to obtain necessary eligibility verification, she should greet the applicant's 8-year-old son, but direct the interview toward the parent or adult members of the family.

61. **The correct answer is (C).** If an applicant begins to tell you a long personal story once the interview has been completed, it would be best for you to interrupt him tactfully, thank him for the information he has already given, and terminate the interview.

62. **The correct answer is (A).** The information that the interviewer plans to secure from an individual with whom he or she talks is determined mainly by the purpose of the interview and the functions of the agency.

63. **The correct answer is (D).** The most effective way to deal with a person who frequently digresses from the subject under discussion or starts to ramble is to inject questions that relate to the purpose of the interview.

64. **The correct answer is (D).** "Being a good listener" is an interviewing technique that, if applied properly, is desirable mostly because it encourages the giving of information that is generally more reliable and complete.

65. **The correct answer is (B).** When questioning applicants for public assistance or public housing, it is best to ask questions that are direct so that the information received is as pertinent as possible.

66. **The correct answer is (D).** A new applicant is more likely to speak frankly to a social investigator or a housing assistant if the interview is conducted in complete privacy.

67. **The correct answer is (A).** When interviewing clients for public housing eligibility, it is inappropriate to obtain data to determine the applicant's mental health status.

68. **The correct answer is (D).** If an eligibility specialist notices that an applicant suddenly shifts topics during an interview, this indicates that the topic has become too anxiety provoking.

69. **The correct answer is (B).** In an assessment where multiple family members are present, the eligibility specialist focuses on the interaction of the family members.

70. **The correct answer is (B).** During an assessment, you notice that the applicant you are interviewing is especially receptive to your interventions and he seems positive and responsive to you. This may be due to the fact that the applicant is experiencing a state of crisis.

Housing and Social Welfare

1.	D	8.	A	15.	B	22.	A	29.	D
2.	D	9.	C	16.	C	23.	B	30.	C
3.	D	10.	A	17.	C	24.	D	31.	D
4.	C	11.	B	18.	A	25.	D	32.	B
5.	D	12.	D	19.	B	26.	D	33.	D
6.	B	13.	A	20.	C	27.	D	34.	A
7.	A	14.	D	21.	C	28.	D	35.	A

1. **The correct answer is (D).** The substandard dwelling units will be required to be replaced in order to meet the shortage and raise standards for housing in the next decade.

2. **The correct answer is (D).** Slum dwellings and slum areas are found in the United States in nearly all towns and cities of every size and in nearly all rural areas.

3. **The correct answer is (D).** While high disease rate, high incidence of fires, and a high rate of juvenile delinquency are all characteristics of slum areas, a high tax rate is not.

4. **The correct answer is (C).** The most important step in improving the housing conditions of low-income families living in slum dwellings is to provide satisfactory housing at rents that are affordable. Otherwise, people will not have access to this housing.

5. **The correct answer is (D).** It is untrue that "slum dwellers create the slums"; slums are caused by conditions that are not under the control of the slum dweller.

6. **The correct answer is (B).** New housing in a slum area is generally undesirable because it most likely will not be maintained against the surrounding slum.

7. **The correct answer is (A).** The high tax expenditures in slums decrease when the people are rehoused and slum buildings are demolished; however, the expenditures that decrease least rapidly are those for delinquency prevention.

8. **The correct answer is (A).** The chief limitation for every family in the country to own its own home is that families are dependent on the changes in their economic and labor conditions.

9. **The correct answer is (C).** Slum areas and bad housing are expensive to a city since there are more city services that need to be provided.

10. **The correct answer is (A).** Tenancy in low-rent government housing projects is usually limited to people of low income because private industry cannot provide decent housing for those low-income groups at a profit.

11. **The correct answer is (B).** Studies of cities have shown that the rate of juvenile delinquency was highest in areas where housing was least adequate. Therefore, provision of adequate housing is probably the most effective tool in combating juvenile delinquency.

12. **The correct answer is (D).** Research on the relationship between juvenile delinquency and poor housing indicates that the size of a city has little significance on the relationship of juvenile delinquency.

13. **The correct answer is (A).** The term "site coverage" means the area occupied by the buildings alone divided by the total area of the project.

14. **The correct answer is (D).** Obsolescence is "the impairment of desirability and usefulness resulting from changes in the arts or in design, or from internal influences that make a property less desirable for continued use."

15. **The correct answer is (B).** A "building code" is the collection of legal requirements for the purpose of protecting the safety, health, morals, and general welfare of those in and about buildings.

16. **The correct answer is (C).** A "slum area" is an area in which the majority of dwellings are detrimental to safety, health, or morals because of dilapidation, overcrowding, lack of ventilation, and other similar faults.

17. **The correct answer is (C).** The theory that the housing needs of the lower-income groups will be met when the higher-income groups move out of their present housing into newly constructed homes and buildings is known as "filter down."

18. **The correct answer is (A).** NORC stands for "naturally occurring retirement community."

19. **The correct answer is (B).** In order to access funds to establish a NORC, social service agencies apply for funds through a granting process referred to as a "Request for Proposal" (RFP).

20. **The correct answer is (C).** If a disabled person requests to have a ramp built on her city-funded apartment building, the building management must comply because buildings that receive city funding are required to do so according to the Americans with Disabilities Act.

21. **The correct answer is (C).** The landlord can bill the tenants for the repairs if an emergency condition is verified by the inspector and if the last validly registered owner and managing agent of the property are notified of said emergency condition by letter and/or by phone and instructed to repair the condition.

22. **The correct answer is (A).** The City Housing Maintenance Code and Multiple Dwelling Law requires landlords to provide heat and hot water to all tenants.

23. **The correct answer is (B).** The Department of Housing Preservation and Development provides new home construction and vacant building renovation with for-profit and not-for-profit partners.

24. **The correct answer is (D).** SCRIE stands for "Senior Citizen Rent Increase Exemption Program."

25. **The correct answer is (D).** A disabled person is not protected from being evicted if the owner provides an equivalent or superior apartment at the same or lower rent in an area near the tenant's present apartment.

26. **The correct answer is (D).** Understanding is the most helpful law of learning in securing tenants' compliance with the rules and regulations of a housing project.

27. **The correct answer is (D).** As the population of cities increases, there is a decrease in the proportion of the developed urban area that is used for residential purposes.

28. **The correct answer is (D).** The building of new homes for the upper-income groups, creating a supply of older buildings for the lower-income groups, is not tenable unless the low-income groups are able to afford the buildings that were vacated.

29. **The correct answer is (D).** The most effective way to reduce the monthly cost of home ownership is to secure reductions in the capital cost of the house.

30. **The correct answer is (C).** The neediest families receive the greatest proportion of assistance for tenant selection for public housing projects.

31. **The correct answer is (D).** Wages have not been high enough in the past, prior to the time subsidized housing became available, to enable the average worker to secure good housing.

32. **The correct answer is (B).** Although the enforcement of existing or procurable legislation regarding public health, safety, and morals would eliminate slums without the use of public funds, existing acceptable housing is still insufficient to meet housing needs.

33. **The correct answer is (D).** The study shows that the data are insufficient to make any of the conclusions presented.

34. **The correct answer is (A).** The families on the public assistance caseload who require some assistance because of high rental payments could be helped by providing satisfactory housing at rents they can afford.

35. **The correct answer is (A).** The difference in the customs and patterns of the present and former environments is the greatest obstacle in the assimilation of immigrant groups.

answers

Judgment

1.	A	9.	C	17.	B	25.	A	33.	D
2.	D	10.	D	18.	A	26.	D	34.	D
3.	A	11.	A	19.	C	27.	B	35.	D
4.	B	12.	C	20.	A	28.	A	36.	D
5.	B	13.	D	21.	B	29.	A	37.	C
6.	C	14.	C	22.	C	30.	A	38.	A
7.	A	15.	A	23.	D	31.	C	39.	B
8.	B	16.	B	24.	D	32.	B	40.	C

1. **The correct answer is (A).** An eligibility specialist should use the services of the home economist for consultation for the management problem that has developed.

2. **The correct answer is (D).** In the case of personal problems that are unrelated to the individual's case, the eligibility specialist should always refer a client to discuss the issue with a private family agency.

3. **The correct answer is (A).** Knowing that a client needs a period of rest and that another agency can arrange this, it would be the responsibility of an eligibility specialist to notify the client of this resource and suggest that he apply there if he wishes to do so.

4. **The correct answer is (B).** It would be inadvisable for the eligibility specialist assigned in any case where a mother's aide is furnished to use the mother's aide as a source of obtaining confidential information for the department.

5. **The correct answer is (B).** When considering the situation, you should let the grant continue because the temporary planned absence of the client does not affect her eligibility.

6. **The correct answer is (C).** If an applicant for public assistance refuses to consent to the necessary procedures to establish his eligibility for aid, the eligibility specialist should try to ascertain why the applicant feels as he does but respect his decision if he refuses to change his mind.

7. **The correct answer is (A).** A public assistance agency should not insist on certain standards of cleanliness as a factor in eligibility to receive public assistance because people have a right to decide how they will live, provided their mode of living does not hurt others.

8. **The correct answer is (B).** The eligibility specialist should encourage Mr. Sears' offers to expedite matters by getting in touch with the employer himself.

9. **The correct answer is (C).** The families' social adjustment is more likely to be achieved if they move to a neighborhood they choose because people should be permitted to make their own plans.

10. **The correct answer is (D).** It is generally understood within the social work community that financial dependency should be treated as a symptom of economic and personal problems.

11. **The correct answer is (A).** The eligibility specialist should not assume that John Smith should be classified as permanently unemployable.

12. **The correct answer is (C).** When conducting a first interview with an international client who is applying for aid, the skill of the eligibility specialist is indi-

cated by utilizing his or her familiarity with the cultural background of the client in order to promote the purpose of the interview.

13. **The correct answer is (D).** It is important for the eligibility specialist to realize that the use of authority is inherent in his or her role and he or she should be aware of its potential uses and abuses.

14. **The correct answer is (C).** As an eligibility specialist, you would be complying with the best case work principles by explaining to the client how planning to repay the loan at the rate of $1 a week will make it more difficult for the family to get along on their limited grant.

15. **The correct answer is (A).** It is important to keep in mind that not all individuals who come to a social agency are destitute.

16. **The correct answer is (B).** As a case worker, if you have reason to believe that an individual on public assistance is working regularly, you should investigate the matter further before taking action.

17. **The correct answer is (B).** As a case worker working with the Drover family, you should determine whether the allowance should be increased to permit Mrs. Drover to stay home.

18. **The correct answer is (A).** The best action to take is to refer Mrs. Semple to the Division of Aid to Dependent Children.

19. **The correct answer is (C).** The case worker should leave the health matters of the man in the hands of the medical social worker since James had asked the medical social worker not to tell his sister of his condition and there is no danger of contracting the disease.

20. **The correct answer is (A).** When handling cases in social agencies, it is best to use indirect questioning because this elicits more complete information from the client.

21. **The correct answer is (B).** In this case, you should inform the applicant that her application will be investigated and her eligibility determined.

22. **The correct answer is (C).** In this case, you should inform the girl that you will take this matter up with her mother and see her again at some future time.

23. **The correct answer is (D).** The case history for this client highlights areas of social isolation, which is commonly associated with poverty and delinquency.

24. **The correct answer is (D).** Mr. and Mrs. Nolan must find a way to better manage their budget. You should suggest that they decide with their family on ways that they can meet their budget. If necessary, you should also seek the assistance of the professional economists on staff.

25. **The correct answer is (A).** In this situation, Mrs. Berry may benefit from the help of a professional counselor to deal with her son. You can best help her by referring her to a counseling agency.

26. **The correct answer is (D).** You should be sensitive to Mr. Dunne's situation and explain to him that he has an illness that makes him unable to do certain things for himself. Then help Mr. Dunne understand that his intentions are righteous but this grant money is to help him be strong.

27. **The correct answer is (B).** Mr. Jones needs to apply for public assistance because his disability limits his ability to be employed.

28. **The correct answer is (A).** It is essential to have knowledge about someone's culture because it helps you build a rapport with the individual.

29. **The correct answer is (A).** The degree of social intelligence a person possesses can best be determined by the extent of success the person has in getting along with people.

30. **The correct answer is (A).** It is important to create an environment that makes the most of one's intelligence by learning to read and write.

31. **The correct answer is (C).** If your client tells you he thinks he may have AIDS, you should first refer him to his doctor or to a health provider who is knowledgeable about AIDS to learn the truth.

32. **The correct answer is (B).** In planning your activities for Thursday, your most efficient and correct use of time would be to plan to visit one AFDC family near the training center whose previously scheduled visit you had to cancel.

33. **The correct answer is (D).** If a client calls with an emergency problem that appears to require an immediate home visit, you should request another case worker to handle the phone and leave a note for your supervisor explaining the situation so you can visit the client immediately.

34. **The correct answer is (D).** You should understand that this client may be lonely and seeking the companionship of other people but doesn't know about community programs and activities that might be of interest to her.

35. **The correct answer is (D).** You should initially explain to the new worker that you will be glad to answer pertinent questions related to her duties but that you must complete your own work on time.

36. **The correct answer is (D).** A case worker who attempts to impose his or her judgments on clients is most likely to run into resistance.

37. **The correct answer is (C).** You should not notify the foster parents of this 16-year-old client in foster care but refer her for counseling.

38. **The correct answer is (A).** You should advise the father to consider calling the police if his son does not stop his threats and reassure him that he has a right to be fearful and anxious about his son.

39. **The correct answer is (B).** You can validate your client's feelings by saying, "I guess you are hurt and angry about not getting the job."

40. **The correct answer is (C).** You would not be showing discrimination in a job interview or on a job application if you asked an applicant to list his or her last three jobs.

Public Health

1.	D	5.	A	9.	C	13.	B	17.	A
2.	C	6.	A	10.	B	14.	D	18.	B
3.	C	7.	A	11.	C	15.	D	19.	C
4.	B	8.	A	12.	A	16.	C	20.	A

1. **The correct answer is (D).** Blind individuals that display a range of experience similar to sighted people have been encouraged to understand their potential and limitations and have made the most of their opportunities.

2. **The correct answer is (C).** Medical social work is distinguished from other forms of case work because it focuses on the medical treatment and recovery of the patient.

3. **The correct answer is (C).** The nutritive value of foods is determined principally by mineral content.

4. **The correct answer is (B).** Knowledge of nutrition is important to a case worker because it helps him or her understand the client's needs and may assist in formulating a plan for meeting these needs.

5. **The correct answer is (A).** The term "vital statistics" is applied to data relating to births, deaths, and marriages.

6. **The correct answer is (A).** Occupational diseases arise from continuing to work in certain places.

7. **The correct answer is (A).** The part of medicine that relates to foods is called mastication.

8. **The correct answer is (A).** Diphtheria is a disease in connection with the Schick Test.

9. **The correct answer is (C).** The decline in the incidence of infectious diseases in childhood in recent years has been a contributing factor to the decline in the death rate in the United States.

10. **The correct answer is (B).** The constantly declining birth rate and immigration rate is attributed to the growth in the aging of the population of the United States.

11. **The correct answer is (C).** The essential purpose of health education is to instruct the public in the value of good medical services.

12. **The correct answer is (A).** Visiting nurses may visit families independently of a physician to give instruction in hygiene or to provide minor services such as baths to patients.

13. **The correct answer is (B).** The authorities of the public health administration are effective when there is a noted decrease in death rates from typhoid, diphtheria, and tuberculosis.

14. **The correct answer is (D).** The best method of combating communicable diseases is to enforce the law requiring the reporting of communicable diseases.

15. **The correct answer is (D).** The most important preventive measure emphasized by the authorities on health education is an annual medical examination.

16. **The correct answer is (C).** The best way to stop the spread of infectious diseases is to wash your hands.

17. **The correct answer is (A).** Alcohol offers no nutritional value.

18. **The correct answer is (B).** Abuse can be physical, sexual, or financial.

19. **The correct answer is (C).** Women who are pregnant are advised to avoid alcohol because drinking when pregnant increases the chance of low birth weight and fetal alcohol syndrome.

20. **The correct answer is (A).** Heart disease can be attributed to family history of heart disease, smoking or use of smokeless tobacco, or the inability to handle stress.

Procedures and Records

1.	A	4.	D	7.	D	10.	D	13.	D
2.	A	5.	B	8.	C	11.	B	14.	C
3.	D	6.	D	9.	C	12.	A	15.	C

1. **The correct answer is (A).** It is difficult to establish protocols based on a model case record; therefore, records should be written to suit the case.

2. **The correct answer is (A).** The clerical efficiency of the eligibility specialist in a public assistance agency automatically speeds up the satisfaction of clients' needs.

3. **The correct answer is (D).** When referring this case to a case worker, the eligibility specialist should not note if an individual in the family has been committed to an institution for alcoholics, taken to court and ordered to keep the peace, or referred to a psychiatric clinic.

4. **The correct answer is (D).** The face sheet of a case record offers a social diagnosis of the family for reference purposes.

5. **The correct answer is (B).** Interviewing applicants for aid is one of the primary functions of an eligibility specialist.

6. **The correct answer is (D).** When writing a case record, it is essential to give a picture of the problem as it appears to the family.

7. **The correct answer is (D).** A lengthy report does not necessarily mean a good report.

8. **The correct answer is (C).** The maintenance of the case record in public assistance administration is to furnish reference material for other case workers, reduce the complexities of the case to manageable proportions, and improve the quality of service to the client. However, it should not be used to show how the public funds are being expended.

9. **The correct answer is (C).** A public assistance agency will lean more on forms than a private agency in the same field of activity because the government framework requires a greater degree of standardization.

10. **The correct answer is (D).** You should explain to the applicant that he should not share any information with you that he wants withheld from his record since you must report all information as part of the case record.

11. **The correct answer is (B).** A face sheet does not include information regarding the client's prior sexual relationships.

12. **The correct answer is (A).** A case record should be kept brief, succinct, and clear.

13. **The correct answer is (D).** A burial fund is not considered an asset that would be included in someone's budget.

14. **The correct answer is (C).** A case record does not include the family's perception of each other's problems.

15. **The correct answer is (C).** The medical history of each client is the least needed information to be included in most cases.

Interpretation of Social Work Problems

1.	C	9.	C	17.	A	25.	D	33.	B
2.	B	10.	B	18.	C	26.	H, J, K	34.	A
3.	C	11.	B	19.	A	27.	B, G, K	35.	A
4.	B	12.	B	20.	B	28.	C, D, H	36.	C
5.	B	13.	D	21.	D	29.	C, D, J	37.	B
6.	C	14.	D	22.	C	30.	A, D, I	38.	A
7.	D	15.	B	23.	B	31.	D	39.	B
8.	C	16.	B	24.	C	32.	A	40.	D

1. **The correct answer is (C).** To find the appropriate grant for the family, you must add all of the individual allowances.

	Food	Clothing	Utilities	Incidentals
2 adults	$35.92	$36	$4.80	$2.80
2 children 13–18	$140	$33.60	$4.80	$2.80
2 children under 13	$120	$31.60	$4.80	$2.80
TOTALS	$295.92	$101.20	$14.40	$8.40

Adding these totals together, you get $419.92. To that, add the rent. $419.92 + $160 = $579.92. However, the question asks for the "semimonthly grant," which is approximately one half of the month. Therefore, $579.92 ÷ 2 = $289.96.

2. **The correct answer is (B).** The monthly total, excluding rent, as calculated above is $419.92. $419.92 × 12 months = $5,039.04, which is the annual cost to the city.

3. **The correct answer is (C).** Add up only those items for which Mrs. Peet is responsible. Keep in mind that her niece is paying for utilities, her personal incidentals, and four fifths of the rent.

Food	$17.96
Clothing	$18.00
Special diet allowance	$15.44
Rent	$22.40
($112 ÷ 5 = $22.40, or one fifth of the rent.)	
TOTAL	$73.80

4. **The correct answer is (B).**

	Food	Clothing	Utilities	Incidentals
1 adult	17.96	$18.00	$2.40	$1.40
2 children under 13	$120	$31.60	$4.80	$2.80
TOTALS	$137.96	$49.60	$7.20	$4.20

Adding these totals, you get $198.96. Now add the rent. $198.96 + $130 = $328.96. However, she also receives $36 a week from her husband and $22.40 a week from working = $58.40 a week. To find the monthly total, using the number 4.3 (number of weeks in a month) given in the question, $58.40 × 4.3 = $251.12. Subtract this income from the allowance: $328.96 − $251.12 = $77.84 a month.

5. **The correct answer is (B).** The widower would receive the following amounts.

Food	$17.96
Clothing	$18.00
Incidentals	$17.40
TOTAL	$53.36

All of his other expenses are paid for by relatives.

6. The correct answer is (C).

Food	$17.96
Clothing	$18.00
Rent	$74.00
Utilities	$2.40
Incidentals	$1.40
TOTAL	$113.76

He also earns $84 a month from working.
$113.76 – $84.00 = $29.76.

7. The correct answer is (D). The most logical assumption that the social case worker can draw from the statement made above is that knowledge of the individual attained through social case work can be effectively utilized in planning a broad social welfare program.

8. The correct answer is (C). The inability of people to obtain employment during a time of economic depression is an example that at certain times employment is not available for many people irrespective of their ability, character, or need.

9. The correct answer is (C). The correct formula is P times $\dfrac{W}{X}$.

10. The correct answer is (B). The real worth of the family court cannot be estimated in dollars and cents. This statement most nearly means that the importance of this court to the community is the service that it renders in the preservation of family life.

11. The correct answer is (B). The correct formula is N minus M minus $\dfrac{P}{R}$.

12. The correct answer is (B). If it was true that the study of anthropology has no value for social work, then it can be understood that no primitive cultures have any meaning for social workers.

13. The correct answer is (D). This research shows that this decrease in the consumption of alcohol may be related to the receipt of social insurance.

14. The correct answer is (D). That the Minimum Wage Act sets up minimum wages and hours for children who are legally permitted to work may or may not be true and cannot be answered on the basis of the facts as given in the excerpt.

15. The correct answer is (B). It is not true that the Minimum Wage Act makes no provision for children over 16 years of age.

16. The correct answer is (B). It is not true that the employment of children of any age in a hazardous occupation is considered oppressive child labor.

17. The correct answer is (A). According to the Act, it is true that a producer in New York State may not employ oppressive child labor for goods that he intends to ship to New Jersey, but is not affected if he sells the goods within New York State.

18. The correct answer is (C). It is partly true and partly false that the Chief of the Children's Bureau may determine what exceptions may be made for children age 14 engaged in farming, and for children age 16 engaged in only manufacturing and mining.

19. The correct answer is (A). The statement should read: "Efforts to deal constructively with the mentally challenged have been thwarted by the commonly held beliefs of a decade or two ago that most of them are social failures. The evidence against that today is overwhelming."

20. The correct answer is (B). The statement should read: "Perhaps startling to some people, although a commonplace to the public assistance workers themselves, is the recently ascertained fact that of those people who became eligible for unemployment compensation, more than 90 percent had notified the assistance offices of the receipt of their benefit checks from the agency before official notification was received from the unemployment compensation authorities."

21. **The correct answer is (D).** The statement should read: "The public aid program must focus on means of training and maintaining the skills of its clients, must play an aggressive leadership role in the placement of its clients in private industry, and must do this fully aware of the importance of preventing the flooding of the labor market with people forced to accept substandard sweatshop wages."

22. **The correct answer is (C).** The statement should read: "The psychoanalysts evolved theories as to the stages of emotional development through which the personality matures and threw much light on the life situations and mental mechanisms by which this process is thwarted."

23. **The correct answer is (B).** The statement should read: "Popular belief in the efficacy of punishment by imprisonment is apparently based on ignorance of the statistics on recidivism. While the figures supplied by prison officials are as low as 39 percent for some states, they are as high as 78 percent in others, and the general average for the whole country is approximately 64 percent. Some authorities frankly express their opinion that large numbers of prisoners emerge from existing institutions worse than when they entered."

24. **The correct answer is (C).** The statement should read: "When aid standards are discussed, it is often difficult to work out the problem that centers on granting allowances to provide health and decency standards and what the self-supporting family can afford. The subsistence diet procedure in aid administration has been

one method used to meet this budgetary deficiency."

25. **The correct answer is (D).** The statement should read: "With the increasing interest in the contribution of group work to individual growth, there has developed within the past few years, in several communities, considerable cooperation between case work agencies and those agencies in the public welfare field."

26. **The correct answers are (H), (J), and (K).** This paragraph best illustrates the points that social change creates problems for the individual as well as for the family, that the children in the modern family may not depend upon their families for definitions of right and wrong, and that the family is no longer a unit of society because modern urban conditions have broken down parental authority.

27. **The correct answers are (B), (G), and (K).** This paragraph best illustrates the points that a family's experience with assistance today vitally influences the pattern of its life tomorrow, that fairness on the part of the eligibility specialist does not depend upon determining financial need on the basis of the client's behavior, and that the client's civility or rudeness may not be an indication of the extent of his or her financial need.

28. **The correct answers are (C), (D), and (H).** This paragraph best illustrates the points that investigation tends to clear up the client's fears of arbitrary action by defining his or her status and responsibilities in relation to the agency; that it is both administratively sounder and psychologically easier for clients that there should be, in general, basic requirements in any determination of eligibility; and that the client's potential for independence may be discovered or developed during the investigation process.

29. **The correct answers are (C), (D), and (J).** This paragraph best illustrates the points that the three major purposes for which professional social work uses publicity today are to enlist public assistance in securing or enforcing social legislation, secure necessary financial support for social services whether publicly or privately financed, and increase understanding of social needs and social purposes.

30. **The correct answers are (A), (D), and (I).** This paragraph best illustrates that in working with the problems of American-born children of parents born in other countries, modern social workers are concerned with helping the children to have a sense of pride in their backgrounds; mediating in conflicts of cultural differences between parents and children; and knowing the culture and resources of ethnic communities.

31. **The correct answer is (D).** An eligibility specialist should never assume anything merely by looking at a client.

32. **The correct answer is (A).** The correct formula is K plus 2L minus 3M.

33. **The correct answer is (B).** The correct formula is P minus $\dfrac{Q}{N}$.

34. **The correct answer is (A).** Citizens of a community forming a committee for the purpose of building a school is an example of cooperative behavior that results from loyalty to the same objective.

35. **The correct answer is (A).** There is no necessary discrepancy or conflict between selfishness and cooperation.

36. **The correct answer is (C).**

Food (special allowance)	$12.44
Clothing	$18.00
Rent	$96.50
Utilities	$2.40
Incidentals	$1.40
TOTAL	$130.74

37. **The correct answer is (B).**

	Food	Clothing	Utilities	Incidentals
1 adult	$17.96	$18.00	$2.40	$1.40
1 child 13–18	$70	$16.80	$2.40	$1.40
2 children under 13	$120	$31.60	$4.80	$2.80
TOTALS	$207.96	$66.40	$9.60	$5.60

The totals add up to $289.56. Add the rent of $145.20 + $289.56 = $434.76. Now add to that the additional stipend of $14.40. $434.76 + 14.40 = $449.16.

38. **The correct answer is (A).** Identifying and bringing public attention to the social problems that they encounter in their daily work is one of the roles of human service workers.

39. **The correct answer is (B).** The most common state fiscal year in the federal government is July 1 to June 30.

40. **The correct answer is (D).** Giving people cash payments in cases of unemployment, old age, and loss of the family breadwinner has helped prevent destitution and dependency in a way that maintained individual freedom and human dignity.

Case Worker Techniques

1.	C	6.	C	11.	C	16.	B	21.	B
2.	B	7.	C	12.	C	17.	A	22.	B
3.	D	8.	C	13.	B	18.	B	23.	C
4.	C	9.	B	14.	D	19.	B	24.	C
5.	B	10.	C	15.	C	20.	A	25.	A

1. **The correct answer is (C).** The skill of the eligibility specialist in conducting the first interview with a client in a public assistance agency is important because it may establish a mutual understanding between the client who expresses needs and the worker who interprets the agency.

2. **The correct answer is (B).** A significant result of doing a good job is that the functions of the agency will be interpreted to the community.

3. **The correct answer is (D).** From the social point of view, the most desirable requisite for a potential eligibility specialist to have at the outset is a desire to help people work through their problems.

4. **The correct answer is (C).** Your function would be to determine the underlying cause of your client and his wife quarreling since this is having a bad effect upon the children and causing friction in the home.

5. **The correct answer is (B).** You would need to attempt to verify the information.

6. **The correct answer is (C).** You would need to determine the length of his employment and wages.

7. **The correct answer is (C).** You would need to make efforts to verify his residence.

8. **The correct answer is (C).** You would need to obtain a mental examination for the member of a client's family who is suspected of developing a mental condition.

9. **The correct answer is (B).** If a client obtains work that lasts for two months at wages that are twice as much as his assistance allowance, you would have to cut off assistance temporarily.

10. **The correct answer is (C).** If a husband on assistance has an accident and is taken to the hospital, you would need to adjust the family budget during his absence in the hospital.

11. **The correct answer is (C).** If this family applies for assistance, you would refer the man for old-age assistance. The man was born in Ireland but is a citizen.

12. **The correct answer is (C).** If a client brings to his home the family of an unemployed married son from another state and asks for increased assistance to cover additional needs of the son's family, you would communicate with the legal residence of son's family for reimbursement of additional assistance.

13. **The correct answer is (B).** You should discontinue aid because of fraudulent statements regarding assets on the part of the client.

14. **The correct answer is (D).** If you find that an applicant has a war-connected disability for which he never thought he could receive a veteran's pension, you would refer him to the Department of Veterans Affairs for assistance.

15. **The correct answer is (C).** If a child of one of your clients develops tuberculosis of the lung and is rapidly getting worse, you should arrange hospital care for the child.

16. **The correct answer is (B).** You should grant assistance because the son now lives independently.

17. **The correct answer is (A).** You should reason with him, pointing out the cause of your action.

18. **The correct answer is (B).** You should interview the brother and attempt to obtain help for the applicant.

19. **The correct answer is (B).** When a client receives assistance, he or she is justified in assuming that he or she has proved eligible for assistance and is free to use the money according to his or her best judgment.

20. **The correct answer is (A).** If this widow applies for aid, you need to ascertain the facts and grant aid if warranted.

21. **The correct answer is (B).** You should refer Mary to Child Protective Services so the agency can find a homemaker to help her care for her children in her home.

22. **The correct answer is (B).** You should inform Mr. Stuart that you are a mandated reporter and explain to him that you need to report such information to the appropriate authorities.

23. **The correct answer is (C).** You should discuss Mr. Carnes' income with him and find out how long he has been receiving this income.

24. **The correct answer is (C).** You should ask this client to discuss the matter in further detail and try to determine how she will manage financially.

25. **The correct answer is (A).** You should address this issue with your client at your next meeting and find out how she plans to financially manage such a large purchase.

answers

Social Work with Children

1.	B	5.	B	9.	A	13.	B
2.	A	6.	D	10.	D	14.	B
3.	D	7.	D	11.	D	15.	C
4.	B	8.	C	12.	D	16.	A

1. **The correct answer is (B).** As the case worker, you should tell Johnny's mother that she can be referred to a specialized agency in the community to help her stop Johnny's truancy.

2. **The correct answer is (A).** As the eligibility specialist, you should advise this woman to apply for Aid to Dependent Children.

3. **The correct answer is (D).** Parental attitudes that are inadequate do not give the child feelings of belonging and freedom for experience.

4. **The correct answer is (B).** One of the deleterious effects of child labor from the social work point of view is that it inevitably deprives the child of opportunities for play.

5. **The correct answer is (B).** The philosophy behind Aid to Dependent Children is premised upon the assumption that children should not be removed from their homes because of poverty alone.

6. **The correct answer is (D).** In this case, Ms. Smith has the same right as any other mother to visit her child.

7. **The correct answer is (D).** The best thing to do with a problem child is to follow an individual plan after analysis of the case.

8. **The correct answer is (C).** The modern practice in the child-care field recognizes that the boarding care of children is desirable, provided there is adequate supervision of the boarding home.

9. **The correct answer is (A).** Foster homes in which children are placed should be of the same religious persuasion as that of the child.

10. **The correct answer is (D).** You should give Anthony a chance to get to know you before he is moved and to express his feelings in relation to the plan that is being made for him.

11. **The correct answer is (D).** It would be unsuitable for you to place the girl in institutional care.

12. **The correct answer is (D).** It is generally agreed among psychologists that in order to develop into healthy, well-integrated adults, children need to have the feeling they are loved and wanted by their parents.

13. **The correct answer is (B).** As her case worker, you should discuss with Ms. Hanson how she is going to manage her home and plan for this new baby.

14. **The correct answer is (B).** Abusive parents are not considered people that provide significant help to children.

15. **The correct answer is (C).** Donors from local restaurants are not involved in the nutritional assistance to Child Care Facilities.

16. **The correct answer is (A).** The licensing of facilities for children does not require a solid recreational program that addresses each physical need for development.

General Review

1.	A	7.	D	13.	D	19.	B	25.	D
2.	D	8.	B	14.	A	20.	A	26.	B
3.	D	9.	A	15.	C	21.	A	27.	B
4.	C	10.	A	16.	D	22.	B	28.	D
5.	B	11.	B	17.	C	23.	B	29.	A
6.	A	12.	D	18.	A	24.	A	30.	C

1. **The correct answer is (A).** Cerebral arteriosclerosis is a type of mental breakdown that ordinarily occurs at the most advanced age.

2. **The correct answer is (D).** The cost of old-age assistance is sustained by the federal, state, and local governments.

3. **The correct answer is (D).** Most old-age assistance programs have been limited in general to the financial and physical needs of the aged because the social service administrators have not been given the means to take on more enlarged programs.

4. **The correct answer is (C).** The invention of a labor-saving device would be an excellent economical and cultural decision during a period of economic adjustment because the rise of unemployment is a temporary phenomenon, while the labor-saving device would add permanent values.

5. **The correct answer is (B).** The principal reason for insurance adjustment is to reduce the number of people receiving assistance.

6. **The correct answer is (A).** The taxpaying public generally understands the parole movement of releasing prisoners before the expiration of their sentences to be based on the assumption that the prison officials and parole officers can watch the paroled prisoners closely and help them adjust themselves in the community at the same time.

7. **The correct answer is (D).** In this example, it can be inferred that the deaths of nonresidents have boosted the death rate of the large city.

8. **The correct answer is (B).** The general effectiveness of marriage courses in college curricula is limited. There is no way to determine if a student, who successfully completes a course in marriage studies, has applied the knowledge that was contained in the course.

9. **The correct answer is (A).** It would be inaccurate to state that a person's intelligence is not directly related to biological factors.

10. **The correct answer is (A).** The family is the only educative agency that starts with a "clean slate" in developing a person's behavior.

11. **The correct answer is (B).** Councils of social agencies or welfare councils are federations or associations of agencies who determine the needs of the community, and by working together, avoid duplication of services.

12. **The correct answer is (D).** According to research, it appears that medical social work seems to be the least needed in cases of acute illness.

13. **The correct answer is (D).** Adoption is a method through which a person legally assumes full parental responsibility for a child that is not his or her own under the authority of a court having suitable jurisdiction.

14. **The correct answer is (A).** A "pay as you go policy" would prevent an individual's annual expenditures to exceed annual income.

15. **The correct answer is (C).** The cost of new construction on modern standards cannot provide affordable apartments for low-income rent and still be profitable for investment.

16. **The correct answer is (D).** Social Security legislation, as enacted by the federal government, carries a combination of state and federal operation, of employer and employee contribution, and a gradual development of the system over the years.

17. **The correct answer is (C).** The visiting teacher may be of assistance to the case worker in understanding family problems because the visiting teacher is able to explain the social and educational maladjustments of school children and assist in meeting their needs.

18. **The correct answer is (A).** The philosophy on in-kind assistance among the social work community is that it tends to be inflexible and develops dependent attitudes in clients.

19. **The correct answer is (B).** The current understanding on public welfare agencies is that they should cooperate with and seek the advice and support of private agencies.

20. **The correct answer is (A).** Need is the basic determinant of eligibility for assistance in the public assistance administration.

21. **The correct answer is (A).** Based on current analysis, it can be determined that the most characteristic definition of migratory agricultural workers are that they are a well defined, distinguishable group that is concerned with acquiring a steady occupation.

22. **The correct answer is (B).** The work of the case worker protects the community because it recognizes potentially serious health and behavior problems and refers them to the appropriate services for care.

23. **The correct answer is (B).** Treatment of the blind community should be based on their total situation rather than their disability because many of the difficulties in which blind persons find themselves come from causes other than their blindness, which serves to heighten their difficulties.

24. **The correct answer is (A).** Parole can be defined as a continuation of the social policy, or social control, instituted by the state when it first places the lawbreaker under apprehension.

25. **The correct answer is (D).** The provision of free hot lunches to needy schoolchildren may stigmatize those who cannot afford to buy their lunches and identify them as dependent children.

26. **The correct answer is (B).** A predominantly male resident population would probably be found in an area that is comprised of made-over private dwellings, rooming houses, cheap hotels, pawnbrokers, and wholesale business establishments.

27. **The correct answer is (B).** If a "slum" were located in the city, it would be comprised of made-over private dwellings, rooming houses, cheap hotels, pawnbrokers, and wholesale business establishments.

28. **The correct answer is (D).** The area in which the most prominent citizens of the community live could best be described as fashionable suburbs, homes of professional and business leaders, and homes that are relatively clean and modern.

29. **The correct answer is (A).** The area likely to contain the sparsest resident population would include retail stores, eating establishments, movie theaters, and offices of professional people and business organizations.

30. **The correct answer is (C).** Middle-class families tend to live in areas that are less crowded than other areas, contain more modern houses, and have fewer children.

answers

PART III

THE INVESTIGATION PROCESS

CHAPTER 3   Principles of Investigation

Principles of Investigation

OVERVIEW

- **Responsibilities of the investigator**
- **The intake process**
- **The investigation**
- **After the investigation**

One area that is extremely important is the investigation process into a client's eligibility for public financial assistance and services. Toward this end, this section provides an overview of the general principles necessary for the case worker, eligibility specialist, and the social investigator to employ in determining one's needs and eligibility.

The initial investigation and the reinvestigation consist of collecting, verifying, analyzing, and appraising pertinent information by which a determination of eligibility or ineligibility for public financial assistance and service is made. The principles and techniques given below, except where indicated, refer primarily to establishing eligibility for financial assistance, including the programs of Aid to Families with Dependent Children (AFDC) and financial assistance to needy individuals and families not eligible for the special programs of AFDC or the Supplementary Security Income (SSI) programs administered by the federal government.

These same principles and techniques are also generally applicable to establishing eligibility for other programs providing assistance to the poor, including the Food Stamp and Medicaid programs and the various assistance programs under SSI (Aid to the Disabled, Aid to the Blind, and Old-Age Assistance). You will learn the more specialized requirements for the programs for which your agency is responsible once you are on the job, but you will find that the process given here is generally applicable to them all.

In some jurisdictions, a case worker may be responsible for both establishing eligibility and providing services to clients, while in other jurisdictions, one person may be responsible only for establishing financial need, while another provides related ancillary services. For example, in New York City, eligibility specialists solely establish financial need, while case workers provide services such as foster care and nursing home placement. The examination and job announcements will show you just what the responsibilities of the job entail. In

chapter 3

NOTE

Cities and states differ in specifying which public employees are responsible for what aspects in determining eligibility for financial assistance.

any event, the material in the following pages should be understood by everyone in the public welfare field, including those who are not directly responsible for granting or denying assistance, whether it is financial aid, Medicaid, or food stamps.

The investigation is a businesslike and individualized process that involves inquiring into the applicant's past and current maintenance, employment, resources, and employability. The necessary information and documentation varies according to the individual factors presented by each applicant and the type of assistance for which eligibility is being investigated or reinvestigated. Note especially that in most jurisdictions, and especially with reference to programs administered or funded by the federal government, no applicant may be discriminated against because of religion, race, color, or national origin. Applicants must be informed of their right to protest against alleged discrimination and be given information, if desired, regarding procedures for filing a discrimination complaint.

The applicant has specific responsibilities in establishing eligibility or ineligibility for assistance and care. The applicant not only must give factual information about the situation but also must submit proof of initial and continuing financial need. The applicant has a responsibility—from the time the application is presented until contact with the agency is terminated—to submit full information regarding eligibility and any changes in the situation that affect initial or continued eligibility for assistance, as well as to cooperate in the verification of these factors. In every instance, the burden of proof rests with the applicant except when he or she is mentally or physically incapable of producing such proof. Therefore, the applicant must understand the eligibility requirements to be able to: (a) provide the necessary information; (b) help verify it; and (c) report promptly any change in the situation affecting initial or continuing eligibility for assistance.

NOTE

For purposes of consistency, we are calling the person responsible for establishing eligibility an "investigator."

The investigation process begins with an intake interview and continues in the field investigation through interviews in the home and with collateral references. The applicant's contact with the department during both the application and assistance periods should be channeled through the investigator. If necessary, consultant services related to employment, resources, housing, health, and management may be available to both the investigator and the applicant. These consultant services can help accelerate the decision-making process, if assistance is unnecessary or that assistance should be withdrawn. In addition, through the use of these consultant services, the investigator gains increased knowledge in the management of the caseload and receives assistance in formulating plans to meet specific problems through the agency or appropriate outside sources.

RESPONSIBILITIES OF THE INVESTIGATOR

The responsibilities of the investigator and of all the other members of the social service staff are as follows:

- Ensure that no needy person eligible for assistance is denied assistance and that no ineligible person receives assistance.

- Verify and evaluate resources and make sure that all available resources that reduce or eliminate the applicant's condition of need are utilized.

- Issue assistance in eligible cases in strict compliance with the policies and the established budget schedules of the agency.

- Issue emergency assistance only when absolutely necessary to meet an acute need and only for essential items until the investigation is complete.

- Render such services that would reduce or eliminate the condition of need. In cases in which other services not provided by the department are needed, the investigator will refer the applicant to the appropriate agency.

- Establish clearly in a written record the initial or continuing eligibility or ineligibility for public assistance. The record should show why assistance is given, denied, or withdrawn, and, if given, the amounts and kinds of assistance.

- Organize and execute work on a planned basis and with the most effective use of time.

- Perform these functions in such a way as to enable the applicant to retain self-respect and his or her capacity for self-direction.

THE INTAKE PROCESS

In large jurisdictions, an appointment interviewer may conduct the initial interview for all applicants and then refer him or her to an intake interviewer or investigator for follow-up. In smaller jurisdictions, a receptionist may merely refer applicants to an interviewer or even to the investigator ultimately responsible for the case. Regardless of who actually conducts this initial interview, certain procedures must take place.

1 **All applicants must be interviewed.** Any person who wishes to apply for assistance may do so. However, assistance may not be granted until eligibility to receive assistance has been established, except in emergency situations.

2 **In most instances, applications for assistance should be made in person.** In some situations of advanced age, ill health, or other special problems, a client or an agency or individual interested in the client's welfare may apply by mail or telephone. The investigator or interviewer must determine that the applicant has not already requested or is receiving assistance; that the applicant registered with the Social Service Exchange, if required; and that appropriate arrangements have been made for either an interview in the office or a visit to the home, if necessary.

❸ The following determinations must be made:

- The client is applying for assistance and care administered by the agency.

- The client resides within the jurisdiction of the welfare center.

- The applicant and the members of his or her family have state residence.

- The applicant and the members of his or her family are not eligible for veteran certification, if the jurisdiction has provision for such special certification forms required by agency procedure.

❹ If the applicant meets the conditions outlined in number three, the investigator:

- Determines the type of assistance for which the applicant and each member of the family is presumed eligible

- Prepares and signs all additional forms required by current procedure

- Issues the appropriate pamphlet describing eligibility requirements for each type of assistance for which the applicant may be eligible

- Issues a separate application blank for the applicant and for each member of the family who is presumptively eligible for another type of assistance, or who is presumptively eligible for the same type of assistance, if separate cases are required

The Intake Interview

After completing the four steps listed above, the interviewer or investigator is ready to conduct the actual interview and carry out the following functions:

- Determining the applicant's eligibility for assistance on the basis of need

- Determining the type(s) of assistance being requested and the type(s) of assistance for which there may be eligibility

- Obtaining information regarding the residence status of each member of the family

- Reviewing previous available records of any family reapplying for assistance to determine why previous assistance was discontinued or denied and to relate the past records to the current information in order to help determine present eligibility

- Advising the applicant of his or her rights under the law

- Ensuring that the applicant has received the appropriate eligibility pamphlet for the type of assistance for which he or she is making the application

- Rejecting at intake ineligible applicants and explaining the reasons for ineligibility both verbally and in writing

- Referring ineligible applicants to other agencies who may be able to provide more appropriate assistance (i.e., Medicaid; food stamps, etc.)

- Determining those situations where the applicant's financial need could be met in full by a referral to special employment or resource units if they exist in the agency and making the necessary referrals to those units

- Deferring decisions, when appropriate, to give the applicant an opportunity to clarify his or her eligibility or to explore further his or her own resources
- Interpreting agency policies for the applicant so that he or she understands the investigation process
- Recognizing emergency situations, giving such situations prompt and effective attention, and arranging for immediate financial assistance where there is substantial evidence that emergency assistance is essential

The nature and direction of the interview is determined primarily by the applicant's reason for his or her need for public assistance, including why the applicant is unable to meet his or her own maintenance problem in whole or in part. To understand the basis for dependency at the point of application, the investigator or interviewer must know how the applicant has maintained him- or herself before applying, why the applicant is no longer able to manage without assistance, and what efforts have been made to utilize actual or potential resources that may be available directly or through other sources. Obtaining such information from the applicant often can be a difficult job. There are many techniques that can be used, depending on the client's personality and the situation. When reading the application, look for:

- Consistency in the facts presented. Is there evidence of unexplained apparent contradictions?
- Long periods of time not accounted for by the applicant.
- Signs of applicant's lifestyle. One may not expect, for example, that an applicant with an arrest record gives as clear an explanation of his past maintenance (outside of prison) as an applicant with a consistent work record.

The statement of the applicant, augmented by the application blank, the Social Service Exchange report, previous records, and any other documents that the applicant presents, are the basis upon which the investigator or interviewer makes a decision to have the case investigated or to reject the application at this point.

THE INVESTIGATION

After the initial intake interview, the actual investigation begins. It starts with a study of the content of the intake interview, the application blank, the Social Service Exchange report, and, in cases of reapplication, a review of the previous record. The investigator's job in a reinvestigation begins with a review of the case record and other pertinent records. Through the use of this available material, the investigator determines:

- What facts are already known
- What additional facts are needed
- What sources of information are available for securing these facts

Home and Office Visits

Many jurisdictions mandate that field investigations be made to applicants' homes before determining eligibility to obtain whatever additional data are necessary from the applicant and the family, to observe the living conditions, and to interpret agency policy procedure to the family.

Since the applicant and all other adult members of the family are primary sources of information, the investigator should always interview these individuals in the home or in the office to verify family circumstances.

Collateral Contacts

Collateral contacts are contacts with individuals outside the immediate family. These contacts may be with relatives, employers, landlords, physicians, hospitals, government departments, social agencies, fraternal and religious organizations, unions, the clergy, friends, and any others who can give pertinent information concerning the family's need for public assistance.

Collateral contacts assist the applicant as well as the agency in determining eligibility for assistance and care, in securing complete or partial support for relatives, and in clarifying employment possibilities and developing resources useful to the applicant.

When collateral contacts are discussed with the applicant, it is not for the purpose of gaining permission to make such visits but to give an explanation of the procedure regarding collateral visits and the necessity for making them. If the applicant refuses a necessary collateral visit and another reference cannot be substituted, the investigator must explain to the applicant the agency's inability, under these circumstances, to continue with the investigation or to grant or continue assistance.

In making collateral contacts, the investigator should reveal no more than the minimum information necessary to accomplish his or her purpose and should limit the discussion to relevant material. The investigator should use the opportunity to interpret agency policies with respect to the particular point in question since such interpretation may enlist a more active cooperation with the person being interviewed.

The method that the investigator uses in making collateral contacts is selected with regard to agency policy and the purpose of the contact. It may be by personal visit, telephone call, or correspondence. Generally, correspondence is suitable for contacts with large organizations. Whenever possible, a personal interview should be arranged if the contact is with an individual who has a personal relationship with the applicant, such as a relative or friend, or an employer who has had direct or close contact with the applicant.

Information Relating to Eligibility

Any or all of the following items (the list below is not all-inclusive) should be investigated in relation to the determination of eligibility. All available or potential resources should be thoroughly explored and discussed.

Past Maintenance

In an initial investigation, information should be obtained regarding maintenance prior to application for assistance. This information should establish clearly the exact way in which the present situation differs from the past, why public assistance is now necessary, and what resources are still available. In a reinvestigation, the investigator should obtain information regarding past maintenance and verification thereof (if pertinent to the determination of continuing eligibility) and management while the applicant was receiving assistance. This information should establish present and continuing need and ensure that the public assistance grant meets the purpose for which it is issued.

Employment

The investigator is responsible for determining if the applicant or any member of the family is employed.

 The investigator should secure and verify the following information for each member of the family that is of employable age.

- Names and addresses of employers
- Earnings
- Length of employment
- Reasons for termination
- Type of work the family member is qualified to do
- Job prospects in the family member's field
- Efforts and results made to secure employment
- Efforts made to secure employment outside the family member's field
- Registration with the state's Employment Services and eligibility for Unemployment Insurance Benefits
- Union affiliations
- Odd jobs—For those workers who have had "odd jobs," the investigator should determine: (a) the present availability of odd jobs; (b) the source the applicant has used to secure these jobs; and (c) whether these jobs have been in the applicant's trade. The investigator should also obtain addresses, periods of employment, and earnings for each job that is secured.

- Seasonal employment—Those workers who have been engaged in industries that have seasonal slack periods would normally be expected to plan through their own resources for these downtimes. In these instances, the investigator should explore: (a) the resources the applicant has used to manage previously during downtimes; (b) why these resources are not available now; (c) whether the present slack period is longer than usual; (d) when the work season begins; (e) whether the applicant has any borrowing capacity; and (f) if the applicant is eligible for unemployment insurance benefits.

- Educational or trade training as it relates to employment or reemployment possibility

2 In addition to the information collected above, the investigator should obtain and verify the following information from each employed applicant or any member of the family whose earnings are not sufficient to enable the applicant to maintain him- or herself or his/her family without public assistance supplementation.

- What are the wages paid, the work schedule, and the nature of the employee's duties?

- Is the employee employed at maximum capacity?

- Does the employee's work schedule permit additional employment?

- Could the employee increase wage-earning capacity with training?

- Does the employee's field of employment have slack periods? If so, how does the employee support himself or herself during these downtimes?

- What opportunities does the family have for supplementing income through its own resources?

3 If the applicant is unable to continue working because of ill health, the investigator should ascertain:

- The nature of the applicant's health problem

- The medical care the applicant is receiving

- Information regarding the probable duration of the illness and incapacity

- Whether the applicant is receiving any wages or disability payments during his or her illness

- Whether the applicant's employer is holding his or her job during the illness

- Whether the applicant may work part time during the illness

- Whether the applicant is fully or partially employable at an occupation other than his or her regular trade

The investigator should verify all applicant statements on this matter. When an investigator makes a collateral visit to the applicant's employer, he or she should not only verify the applicant's employment status and determine the possibility for reemployment, but also should obtain information regarding other possible openings in the industry, its seasons of greatest activity, its wage scale, and its method of employing.

This enables the investigator to discuss employment possibilities intelligently with the applicant and to stimulate interest in seeking employment in his or her trade. If any of the applicants are employed or employable, current procedure with respect to payroll clearances with the state's Division of Placement and Unemployment Insurance should be followed.

Relatives

Relatives of applicants constitute an invaluable resource because they can often supply necessary and pertinent information regarding the eligibility of the applicant and his or her past maintenance and present need. In addition, relatives can often suggest employment opportunities that would be available.

A careful and individualized consideration of the ability of relatives to support an applicant is essential to determine the applicant's eligibility and degree of need. For this purpose, all legally responsible relatives must be contacted. Every effort should be made to obtain full support from the relatives. If the relatives' resources are insufficient to provide full or partial maintenance for the applicant, effort should then be directed toward obtaining their assistance in supplying such special needs as clothing, medical care, surgical appliances, care of children during employment of the applicant, or help with housekeeping during illness.

In situations where there is a deserting spouse—or a putative or adjudicated parent—who is not contributing to the support of the family, it is the primary responsibility of the applicant to make every effort to find the missing spouse or parent and obtain support. When relatives who are legally responsible for the support of the applicant are able but unwilling to provide such support in full or in part in accordance with the relatives' circumstances, the applicant must seek support through appropriate court action. When court action is indicated or necessary, failure on the part of the applicant to institute or cooperate with the agency in the necessary legal proceedings may result in ineligibility for assistance.

Friends

When friends have assisted an applicant in the past, it is important to know the names, addresses, the extent of their assistance, and under what circumstances the assistance was given. The investigator should explore their present willingness and ability to assist the applicant. Can any other friends be of assistance?

Landlords

The investigator should ask current landlords for the following information:

- What is the rent?
- Is the rent paid to date?

- Does the applicant pay his or her rent regularly?
- What amount has he or she paid?
- By whom has the rent been paid?
- Is the applicant a janitor or superintendent? If so, what is his or her compensation for this service?
- Can the landlord give any information regarding boarders or lodgers?
- Has rent been established in accordance with legal controls, or is rent not subject to control?

NOTE

In some instances the investigator may need to contact a previous landlord for information concerning the applicant's eligibility for assistance.

Resources

The investigator is responsible for determining the total available resources of each applicant and each member of the family.

① **Insurance.** What insurance policies does each family member carry? Have they been reviewed by anyone in the agency? Has any cash or benefits been realized from the selling of policies or from death benefits, loans, disability or accident insurance? Is sickness or disability insurance carried now? How is the family paying the insurance premiums?

② **Banks.** In the initial investigation, the investigator inquires into present or past bank accounts and safe deposit boxes. Whenever there has been or is an indication of a bank account, this should be cleared in accordance with current procedure. The investigator should see the bank book or bank statement to correlate withdrawals and deposits with the story of past management and assets. A review of the amount of the withdrawals is important since cancellation of an account in one bank does not necessarily mean there is no account in another bank.

③ **U.S. Savings Bonds.** United States Savings Bonds have cash value and must be considered a liquid asset. The investigator must ascertain location and total current value of any bonds held by the applicant.

④ **Property.** The investigator must discuss with each applicant what real or personal property he or she has had in the past or now has, and such property must be evaluated with the appropriate consultant in the agency to determine how it can be utilized for the applicant's present maintenance. In a reinvestigation, the investigator must determine whether he or she has obtained adequate information concerning real or personal property the client has had or now has. When necessary, clearances or re-clearances should be initiated.

⑤ **Additional compensation:** The investigator should ascertain the following information regarding additional compensation:

- Has the applicant or any member of the family had an industrial accident? Is workers' compensation possible? Is a claim pending? Has the applicant ever received an award?
- Is the applicant or any member of the family receiving disability insurance or allowance?

6 **Pending civil suits.** The investigator should find out the following information:

- Are there any pending civil suits?
- Can damages for personal injuries (accidents) be collected?
- Can outstanding loans be collected?

7 **Pensions and benefits:** Is any member of the family eligible for:

- Pension for service in a public department, such as police, fire, education, or other department
- Pensions or benefits from private industry; for example, from railroads or for personal service over an extended period
- Unemployment insurance benefits
- Veteran's bonus, pensions, benefits, and other allowances

8 **Allowances.**

- Is the applicant or any member of the family receiving an allowance through your state or county's family court, Supreme Court, or court of special sessions, or other legal process?
- How often are these payments made? What is the amount?
- Should the applicant be referred to one of these sources?

9 **Trust funds and estates.** Can funds be obtained from these resources at this time?

10 **Other resources.** The investigator should determine whether the family has access to additional resources such as:

- Free rent, utilities, etc.
- Income from lodgers or boarders
- Benefits received from and dues paid to lodges and unions

Debts

The investigator must determine if the applicant is in any debt and by how much. To whom is the money owed, and under what circumstances was it borrowed? Has any part of the debt been repaid? What arrangements have been made for payment? Does the applicant have further borrowing facilities? If money has been borrowed, did the applicant have cosigners on the loan? If so, who were they? Have they been contacted?

Residence

Although state residence may not be required for eligibility for financial assistance in many jurisdictions or for participation in the Medicaid or food stamps programs, information must always be available as to the residence status of each person included in the application. It should be included in the application for financial assistance or in the grant, unless the previous case record contains acceptable documentary evidence for each individual and the residence has not changed since that time. The investigator should give the applicant such assistance as he or she may require in obtaining of proof of residence. Every case record must contain proof of the applicant's living arrangements, be it a hotel, subsidized housing project, apartment, living arrangement with non-welfare relatives, friends, etc.

Eligibility for Aid to Families with Dependent Children (AFDC)

All applicants and cases must be investigated to determine whether the applicants are eligible for this type of assistance. If so, all legal requirements regarding their eligibility must be investigated and documented. These requirements include such factors as relationship of the adult to the minor child or children, actual presence of the child or children in the home, school attendance, presence or absence of one or more parents, reasons for inability of parents or guardians to support the child or children, etc. All of these factors must be verified, documented, and evaluated in order for AFDC to be granted. If eligibility for AFDC has been established but all documentary evidence has not been secured, assistance may be given only through the preinvestigation grant procedure.

Eligibility for Supplemental Security Income (SSI)

Programs giving financial assistance to individuals who are aged, disabled, or blind are administered by the federal government through the Social Security Administration. Applicants must meet most, or all, of the requirements referred to above and also meet the specific requirements of the assistance program for which they are applying. Note that a family cannot receive both SSI payments and AFDC payments, but must choose the program that best fits their needs.

Methods and Sources of Proof

General Considerations

The investigator must obtain proof of the financial and social data that the applicant supplies. The applicant should have the opportunity to produce proof and to exercise some choice, if possible, in the manner or method of obtaining this. The investigator should offer suggestions, if necessary. For example, an applicant for SSI may be able to produce a birth certificate to establish an age of 65 or older. If no proof is readily at hand, the applicant may prefer to apply for a birth certificate copy, or, if ill or otherwise not able to assume this responsibility, it may be necessary for the investigator to obtain this verification for the applicant.

The investigator needs to evaluate the reliability of the proof since records vary in accuracy, and statements offered by individuals such as employers, relatives, or landlords may be biased toward or against the family. It is therefore important to determine the validity of records and testimonial evidence. The following criteria may be helpful.

- If the information for the record was supplied by the applicant, when was it given and under what circumstances would it have been in the applicant's interest to falsify it?
- If the information was given by someone other than the applicant, when and under what circumstances did the other person acquire such information?
- What is the nature of the other person's attitude toward the applicant?
- Is there any reason why the other person might have motivation for misrepresenting or withholding information?

When a record conflicts with the applicant's statements or other evidence, the conflicting data should be compared. If possible, more conclusive proof should be obtained. If conclusive proof is not available, the investigator must select the most reliable source as the basis for determining the fact to be established and explain this in the case record.

Sources of Proof

1 **Age.** The following may be accepted as proof of age:

- Birth certificate—original, transcript, or a written notification from the municipal or state Bureau of Vital Statistics.
- Baptismal certificate—original or transcript from the church, duly certified by the custodian of such records.

If these records cannot be produced, proof of age may be obtained by secondary evidence, such as the sources listed below. (It should be noted that this listing is alphabetical for easier reference. The reliability of these sources may vary.)

- Affidavits of reliable and disinterested persons
- Bank and postal saving records
- Bible or family records
- Birth certificates of children
- Birth or baptismal certificates (when based upon information filed at a later date)
- Census records, state and federal
- Church records
- Court records
- Hospital and clinic records
- Immigration records
- Insurance policies
- Naturalization records
- Passports
- Physicians' records
- Records of public or private social agencies
- School records

- Social security records
- Vaccination records

When the possibilities of securing proof of the exact age—the day, month, and year of birth—have been exhausted, an approximate birth date is acceptable by many jurisdictions. This method is used only in extreme situations, such as cases involving foundlings, children placed for adoption, and persons who were born in communities in which such registration was not a legal requirement or when a requirement was not enforced. Such people might have no way of ascertaining their exact birth date and yet would be permanently denied the right to receive SSI benefits or AFDC benefits unless this modification is permitted.

A signed statement of medical findings by a physician where the age of an individual is not unreasonably close to the minimum prescribed by law may be accepted in support of the information.

2 **Residence:** The following sources may be used to verify the applicant's address:

- Automobile registration
- Bank records (deposit slips and records at time of opening account)
- Bills, such as utilities, telephone, or tax
- Birth certificates of children born in the jurisdiction where financial assistance is being sought
- Census records
- Citizenship papers
- Civil service records
- Employment registration cards of the United States and the jurisdiction's services
- Hospital and clinic records
- Installment purchase books
- Insurance payment books
- Library cards
- Licenses such as barber's, chauffeur's, driver's, marriage, or peddler's
- Rent receipts, records of landlord or landlord's representatives, leases, and dispossession and eviction notices
- School records
- Social agencies' records
- Social Security registration
- Statements and receipts of service from utility companies
- Voting records

Many of these sources need to be carefully evaluated with regard to reliability. Postmarked envelopes are poor evidence of proof of residence since letters may be sent to mailing addresses while the addressee lives elsewhere. A statement from an individual or organization is not always sufficient proof of residence and it may be necessary to interview the writer. A statement regarding residence does not have increased value by being notarized.

Sufficient proof of residence should be secured to cover the total period being used as the basis for establishing the residence status of the individual.

3 **Death.** The following are acceptable as proof of the death of an applicant's family member or relative:

- Cemetery, hospital, insurance, and physician's and undertaker's records
- Diaries or letters written near time of death
- Family bibles
- Newspaper items
- Registration of death in the jurisdiction's or the state's Bureau of Vital Statistics

4 **Military service.**

- Certificates of eligibility for allotments, disability pensions, educational benefits, etc.
- Certification of veteran status by an approved veteran organization
- Discharge papers or photocopy thereof
- Signed statements of responsible individuals who have knowledge of the fact to military service

5 **Imprisonment.**

- Court record
- Penal institution

6 **Marriage.** The following items are acceptable for both a civil and ceremonial (religious) marriage.

- Marriage certificate
- Records of marriage in the jurisdiction's or the state's Bureau of Vital Statistics

Where records have been destroyed, verification may be through church records, citizenship papers, deeds, insurance policies, mortgages, and passports. In addition, statements about the time and place of marriage by people who performed the ceremony or those who were present or knew of the marriage are satisfactory verification.

AFTER THE INVESTIGATION

Upon completing the investigation or reinvestigation and the budget computation, the investigator recommends whether an application should be accepted or declined. This recommendation should be based on complete, factual, and verified information. Generally, the supervisor has the responsibility for approving or disapproving the investigator's recommendation.

NOTE

A common-law marriage is one in which a man and woman under no legal disability consent to live together presently as husband and wife, promise in each other's presence to become husband and wife and thereafter live as husband and wife. The validity of common-law marriage varies in each jurisdiction and sometimes depends on the year the marriage was contracted and the state in which it was contracted.

If, after the investigation or reinvestigation, the investigator determines that the applicant is not eligible for public assistance, the basis for the denial of assistance or the closing of the case must generally be given to the applicant and confirmed in writing. If the declined applicant has problems or needs that may be met through services available from another agency, the investigator should explain to the applicant the services or facilities available and to make suitable referral, if the applicant so desires.

If the investigator has determined that the applicant is eligible for public assistance, the family should be informed of the amount of public assistance it will receive and the manner in which the grant will be issued. There should also be an explanation of the specific items that will be included in the regular grant. The investigator should inform the client of the services available through the agency, such as medical or dental care, and ask the applicant to discuss his or her needs for such services if they arise. The investigator should also provide the applicant with a written copy of the budget. Finally, in every instance in which there is a change of grant, a written copy of the new budget should be given to the client.

The investigator should explain to the client his or her responsibility for making continuing efforts toward self-maintenance and legal responsibility to inform the agency of any change in his or her financial or social situation affecting eligibility. A review with the family of the basis on which present eligibility is established helps to define more sharply the factors that are subject to change and that may affect the amount of the grant or the applicant's eligibility for assistance.

Granting of Initial Assistance

It is important that the family's minimum financial needs, if they cannot otherwise be met, be provided in accordance with the agency's budget allowance, but it is equally important that all items should not be granted routinely. Assistance is usually granted on any of the following bases:

- Full assistance
- Supplementary assistance
- Short-term assistance
- Emergency assistance

Full assistance is the budget allowance granted by the agency when there are no other resources available and shall be granted only after eligibility has been determined.

Supplementary assistance is partial assistance that supplements the family's financial resources. This should be given in accordance with the agency's budgetary policy and shall be granted only after eligibility has been determined.

Short-term assistance is full or supplementary assistance given to meet a critical, immediate, and isolated situation, such as illness, after which the client can manage for him- or herself. The inability of the applicant to meet his or her needs during this short period shall be fully documented in the case record. A clear notation regarding the probable duration of the need for short-term public assistance should be made in the case record, and there shall be immediate and continued follow-up to ensure the prompt withdrawal of assistance when the period of temporary need terminates. Short-term assistance is usually granted only after eligibility has been determined. Recurring allowances for certain items of the budget such as clothing, household equipment, and supplies, and recurring allowances for items required only during certain seasons, such as fuel for heating and school expenses, are not routinely included in the grant in short-term cases.

Emergency assistance is sometimes granted to meet an acute need until the investigation is completed. The amount and kind of assistance depend upon the circumstances. This involves a careful consideration of all the facts to ascertain if there is any other way that this emergency can be met. Telephone verification and, wherever possible, a home visit, must be made prior to the granting of emergency assistance.

Investigator Caseload Responsibilities

General Considerations

After assistance has been approved, it is the investigator's responsibility to be certain:

- That there is continued eligibility for the assistance granted to his or her under-care cases
- That there has not been any undisclosed employment or change in the financial status of the family (income, earnings, and other resources) since the last contact with the client
- That cases are given services that can help restore the family to self-support

The frequency and purpose of further contacts with the client are based upon discharging the functions of the agency efficiently and appropriately and rendering adequate service to the client. In larger jurisdictions, these contacts are usually made at the public assistance center rather than through visits to the home.

Mandatory contacts must be made in accordance with the specific laws or rules of the agency. Cases in which eligibility has been fully established and in which there is little likelihood of change need not be contacted more frequently than the statutory requirements. More frequent contact than the minimum required should be maintained in cases where there is likelihood of any changes affecting eligibility status or where the family is in need of specific services in meeting essential needs or in being helped to return to self-support.

Continued Purposeful Contacts with Clients

The investigator should remain in contact with his or her clients to stay informed about the following areas:

1 **Employment**

2 **Odd Jobs.** The investigator should discuss this topic frankly and regularly with the client. The investigator should know the addresses, the periods of employment, and the earnings in each job so that any earnings can be correlated with budgetary needs and changes in the amount of assistance granted. Suggested topics for discussion with the client include the following questions:

3 **Seasonal Employment**

4 **Unions**

5 **Family Composition**

6 **Resources**

- Insurance
- Pensions or benefits
- Lodges and unions
- Property
- Bank accounts
- Boarders and lodgers
- Civil suits
- Support fixed by order of the court
- Trust funds
- Frozen assets
- Relatives

7 **Health.** A client's health problems can be funded by the medical assistance that the agency gives in addition to Medicaid. When a client's health affects employability, the investigator should find out:

- If the employable member is receiving treatment
- If the client should be referred
- If a follow-up has been made to ascertain how the client's health condition affects present and future employability
- If physical condition makes former employment impossible, has the client been considered for other types of employment or has he or she been referred to an agency for vocational training

Health problems such as tuberculosis may involve a referral to another agency for treatment. In these instances, the investigator needs to determine whether continued financial assistance is necessary or whether another agency should assume complete responsibility. Health problems may involve potential resources that may be available. The investigator should ask about these possible resources.

8 **Management of Public Assistance.** It is the responsibility of the investigator to relate the assistance grant to the client's current needs.

9 **Continued Contact with Collateral Sources.** Although contact with collateral sources may have been made during the initial investigation, further visits are necessary. This applies to previous references as well as others that may be able to offer significant information at this time.

- **Employers.** It is important to consider recontacting employers.

- **Relatives.** Contact with certain relatives and others may be necessary. During continued contact with the family, the investigator may become aware of relatives previously not mentioned to whom a visit or call may be advisable. The investigator should always bear in mind that certain relatives are legally responsible and that he or she has an obligation to secure current knowledge of their ability to assist in whole or in part.

- **Others.** The investigator's discussion with the client may reveal the need for interviews with other collateral sources or for appropriate clearances or reclearances. He or she should be alert to and follow up on any previously unknown leads.

10 **Withdrawal of Assistance.** Assistance is generally withdrawn when:

- There is no further need

- There is lack of proof of need

- There is income from any source, which covers the budget

- There are available assets or resources, such as trust funds, bank accounts, or insurance from which the client can be maintained

- The client refuses to allow the investigator to verify his or her financial need

- There is a job refusal

- There is refusal to comply with agency policies

- The client has been admitted to an institution or hospital making continued assistance unnecessary

- The client dies

- The client's whereabouts are unknown

- The client has moved permanently out of the state

SUMMING IT UP

- The investigation process is extremely important in determining a client's eligibility for public financial assistance and services. Toward this end, a case worker, eligibility specialist, and social investigator must understand the principles to be employed in determining one's needs and eligibility.

- The Investigator is responsible for determining the total available resources of each applicant and each member of the family.

PART IV
FIVE PRACTICE TESTS

Practice Tests 2–6

The following practice tests will test your knowledge about various areas of social work, and more specifically, those of case worker, eligibility specialist, and social investigator. Most of these types of questions will appear on your actual exam. Following is a list of topics you can expect to be tested on:

- Social Work Vocabulary
- Reading Interpretation
- Eligibility for Public Assistance and Housing
- Housing and Social Welfare
- Judgment
- Public Health
- Procedures and records
- Interpretation of Social Work
- Case Work Techniques
- Social Work with Children
- General Review

ANSWER SHEET PRACTICE TEST 2

1. Ⓐ Ⓑ Ⓒ Ⓓ   21. Ⓐ Ⓑ Ⓒ Ⓓ   41. Ⓐ Ⓑ Ⓒ Ⓓ   61. Ⓐ Ⓑ Ⓒ Ⓓ
2. Ⓐ Ⓑ Ⓒ Ⓓ   22. Ⓐ Ⓑ Ⓒ Ⓓ   42. Ⓐ Ⓑ Ⓒ Ⓓ   62. Ⓐ Ⓑ Ⓒ Ⓓ
3. Ⓐ Ⓑ Ⓒ Ⓓ   23. Ⓐ Ⓑ Ⓒ Ⓓ   43. Ⓐ Ⓑ Ⓒ Ⓓ   63. Ⓐ Ⓑ Ⓒ Ⓓ
4. Ⓐ Ⓑ Ⓒ Ⓓ   24. Ⓐ Ⓑ Ⓒ Ⓓ   44. Ⓐ Ⓑ Ⓒ Ⓓ   64. Ⓐ Ⓑ Ⓒ Ⓓ
5. Ⓐ Ⓑ Ⓒ Ⓓ   25. Ⓐ Ⓑ Ⓒ Ⓓ   45. Ⓐ Ⓑ Ⓒ Ⓓ   65. Ⓐ Ⓑ Ⓒ Ⓓ
6. Ⓐ Ⓑ Ⓒ Ⓓ   26. Ⓐ Ⓑ Ⓒ Ⓓ   46. Ⓐ Ⓑ Ⓒ Ⓓ   66. Ⓐ Ⓑ Ⓒ Ⓓ
7. Ⓐ Ⓑ Ⓒ Ⓓ   27. Ⓐ Ⓑ Ⓒ Ⓓ   47. Ⓐ Ⓑ Ⓒ Ⓓ   67. Ⓐ Ⓑ Ⓒ Ⓓ
8. Ⓐ Ⓑ Ⓒ Ⓓ   28. Ⓐ Ⓑ Ⓒ Ⓓ   48. Ⓐ Ⓑ Ⓒ Ⓓ   68. Ⓐ Ⓑ Ⓒ Ⓓ
9. Ⓐ Ⓑ Ⓒ Ⓓ   29. Ⓐ Ⓑ Ⓒ Ⓓ   49. Ⓐ Ⓑ Ⓒ Ⓓ   69. Ⓐ Ⓑ Ⓒ Ⓓ
10. Ⓐ Ⓑ Ⓒ Ⓓ   30. Ⓐ Ⓑ Ⓒ Ⓓ   50. Ⓐ Ⓑ Ⓒ Ⓓ   70. Ⓐ Ⓑ Ⓒ Ⓓ
11. Ⓐ Ⓑ Ⓒ Ⓓ   31. Ⓐ Ⓑ Ⓒ Ⓓ   51. Ⓐ Ⓑ Ⓒ Ⓓ   71. Ⓐ Ⓑ Ⓒ Ⓓ
12. Ⓐ Ⓑ Ⓒ Ⓓ   32. Ⓐ Ⓑ Ⓒ Ⓓ   52. Ⓐ Ⓑ Ⓒ Ⓓ   72. Ⓐ Ⓑ Ⓒ Ⓓ
13. Ⓐ Ⓑ Ⓒ Ⓓ   33. Ⓐ Ⓑ Ⓒ Ⓓ   53. Ⓐ Ⓑ Ⓒ Ⓓ   73. Ⓐ Ⓑ Ⓒ Ⓓ
14. Ⓐ Ⓑ Ⓒ Ⓓ   34. Ⓐ Ⓑ Ⓒ Ⓓ   54. Ⓐ Ⓑ Ⓒ Ⓓ   74. Ⓐ Ⓑ Ⓒ Ⓓ
15. Ⓐ Ⓑ Ⓒ Ⓓ   35. Ⓐ Ⓑ Ⓒ Ⓓ   55. Ⓐ Ⓑ Ⓒ Ⓓ   75. Ⓐ Ⓑ Ⓒ Ⓓ
16. Ⓐ Ⓑ Ⓒ Ⓓ   36. Ⓐ Ⓑ Ⓒ Ⓓ   56. Ⓐ Ⓑ Ⓒ Ⓓ   76. Ⓐ Ⓑ Ⓒ Ⓓ
17. Ⓐ Ⓑ Ⓒ Ⓓ   37. Ⓐ Ⓑ Ⓒ Ⓓ   57. Ⓐ Ⓑ Ⓒ Ⓓ   77. Ⓐ Ⓑ Ⓒ Ⓓ
18. Ⓐ Ⓑ Ⓒ Ⓓ   38. Ⓐ Ⓑ Ⓒ Ⓓ   58. Ⓐ Ⓑ Ⓒ Ⓓ   78. Ⓐ Ⓑ Ⓒ Ⓓ
19. Ⓐ Ⓑ Ⓒ Ⓓ   39. Ⓐ Ⓑ Ⓒ Ⓓ   59. Ⓐ Ⓑ Ⓒ Ⓓ   79. Ⓐ Ⓑ Ⓒ Ⓓ
20. Ⓐ Ⓑ Ⓒ Ⓓ   40. Ⓐ Ⓑ Ⓒ Ⓓ   60. Ⓐ Ⓑ Ⓒ Ⓓ   80. Ⓐ Ⓑ Ⓒ Ⓓ

answer sheet

Practice Test 2

HOSPITAL ENVIRONMENT

80 Questions • 3 Hours

Directions: Each question has four possible answers. Choose the letter that best answers the question and mark your answer on the answer sheet.

1. You have scheduled an hour's time for an interview with a patient. As the time is almost up and you must go on to your next patient, the patient suddenly begins to talk about what he believes to be a new problem. It would be best for you to

   (A) conclude the interview and schedule another appointment with the patient in the near future.

   (B) permit the patient to take all the time he needs and skip your next scheduled interview.

   (C) request the patient's reason for bringing up the problem as the interview is about to end.

   (D) tell the patient that you have no more time to spend with him.

2. You are meeting with a patient for the first time. This patient has some questions about resources. You observe the patient to be exhibiting shaky and anxious behaviors. At this meeting you should

   (A) confront the patient, and tell her that she is acting strangely.

   (B) ignore the behavior and answer her questions to avoid offending her.

   (C) be direct and ask her if she has ever been treated for any mental health problems in the past.

   (D) do a thorough assessment and once you have achieved a comfort level, ask the patient how she is feeling because she seems to be anxious.

3. An infant showing drug withdrawal symptoms at birth is ready for adoptive care placement following a medical follow-up and the completion of the appropriate paperwork. To prepare the adoptive parents, the case worker should

   (A) not mention the birth parents' drug background.

   (B) inform the adoptive parents of the child's drug background and new treatments provided and answer any questions that they have about any medical problems that the child may be experiencing.

   (C) inform them about the child's background but be careful not to offer any information unless they ask for it.

   (D) inform them that the biological parents had suffered from drug addictions but reassure them that it is very unlikely that the child will experience such problems.

173

4. A newly admitted elderly female patient has been assigned to you. The woman is unable to make her needs known and is unable to coherently identify herself. However, a card containing her name and an address has been found in her possession, which is a short distance from the hospital. The telephone company has no listing of the woman's name at any address. The patient is verbal, yet her statements are illogical and repetitious. The patient keeps commenting that she must take care of her sick daughter. You should

(A) send someone to the address to take care of her sick daughter.

(B) send security guards to the address and tell the people who live there that this patient has been hospitalized.

(C) after confirming the address with a local police precinct, refer the case to Adult Protective Services and put home care in place for the patient so that she can be discharged home safely.

(D) call the public assistance office and find out if the patient is receiving any services.

5. Assume that you are a case worker assigned to the alcoholism clinic. One of your clients appears for a scheduled interview intoxicated. It would be best for you to

(A) conduct a session completely devoted to the evils of drinking.

(B) cancel the interview, make another appointment for the client, and tell him that you cannot interview him while he is intoxicated.

(C) tell the client in an authoritative manner that you are about to close his case.

(D) recommend that he be referred for further medical assistance because your counseling is not of any help.

6. Assume that you are a case worker in a family planning clinic. One of your clients is an 18-year-old unmarried pregnant woman who wants an abortion even though her boyfriend is encouraging her to have the child after marrying him. She is bewildered and does not know what to do. It would be best for you to

(A) lecture her, emphasizing that it was her carelessness that caused her present predicament.

(B) encourage her to make up her own mind and you will support her decision.

(C) encourage her to do what her boyfriend wants her to do because he is offering to marry her.

(D) try to determine if the girl's uncertainty in this matter is a result of her religious upbringing.

7. You are interviewing a new client who tells you that he is on public assistance and is receiving as much money as when he was working. He further states that he cannot understand why anyone would really want to work when they can receive as much money by being on assistance and not working. In response, it would be most appropriate for you to

(A) strongly state that you disagree with the client.

(B) state that it all depends on an individual's values.

(C) agree with the client.

(D) refuse to discuss this matter with the client.

8. During a follow-up interview with a young female client, the client suddenly states, "Stop all this professional stuff, let's chat about this like friends." It would be best for you to respond by saying

    (A) "If we were friends, it would be very difficult for me to help you as I should."

    (B) "We can be friends, but I will have to get you assigned to someone else."

    (C) "Our rules and regulations prohibit this."

    (D) "I am too busy to make any new friends."

9. On the basis of an interview with a new male client you discover that he is on probation, having been recently released from prison. You feel that it would be desirable to contact the client's probation officer in order to secure additional information concerning the client. It would be appropriate for you to contact the probation officer

    (A) after the interview, only with the client's consent.

    (B) after the interview, without the client's consent.

    (C) at the completion of the interview without telling the client.

    (D) only if the client can be present during the discussion.

10. During your first interview, a newly hospitalized patient tells you of her son's truancy from school. She seems to be very concerned about this matter. Your initial response should be

    (A) "This is your son's problem, your problems are more important at this point."

    (B) "Will this matter bother you during your hospitalization?"

    (C) "Has your son failed any subjects because of his truancy?"

    (D) "I am too busy to discuss your son with you today."

11. A young woman, one of your clients, gave birth three days ago. She refuses to see her baby and is very abusive to the staff. At this point it would be most appropriate for you to

    (A) remonstrate with the woman, pointing out that she is acting like a child.

    (B) speak to the woman, telling her that she will feel differently after she sees her child.

    (C) interview the woman in an effort to understand why she is acting like she is.

    (D) threaten the woman with a transfer to the psychiatric ward if she does not conform to acceptable behavior.

12. In a first interview with a battered woman who wants to leave a violent husband, a case worker must first be aware that

    (A) women often make false claims of abuse in order to improve their situations in custody battle relating to divorce.

    (B) the husband must be contacted to try to repair the relationship and reduce the level of violence.

    (C) the woman may be in great danger as men who batter are often enraged by the woman's efforts to seek outside help.

    (D) court orders of protection, social services, and community supports are readily available and accessible to most battered women.

13. You are a case worker in a methadone maintenance clinic. As you complete a scheduled interview with one of your clients, he asks to borrow $10 from you. In this instance you should

    (A) tell your client that rules and regulations prohibit you from lending him the money.

    (B) lend the client the $10.

    (C) suggest he borrow it from a friend or a relative.

    (D) tell him to request the loan from another member of the staff.

14. You have been assigned as a client a young woman who is pregnant but wants to have an abortion because she feels that she may not be able to properly care for her baby. An appropriate first response would be for you to say

    (A) "What do you consider to be proper care?"

    (B) "You are going to be an excellent mother."

    (C) "Who is the baby's father?"

    (D) "In what month of your pregnancy did you start to have these thoughts?"

15. In your capacity as a case worker, the best reason for you to utilize the questioning technique while interviewing your clients is to

    (A) reinforce your own impressions concerning the case.

    (B) obtain necessary information to process the case.

    (C) bring to light any fraudulent intent on the part of the client.

    (D) reveal misinformation given by the client.

16. Properly acting case workers should accept a client even though they may differ with the client in his or her feelings, attitudes, and general behavior. This means that case workers should

    (A) agree with the client as to what he or she says, feels, and does.

    (B) indicate their respect for the client as a person.

    (C) form no strong opinion concerning their client's beliefs.

    (D) attempt to change their sense of values so that they coincide with the client's.

17. You are asked to meet with a patient who recently delivered a baby. This patient has allowed the daughter of the father of the baby from a previous relationship to sleep over in the hospital with this patient. This is against hospital policy. You should

    (A) briefly go in and meet with the mother and see if she and the baby are comfortable. If everything is okay you should not be concerned since the patient will be leaving the hospital that day to go home.

    (B) report the case to Child Protective Services immediately as this shows tremendous neglect.

    (C) meet with the patient privately and try to determine why this girl stayed with her overnight.

    (D) meet with the patient and the girl, and explain that she should not have stayed with her overnight. Then educate the parent on proper parenting skills.

18. Following your introduction to a new client, which of the following questions is the most appropriate to ask first?

    (A) "Will you be having visitors today?"

    (B) "Which doctor is treating you?"

    (C) "How can I help you?"

    (D) "Do you carry hospitalization insurance?"

19. You can best clarify a statement made by a client during an interview by

   (A) asking the client to rephrase his or her statement.

   (B) rephrasing the statement and asking the client if that is what he or she meant.

   (C) telling the client that you do not understand what he or she is saying.

   (D) making your own assumptions where necessary.

20. In the midst of interviewing a married patient who is about to undergo surgery, she asks if you are married. You should reply by

   (A) stating in a friendly manner, "You know we are here to talk about you," and continue with your questions.

   (B) tell the patient your marital status and proceed to show her the pictures of your spouse.

   (C) tell her that the question is entirely inappropriate.

   (D) share with her that you are having difficulties in your personal life, and you would rather not discuss it.

21. A 13-year-old adolescent in treatment at a family agency mentions that he is having suicidal thoughts. The worker believes this to be serious. What should be done first?

   (A) Respect the confidential relationship between the case worker and the adolescent.

   (B) Consult your supervisor.

   (C) Refer the teen to the staff psychiatrist for an appointment after consulting with your supervisor.

   (D) Call the client's family after telling him that you are required to do so.

22. After you've introduced yourself to a new patient, she proceeds to give you a lengthy description of her illness. It would be proper for you in this instance to show your concern by

   (A) making brief comments and asking relevant questions.

   (B) making no comments so that the patient is not interrupted.

   (C) interrupting frequently so that you may clear up in your mind points you do not understand.

   (D) requesting that the patient pause at specific intervals so that you may ask pointed questions.

23. An adult patient in your care has been receiving your counseling for about a month. He is about to be discharged from the hospital but his place of residence is still an undecided issue. The final decision concerning this matter should be made by

   (A) you in the capacity of his case worker.

   (B) the patient's relatives.

   (C) the patient, with the assistance of the case worker if it is required.

   (D) the patient, based upon the advice of the doctors.

24. You are seeing a patient who recently delivered a baby. This patient has developed low iron and requires a blood transfusion. This patient's mother died many years ago when she was transfused with the wrong blood. You should

   (A) be supportive and sensitive to the patient's family history and encourage her to think of the health of her new baby and to follow through with the blood transfusion.

   (B) accept the patient's right to choose.

   (C) refer the case to Child Protective Services because of neglect.

   (D) tell the patient that you will refer the case to Child Protective Services because of neglect if she does not follow through on the doctor's orders.

25. Good case work technique indicates that while interviewing a young child, close attention should be paid to the child's behavior, feelings, and mood, in addition to what the child says. Close observation is necessary because it

(A) provides pertinent information about the child.

(B) aids the relationship.

(C) warns the case worker about the proper time to offer consolation.

(D) offers clues about the proper time to humor the child.

26. You decide it would be proper to refer one of your patients who is about to be discharged for psychiatric help. He agrees to cooperate but requests that you withhold in your report certain information that he has given to you in confidence. For you to include this information in your report to the psychiatrist without the patient's permission would be

(A) proper because the psychiatrist will need this information.

(B) improper because you would be violating a confidence.

(C) proper because the client's welfare is of utmost importance.

(D) improper because the patient would probably find out eventually that the confidence was breached.

27. One of your clients, a woman who had been severely beaten by her husband, is visibly upset and embarrassed about relating detailed information concerning the beating to you. It would be best in this instance for you to

(A) insist that she tell her entire story of the beating, including details.

(B) tell the patient you are leaving and will return when she is ready to tell her story.

(C) tell the woman that she doesn't need to tell you the details of the beating at this time and ask her how you can help her.

(D) put off the interview until such time that the husband can be present to give his side of the story.

28. A retired 78-year-old schoolteacher is about to be discharged from the hospital after a brief illness. Up to this point, he has spoken clearly and seems to be well oriented. As you enter his room to confer with him he fails to recognize you, and his speech is rambling and incoherent. It would be most appropriate for you to react to this change of behavior by

(A) telling the patient in an authoritative tone to come to his senses.

(B) leaving the room and telling the patient you will return when he comes to his senses.

(C) advising the patient's physician of the change of behavior.

(D) telling the patient that discharge plans will be canceled and a transfer to a state hospital will be processed.

29. An elderly woman comes into the emergency room with a diagnosis of terminal cancer. The patient is unaware of her diagnosis. She is the primary caregiver for her 2 grandchildren who were abandoned by their parents. You ask the patient for an emergency contact so you can arrange for the care of her grandchildren while she resides in the hospital. She declines, stating that no one is good enough to care for her grandchildren except for her. You should

(A) threaten the patient by telling her that her grandchildren need an alternative caregiver because she is too ill to care for them.

(B) let the children care for themselves and trust that the patient will come up with a better plan once the doctor has informed her of her diagnosis.

(C) meet with the patient and explain to her that she may have to stay in the hospital overnight. Then discuss the various options available for caring for her grandchildren and assist her to put a plan in place.

(D) meet with the patient and tell her that you will have to call in Child Protective Services to take the children into their care.

30. One of your clients who has been admitted to the hospital on a medical emergency appears to be depressed over the fact that he has become ill during a period when his wife and children are away. In the past, you have had a similar experience that you dealt with successfully. In this instance, it would be most appropriate for you to

(A) tell the man of your experience and tell him to use the same approach.

(B) tell the man of your experience and show your sympathy.

(C) tell the man to get a good night's sleep and he will feel better tomorrow.

(D) tell the man you dealt with this situation and find out how he feels about taking the same approach as you did.

31. You are assigned as a case worker in pediatric services and you receive a phone call from a woman who reports that her neighbor's infant has black and blue marks all over his body. She says that she has heard sounds from her neighbor's apartment that lead her to believe that the child has been beaten. It would be most proper for you to respond to this call by

(A) referring the matter to the proper agency responsible for the welfare of children.

(B) advising the caller that you cannot act on the basis of a phone call.

(C) informing the caller to mind her own business.

(D) telling the woman to call the police and have the parents of the child arrested.

32. You have been assigned a long-term patient and have been advising her for a considerable period of time. However, due to an impending reorganization, this patient is about to be assigned to a new case worker. It would be most appropriate for you to tell the patient of her imminent reassignment to a new case worker

(A) at once so that the patient may prepare herself for the change.

(B) at the first visit of the new case worker so that the patient will not attribute the change to you.

(C) at your final visit and at the same time telling the patient what you know about the new case worker.

(D) at the conclusion of your final visit in order to avoid a sentimental farewell.

33. While working in a psychiatric clinic as a case worker, you receive a call from an individual who is not a clinic patient at the hospital. The person tells you that he has tried committing suicide by ingesting pills. You should

(A) try to encourage the person to regurgitate and then provide counseling over the telephone.

(B) take down his information and inform him that you would like to help him and arrange for emergency help immediately.

(C) tell him to jump into a cab and to come over to meet with you for an appointment as soon as he can make it.

(D) give him the number of a walk-in clinic.

34. As you enter the hospital, your place of employment, you see an elderly man trip over the curb and fall to the ground. You should first

   (A) inform the hospital administrator of the accident.

   (B) help the man to his feet and walk him into the hospital where he can sit down.

   (C) stay with the man and caution him not to move until help can be summoned.

   (D) call the police from the nearest phone.

35. One of your clients is in the midst of relating to you the details of her previous surgery and the problems she had with it, including her postoperative treatment. She encountered many adverse reactions from her family during this period. She is now scheduled to undergo similar surgery and she is anxious to avoid the same problems she encountered before. The amount of notes taken during this interview should have been

   (A) extensive; there were many details related in the interview.

   (B) minimal; the discussion demanded your entire attention and notes should have been recorded after the interview was completed.

   (C) extensive; the client will then be impressed by your apparent interest.

   (D) minimal; the details of this case are best left in your memory.

36. As a case worker, you are interviewing a patient for the second time and you find your relationship considerably strained. You can best handle this situation by first

   (A) considering this situation to be routine and reviewing your own attitudes and reactions towards the client during your initial interview.

   (B) considering this to be unusual and trying to analyze your client's reasons for his or her attitude.

   (C) considering it to be routine and request that the client be assigned to another case worker.

   (D) considering it to be unusual and requesting the client to explain his or her hostility toward you.

37. You are working with a 43-year-old male who is a noncompliant diabetic patient at your medical clinic. His refusal to administer his own insulin injections has resulted in his admission to the emergency room in a diabetic coma on two occasions. You should

   (A) request a home-care evaluation to educate both the patient and his wife on how to give the injections.

   (B) tell the patient to forget about the shots and control his diabetes through dietary changes.

   (C) speak to his wife to enforce the severity of the situation and ask why she is not following through on these shots.

   (D) refer him for psychiatric treatment as soon as possible.

38. A young waitress has been to the emergency room twice in the last few days because of on-the-job accidents. On both occasions, she has indicated to the physicians who have treated her that she is tired and tense almost continuously. She has been referred for a complete medical workup and you have been assigned to counsel her. You can be of assistance to her by

   (A) requesting copies of all medical tests as they are taken.

   (B) interviewing the waitress to ascertain if any nonmedical problems are contributing to her condition.

   (C) recommending her for an immediate psychiatric evaluation.

   (D) not interviewing her until the results of the medical workup are made available to you.

39. A female patient frequently fails to keep clinic appointments because she is more interested in coping with nonmedical problems than with her medical condition, which the doctor feels is sufficiently significant to warrant frequent and regular treatment. You are assigned to counsel her and attempt to convince her of the importance of keeping her medical appointments. You can best accomplish this by

(A) telling her no problem could be more important than her medical problem.

(B) interviewing her in an attempt to evaluate her other problems and ascertain just how much help you can supply to her.

(C) telling her you will be happy to help her with her other problems only after she keeps all of her medical appointments.

(D) warning her she will be discharged if she misses one more medical appointment.

40. A case worker assigned to a hospital would have the primary responsibility of

(A) instructing the nurse concerning the patient's medication.

(B) contacting relatives as to when they should visit.

(C) observing a patient for signs of anxiety concerning his or her illness.

(D) keeping full records of the patient's visitors.

41. You have been assigned to look after the welfare of a young child whose parents have both been hospitalized following an automobile accident. Of the following, your primary concern would be to

(A) encourage the child to react as a grown-up because that is what is expected of him.

(B) spend your time playing games with the child.

(C) get the child to tell you his true feelings and reassure him that you will give him help when he needs it.

(D) convince the child that he has no real fears.

42. Following an initial visit to an elderly client, you notify your client that you and he will meet again in six weeks. For the next several days, the elderly man continues to call with trivial and unimportant concerns that do not appear to be pressing issues. You should

(A) answer the questions and not schedule another visit.

(B) ask the client if he would like to meet sooner.

(C) confront the client and ask him if he is feeling anxious because he is calling so frequently.

(D) transfer the case.

43. A case worker has been treating a patient on a weekly basis for several months. During the past month, the patient has been complaining of a strong headache. The case worker should

(A) offer the patient aspirin.

(B) change the treatment modality.

(C) refer the patient for psychological testing.

(D) refer the patient to a neurologist.

44. A newspaper reporter approaches you and says he has received many complaints concerning long waits for emergency treatment. Your most appropriate response would be to

(A) tell the reporter that there are more cases with less help available.

(B) refer the reporter to the head of your division.

(C) assure the reporter that the emergency room is most efficient.

(D) direct the reporter to speak to the hospital employee responsible for public relations.

45. You are assigned a client whose problems seem to be typical of those of many of your other clients. Of the following, it would be most appropriate to

    (A) attempt to learn more about the client to ascertain if there are significant differences.

    (B) just handle this client as you do your other clients.

    (C) discuss the matter with another case worker.

    (D) tell the client that there are many others with similar problems.

46. A patient informs you that someone has stolen his shoes. He is about to be discharged and he tells you that he has no means for replacing them. It would be most appropriate for you to first

    (A) suggest he speak to the unit nurse about that matter.

    (B) advise him to buy a new pair in a neighborhood store.

    (C) tell him you will see if there is an available pair in the hospital clothing room.

    (D) question him to find out if he was wearing a pair when he was admitted.

47. A 14-year-old girl stops attending school and stays home. The social worker has ruled out school phobia and trauma as a reason. The case worker should

    (A) let the girl stay home.

    (B) get the girl a tutor.

    (C) explore her resistance and encourage her parents to urge the child to go back to school as soon as possible.

    (D) refer her to a psychiatrist for medication.

48. For clients beginning treatment, the primary focus of the case worker is to

    (A) establish a warm relationship with the client.

    (B) engage the client in treatment.

    (C) gather information for a psychological diagnosis.

    (D) understand why the client is seeking help.

49. A man enters your office without an appointment and tells you that he is a close friend of one of your clients who is a terminal cancer patient. He seats himself in a chair next to your desk. Your first remark to the man should be

    (A) "You probably want to know how your friend is doing."

    (B) "You know that your friend is dying of cancer."

    (C) "May I help you?"

    (D) "Do you have a problem?"

50. While conducting an interview with a new client, your mind wanders and you feel that you might have missed some important details that your client has been telling you. At that point it would be best for you to

    (A) let the patient continue and hope that he or she will repeat what you may have missed.

    (B) tell the client to rephrase what he or she has been saying.

    (C) admit that you did not get part of the client's story and ask him or her to repeat it from the part you last remember.

    (D) assume the part you may have missed was not important.

51. In the midst of your client relating to you her family makeup, she suddenly says, "Three of my children go to school and my oldest, who is 18 . . ." At this point she stops speaking. The most appropriate action that you could take at this point is to

(A) say "Works?"

(B) say "Left school?"

(C) prompt "What about the fourth child?"

(D) remain silent for a short time and hope your client will continue.

52. An 8-year-old boy has been referred to the pediatric clinic because he frequently falls asleep in class. The examining pediatrician can find no medical reason for this behavior. You decide to pay a visit to the boy's home where you determine that there is continual quarreling between the boy's parents. The boy has 2 younger brothers. The father has been unemployed for several months. Your best course of action at this point would be to

(A) refer the case to the agency that has jurisdiction over cases of child neglect.

(B) take immediate steps to place the 3 boys in foster homes.

(C) offer to obtain a job for the father and to seek a second medical opinion.

(D) ask your superior to refer this case to a social worker in order to obtain a proper evaluation of the overall family situation.

53. A 10-year-old boy who requires a complete body cast to correct an orthopedic condition will be ready for discharge in about two weeks. He will be required to return weekly to the orthopedic clinic. His mother is the sole support of the child, and you are asked to prepare for the discharge and the subsequent follow-up treatment. You should

(A) recommend that she use her vacation time during her son's convalescence.

(B) suggest that she place her son in a rehabilitation center until he is completely well.

(C) advise her to quit her job until he is completely well.

(D) help her decide what will be best for both herself and for her child.

54. A 5-year-old boy is required to take oral medication five times daily to control a chronic condition. This type of therapy is almost always successful in treating this type of medical condition. However, the boy does not seem to respond to the medication, even though his mother insists she follows the doctor's orders religiously. In this situation it would be best for you to

(A) direct the mother to keep a complete record of just when she gives her son the medication.

(B) discuss the matter with the boy's father, asking him to make sure his wife administers the medication as required.

(C) interview the mother and father at the same time, evaluating if the medicine is actually being given to the child as required.

(D) suggest to the doctor that the child be hospitalized until it can be definitely determined whether the medication will help the child.

55. In a previous children's day hospital visit with a withdrawn child, you had introduced play therapy in your treatment. Presently, the child seems disinterested. You should

    (A) evaluate your treatment with a supervisor.

    (B) transfer the case to a worker with a more proactive style of treatment.

    (C) seek consultation with a medical professional.

    (D) go on with the therapeutic treatment as if nothing has changed.

56. Which of the following would be an appropriate health facility for an aged disabled individual who becomes acutely ill at home?

    (A) Nursing home

    (B) Hospital

    (C) Extended day facility

    (D) Home attendant

57. You have been assigned to place an elderly patient who is ready for discharge from a hospital and who will be able to take care of herself but will require some supervision. The most suitable accommodation that you could place her in would be a

    (A) nursing home.

    (B) rehabilitation center.

    (C) chronic-care facility.

    (D) health-related facility.

58. One of your clients, a married woman with 3 children, will be hospitalized for some time. Her children are all younger than 10 and her husband works days regularly. In this instance, it would be best for you to arrange for the children's care that would provide for

    (A) a foster home.

    (B) services at a day-care center.

    (C) a homemaker.

    (D) a visiting nurse.

59. One of your clients, an elderly woman, is getting ready to be discharged. She will need a significant amount of attention for her personal needs because she lives alone. You should therefore recommend a

    (A) housekeeper.

    (B) homemaker.

    (C) home attendant.

    (D) companion.

60. Which type of facility would be suitable for a patient in a psychiatric facility who is scheduled to be returned to community living?

    (A) A halfway house

    (B) A rehabilitation center

    (C) A community center

    (D) A nursing home

61. One of your clients requires services from another city agency. The proper way to make this referral is to

    (A) telephone the agency and advise them he is on his way.

    (B) have the client contact the agency on his own.

    (C) write a referral letter for the client and have him bring it with him.

    (D) have the client execute a release of information and forward it to the agency with a summary of the client's problem and request that an appointment be set up for him.

62. A woman who speaks little English is having great difficulty in setting up an appointment for her youngest son who is afflicted with a severe behavioral disorder. A physician who found no medical reason for the child's erratic behavior has referred him to the psychiatric clinic. You determine that the woman has not filled out and returned the required forms, and in the interim the child's behavior has worsened. You should

(A) tell the woman that nothing can be done until she completes and returns the required forms.

(B) send the woman to the clinic to explain her problem.

(C) help the woman complete the forms.

(D) tell the recommending physician about the child's deteriorating condition and request that he or she seek immediate help for the child.

63. A client requests to see a case worker after finding out that her 1-year-old baby boy has been diagnosed with childhood diabetes. The client is anxious and states that she is depressed over her child's health problem. The client would be best helped by

(A) having the case worker conduct an assessment of the client's psychological history and family dynamics to better understand her capacity to take care of her child.

(B) referring the client to your sleep clinic for a study you know about that will pay her $50 since you know she could use the money.

(C) refocusing the client on learning how to take care of her child.

(D) discussing her growing up experiences and why she believes she is responding so strongly to this situation.

QUESTIONS 64–66 ARE BASED ON THE FOLLOWING REPORT.

Name: Margaret Brown

Age: 54

Marital Status: single

Parents: deceased

Closest Living Relative: Myra Farlow, sister, age 56, married

Diagnosis: muscular dystrophy

The patient, a high school graduate, supported herself as a typist since graduation. She lived at home with her parents until their death in an automobile accident fifteen years ago. After their death, she maintained her own apartment until she became ill and could no longer work. A medical workup resulted in the diagnosis of muscular dystrophy, which has proved to be progressive. The time came when she could no longer take care of her needs, and when she took a serious fall, she was hospitalized. Arrangements have been made to have her placed in a nursing home, to which she will be released in a short time. Her sister will be unable to take care of her because she has to maintain a home for her family. Margaret Brown is unhappy over the prospect of going to a nursing home, and she is under the impression that her sister, Myra Farlow, is putting her there to be rid of her. Ms. Farlow is requesting assistance from the case worker assigned to her sister.

64. Margaret Brown is probably most resentful of the decision to put her in a nursing home for which of the following reasons?

   (A) Her illness has warped her thought process.

   (B) She has disliked her sister all of her life.

   (C) She had no say in the decision to place her in the nursing home.

   (D) She always sought help from others before she became ill.

65. The case worker can be of most assistance to Myra Farlow in this situation by

   (A) assuring Ms. Farlow everything will come out right.

   (B) telling Ms. Farlow you are sure you can straighten out her sister's thinking about the matter.

   (C) helping Ms. Farlow to understand her sister's feelings concerning her imminent transfer to a nursing home.

   (D) requesting that Ms. Farlow visit her sister and explain why she is being put into a nursing home.

66. A nursing home for Margaret Brown should be selected on the basis of giving primary consideration to which one of the following four factors?

   (A) The number of male residents in the nursing home

   (B) An accessible location to Ms. Farlow's home

   (C) The availability of a private room for Margaret Brown since she has always had her own bedroom

   (D) The average age of the nursing home's residents

QUESTIONS 67–69 ARE BASED ON THE FOLLOWING CASE RECORD.

Name: Mary Jordan

Age: 38

Marital Status: single

Children: Robert, 8, and Geraldine, 4

Diagnosis: paralysis of left side following stroke

Patient completed eighth grade before leaving school to work at variety of jobs in factories and as a lunchroom waitress. She is now supported by public assistance. In May 2003, a hysterectomy was performed as well as the removal of a benign tumor on her left kidney. In February 2004, she suffered a cerebrovascular episode that was diagnosed as hemiparesis left. In May 2005, she had a cystoscopy operation. Discharged in July 2005, the patient was scheduled for biweekly visits to the rehabilitation clinic for treatment of paralysis. She has followed therapy faithfully and has recovered to the point where she can walk with the aid of a cane. However, her left hand and arm have not responded well to treatment.

Patient displays a poor attitude during interviews with the case worker. She feels she is being punished for a sin she has committed. She is very concerned about the welfare of her children who appear to be doing well in school and are healthy.

67. The most important reason for the case worker's ability to understand the medical terms in this report is that it will

(A) enable the case worker to participate in medical discussions with the treating physicians.

(B) enable the case worker to understand the patient's symptoms.

(C) enable the case worker to sound professional.

(D) enhance the promotional opportunities of the case worker.

68. The case worker will best be able to handle Mary Jordan's fear that she is being punished for sins she has committed by

(A) discussing with her superior the possibility of referring Mary Jordan for psychiatric evaluation.

(B) advocating that the fear be treated psychiatrically.

(C) reassuring Mary Jordan that what she thinks is definitely not so.

(D) accepting Mary Jordan's fears as an indication that she is psychotic.

69. The case worker should understand that the reason that Mary Jordan is overly concerned about the children's welfare is that

(A) she doubts her future ability to take care of her children adequately.

(B) she is convinced that she has not properly brought up her children.

(C) she depends on her children to make her feel worthy.

(D) she has ambitions to provide for her children better than she was provided for in her childhood.

QUESTIONS 70–73 ARE BASED ON THE FOLLOWING PASSAGE.

At the completion of an interview, the case worker should record the essential points in a manner so that it serves several purposes. The record of an interview can ensure continuity of service to a client by an agency even though a client is to be served by several case workers for one reason or another. The record also serves as a permanent record of the service extended to a client and is also an indicator of the agency's accountability to the community. The case worker who is about to record the results of an interview is faced with the problem of just what is to go into the record and the manner in which the essential information brought to light during the interview is to be presented. The purpose of a record is not an end in itself. However, it does provide a means to an end in that it may provide the basis for required training of the staff, or it can be an indicator for improvement of methods and procedures and used for purposes of research. There is no universal opinion of the most important reason for the recording of case work interviews; therefore, in reality, recording has proved to be limited in its effectiveness and has not truly served any of its purposes with true efficiency.

The cost of recording is considerable and it usually takes three times as much worker time as the actual interview. Not to be overlooked is the time of the transcriber, the filing time, and the time of the record reviewer. In addition, there is the expense of the filing equipment and the space that this equipment occupies. There is no question that the recording of interviews is of utmost importance but the value of interviewing in such a way is questionable.

70. The passage indicates that the recording of an interview for social work purposes
   (A) takes three times as long as the actual interview.
   (B) is a less expensive process than the actual interview.
   (C) is equal to the money expanded for the actual interview.
   (D) is too expensive to serve any worthwhile purpose.

71. A specific purpose of the recording process mentioned in the passage is
   (A) conservation of time.
   (B) overall economy.
   (C) a source of research.
   (D) a labor-saving device.

72. According to the passage, one of the major expenses that a social agency may incur by its recording process is
   (A) supervision.
   (B) on-the-job training.
   (C) research.
   (D) record reviewing.

73. From this passage, you may infer that the author's opinion regarding the ultimate usefulness that social work recording achieves is that it is
   (A) very useful.
   (B) limited.
   (C) not readily measured.
   (D) of no value.

QUESTIONS 74–76 ARE BASED ON THE FOLLOWING PASSAGE.

The governor, in an effort to improve the administration of the medical program so that it can deliver services to its beneficiaries, has appointed a committee whose purpose will be to advise the State Commissioner of Social Welfare concerning medical care services. This committee is composed of members of the medical, dental, pharmaceutical, nursing, and social work professions and also includes representatives from the fields of mental health, home health agencies, nursing homes, educational facilities, public health and welfare administrations, and the public. The committee includes a number of physicians in private practice who look after the interests of all private physicians who treat Medicaid patients.

The committee makes appropriate recommendations concerning the standards, quality, and costs of medical services, personnel, and facilities and helps to bring to light unmet needs. It also assists in long-range planning and serves to evaluate the effectiveness and utilization of services. When requested, it advises on administrative and financial matters and acts to interpret the program and its goals to professional groups. Midland City contributions to the effort are depicted in the process of representatives of the medical societies meeting periodically with administrators representing Medicaid to discuss problems and to mull over proposals. One objective is to gain the cooperation of the county medical societies so that they will eventually inform the citizenry of just where they can avail themselves of medical care under Medicaid.

74. One might infer that the group on the advisory committee least likely to be objective in their recommendations would be
   (A) public health and welfare administrations.
   (B) representatives of the general public.
   (C) private physicians.
   (D) schools of health science.

75. You may infer from the passage that a major problem of the Medicaid program in Midland City is that
   (A) the mayor has not appointed a committee to assist in improving Medicaid's operation.
   (B) a sizeable number of citizens do not know where to go to obtain medical care under Medicaid.
   (C) insufficient meetings are held by the committee members to deal effectively with the problems at hand.
   (D) citizens are lacking the initiative to seek medical care offered under the Medicaid program.

76. The passage states that the governor's purpose in appointing the committee to act in an advisory capacity concerning Medicaid was to
   (A) obtain increased cooperation from the county medical societies.
   (B) encourage committee members to provide medical care to Medicaid beneficiaries.
   (C) assist in improving the Medicaid program all around and to make for better administration and provision of services.
   (D) indicate to private physicians and other health-care professionals that it would be to their benefit to accept Medicaid patients.

77. You have been assigned a very difficult case. You are to counsel and provide for an 8-year-old boy whose parents have been seriously injured in an automobile accident. Your initial approach should be to

   (A) convince the child that he will be able to handle the situation without difficulty.

   (B) play games with him and always let him win.

   (C) permit the child to open up and tell you of his fears and reassure him that you and others will provide him with the assistance he will need.

   (D) tell the child he really does not have any problems.

78. An 80-year-old frail patient in your clinic is requesting a prescription over the telephone for adult incontinence products. He is new to your clinic and his chart does not indicate any need for such an item. You should

   (A) give him the prescription because you would humiliate the gentleman if you rejected his request.

   (B) tell him that he must drink less at night and provide the patient with resources on urinary problems from the Internet for him.

   (C) recommend that he come to the clinic to meet with the medical staff first so that they can better assist him with his incontinence problems.

   (D) arrange for a physician who you know privately to write a prescription for this patient.

79. A patient comes to you asking for resources for physical therapy in another state to which he is relocating. You are not familiar with these resources. You can best help your patient by

   (A) suggesting that she make phone calls herself using a phone book from that state and tell her to ask if they will accept her insurance.

   (B) telling her that because she is very busy with the move, you will make phone calls and research this for her.

   (C) having her assessed to make sure she is capable of such a move.

   (D) offering to help her move since she is weak and not capable of moving by herself.

80. Of the following records, the most useful to you as a case worker in the preparation of a treatment plan for a patient is the

   (A) medical services order.

   (B) fact sheet.

   (C) social service medical record.

   (D) psychosocial summary.

ANSWER KEY AND EXPLANATIONS

1. A	17. C	33. B	49. C	65. C
2. D	18. C	34. C	50. C	66. B
3. B	19. A	35. B	51. D	67. B
4. C	20. A	36. A	52. D	68. A
5. B	21. D	37. A	53. D	69. A
6. B	22. A	38. B	54. D	70. A
7. B	23. C	39. B	55. A	71. C
8. A	24. A	40. C	56. B	72. C
9. A	25. A	41. C	57. D	73. B
10. B	26. B	42. B	58. C	74. C
11. C	27. C	43. D	59. C	75. B
12. C	28. C	44. D	60. A	76. C
13. A	29. C	45. A	61. D	77. C
14. A	30. D	46. C	62. D	78. C
15. B	31. A	47. C	63. C	79. A
16. B	32. A	48. D	64. C	80. D

1. **The correct answer is (A).** Good case work practice requires that appointment schedules be kept unless emergency situations arise. There is nothing in the situation presented to indicate the client's "new" problem is actually a new one or requires immediate discussion. Concluding the interview and scheduling the next meeting for the near future to discuss the new problem will solve the issue.

2. **The correct answer is (D).** It is essential to create a bond between the case worker and the patient. The relationship is the essential building block in any work you will do with a patient. There may be many reasons for the patient's increased level of anxiety.

3. **The correct answer is (B).** A case worker must ensure a safe discharge and be sure that the adoptive parents are well informed and prepared to care for this baby with complete awareness of their new child. A case worker cannot determine how people will cope with problems without being direct.

4. **The correct answer is (C).** This patient may have no family support system and lack resources. This may also be a case of neglect on the part of the family, who may be living in the home. This is established if Adult Protective Services determines that it is a reportable case. In addition, see that home care is in place so that the patient's needs are attended to safely.

5. **The correct answer is (B).** In the situation described, no practical purpose is served by attempting to interview the client. A client who is drunk may not absorb a lecture on the evils of drinking or may threaten to close the case. Recommending further medical assistance without counseling is an abdication of your responsibility as a counselor for an alcoholism clinic. Since there is no indication that the patient has been intoxicated persistently at interviews, your best

procedure is to cancel the interview. Schedule another and impress upon the client that he will not be counseled unless he is sober.

6. **The correct answer is (B).** Good case work practice requires that you be concerned with solutions, not past actions, and that you *not* make decisions for the client. It is your responsibility to discuss with the client all social, economic, religious, and moral factors involved. Help the client see all the possible consequences of selecting the easiest alternative and, when she arrives at a decision, assure her of your full support, regardless of your personal opinions on the matter.

7. **The correct answer is (B).** Good case work procedure requires that a client's viewpoint be discussed and respected but that society's values be fully understood by the client as well. Your personal attitude toward receiving public assistance is *not* at issue. In this instance, the case worker must explain society's values towards work and must explore with the client his own attitudes towards self-support.

8. **The correct answer is (A).** Good case work practice demands the maintenance of a professional client–worker relationship. You must make the client understand that failure to maintain such an objective relationship may impair your ability to help her reach the correct decisions about her problems.

9. **The correct answer is (A).** Confidentiality of information received from or about a client and complete honesty with the client are basic requisites in any client–case worker relationship. The client must be made aware of and agree to your need to consult with his probation officer in order for you to help the client reach any decisions.

10. **The correct answer is (B).** Your primary concern must be the welfare of the newly hospitalized client. You must therefore initially determine whether her son's truancy will adversely affect her medical condition.

11. **The correct answer is (C).** In the circumstances given, the first item that must be determined is the reason the client thinks is the cause of her actions. Only after you understand her feelings can action be taken toward protecting the future well-being of the infant and toward correcting the abusive relationship with hospital staff.

12. **The correct answer is (C).** An effort must be made to comfort and secure placement in a shelter or other environment where this patient will be free of contact from her abuser. The patient must stay in the hospital until a safe placement is made.

13. **The correct answer is (A).** Good case work procedure and public welfare regulations mandate that neither the individual case worker nor any employee of the facility lend or give money to clients. This must be carefully explained to the client so that a good relationship continues between you and the client and so that future requests to you or to other staff members are prevented.

14. **The correct answer is (A).** You are asked for the correct *first* response to the client's stated desire for an abortion. You only know that she believes she may not be able to take proper care of a baby. Only when you know what she believes "proper care" to be can you fully discuss with her the many aspects connected with this request. The other proposed answers will not give you any basic information to help you begin the discussion.

15. **The correct answer is (B).** Correct case work procedure mandates that you seek information from the client, accept this

information as true, and form no opinions without first obtaining needed data from the client. Only by asking pertinent questions can a case worker obtain the necessary data to determine eligibility for public assistance for any specific service requested by the client.

16. **The correct answer is (B).** The statement given in this question is one of the most basic tenets of good case work practice. *Acceptance* of the client does *not* mean case workers must either adopt clients' values for themselves or attempt to change the client in these respects. The *acceptance* of the client means that workers realize and understand that the clients are entitled to their own feelings and attitudes. A solution to any problem must conform to those individual attitudes and beliefs and be acceptable to the client.

17. **The correct answer is (C).** It is important to find out the patient's reason for making this decision—there may be a problem at home or a lack of appropriate child care. You may be able to provide this patient with helpful resources.

18. **The correct answer is (C).** Good case work procedure mandates that the hospitalized client learns immediately that you, the case worker, are there to assist with problems. Only after this is fully understood and accepted by the client can you ask the questions needed to elicit information to help the client.

19. **The correct answer is (A).** Good case work interviewing technique requires that you obtain the most complete and accurate statements possible. By asking clients to rephrase a response you didn't fully understand, you enable them to rethink the statement and tell you what they really meant to say. Rephrasing the statement yourself may result in a client's apparent agreement to something not really meant. Explaining you didn't un-

derstand may cause loss of confidence in you, resentment, or agitation. Making your own assumptions can be fatal to full understanding of the statement.

20. **The correct answer is (A).** It is important to create boundaries with and stay focused on the patient.

21. **The correct answer is (D).** It is the duty of a case worker to follow up on issues as serious as suicide, especially in the case of a minor. In this situation, a child's guardians must be notified of any suicidal thoughts on the part of a child.

22. **The correct answer is (A).** The first meeting is primarily an exploratory one in which you and the client begin to understand and respect each other while the client is made confident of your desire and ability to help her. The best way to do this is to allow her to freely discuss the problem that is bothering her the most—her illness. By making brief comments and asking pertinent questions you are indicating both sympathy with her illness and awareness of related social, marital, and economic problems but *not* interrupting her train of thought. This will increase her confidence in your sympathy and ability and will help you to prepare for the next meeting where problems relevant to her situation can be discussed. Choice (B) may lead her to think you are not really listening; choice (C) disturbs her thoughts and may result in her feeling the interview is too regimented.

23. **The correct answer is (C).** In the situation described, there is no indication that the client is unwilling or unable to arrive at his own decision regarding his residence after discharge from the hospital. Good case work procedure requires that the patient make the decision himself. Your suggestions or advice should be made available to him as well as your assistance in obtaining the residence he

desires, but the final decision is his to make. Doctors' advice is limited to physical necessities (e.g., client can't climb stairs). Relatives cannot make the decision; they can only offer or refuse to offer financial help or the availability of their own residence for his consideration.

24. **The correct answer is (A).** Support the patient's wishes and validate and support her feelings while pointing out the patient's new role as a parent. Maintain the patient's focus on her new child and the relationship between them.

25. **The correct answer is (A).** A child is usually unable to hide his feelings, emotions, and moods, but may often be unable to verbalize them. Good case work technique requires you to observe these nonverbal actions and learn the reasons for them in order to understand the child's problems fully. Thus, for example, the child who says school is "okay" but who is always feeling sick at breakfast probably is indicating problems at school.

26. **The correct answer is (B).** In most situations, the information given to you "in confidence" should *not* be released to anyone else without the client's consent. The situation described in this question contains no extenuating circumstance that merits your violating that confidence.

27. **The correct answer is (C).** From the situation described, good case work technique requires you to wait until the client is willing to tell you the details of the situation or to respect her inability or unwillingness to tell you anything at all. The best course for you to take is to move on to the practical question of how to help her to handle the situation that has arisen.

28. **The correct answer is (C).** In this situation, an elderly, well-educated, well-oriented person has suddenly exhibited a marked change in ability to speak clearly

and to recognize a familiar face. The best possible response for the case worker is to tell the attending physician about the change as quickly as possible so that the doctor can determine if further medical assistance is needed and whether the immediate hospital discharge is still feasible.

29. **The correct answer is (C).** Be supportive and understand this patient's role. A case worker must be diplomatic and sensitive to the patient's feelings while helping her to exercise her best judgment in caring for her grandchildren and put a plan in place.

30. **The correct answer is (D).** The case worker's responsibility in dealing with this emergency medical problem is to try to relieve any anxieties the patient may have and to assure the patient that you will give all the aid possible in dealing with any problems. The correct answer in the situation presented in this question gives the patient a possible solution to his problem and the opportunity to accept or reject it.

31. **The correct answer is (A).** As a general rule, a case worker should refer all problems that are not the specific responsibility of his or her agency to the proper governmental agency—in this instance to the child welfare or child abuse agency. If uncertain about the proper authority, consult your supervisor.

32. **The correct answer is (A).** When a long-term counselor–patient relationship, as described in this question, is going to be terminated, the best approach is to inform the patient sufficiently before the change in case worker so that the patient has time to prepare. Waiting until your final visit will give the patient no time to ask questions regarding the change, or to bring up important points she has put off telling you and may be even more reluctant to discuss with a new counselor.

Note: This principle applies to *all* types of long-term counselor–client relationships. The client should feel neither deserted nor at fault and must understand that the change in counselor will not be injurious.

33. **The correct answer is (B).** Every potential suicide must be taken seriously. In this case, keep the patient calm and follow through on arranging for help immediately.

34. **The correct answer is (C).** A basic principle in the situation described in this section requires that the injured person *not* move or *not* be moved by an unskilled person. Since you are already on the hospital grounds, you should remain with the man, make sure he does not move or attempt to move himself, and have someone else obtain skilled help to move him.

35. **The correct answer is (B).** The amount of notes taken during the course of an interview depends on the circumstances. In the situation given, the patient is anxious to avoid problems she experienced after the past operation. You should give her your full attention. Both you and she will be disturbed if you take copious notes. Furthermore, the actual amount of notes needed will probably be minimal since it is primarily a personality and factual situation not requiring specific detailed data, statistics, etc. Be sure to record pertinent data and impressions, problems, possible decisions reached, etc., after the interview.

36. **The correct answer is (A).** A second interview is frequently strained since the patient has learned what will be expected of him or her, has had time to reconsider previous statements, and may not, for various reasons, have gained full confidence in or a rapport with you, the case worker. The professional approach is for the case worker to review personal past actions, statements, attitudes, and feelings towards the patient and the situation to make certain that this second interview results in a more positive and productive relationship.

37. **The correct answer is (A).** Very often, patients may require reeducation via a home-care nurse who can supervise the patient at home and review the various aspects of the patient's care.

38. **The correct answer is (B).** In this situation, the possible medical reasons for the patient's past accidents are being studied by professional medical personnel. It is the case worker's role to explore possible nonmedical reasons for the repeated accidents. This *team* approach is the best method to solve the patient's problem.

39. **The correct answer is (B).** The situation presented is one of an adult so preoccupied with real or fancied problems that she neglects her medical problems. Your responsibility is to help her deal with these nonmedical problems so that she will be able to focus her attention on the medical ones. To do this, you must discuss these nonmedical problems, determine their real importance, solvability, and any way you can help her solve them or come to terms with them so that she can be made to realize the need to keep the medical appointments.

40. **The correct answer is (C).** The primary goal of *all* hospital workers is to help the patient achieve the best health possible. The case worker's role is primarily one of making certain that emotional, family, and related social problems do not interfere with reaching that goal. To do this, the case worker must observe any signs of anxiety shown by the patient and work with the patient to relieve such anxiety.

41. **The correct answer is (C).** In this situation, the case worker has a most important role: to help the young child understand and cope with the frightening situ-

ation confronting him and to give him the assurance that there are adults around who care for his well-being and will help him with his problems.

42. The correct answer is (B). This patient may have other needs that may be prompting this action, and he may not feel comfortable discussing them over the telephone. But by expediting the appointment, you may relieve his anxiety as well.

43. The correct answer is (D). A case worker must never dispense medication or medical advice. Be careful not to confuse your role, but refer your client to trained professionals as you see fit.

44. The correct answer is (D). A case worker in a government hospital *or* in any government welfare agency must *never* attempt to answer questions of a general public relations nature single-handedly. All such questions should be referred to the office or individual responsible for such matters.

45. The correct answer is (A). All of us have problems similar in nature to those of other people and yet each individual has a unique set of circumstances and attitudes that may be sufficiently unique to result in a solution different from the one appropriate to another person. A good case worker knows that as much as possible must be learned about the individual client and his problem before attempting to work with that client toward finding an acceptable solution that may or may not be the same solution which was successfully utilized in other cases.

46. The correct answer is (C). The patient is ready for discharge and such discharge should not be delayed. There are several possible reasons for the occurrence, including the patient's subconscious fear of being discharged. Good case work practice requires you to help the patient leave the hospital as soon as possible by trying to find him shoes without cost to him and by following up on the actual situation with the unit nurse or with other appropriate hospital personnel.

47. The correct answer is (C). A change in a child's behavior can be a tremendous indicator of other problems. This would be an important case to follow up on and investigate what is going on at both school and home.

48. The correct answer is (D). Once the case worker can begin to understand what prompted the client to seek treatment, then treatment goals can be developed. This also gives the worker a greater understanding of where the patient is coming from and what their needs are.

49. The correct answer is (C). In this situation, the man knows his friend's condition. You have no idea why he is seeking your aid and your best approach is simply to ask in what way you can assist him.

50. The correct answer is (C). Even the most experienced case worker will sometimes miss part of what a client was saying. The best way to handle this is to admit your failure to listen and have the client repeat exactly what was said from the point where your mind began wandering. The new client will appreciate your concern to get the full story. The other solutions given in the wrong answers may result in your failure to grasp important details you will need in order to work with this new client successfully.

51. The correct answer is (D). Interviewers will often find that clients will stop in the middle of a discussion if another thought occurs to them about their topic. The best procedure is to give clients time to think through their thoughts. Don't put words in a client's mouth—as in choices (A) or (B)—or prompt the client. You may cause the client to omit something important.

52. The correct answer is (D). This situation calls for professional social work evaluation and action. A case worker should be aware of situations requiring *professional* help and is responsible for alerting the appropriate personnel of the need.

53. The correct answer is (D). Good case work procedure requires that the client, or in this case, the patient's mother, arrive at a decision she fully understands and accepts and is prepared to take responsibility for any consequences resulting from *her* decision. Your role is to help her see alternatives and possible consequences and arrive at a decision that is right for her.

54. The correct answer is (D). Although the medication prescribed is *almost always* successful, it may not have been in this case. Further, you are not certain that the medication has been taken as prescribed. Your best procedure is to inform the doctor of the situation and suggest hospitalization for the child. If the medication is successful under the controlled conditions in the hospital, you will then have to work with the patient to ensure that it is properly administered at home.

55. The correct answer is (A). Play therapy can be very challenging when new. It is important to review your style in supervision to increase your awareness of your actions and gain insights into the child's behaviors.

56. The correct answer is (B). Study the glossary and other appropriate sections of this book. A hospital is the appropriate health facility for the care of an acutely ill person.

57. The correct answer is (D). Your study of the glossary will show you that an elderly person released from a hospital that can manage for herself but needs some supervision should be placed in a health-related facility.

58. The correct answer is (C). Your study of the glossary will teach you that a homemaker will be the best person to provide the all-day and perhaps all-night care for the children while the mother is hospitalized and the father works.

59. The correct answer is (C). Note that this situation does not require the client to have medical service and that housekeeping needs are minimal. The glossary will show you that a home attendant will solve the problem.

60. The correct answer is (A). Study the glossary to learn the differences between the services provided in the different facilities mentioned in the four possible answers. You will discover that a halfway house is the appropriate facility in this instance.

61. The correct answer is (D). This situation occurs frequently. Correct case work procedure requires that you obtain a release from the client before forwarding confidential data to another governmental agency. In the situation described, the most expeditious way to process the referral is for you to obtain the release, give all the information you have available that will be needed by the other agency, and request an appointment for her. The other answers will delay or hinder correct and expeditious handling of the referral.

62. The correct answer is (D). One of the most important lessons a case worker must learn is when to refer a problem to a professional in another discipline. In this situation, the child's condition is becoming worse, so the recommending doctor must be alerted to expedite the proper referral and treatment. The other answer choices for this question will delay the receipt of immediate care.

63. The correct answer is (C). Stay with the presenting problem, and help the client to problem solve by alleviating her anxiety about what she can expect from this medical diagnosis.

64. The correct answer is (C). There is *no* indication given in this report that choice (A) or (B) are true and there *is* indication that choice (D) is contrary to the facts given. The correct answer is borne out of the facts given in the case report.

65. The correct answer is (C). Your client's well-being is your primary concern and it is most important that a good relationship between the sisters be maintained. The client's sister has come to you for assistance. Your best approach is to try to help her understand her sister's feelings and work with her to either accept the client into her household or help you convince the client that her sister maintains her affection and support for the client even though she cannot bring her into her home.

66. The correct answer is (B). As noted above, a good relationship between the sisters is vital to your client's well-being. The ability of Ms. Farlow to visit her sister as frequently as possible is most important in helping your client—who up to this point has been independent and self-sustaining—maintain a relationship with her family and with the world outside of the nursing home.

67. The correct answer is (B). The case record contains medical data the case worker must understand to comprehend the client's state of mind, physical limitations, and reasons behind her reactions and to be able to help the client resolve her problems. The other answer choices will not help the case worker carry out her primary role and are trivial reasons for understanding the medical terminology.

68. The correct answer is (A). The client has demonstrated a poor attitude and a belief she is being punished for past sins. A good case worker must realize his or her own limitations in dealing with what may

be deep psychological problems requiring expert psychological counseling. In this situation, the case worker should discuss the matter with the supervisor to determine the need for a psychiatric evaluation and possible psychological or psychiatric counseling for the client.

69. The correct answer is (A). The case record shows that the children are well and have no school problems. There is nothing in the record to indicate that the client's concern for the children is connected with anything other than her future ability to maintain the children's health and well being.

70. The correct answer is (A). Based *solely* on the information given in the passage, the correct answer is clearly stated in the second paragraph. None of the other possible answer choices can be deduced from the passage.

71. The correct answer is (C). The passage *only* dictates that the recording process is a source of research. The other possible answer choices are *not* given in the passage as purposes of the recording process.

72. The correct answer is (C). The passage indicates that the cost of research is considerable. There is *no* indication in the passage regarding the expenses incurred for the recording processes that are referred to in the other possible answer choices.

73. The correct answer is (B). The passage clearly implies that the author believes that the recording process is of limited ultimate usefulness.

74. The correct answer is (C). The passage clearly states that the advisory committee includes "a number of physicians who look after the interests of all private physicians who treat Medicaid patients." From this, you can infer that private physicians on the committee are less likely to be objective than the groups of people indicated in the other answer choices.

75. **The correct answer is (B).** The passage indicates that in Midland City, administrators of the Medicaid program meet with representatives of the medical societies to gain their cooperation in informing citizenry where they can receive Medicaid. The correct answer can be inferred from that fact.

76. **The correct answer is (C).** The governor's purpose in appointing an advisory committee is clearly stated in the first sentence of the passage. The correct answer paraphrases that sentence. The other possible answers cannot be inferred from the passage.

77. **The correct answer is (C).** The question emphasizes your first action, which is to get the child to talk about his fears, then reassure him. Further help that is needed will follow.

78. **The correct answer is (C).** A prescription cannot be given without proper medical authorization. It is a case worker's responsibility to honor professional practices.

79. **The correct answer is (A).** It is perfectly fine, depending on the individual's abilities, for a case worker to empower a patient by having him or her locate some resources on his or her own. Case workers must be careful not to enable people when they can increase their ability to help themselves.

80. **The correct answer is (D).** A treatment plan prepared by a case worker requires utilization of the psychological and social problems of the patient, not the medical problems, so that the psychosocial summary would be a source of data for your treatment plan.

answers

Practice Test 3

SOCIAL SERVICES

100 Questions • 3 Hours 30 Minutes

Directions: Each question has four possible answers. Choose the letter that best answers the question and mark your answer on the answer sheet.

1. In case work, there is implicit acceptance of a client's value system that may be different from that of the case worker. Of the following, the most valid conclusion to be derived from this statement is that

    (A) clients do not have moral standards.

    (B) the case workers' standards are always stricter than the clients' standards.

    (C) cultural patterns have little effect on value systems of either clients or case workers.

    (D) a case worker has no right to insist on conformity of a client's behavior with his or her own standards.

2. The establishment and maintenance of a professional relationship with a client is stressed in case work. This relationship should be

    (A) clear, businesslike, and delimited by the agency function.

    (B) permissive, friendly, and kind, with the pace determined by the client.

    (C) warm, enabling, and consciously controlled by the case worker.

    (D) variable and unpredictable because of the fluctuations in client need.

3. There is great interest being shown currently in the possible merger of the child welfare and family case work fields, in private as well as public agencies. The best argument in support of such a merger is that

    (A) families with child-care problems would not be broken up through placement of children.

    (B) the taxpayers' and the voluntary contributors' money would be saved.

    (C) through intensive work with children, prevention of the development of behavior problems would be possible.

    (D) new techniques in family case work treatment and the development of new community resources would probably result.

4. There is general agreement among experts in the field that, when dealing with a client or handling a case, a case worker should

   (A) place emphasis on the objective aspects, directing his or her work primarily to the physical factors in the client that indicate need for change.

   (B) place emphasis on the environmental factors, especially those surrounding the client that have caused him or her to be in this present state.

   (C) give attention not only to the environmental factors and social experiences, but also to the client's feelings about, and reactions to, his or her experiences.

   (D) consider each factor in the case as a separate unit after carefully distinguishing between the truly environmental and the truly emotional factors.

5. In case work practice, the unit of attention is generally considered to be the family, although in some agencies, the client or patient is often viewed as being outside of the family. The trend in modern case work, with respect to the family of a client, is to

   (A) involve the family wherever feasible in the total work process.

   (B) scientifically determine how the family is harmful to the client and try to make plans for the client to leave her family.

   (C) educate the public so that families of clients will not interfere with agency plans.

   (D) refer every member of the family for case work help.

6. John, age 15, was referred to a youth counseling agency by the principal of the high school he attends because he has been truant for the past six months. He is of above-average intelligence, is in the tenth grade, and is currently failing four of his five courses. His mother says that he frequently comes home after midnight and is friendly with two boys with court records. The family group consists of John and his mother who supports the two of them by working as a secretary. Two sisters, 19 and 21, are married and out of the home. John's father deserted when John was 3. The principal told John he would have to go to the youth counseling agency or be brought into court by the truant officer. In beginning to work with John, the case worker should first

   (A) recognize that since John did not come voluntarily he will refuse case work treatment.

   (B) establish himself or herself as an adult who will keep John in line.

   (C) secure more facts about John and his situation in order to determine further case activity.

   (D) promise that the agency will keep John from being sent to juvenile court.

7. A client discusses her plans to leave her current position as a commodities trader so that she can go back to school to pursue a career as a teacher. The case worker thinks this client will not only earn less but she will have to take out large student loans, which will create a large debt for this client. The case worker should

   (A) refuse to give the client permission to change jobs without an attempt to counsel her.

   (B) allow the client to change her career without inquiring as to her rationale.

(C) try to dissuade this client because it would be a much better choice for this client to increase her salary and avoid taking out any loans.

(D) find out why the client wants to make this career choice and offer points that support both sides, while allowing her to make the choice for herself as long as it does not hurt her or someone else.

8. Case work interviewing is always directed to the client and his or her situation. Which of the following is the most accurate statement with respect to the proper focus of an interview?

(A) The case worker limits the client to concentrate on objective data.

(B) The client is generally permitted to talk about facts and feelings with no direction from the case worker.

(C) The main focus in case work interviews is on feelings rather than facts.

(D) The case worker is responsible for helping the client focus on any material that seems to be related to his or her problems or difficulties.

9. A case worker is faced with the problem of interviewing dull clients who give slow and disconnected case histories. Which of the following interviewing methods is best to use to ascertain the facts?

(A) Ask the clients leading questions that require simple "yes" or "no" answers.

(B) Request the clients to limit their narration to the essential facts so that the interview can be kept as brief as possible.

(C) Review the story with the clients, patiently asking simple questions.

(D) Tell the clients that unless they are more cooperative they cannot be helped to solve their problems.

10. A case record includes relevant social and psychological facts about the clients, the nature of their requests, their feelings about their situation, their attitudes towards the agency, and their use of and reaction to treatment. In addition, the record should always contain

(A) a routine history.

(B) complete details of personality development and emotional relationships.

(C) detailed process accounts of all contacts.

(D) data necessary for understanding the problem and the factors important to arriving at a solution.

11. The chief basis for the inability of a troubled client to express her problem clearly to the case worker is that the client

(A) sees her problem in complex terms and does not think it possible to give the case worker the whole picture.

(B) has erected defenses against emotions that seem inadmissible or intolerable to her.

(C) cannot describe how she feels about the problem.

(D) views the situation as unlikely to be solved and is blocked in self-expression.

12. Which of the following statements is most accurate in giving case work service to medically ill clients?

(A) The case worker should understand the general aspects of medical treatment of the client's illness.

(B) The case worker should refrain from any involvement in the client's medical care or treatment routine.

(C) The case worker should be concerned only with problems directly relating to the client's illness.

(D) The case worker should consider problems of the client apart from the medical setting.

13. A 70-year-old grandmother comes to a case worker for individual therapy to help her cope with many losses she has suffered in her life. This patient's daughter has abandoned her 2 grandsons who have special needs and she has taken on the responsibility of caring for them. In counseling this patient, your primary focus would be to

(A) get the patient to identify her stressors and discuss how she can manage each of these areas better.

(B) help this patient find alternative care for these boys, as she is old and should not be taking care of them.

(C) bring the children in for counseling so you can help facilitate conversation between the grandmother and her grandsons, as you have determined there to be poor communication in the family.

(D) have the patient hire a baby-sitter so that she can have some free time and work on her personal interests free from the burden of her grandchildren.

14. You are counseling a married couple having difficulty coping with their child who has just been placed in foster care due to a prior episode of domestic violence. Your goals in working with this family would be to

(A) have the parents decide if they want to stay married and then review who will be taking custody of this child.

(B) work with the family together while the parents are simultaneously seeking treatment for their domestic violence issues. Together in treatment you will focus on ways to change their family to create a more supportive and functional household so that their child will have a stable home to return to.

(C) help the family identify areas that they want to improve so that they will increase their level of self satisfaction.

(D) identify them as the sole reason their child is in foster care and point out how this experience will emotionally scar their child for life.

15. When a decision has been reached that a wayward boy's needs can best be met by foster home placement, which of the following approaches is best for the case worker assigned to the case to use in order to break the news to the child?

(A) Inform the child that, although he is being punished in this manner for his bad conduct, he is being separated from his family only temporarily until home conditions are good enough for him to return.

(B) Point out to the child that he is being placed in a fine home with foster parents.

(C) Reassure the child that no punishment is involved in his separation from home and that efforts will be made to help him and his parents achieve the needed changes that will enable him to return home.

(D) Tell the child in a friendly but frank manner that he is being removed from the home because of his parents' inability and lack of intent to help him to become better adjusted.

16. A woman referred to a community mental health agency has been tested twice for HIV. Though her tests were both negative, she is requesting to be tested for a third time. The case worker should assess

(A) her current mental health diagnosis.

(B) her involvement with HIV risk behaviors.

(C) her knowledge of HIV.

(D) the reasons surrounding her concern.

17. While working on a hot line you receive a phone call at 4:00 a.m. from an individual reporting that he is depressed and having suicidal thoughts. The staff psychiatrist will be unavailable until 9 a.m. When you inquire further, he explains his plan is to take sleeping pills. You should

    (A) tell him to go to a mental health agency in the morning.

    (B) tell him that no one is available to help him now and that he should call back in the morning.

    (C) convince him to go to a hospital emergency room and call the police to follow up on him.

    (D) try to counsel him on the telephone and keep him occupied until the therapist comes in to work.

18. A married couple has been arguing and disagreeing continuously, though they agree about one area: the husband's career. The husband is about to begin his first year as a professor; however, he has become very anxious and stressed about his fears of beginning a career and the stress of trying to complete a doctorate. The wife demands attention and interferes with his work. The case worker's primary focus in treatment would be to

    (A) modify the attitudes that created the marital crisis.

    (B) give support to the husband in his academic career.

    (C) examine and interpret the couple's underlying causes of the marital conflict.

    (D) help the wife minimize her destructive attacks on her husband.

19. A 9-year-old boy is living at home with his remarried widowed mother, his stepfather, and his 3-year-old half-sister. The boy is being neglected and is often severely mistreated by his mother and stepfather. The stepfather resents the boy's presence in the home. After failing to correct the situation by discussions with the boy's mother and stepfather, the case worker should recommend which of the following for the boy's welfare?

    (A) Foster-home placement in order to prevent his further mistreatment while corrective educational therapy is used on the parents

    (B) Permanent separation of the boy from his family as the best means of preventing his continued exposure to the unsatisfactory pressures in the household

    (C) Placement of the boy outside the household and a stern warning to the parents that similar action will be taken on behalf of the younger child should the situation warrant it

    (D) Temporary placement of the boy with a foster family until such time as the stepfather is no longer in the household

20. In treating a client diagnosed as schizophrenic, the case worker's most important task is to

    (A) distinguish fantasy from reality.

    (B) establish a positive relationship with the patient.

    (C) examine the individual's psychological background and any potential of a psychotic episode in childhood.

    (D) listen to the individual in a sympathetic manner while shifting the conversation to focus on the matters at hand.

practice test

21. In contracting with a client, a case worker's primary function in the relationship is to

   (A) confirm the roles for both the client and the worker while discussing the expectations and tasks to be achieved.

   (B) hold him- or herself accountable.

   (C) hold the client accountable.

   (D) None of the above

22. A widowed father who lives with his 2 adult sons also lives close to his parents. This client sees his mother often and talks to her on the phone. This client appears to be dependent on his mother, and in general seems to be helpless. The case worker should focus on

   (A) the suggestions of this client's mother that may feed into his dependence.

   (B) the relationship that has existed between him and his mother.

   (C) a poorly developed past that is now being repeated in his present.

   (D) the impact of his family on his behavior.

23. Alcoholism may affect an individual client's ability to function as a spouse, parent, worker, and citizen. A case worker's main responsibility to a client with a history of alcoholism is to

   (A) interpret to the client the causes of alcoholism as a disease syndrome.

   (B) work with the alcoholic's family to accept him or her and to stop trying to reform him or her.

   (C) encourage the family of the alcoholic to accept case work treatment.

   (D) determine the origins of her particular drinking problem, establish a diagnosis, and work out a treatment plan.

24. There is a trend to regard narcotic addiction as a form of illness for which the current methods of intervention have not been effective. Research on the combination of social, psychological, and physical causes of addiction would indicate that social workers should

   (A) oppose hospitalization of addicts in institutions.

   (B) encourage the addict to live normally at home.

   (C) recognize that there is no successful treatment for addiction and act accordingly.

   (D) use the existing community facilities differently for each addict.

25. A case worker in a community agency is treating a patient who reports that her husband drinks a great deal. She explains that he may lose his job as a result of his drinking. The case worker should

   (A) call Alcoholics Anonymous.

   (B) determine whether she and the husband are both in need of support from a case worker.

   (C) encourage the wife to call her husband's boss and discuss his problems with him, in hopes of enlightening him and making him more sensitive.

   (D) ask to meet with her husband.

26. Assume that a case worker has been newly assigned to a load of about seventy cases. In order for her to be able to meet the needs of the clients in this caseload promptly, she should first

   (A) arrange for each client to come to the office for a brief interview.

   (B) read the case history of each client to get a general understanding of the problems involved.

   (C) concentrate on those cases having the most serious problems.

   (D) make a short visit to the home of each client to determine immediate needs.

27. A patient readmitted to a psychiatric hospital complains to you that the doctors have never understood him. In this situation, you should

    (A) tell the medical staff so that they can meet with the patient to discuss this.

    (B) tell the patient that this is a problem that happens with most patients and that he should try to minimize his hostility.

    (C) explore with the patient why he feels this way and offer to discuss them with the doctor.

    (D) explore the reasons for his feelings and help him to discuss them with his doctor.

28. An increase in the size of the welfare grant may increase the cost of the welfare program not only in terms of those already on the public assistance rolls, but also because it may result in an increase in the number of people on the rolls. The chief reason that an increase in the size of the grant may cause an increase in the number of people on the rolls is that the increased grant may

    (A) induce low-salaried wage earners to apply for assistance rather than continue at their current jobs.

    (B) make eligible for assistance many people whose resources are just above the previous standard.

    (C) induce many people to apply for assistance who hesitated to do so because of meagerness of the previous grant.

    (D) make relatives less willing to contribute because the welfare grant can more adequately cover their dependent's needs.

29. All definitions of case work include certain major assumptions. Of the following, the one that is NOT considered a major assumption is that

    (A) the individual and society are interdependent.

    (B) social forces influence behavior and attitudes, affording opportunity for self-development and contribution to the world in which we live.

    (C) reconstruction of the total personality and reorganization of the total environment are specific goals.

    (D) the client is a responsible participant at every step in the solution of his problems.

30. In establishing a professional relationship, a case worker must convey to the client

    (A) positive acceptance.

    (B) a sense of natural caring.

    (C) a feeling of being seen objectively.

    (D) health disagreement.

31. In approaching the client, a case worker should

    (A) be open and permissive.

    (B) accept the client with positive but restricted consideration.

    (C) accept the client completely.

    (D) be in favor of moral responsibility.

32. From the point of view of the case worker in a public welfare agency, the assignment of welfare clients to different categories of assistance serves to

    (A) establish uniform standards of need and factors of eligibility.

    (B) ensure an adequate level of assistance by providing federal grants.

    (C) provide a source of statistical data from which plans for improved services can be drawn.

    (D) identify those social and health problems upon which case work services should be focused.

33. A significant factor in the United States' economic picture is the state of the labor market. Of the following, the most important development affecting the labor market has been

(A) an expansion of the national defense effort creating new plant capacity.

(B) the general increase in personal income as a result of an increase in overtime pay in manufacturing industries.

(C) the growth of manufacturing as a result of automation.

(D) a demand for a large number of new jobs resulting from new job applicants as well as displacement of workers by automation.

34. A working man becomes disabled and is unable to engage in any substantial gainful activity. He applies for benefits under the Social Security law. According to the Social Security regulations, his benefit payment would be based on

(A) a prorated benefit for him and his dependents based on his current age.

(B) a monthly amount depending on the specific limb or bodily organ injured.

(C) the length of time he will probably be disabled.

(D) a monthly amount equal to the old-age insurance benefit he would receive if he were 65.

35. According to the Social Security law, the eligible dependent wife of a man who is receiving old-age benefits is entitled to receive

(A) up to one half of the husband's monthly benefit payment.

(B) a payment of 10 percent less than her husband's monthly benefit payment.

(C) up to three quarters of the husband's monthly benefit payment.

(D) a payment equal to her husband's monthly benefit payment.

36. When a client is presenting material, a case worker should

(A) be gently teasing and thought-provoking.

(B) provide a tolerant and encouraging attitude.

(C) make inferences from nonverbal behavior.

(D) ask leading questions.

37. You are meeting a client for the first time, and he appears reluctant. You should first

(A) allow the client to freely express his ideas, understanding that a relationship will develop and change over time.

(B) try to establish a positive relationship immediately by agreeing with whatever the client says.

(C) establish conditions for going forward.

(D) consider professional goals and try to persuade the client to agree with you.

38. A woman comes to the intake section of the Department of Social Services. The intake worker discovers, fairly early in the interview, that the applicant has come to the wrong agency for the special help she needs. For the worker to continue the interview until the applicant has explained her need is

(A) advisable, mainly because the intake worker should create an atmosphere in which the client can talk freely.

(B) inadvisable, mainly because the applicant will have to tell her story all over again to another agency's intake worker.

(C) advisable, mainly because the proper referral cannot be made unless the worker has all the pertinent data.

(D) inadvisable; the applicant should not be permitted to become too deeply involved in telling her story to an agency that cannot help her.

39. A man has been referred to the Department of Social Services by another agency. The intake worker has reviewed the detailed case history forwarded by the referring agency. When the client comes in for his initial interview, he proceeds to go into detail about his past situation. For the intake worker to allow the client to relate his history at this point is

(A) inadvisable, chiefly because allowing the client to give a detailed account of his past would allow him to control the course of the interview.

(B) advisable, chiefly because the case history may not fully cover some essential areas.

(C) inadvisable, chiefly because the facts are fully recorded and valuable time would be wasted in allowing the client to retell them.

(D) advisable, chiefly because this will give the client the feeling that the worker is interested in him as an individual.

40. A 15-year-old requests to meet with you after an altercation at school. In reacting to what he shares with you, you should

(A) expand the material in a more sophisticated level.

(B) deal with the concrete data only as it is presented to you.

(C) break down the basic theme of communication and reflect back to a broader view.

(D) speak to the teen in the same language that he is speaking to you using his same words whenever possible.

41. In handling a case, an investigator should summarize the facts he has gathered and the observations he has made about the family and incorporate this material into a formal social study of the family. Of the following, the chief advantage of such a practice is that it will provide a(n)

(A) picture of the family on the basis of which evaluations and plans can be made.

(B) easily accessible listing of the factors pertaining to eligibility.

(C) simple and uniform method of recording the family's social history.

(D) opportunity for the investigator to record his evaluation of the family's situation.

42. An applicant for public assistance tells the worker who is investigating his case that he has always supported himself by doing odd jobs. While attempting to verify the applicant's history of past maintenance, it is most important for the worker to determine, in addition,

(A) how the applicant was able to obtain a sufficient number of odd jobs to support himself.

(B) what skills the applicant has that enabled him to obtain these jobs.

(C) why the applicant never sought or kept a steady job.

(D) whether such jobs are still available as a source of income for the applicant.

43. For a worker to make a collateral contact with a client's legally responsible relative when that relative is also receiving public assistance is

   (A) advisable, mainly because the relative may be able to assist the client with needed services.

   (B) inadvisable, mainly because the relative is in receipt of assistance and cannot assist the client financially.

   (C) advisable, mainly because the worker may obtain information concerning the relative's eligibility for assistance.

   (D) inadvisable, mainly because any information concerning the relative can be obtained from the other welfare center.

44. An applicant for public assistance tells the worker that her bank savings are exhausted. While a bank clearance can verify her statement, it is still important for the worker to see her bankbook chiefly in order to

   (A) determine when the account was first opened and the amount of the initial deposit.

   (B) correlate withdrawals and deposits with the applicant's story of past management.

   (C) learn if the applicant had closed this account in order to open an account in another bank.

   (D) verify that the last withdrawal was made before the applicant applied for assistance.

45. An unemployed father whose family is on public assistance has refused to take a job as a laborer because he has enrolled in a training course that will enable him to become an electrician's helper. He states that once he has completed the course, he is sure that he can get a job and support his family. However, you learn that because of the long waiting list for this course, he cannot begin classes for four months. For his refusal to accept this laborer's job to be treated as a job refusal is

   (A) proper; there is no guarantee that he will be able to obtain employment when he has completed the course.

   (B) improper; he should be encouraged to engage in a training program that will increase his job skills and earning capacity.

   (C) proper; his working as laborer will not interfere with his starting the training course when he is reached on the waiting list.

   (D) improper; he has a right to refuse a low-paying job in view of his potential skills.

46. Because of the heavy load of mail at Christmas time, a welfare family's check has not arrived on the expected date. The investigator visits the family and finds that they are without food or funds. For the investigator to ask the local grocer to extend credit to this family until their check arrives is

   (A) advisable, mainly because the family's needs will be met and there will be no need to duplicate assistance.

   (B) inadvisable, mainly because the worker is sanctioning the family's use of credit buying and this might encourage them to make larger purchases with the credit.

(C) advisable, mainly because this is the simplest and fastest way of meeting the family's needs, and the debt can be repaid when the check arrives.

(D) inadvisable, mainly because the family may not repay the debt when they receive their check, and the grocer might sue the worker.

47. When the case of an applicant who lives in a public housing project has been accepted, the authorities in charge of such projects should be notified, chiefly in order to ensure that the

(A) special services available to tenants in public housing projects are utilized.

(B) schedule of rents established for welfare recipients is used.

(C) family consists of only those people indicated on the welfare application.

(D) housing authorities are informed of the applicant's reduced income.

48. A client who is receiving supplementary assistance tells his case worker that he has been offered a higher paying job. He states, however, that he is not sure that he has the skill to handle the increased job responsibilities and asks the case worker for advice. The case worker should

(A) suggest that he take the job because he will then be able to support his family without help from the Department of Welfare.

(B) allow the client to make his decision independently since only he can make such a decision.

(C) help him to evaluate his level of skill and his ability to accept the new responsibilities.

(D) recommend that the client refuse the job because he may not be able to keep it.

49. It has been suggested that all case workers be kept currently informed about general departmental actions taken, changes in other departmental work units, and new developments of general interest in their department. For a welfare department to put this suggestion into effect is generally

(A) inadvisable; case workers should perform the duties specifically assigned to them and not get involved in matters that do not concern them directly.

(B) advisable; case workers may often need to know such information in order to coordinate their work properly with that of other work units.

(C) inadvisable; changes in other work units have little effect on the work performed by case workers not assigned to these units.

(D) advisable; broad knowledge of the activities in an agency tends to improve social work skills.

50. A training program for workers assigned to the intake section should include actual practice in simulated interviews under simulated conditions. Which of the following education principles is the chief justification for this statement?

(A) The workers will remember what they see better and longer than what they read or hear.

(B) The workers will learn more effectively by actually doing the act themselves than they would learn from watching others do it.

(C) Watching one or two simulated interviews will enable workers to cope with the real situation with little difficulty.

(D) A training program must employ methods of a practical nature if the workers are to find anything of lasting value in it.

51. A divorced mother of two whose husband was abusive comes to you. As a case worker, you must be an active listener. This means that you should primarily

    (A) offer verbal and nonverbal cues that show continued interest.

    (B) make comments that keep the client directly involved in the material.

    (C) convey good listening through non-verbal cues.

    (D) allow your attention, concern, and empathy to be communicated through your presence and style.

52. In the evaluation process, the employee who performs all or the greater portion of his job responsibilities in a satisfactory manner is considered standard in performance. Which of the following factors is NOT significant in choosing between a standard or below-standard evaluation for a particular employee?

    (A) Growth potential in terms of his ability to handle duties that pertain to higher-level positions

    (B) Potential for improvement in areas where he is deficient

    (C) The extent of supervision necessary for satisfactory performance

    (D) Work habits and adherence to the rules of the agency

53. In a large city, an intake worker determines that an applicant who was referred to this welfare center by the Homeless Women Emergency Assistance Unit of the agency, although apparently in need of assistance, has been referred to the wrong welfare center. The worker should

    (A) refer the applicant back to the Homeless Women Emergency Assistance Unit after the case has been processed and the investigation completed.

    (B) process the referral and complete the investigation before transferring the case to the appropriate welfare center.

    (C) process the referral only if the applicant is in need of emergency assistance; otherwise, refer the case to the appropriate center.

    (D) refer the applicant back to the Homeless Women Emergency Assistance Unit if she is in need of emergency assistance; otherwise, refer her to the appropriate center.

54. When a restricted or indirect payment method is used by a local welfare agency, reimbursement by the federal government will be made only for

    (A) medical care.

    (B) finder's fees.

    (C) security deposits.

    (D) utility payments.

55. Income resulting from a current court support order may be removed from the budget if the relative under court order ceases to make payments and if he

    (A) presents verification to the investigator that he is now financially unable to assist.

    (B) has made no contribution under the court order for twelve consecutive months.

    (C) has disappeared and it is established that his whereabouts cannot be ascertained.

    (D) moves to another state and refuses to continue his contribution.

QUESTIONS 56–61 ARE BASED ON THE FOLLOWING TABLE.

MIDVALE CITY

Number of Persons Receiving Assistance and Cost of Assistance in 2004–2005

Type of Assistance	Average Number Receiving Assistance/ Month		Total Cost Per Year in Millions		Cost to Midvale City Per Year in Millions Per Year	
	2004	2005	2004	2005	2004	2005
PA	36,097	38,263	$19.2	$17.4	$9.7	$8.7
VA	6,632	5,972	2.5	1.6	1.3	.8
OAA	32,545	31,804	33.7	29.7	6.5	5.0
MAA	13,992	11,782	13.2	21.3	3.3	5.3
ADC	212,795	228,795	108.3	121.4	27.5	31.3

56. Assume that the total cost of the public assistance category decreases by 10 percent each year for the next three years after 2005, and that Midvale City continues to pay a portion of the costs. The public assistance (PA) category for 2008 will be, most nearly,

(A) $11.5 million.

(B) $12.7 million.

(C) $14.1 million.

(D) $14.5 million.

57. The category for which Midvale City paid the smallest percentage of the total cost was

(A) OAA in 2004.

(B) OAA in 2005.

(C) VA in 2004.

(D) ADC in 2005.

58. The monthly cost to Midvale City for each person receiving MAA during 2005 was, most nearly,

(A) $67 more than in 2004.

(B) $26 less than in 2004.

(C) $20 more than in 2004.

(D) $18 more than in 2004.

59. Assume that 40 percent of the number of persons receiving ADC in 2004 were adults caring for minor children. If Midvale City's contribution toward maintaining these adults was only 36 percent of its total contribution to the ADC program in 2004, then the amount paid by the city for each adult per month in 2004 was, most nearly,

(A) $10.

(B) $14.

(C) $31.

(D) $36.

60. Assume that if 10 percent of the persons receiving OAA in 2005 will be transferred to MAA in 2006 and 6 percent of the persons receiving MAA in 2005 will no longer need any public assistance in 2006, then the percentage change from 2005 to 2006 in the monthly average number receiving MAA would be, most nearly, a(n)

(A) increase of 4 percent.

(B) increase of 21 percent.

(C) decrease of 6 percent.

(D) increase of 27 percent.

61. (This question is based only in part on the previous table.) The change from 2004 to 2005 in the monthly average number of persons stated in the table as receiving old-age assistance (OAA) may be best explained by the fact that the

(A) number of aged persons in our population is on the rise.

(B) movement of population out of the city included more younger families than older single persons.

(C) number of persons receiving Social Security benefits and the amount of benefits have increased.

(D) cost of living for older persons is lower than that for the population as a whole.

QUESTIONS 62–64 ARE BASED ON THE FOLLOWING PASSAGE.

Toward the end of the nineteenth century, as social work principles and theories took form, areas of conflict between the responsibility of the social worker to the client group and to the status quo of social and economic institutions became highlighted. The lay public's attitude toward the individual poor was one of emphasis on improvement through the development of the individual's capacity for self-maintenance. They hoped to maintain this end both by helping the client rely on his or her unused capacities for self-help and by facilitating his or her access to what were assumed to be the natural sources of help—family, relatives, churches, and other charitable associations. Professional social workers were fast becoming aware of the need for social reform. They perceived that traditional methods of help were largely inadequate to cope with the factors that were creating poverty and maladjustment for a large number of the population faster than the charity societies could relieve such problems through individual effort. The critical view, held by social workers, of the character of many social institutions was not shared by other groups in the community who had not reached the same point of awareness about the deficiencies in the functioning of these institutions. Thus, the views of the social worker were beginning to differ, sometimes radically, from the basic views of large sections of the population.

62. The social workers of the late nineteenth century found themselves in conflict with the status quo chiefly because they

(A) had become professionalized through the development of a body of theory and principles.

(B) became aware that many social ills could not be cured through existing institutions.

(C) felt that traditional methods of helping the poor must be expanded regardless of the cost to the public.

(D) believed that the right of the individual to be self-determining should be emphasized.

63. It was becoming apparent by the end of the nineteenth century that in relation to the needs of the poor, existing social institutions

(A) did not sufficiently emphasize the ability of the poor to utilize their natural sources of help.

(B) were using the proper methods of helping the poor but were hindered by the work of social workers who had broken with tradition.

(C) were no longer capable of meeting the needs of the poor because the causes of poverty had changed.

(D) were capable of meeting the needs of the poor but needed more financial aid from the general public since the number of people in need had increased.

64. Social workers at the end of the nineteenth century may be properly classified as

  (A) growing in awareness that many social ills could be alleviated through social reform.

  (B) very perceptive individuals who realized that traditional methods of help were humiliating to the poor.

  (C) strong advocates of expanding the existing traditional sources of relief.

  (D) too radical because they favored easing life for the poor at the expense of increased taxation to the public at large.

QUESTIONS 65–68 ARE BASED ON THE FOLLOWING PASSAGE.

Form W-280 provides a uniform standard for estimating family expenses and is used as a basis for determining eligibility for the care of children at public expense. The extent to which legally responsible relatives can pay for the care of a child must be computed. The minimum amount of the payment required from legally responsible relatives shall be 50 percent of the budget surplus as computed on Form W-281 plus any governmental benefits, such as OASDI benefits, or railroad retirement benefits being paid to a family member for the child receiving care or services. Because of the kinds and quantities of service included in the budget schedule (W-280), and because only 50 percent of the budget surplus is required as payment, no allowances for special needs are made, except for verified payments into civil service pension funds, amounts paid to a garnishee or to another agency for the care of other relatives for whom the relative is legally responsible, or for other such expenses if approval has been granted after Form W-278 has been submitted. In determining the income of the legally responsible relative, income from wages, self-employment, unemployment insurance benefits, and any such portion of governmental benefits as is not specifically designated for children already receiving care is to be included. Should 50 percent of the family's surplus meet the child-care expenses, the case shall not be processed. Form W-279, an agreement to support, shall be signed by the legally responsible relative when 50 percent of the surplus is $1 or more a week.

65. A family is required to sign an agreement to support

  (A) whenever they are legally responsible for the support of the child under care.

  (B) before any care at public expense is given to the child.

  (C) when their income surplus is at least $2 a week.

  (D) when 50 percent of their income surplus meets the full needs of the child.

66. The reason for allowing a family to deduct only certain specified expenses when computing the amount they are able to contribute to the support of a child being cared for at public expense is that the family

  (A) should not be permitted to have a higher standard of living than the child being cared for.

  (B) budget schedule is sufficiently generous and includes an allowance for other unusual expenses.

  (C) may not be able to verify their extraordinary expenses.

  (D) may meet other unusual expenses from the remainder of their surplus.

67. Mrs. Barrett wishes to have her daughter Mary cared for at public expense. Her income includes her wages and OASDI benefits of $250 a month, of which $50 a month is paid for Mary, and $50 a month for another minor member of the family who is already being cared for at public expense. In order to determine the amount of Mrs. Barrett's budget surplus, it is necessary to consider as income, her wages and

  (A) $50 of OASDI received by Mary.

  (B) $150 of the OASDI benefits.

  (C) $200 of the OASDI benefits.

  (D) $200 of the OASDI benefits if she is legally responsible for the care of the other child in placement.

68. In order to determine a family's ability to contribute to the support of a child, the case worker should

  (A) have the legally responsible member sign Form W-279 agreeing to support the child, and then compute the family surplus on W-281 in accordance with public assistance standards.

  (B) compute the family's income in accordance with the allowance included on Form W-280 and the expenses included on Form W-278 and have Form W-279 signed if necessary.

  (C) use Form W-278 to work out a budget schedule for the family and compute their surplus on W-281 and then have them sign W-279 if necessary.

  (D) compute income and expenses on Form W-281, based on Form W-280, and have Form W-279 signed if necessary.

69. Among the following needy persons, the one NOT eligible to receive veteran assistance is the

  (A) husband of a veteran, if living with the veteran.

  (B) minor grandchild of a veteran, if living with the veteran.

  (C) incapacitated child of a deceased veteran.

  (D) nonveteran brother or sister of a veteran, if living with the veteran.

70. Under the Social Security Act, public assistance payments do NOT provide for

  (A) old-age assistance.

  (B) care of children in foster homes.

  (C) aid to the blind.

  (D) aid to dependent children.

71. The main difference between public welfare and private social agencies is that in public agencies,

  (A) case records are open to the public.

  (B) the granting of assistance cannot be sufficiently flexible to meet the varying needs of individual recipients.

  (C) only financial assistance may be provided.

  (D) all policies and procedures must be based upon statutory authorizations.

72. You are assigned to work with a 55-year-old male pedophile. Which of the following treatment goals would you be most likely to use?

  (A) Encouraging the client to focus on heterosexual relationships

  (B) Encouraging the client to focus on homosexual relationships

  (C) Increasing the client's relationships within his peer group

  (D) Decreasing the client's sexual impulse control

73. After 10 years of marriage, a couple comes to you because of financial problems but you discover they are having marital difficulties. In helping this couple, you should NOT try to

(A) enhance their strengths as a couple as a means of bringing them closer and rekindling their strengths.

(B) focus on the dysfunctional style of the couple and what they are each bringing to the relationship.

(C) focus on one spouse in the couple and his or her poor psychological functioning.

(D) help the couple individually by helping them see their individual strengths.

74. An elderly client who is coping with problems in her public housing reveals anxiety-provoking feelings. This client explains that she was abandoned as a child and is fearful that will occur again now. The worker should

(A) attempt to sustain the client's functioning to alleviate her anxiety, then proceed to focus on the individual issues at hand once the client is in a calmer state.

(B) involve the client in seeing her anxious state and confront her about this anxiety.

(C) not expect the client to return after this meeting.

(D) expect to reveal a deep psychological stressor that occurred when she was abandoned as a child.

75. Your professional opinion of a situation should be formed

(A) within three or four meetings.

(B) immediately after meeting a client.

(C) after each interview.

(D) as the client progresses, with the ability to be flexible and change your opinion as the client progresses.

76. When an applicant for public assistance is repeatedly told that "everything will be all right," the effect that can usually be expected is that he will

(A) develop overt negativistic reactions toward the agency.

(B) become too closely identified with the interviewer.

(C) doubt the interviewer's ability to understand and help with his problems.

(D) have greater confidence in the interviewer.

77. A client has a prison record and is now having trouble seeking employment. In writing an evaluation for this client, the case worker would most likely include

(A) the client's readiness to utilize help.

(B) a description of the client's character.

(C) the client's capacity to function.

(D) All of the above

78. During an interview, a curious applicant asks several questions about your private life. As the interviewer, you should

(A) refuse to answer such questions.

(B) answer the questions fully.

(C) explain that your primary concern is with her problems and that discussion of your personal affairs will not be helpful in meeting her needs.

(D) explain that it is the responsibility of the interviewer to ask questions and not to answer them.

79. You are working with a 15-year-old student who is having difficulties both academically and behaviorally. The student becomes easily distracted and overwhelmed by her studies and she is extremely negative towards herself and others. She is strongly resistant to meeting with you. You would most likely

(A) recommend that she seek long-term therapy with a psychoanalyst.

(B) plan to meet with her on a short-term trial basis.

(C) meet with other students like herself.

(D) make arrangements to meet with her on a long-term basis.

80. "An interviewer's attention must be directed toward himself as well as toward the person interviewed." This statement means that the interviewer should

(A) keep in mind the extent to which his own prejudices may influence his judgment.

(B) rationalize the statements made by the person being interviewed.

(C) gain the respect and confidence of the person interviewed.

(D) avoid being too impersonal.

81. You are seeing a depressed patient at a mental health clinic. After several weeks of working toward getting him housing and strengthening his ties to the community, you and the other staff members begin to see signs of recovery from his depression. At this point, your concern about the patient committing suicide would

(A) depend on the individual's level of medication.

(B) decrease.

(C) increase.

(D) remain the same.

82. When meeting with a client to discuss her eligibility for public assistance, you should do all of the following EXCEPT

(A) assess what the individual can do immediately about her problem.

(B) assist this individual to use her strengths to solve her problems.

(C) discuss what she thinks she can do about her problems.

(D) discuss her reasons for being on public assistance and her inability to function independently.

83. A good technique for the interviewer to use in an effort to secure reliable data and to reduce the possibility of misunderstanding is to

(A) secure the desired information by using casual, undirected conversation, enabling the interviewee to talk about himself or herself.

(B) use direct questions regularly.

(C) extract the desired information from the interviewee by putting him or her on the defensive.

(D) explain to the interviewee the information desired and the reason for needing it.

84. As a case worker interviewing applicants for public assistance, your attitude toward their veracity should be that the information they have furnished you is

(A) untruthful until you have had an opportunity to check the information.

(B) truthful only insofar as verifiable facts are concerned.

(C) untruthful because clients tend to interpret everything in their own favor.

(D) truthful until you have information to the contrary.

85. As a case worker conducting the first interview with a new public assistance client, you should
    (A) ask questions requiring "yes" or "no" answers in order to simplify the interview.
    (B) rephrase several of the key questions as a check on his or her previous statements.
    (C) let him or her tell his or her own story while keeping him or her to the relevant facts.
    (D) avoid showing any sympathy for the applicant while he or she reveals his or her personal needs and problems.

86. An elderly person who is unable to produce immediate proof of age has made an application for old-age assistance. He states that it will take about a week to obtain the necessary proof and that he does not have enough money to provide meals for himself until then. If it appears that he is in immediate need, he should be told that
    (A) the law requires proof of age before any assistance can be granted.
    (B) temporary assistance will be provided pending the completion of the investigation.
    (C) a personal loan will be made to him from a revolving fund.
    (D) he should arrange for a small loan from private sources.

87. Of the sources through which a social service agency can seek information about the family background and economic needs of a particular client, the most important consists of
    (A) records and documents covering the client.
    (B) interviews with the client's relatives.
    (C) the client's own story.
    (D) direct contacts with former employers.

88. Which of the following sources of evidence would most likely provide information needed to verify residence?
    (A) Family affidavits
    (B) Medical and hospital bills
    (C) An original birth certificate
    (D) Rental receipts

89. In public assistance agencies, vital statistics are a resource used by case workers mainly to
    (A) help establish eligibility through verification of births, deaths, and marriages.
    (B) help establish eligibility through verification of divorce proceedings.
    (C) secure proof of unemployment and eligibility for unemployment compensation.
    (D) secure indices of the cost of living in the larger cities.

90. Case records should be considered confidential in order to
    (A) make it impossible for agencies to know each other's methods.
    (B) permit workers to make objective rather than subjective comments.
    (C) prevent recipients from comparing amounts of assistance given to different families.
    (D) protect clients and their families.

91. Because social case workers generally are not trained psychiatrists, they should, when encountering psychiatric problems in the performance of their departmental duties,

(A) ignore such problems because they are beyond the scope of their responsibilities.

(B) inform the affected people that they recognize their problems personally but will take no official cognizance of them.

(C) ask to be relieved of the cases in which these problems are met and recommend that they be assigned to a psychiatrist.

(D) recognize such problems where they exist and make referrals to the proper sources for treatment.

QUESTIONS 92–94 ARE BASED ON THE FOLLOWING PASSAGE.

The problem of homelessness is not unique to the nation's largest cities; rather, it is a growing national problem. The causes of homelessness are deeply rooted in underlying social and economic ills that are pushing an increasing number of formerly normal, well-adjusted, self-sufficient people out of the mainstream of American life. Even the most prosperous cities have only limited ability to address the problem of the homeless. They can only partly ameliorate the situation with the limited money and resources at their command. In every city, there is a chronic and ever-growing shortage of housing that poor families can afford. There are inadequate facilities for the mentally ill who have been released from institutions, without any adequate community-based facilities for their utilization. The homeless problem is only one of the manifestations of a larger one. It is the rapidly changing and complex economic and social structure in the United States that has been the primary cause for an increasing number of families and individuals exhibiting not just housing difficulties but also many other social problems. The recent fiscal and social retrenchment policies of the federal government have further exacerbated these problems.

92. According to the passage, homelessness

(A) could be eliminated if federal funds were extended to build public housing.

(B) is largely the fault of cities' failure to properly utilize their resources to provide affordable housing for the poor.

(C) is increased by the large number of people moving to the cities from rural areas to improve their economic conditions.

(D) is one face of the large problem of the increased inability of many people to cope with the ills prevalent in today's society.

93. Assume that a family that has been self-supporting up to this point has applied for supplementary public assistance because they currently cannot meet their needs. They are in danger of becoming homeless because they cannot pay the interest on their mortgaged home. Based on the passage, the reason for their monetary problems is probably

(A) the result of poor management of their funds.

(B) due to the current practice of mortgage holders to charge exorbitant rates of interest.

(C) the inability of the father to command a higher salary.

(D) a combination of social and economic factors existing in the United States.

94. Assume that the manager of a hotel to which mentally ill people are released by institutions comes to you, a case worker, at the nearby public assistance office. He states that one of the residents receives SSI but frequently tells the manager he has insufficient funds to pay his rent. Based on the passage, it can be inferred that

(A) SSI has incorrectly determined the amount the individual's grant should be.

(B) an attempt should be made to inform SSI or a locally based community organization of the help the individual may need in managing his money properly.

(C) someone else in the hotel, a staff member or resident, is probably appropriating part of the man's monthly check.

(D) the rent payment should be sent directly to the hotel by the SSI office.

QUESTIONS 95–97 ARE BASED ON THE FOLLOWING PASSAGE.

Various laws in New York City and New York State protect the rights of people with AIDS or with AIDS-Related Complex (ARC). These laws prohibit discrimination against people who have disabilities, and AIDS is considered to be a disability. A person with AIDS or ARC cannot be fired from his or her job unless he is incapable of satisfactorily performing it, nor can an employer dismiss a person because he is a homosexual and, therefore, in a high-risk group with respect to AIDS susceptibility, since such action would mean the employer is perceiving the individual to have a disability. In New York City, the law further prohibits any discrimination in employment because of sexual orientation, without reference to AIDS or ARC.

The city and state laws also protect AIDS/ARC victims from eviction provided they pay their rent from a rent-stabilized or rent-controlled apartment. Tenants in a boarding home where the landlord also resides, however, are not protected from eviction under these laws. Failure to pay rent owed the landlord may result in eviction. An AIDS/ARC victim may be unable to work and, therefore, cannot meet his or her financial obligations. If a diagnosis of such inability is obtained, the person may be eligible for financial aid through federal entitlement programs. During the time an application for such assistance is being processed, the city's welfare department may intervene to pay back rent if the rent is reasonable.

95. Assume you are a case worker in Bloomstown, Arkansas. A male client who has been receiving supplementary assistance to augment his weekly salary reports that he has lost his job because his employer has learned that he has AIDS. Based on the passage, you should

(A) advise the client to file an antidiscrimination suit since firing a person because of AIDS is illegal.

(B) personally talk to the employer and try to convince her or him that a person with AIDS can still perform meaningful work.

(C) refer the client for application for a federal entitlement program.

(D) research appropriate material regarding the legality of the employer's actions in your city or state.

96. A man applying for public assistance in New York City shows you a letter of eviction from his landlord. The applicant complains that the landlord is pursuing this action because the applicant is a homosexual. Based on the passage, you should first determine whether the applicant

(A) has filed an antidiscrimination suit.

(B) has AIDS or ARC.

(C) has paid his rent each month.

(D) is a bona fide resident of New York City.

97. A young female client on supplementary public assistance in Owegee, New York, has a work history of frequent changes in employment. She comes to you, her case worker, to report that she has just lost her job as a file clerk in a large company because the personnel office of the company has discovered she is a lesbian. Based on the passage, you should

(A) urge her to file an antidiscrimination suit.

(B) inform her that her work history shows she is unable to hold a job because of reasons other than her sexual preferences and that you cannot accept her reasons for losing her current job.

(C) obtain more information from her and from the employer regarding the reasons for her dismissal.

(D) refer her for possible employment elsewhere without discussing her previous work pattern, since she is able and willing to work.

QUESTIONS 98–100 ARE BASED ON THE FOLLOWING PASSAGE.

AIDS is caused by the Human Immunodeficiency Virus (HIV). The virus attacks a person's immune system, leaving the body susceptible to a large number and variety of life-threatening infections, as well as certain types of cancer. The virus is found in blood, semen, and certain other body fluids such as saliva, tears, and vaginal secretions.

Although the diseases caused by HIV can be devastating, it has been determined that the virus itself is very fragile outside of the human body. Thus, if it is not inhabiting human tissue, it does not survive for a long period of time. It can be inactivated by exposure to drying, chlorine bleach, heat, household disinfectants, and other chemicals used in sterilization.

98. According to the passage, HIV

(A) causes certain types of cancer.

(B) can cause AIDS.

(C) is a dangerous infection affecting the bodily fluids.

(D) can survive for long periods of time within a household.

99. From the passage, it can be inferred that a person with AIDS

(A) is susceptible to many life-threatening infections.

(B) will be very likely to succumb to the diseases.

(C) can be cured if the virus is outside his or her body.

(D) will not contract certain types of cancer.

100. Assume that a suitable, completely vacant apartment has been found for a needy family. The apartment has been vacant for several months. The mother comes to you, the case worker for her case, and expresses fear because the previous tenant of the apartment had died of AIDS. Based on the passage, you should

   (A) immediately require that the family member be examined for AIDS.

   (B) immediately remove the family from the apartment.

   (C) assure the woman that sufficient time has expired so that there is no danger to the family.

   (D) advise the woman to disinfect the kitchen and bathroom facilities thoroughly to make certain no virus remains in the apartment as a precautionary measure.

practice test

ANSWER KEY AND EXPLANATIONS

1. D	21. A	41. A	61. C	81. C
2. C	22. A	42. D	62. B	82. D
3. D	23. D	43. A	63. C	83. D
4. C	24. D	44. B	64. A	84. D
5. A	25. B	45. C	65. C	85. C
6. C	26. B	46. D	66. D	86. A
7. D	27. D	47. B	67. B	87. C
8. D	28. B	48. C	68. D	88. D
9. C	29. C	49. B	69. D	89. A
10. D	30. A	50. B	70. B	90. D
11. B	31. B	51. D	71. D	91. D
12. A	32. D	52. A	72. D	92. D
13. A	33. D	53. B	73. C	93. D
14. B	34. D	54. A	74. A	94. B
15. C	35. A	55. C	75. A	95. D
16. D	36. B	56. B	76. C	96. C
17. C	37. A	57. B	77. D	97. C
18. B	38. C	58. D	78. C	98. B
19. A	39. D	59. A	79. B	99. A
20. B	40. C	60. B	80. A	100. D

1. **The correct answer is (D).** The correct answer is the only one that can be derived from the statement given in the preamble. It states a basic premise that all case workers must fully understand and follow in working with their clients.

2. **The correct answer is (C).** A professional relationship between the case worker and the client requires that a sympathetic atmosphere be created by the case worker so that the client feels able to trust and confide in the worker. At the same time, the case worker must maintain control of the relationship and not allow the client to digress or pursue areas that are not directly related to the worker's responsibility. Nor must the worker permit the relationship to become a friendship that could hinder the worker's maintenance of objectivity and ability to help the client successfully resolve problems.

3. **The correct answer is (D).** Of the possible arguments given in support of the merger of welfare and family case work fields, the best one is that new techniques and new community resources may become available to both fields. This is due to the fact that resources may have been used previously by or known to only one of the fields and that resources have been discovered through the new combination of people and knowledge available as a result of the merger. Choices (A) and (C) are irrelevant to the question, and choice (B) is simply not true.

4. **The correct answer is (C).** Most social work experts believe the best case work practice requires that attention be given both to the physical, environmental, and social factors involved in the situation and to the client's reactions to these factors and to his or her own life experiences.

5. **The correct answer is (A).** Modern case work theory tends to believe the family unit is of great importance in solving a client's problems and will try to involve family members whenever possible. In many instances, the family relationship *is* a central reason for the problem or *is* the problem. In any event, members of the family, and the family as a whole, should be aware of the problem, help solve it if possible, accept the solutions arrived at, and help carry out these solutions successfully.

6. **The correct answer is (C).** In this situation, the case worker merely knows that John is intelligent, is in his proper year in high school, has become a truant, and has been ordered by the school principal to go to youth counseling. You, the case worker in the youth counseling agency, must first learn considerably more about John— what he does during the hours he is not at school, who his friends are, the financial and social scene at home, etc. Only when you have a more complete picture of these factual matters can you properly begin to explore with John his attitudes and the reasons for his relatively sudden change in behavior.

7. **The correct answer is (D).** It is essential for a case worker to remain objective and follow the goals of the client. In addition, it is important to follow a client's psychological reasoning when making drastic changes in her life while keeping in mind any harmful reasons for such a change.

8. **The correct answer is (D).** You are given a statement that is a basic premise in all good case work interviewing in that it requires a particular focus on the client's actual situation. The correct answer amplifies this basic premise.

9. **The correct answer is (C).** Even with the best intentions, some clients cannot give the case worker a crisp, connected story. Good case work requires that in these instances you retain your patience, ask simple questions requiring straightforward responses, and frequently review with the clients what you think they have said to be sure you understand the response. Never ask leading questions since they may confuse the clients or prompt them to give what *for them* is the wrong answer but which they think is the answer *you* want.

10. **The correct answer is (D).** The passage gives you most of the main points that should ordinarily be included in a case record but neglects the case record's vital need for sufficient data for understanding the client's actual problem and information about factors that *must* be known for a solution to be reached. Without such data, a case record will not be of any real use.

11. **The correct answer is (B).** It would be extremely difficult for a "troubled client" to achieve the degree of confidence in the case worker necessary to reveal true feelings during the interview. Therefore, the client is likely to hide such feelings especially in areas where she believes the case worker is unlikely to believe and respond properly.

12. **The correct answer is (A).** The case worker's role is to help the client cope with problems. In working with a sick client, the worker must know and understand enough about the medical condition, limitations, and prognosis to intelligently discuss with the client the specific

problems, including the medical problems that will affect the resolution of other problems. Note that while choice (B) may be a correct statement of fact, it does not answer the question posed.

13. **The correct answer is (A).** By helping the patient identify her stressors, you will begin to follow along with her in her life as she sees her problems. By her identifying her problems, you can set up a plan for your work. Always be where the client is.

14. **The correct answer is (B).** By working with the family together while the parents are simultaneously seeking treatment for their domestic violence issues, you can address the changes that need to be made as they increase their awareness of domestic violence in their life. The goal is to help them to work together as a family unit.

15. **The correct answer is (C).** There is nothing in the passage to indicate the home life is anything but a normal, good one. A positive approach is the most useful one for the case worker to take. The child must be made aware that while he is not being punished, his actions have been such that temporary removal to a foster home will help him and his family achieve changes that will benefit him and enable him to go home.

16. **The correct answer is (D).** By understanding the woman's concerns, the case worker can help educate her about HIV and the risk factors surrounding this virus.

17. **The correct answer is (C).** A person who is in this state of mind must be taken seriously especially if he has a plan. It is your professional obligation to follow through on this case while helping him through your support and concern.

18. **The correct answer is (B).** By giving support to the husband you will alleviate the main cause of stress in the couple's relationship. The wife will be able to decrease her anxiety as her husband becomes more readily available to her emotionally and psychologically.

19. **The correct answer is (A).** In this situation, discussion with the parents has not improved the boy's home life and he is being mistreated. Foster home placement is indicated until the parents are able to accept and properly care for him. Solutions presented in the other possible answers are not indicated in choice (B), not warranted by the facts in choice (C), and are not possible according to the facts given in choice (D).

20. **The correct answer is (B).** The most important factor in any therapeutic relationship is to establish a comfort level. When a client recognizes the sensitivity and understanding on the part of the case worker, he will be more receptive and trusting for the future of their relationship.

21. **The correct answer is (A).** Contracting with a client is the first step in initializing a therapeutic relationship. It is essential for both parties to meet and form a common understanding of the work that they plan on achieving together.

22. **The correct answer is (A).** The client's mother may have a great deal of power over this individual and thus foster feelings of dependency and helplessness on this individual.

23. **The correct answer is (D).** In this situation, the case worker must concentrate on working with the alcoholic client in the direct, positive fashion indicated in choice (D). The other answer choices will not help resolve the client's special problem, which, as noted in the first sentence, must be solved.

24. **The correct answer is (D).** You are told that research shows there are many different social, psychological, and physical reasons for addiction and no one cure for all cases. Accordingly, community facilities dealing with addiction and related problems must be utilized on a differentiated basis, depending on the individual client's background—social, economic, education, physical condition, etc. Thus, one addict may be best treated at home, one in a hospital, another in a group facility, etc.

25. **The correct answer is (B).** By helping both wife and husband with their issues individually, they will be better able to focus on their capacities.

26. **The correct answer is (B).** The best approach in this situation is to first get an overview of all seventy cases in order to learn which ones will need immediate attention, which can be delayed, and which will require deep study before any action can be taken. The new case worker should study each record to set priorities.

27. **The correct answer is (D).** By helping the patient recognize his feelings and explore them with the doctor, he can provide his physician with insight into their relationship as well.

28. **The correct answer is (B).** The number of people on public assistance and the amount of each person's grant are the important factors in determining the cost of a welfare program. If the size of the grant is increased, the standard of eligibility will go down, allowing people who have resources just at or just below the previous standard to be eligible for public assistance.

29. **The correct answer is (C).** Case work theory and practice concentrates on solving individual and family behavior problems and attitudes, on obtaining individual and family participation in the solution of problems affecting their lives, and on helping to change their environments for the welfare of client(s). It is not generally concerned with attempts to reconstruct total personalities or total environments.

30. **The correct answer is (A).** Positive acceptance is the primary ingredient in building a relationship with a client. Although being neutral and nonjudgmental are significant qualities, one must also recognize that all new relationships are built on the foundation of acceptance.

31. **The correct answer is (B).** When working with a client, a case worker must always provide an environment free from judgment, but be aware that there is more to this client than what he or she presents. It helps to be reserved when developing an understanding of a client and his or her patterns.

32. **The correct answer is (D).** The case worker's point of view is primarily one of helping the client. By dividing the cases into different categories, the worker can see a commonality with other clients of similar problems (e.g., problems of disability, of age, etc.) and can draw knowledge and possible solutions from these other cases. The other answer choices are reasons for dividing cases by category from an administrative, policy-making point of view, but *not* from the case worker's primary responsibility or concern.

33. **The correct answer is (D).** The demands of the labor market have resulted in the increase in the number of unskilled or semiskilled persons looking for jobs because automation and computerization have made their former jobs obsolete. At the same time, the need has grown for persons with specialized skills required by the newly computer-automated industries. The influx of women into the job market has further increased the number of job applicants.

34. **The correct answer is (D).** This answer is self-explanatory. If disability is expected to last a minimum of twelve months, and the worker was employed within the last five years in covered employment, then choice (D) is appropriate.

35. **The correct answer is (A).** The wife of a husband declared disabled and receiving benefits under the Social Security law can receive no more than one half of her husband's payments. This can also work the other way: if the wife is disabled and covered by disability payments, the husband can also collect up to one half of the amount involved.

36. **The correct answer is (B).** By waiting with patience and providing an encouraging attitude the case worker will provide the client with a nonjudgmental setting, one on which he or she can safely confide in you.

37. **The correct answer is (A).** To allow the client to freely express his ideas creates an environment that promotes understanding. Through that, a relationship will develop and change over time.

38. **The correct answer is (C).** A case worker in a public agency cannot afford to give a considerable amount of time to a situation known not to be the concern of the agency. Nevertheless, good case work and public relations procedure mandate that the worker listen to enough about the problem to determine what agency can help the woman and direct her to it. Only by listening to her can the worker be of assistance.

39. **The correct answer is (D).** While case workers in public agencies have limited time to spend on a client, it is most important that good rapport be established. By taking the time to hear the client's story, even if it repeats data given in the case record of the referring agency, the client will become comfortable with the new agency and will feel that his individual interests are going to be considered and that he is not merely a "statistic," being transferred from one agency to another.

40. **The correct answer is (C).** By breaking down the basic theme of communication and reflecting back to a broader view, you allow the client to gain insight into his behavior and give way to new awareness.

41. **The correct answer is (A).** The ultimate purpose of a formal social study in a public assistance case is to help evaluate the needs of the family and plan how to meet those needs.

42. **The correct answer is (D).** The first aim of the case worker in this situation is to prevent the family from having to go on public assistance or to achieve a degree of self-support that will necessitate receiving only supplementary assistance. The worker should, therefore, not only verify past work history but also determine if there is the possibility of employment now or in the near future at the client's previous places of employment. The other answer choices are useful steps to be taken after it has been determined that public assistance is needed.

43. **The correct answer is (A).** The proposal to contact the client's legally responsible relative in this situation is a good one. Although the relative is on public assistance and not able to offer financial assistance, she may be able to provide other services your client needs (e.g., helping your client clean the house or mind the children while your client has to go to a job interview). Note that choice (C) is unacceptable because the relative's inability to give financial help has been established and is not yet your concern.

44. **The correct answer is (B).** A case worker must examine a client's closed bankbook to determine past management. Thus, a

closed account showing steady withdrawals for many months prior to closing the account at "zero" amount of money will help establish the lack of present income and that the client had been living on the amount in the bank. A steady addition of small amounts before the withdrawals could help verify that the client had a job at one time. The bankbook may also show the withdrawal of a substantial amount of money just prior to application for public assistance. Explanation and proof of the use of that amount would be required prior to acceptance of the case.

45. **The correct answer is (C).** A client may refuse to accept a job that might give him and his family assistance only for good and sufficient reasons. In the situation presented, the reasons stated are not sufficient to warrant acceptance of the client's job refusal because the laborer position that is available *now* will not interfere with enrolling in the training course several months from now.

46. **The correct answer is (D).** It is not good public policy for the worker to request extension of credit in this instance. There is no guarantee that the client will pay the money owed to the grocer. If the family is in dire need, an emergency check can be issued and the original check stopped at the bank.

47. **The correct answer is (B).** Special rent schedules are utilized for persons on public assistance who live in housing projects.

48. **The correct answer is (C).** Good case work procedure requires you to work with the client to help reach an acceptable decision. In this instance, the case worker must help the client determine whether he can really handle the new job he has been offered, both in terms of the skills needed and the higher level of responsibilities involved.

49. **The correct answer is (B).** A public welfare agency, especially in a large city, is generally organized on a functional basis with separate units handling specialized matters such as housing, resource evaluation, legal matters, etc. A case worker must be aware of all changes in these areas that might affect how cases should be handled.

50. **The correct answer is (B).** A basic training principle is that learning by doing is the most effective way to learn something new. The use of simulated interviews in which the new worker is an active participant is a good learning device for workers whose main activity is conducting actual interviews.

51. **The correct answer is (D).** This client needs the attention, concern, and empathy that you can provide. By providing this, you will establish a relationship that will be communicated through your presence and style.

52. **The correct answer is (A).** An evaluation is of an employee's actual performance for the period covered, and one is evaluated against the agency's or unit's standards of performance. It generally does *not* cover future performance or growth potentiality. In determining an individual's potentiality for promotion to a higher level job, past evaluations may be considered, but that is not the question being asked.

53. **The correct answer is (B).** Here is an area in which an apparent error has been made by a worker from social services. Therefore, it should be corrected without further inconveniencing the client and in a manner that will not reduce the confidence of the client in the operation of the agency as a whole. If a client mistakenly walks into the wrong unit of the agency, she should be directed to the proper unit even if it is some distance away. However,

if the client has been sent to the wrong location by a social services worker, proper corrective measures should be instituted at once.

54. **The correct answer is (A).** This is a factual question. The federal government will not reimburse restricted payments for finder's fees, security deposits, or utility payments, but it will reimburse restricted payments for medical expenses. (See the glossary for the definition of restricted payment.)

55. **The correct answer is (C).** The client's budget provides that under a court order the client receive a degree of financial support from the relative. Agency policy generally provides that the amount remain in the budget unless the court removes or modifies its order or the agency is certain the order will not be followed and the client will not be receiving that amount of money. Choices (A) and (B) do not provide that assurance. When the relative moves to another state, as in choice (D), there are reciprocal agreements between states to provide that the court-ordered amount of money will still be made available for the client. Only when a relative has disappeared and an exhaustive search for his or her whereabouts has proved unsuccessful can the income from the relatives be removed from the budget.

56. **The correct answer is (B).**
    1. $17.4 million in 2005
    2. 10% less in 2005 = $15,660,000
    3. 10% less in 2006 = $14,094,000
    4. 10% less in 2007 = $12,680,000

57. **The correct answer is (B).** Choice (A): Cost of OAA to Midvale City in 2004 = $6.5 million. Total cost of OAA in 2004 = $33.7 million. Percent paid by Midvale City in 2004 = $6.5 million ÷ $33.7 million = 19.29%.

Choice (B): Cost of OAA to Midvale City in 2005 = $5 million. Total cost of OAA in 2005 = $29.7 million. Percent paid by Midvale City in 2005 = $5.0 million ÷ $29.7 million = 16.48%.

Choice (C): Cost of VA to Midvale City in 2004 = $1.3 million. Total cost of VA in 2004 = $2.5 million. Percent paid by Midvale City in 2004 = $1.3 million ÷ $2.5 million = 52%.

Choice (D): Cost of ADC to Midvale City in 2005 = $27.5 million. Total cost of ADC in 2005 = $108.3 million. Percent paid by Midvale City in 2005 = $27.5 million ÷ $108.3 million = 25%.

58. **The correct answer is (D).** 2004: $3,300,000 ÷ 13,992 = $235.85. 2005: $5,300,000 ÷ 11,782 = $449.84. $449.84 − $235.85 = $213.99. 213.99 ÷ 12 = $17.83. $17.83 is most nearly $18.

59. **The correct answer is (A).** Number of persons on ADC per month in 2004 = 212,795. 40% adults = 85,188 per month. Midvale total contributions to ADC in 2004 = $27.5 million per year. 36% of Midvale contribution per month to ADC in 2004 = $27.5 million; .36 ÷ 12 = $825,000. $825,000 ÷ 85,118 = $9.69. $9.69 is most nearly $10.

60. **The correct answer is (B).** Number of persons per month on OAA in 2005 = 31,804. 10% of 31,804 = 3,180 = number transferred per month in 2005. So, 14,962 = number otherwise on MAA per month in 2006. (11,782 + 3,180 = 14,962). But 6% of 11,872 per month will not be on public assistance in 2006 = 706.92 fewer (707). 14,962 − 707 = 14,255. 14,255 will be on MAA in 2006. 14,255 − 11,782 = 2,473 increase (i.e., 2,473 ÷ 11,782 = 21% increase).

61. **The correct answer is (C).** The table shows you that the monthly average of persons on MAA has *decreased* from 2004 to 2005. Choice (A) is known to be true

and, therefore, cannot be the answer for a *decrease* on persons on MAA. Choice (B) has no relevance to the question being asked. While choice (D) may be a true statement, it would not by itself affect the number of persons eligible for MAA, which depends on the resources of the elderly person *and* his living expenses. Choice (C) is correct both in the facts given and the deduction you can make from those facts. Social Security is a financial resource and since *more* people are receiving it, many of those people will now have sufficient funds to no longer need OAA. Furthermore, if the amount of a benefit increases, the amount of their financial resources also increases, so that people who would have heretofore been eligible for OAA would no longer be eligible.

62. **The correct answer is (B).** The passage clearly states that the social workers began to view the character of many social injustices with a critical eye and were becoming aware of the deficiencies in these institutions in curing these injustices.

63. **The correct answer is (C).** The passage clearly states that professional social workers were becoming aware of the need for social reform because the traditional means of helping the poor (e.g., private charitable institutions, families, etc.) were inadequate to cope with the new factors "that were creating poverty and maladjustment."

64. **The correct answer is (A).** The whole tenor of the passage shows that social workers were becoming aware that social reform was needed. None of the other answer choices can be deduced or inferred from the passage.

65. **The correct answer is (C).** The last sentence of the passage states that an agreement to support form is signed by the legally responsible when 50 percent of the weekly surplus is at least $1 a week (50 percent of $2 = $1).

66. **The correct answer is (D).** The passage clearly states that no allowance for special needs is made, except for the certain instances also spelled out in the passage, "because only 50 percent of the budget surplus is required as payment for support of the child or children being cared for at public expense." There is nothing in the passage to indicate the other possible answer choices are correct.

67. **The correct answer is (B).** Mrs. Barrett's OASDI benefits are $250 a month. The passage states that, in determining a legally responsible relative's income, "any portion of a government benefit not specifically designated for children already receiving care" is included as income. Accordingly, the $50 paid for Mary's care and the $50 paid for the other minor's care are deducted from Mrs. Barrett's OASDI benefits from OASDI and must be considered in determining her budget surplus.

68. **The correct answer is (D).** The passage indicates Form W-280 is used to compute family expenses. Form W-281 is used to compute income and budget surplus. If the "bottom line" on Form W-281 (i.e., income as given on Form-281 *minus* expenses as given on Form W-280) indicates a surplus of at least $2 a week, Form W-279 must be signed.

69. **The correct answer is (D).** Most cities and states, if providing for veteran assistance, do *not* consider nonveteran brothers or sisters living with the veteran who is eligible for such assistance as eligible for that form of assistance.

70. **The correct answer is (B).** This is a factual question. Care for children in foster homes is not provided for under the Federal Social Security Act and is, therefore, completely a local or state expense.

71. **The correct answer is (D).** The chief difference between public welfare and private social work agencies is that all major policies and procedures pursued by public agencies have their basis in statutes passed by the legislature of the governmental jurisdiction concerned and are signed by the head of that jurisdiction.

72. **The correct answer is (D).** By focusing the pedophile on decreasing his sexual impulse control, you enhance his ability to function better and learn coping skills and appropriate behavior models.

73. **The correct answer is (C).** It would be detrimental to focus on one spouse in the couple and his or her poor psychological functioning during the meeting. By doing this, you alienate the individual and create a tension-filled environment.

74. **The correct answer is (A).** By attempting to sustain the client's functioning to alleviate her anxiety, you can then focus on the individual issues at hand once the client is in a calmer state. This allows the client to feel safe and heard.

75. **The correct answer is (A).** As a case worker, your opinion should be formed within three or four sessions. In that time period, you would have ample time to make professional judgments.

76. **The correct answer is (C).** Applicants for public assistance, like most people, have problems that are real and complex. By telling a client "everything will be all right," you are misleading the client and making him doubt your ability to understand the complexity of the problem and the difficulty in solving it. This may result in the client's loss of confidence in your interest and competence.

77. **The correct answer is (D).** The client's readiness to utilize help, a description of the client's character, and his or her ca-

pacity to function are all essential components in creating a plan for this client.

78. **The correct answer is (C).** The best way to handle the situation presented is merely to remind the client that together you are focusing *solely* on her problems. A discussion of your personal affairs will not be useful in resolving any of these problems.

79. **The correct answer is (B).** By meeting on a short-term trial basis, you will not pose a threat to the student. This will allow your work to take place so that you can make a proper assessment and then make further recommendations as needed.

80. **The correct answer is (A).** The quotation reminds the interviewer that personal attitude and beliefs, unless understood and accounted for, may distort finding a solution to the client's problems that will be acceptable to the client although not necessarily to the worker.

81. **The correct answer is (C).** Many suicides occur shortly after a period of what appears to be recovery. It is at this time that people stop paying as keen attention to the individual and therefore, they may miss some important signs.

82. **The correct answer is (D).** It is important to maintain an individual's self-esteem and dignity when dealing with such sensitive issues. You want to focus on building up strengths and establishing a sense of trust between the client and yourself.

83. **The correct answer is (D).** The best way to obtain reliable information and lessen the chance of misunderstandings in case work interviewing is to make sure that the client understands both the reasons for the question and how the truthful, accurate answer will help solve

problems or establish eligibility for public assistance. Choice (A) may result in misunderstandings, choice (B) in prevarication, and choice (C) in resentment.

84. **The correct answer is (D).** Basic case work interviewing in a public setting requires that the worker generally assume that information the client furnishes is truthful unless reliable information or documentation to the contrary is in the worker's possession at the time the interview is being conducted or unless the client's information is so contrary to common sense that its truthfulness must be explored. This does not mean that certain required basic data to establish eligibility must be left unverified.

85. **The correct answer is (C).** The first interview with an applicant for public assistance is most important in obtaining facts that will be either accepted at face value or explored and verified in order to establish eligibility for public assistance. This first interview is also important in establishing a good relationship between the client and case worker. Allowing the client to tell his or her story while keeping him or her to relevant facts is the best way to do this. To obtain the more basic data needed to establish eligibility is useful and ensures uniformity and completeness of such data, but it is not as helpful in establishing the real reasons for a problem, the need for public assistance, or the good relationship required for an ongoing rapport.

86. **The correct answer is (A).** The SSI does not give any money in this situation.

87. **The correct answer is (C).** The primary source for information about the family background and economic needs of a client is simply the client. Relatives, friends, records, employers, etc., are secondary sources and may be consulted to verify certain information given by the client, but it is only from the client that the complete picture can be obtained.

88. **The correct answer is (D).** Residence verification is best obtained by the perusal of rent receipts. The other answer choices provide no information and/or no verification of current residence.

89. **The correct answer is (A).** Vital statistics are kept by a local or state government agency and provide official records of births, deaths, and marriages in that locality. Such official information is essential in giving proof of information, such as a client's age or parentage of a child, which is often needed in establishing eligibility for certain types of public assistance.

90. **The correct answer is (D).** A case record contains the client's needs, problems, and other personal data that a client is often willing to impart only to the case worker. To give such information to others without first obtaining the permission of the client would make rapport with the client very difficult. It may result in the client's failure to give the worker information that is very important to a successful working relationship. Furthermore, it may result in actual harm to the client if the data are seen by people outside the agency without the client's permission.

91. **The correct answer is (D).** A good case worker must know when the help of a professional in another discipline is needed and refer the client to this other source. At the same time, the worker must remain responsible for the entire case and coordinate activities with the other professional.

92. **The correct answer is (D).** This choice succinctly states the main point contained in this passage.

93. The correct answer is (D). This choice reflects the socioeconomic problems that exist in this society, which could lead to the predicament this family now finds itself in.

94. The correct answer is (B). Of the choices given, this is the only one that presents a direct attempt at the solution of the problem. The three other choices contain facts that do not appear in the preamble of the question. Therefore, they cannot be given serious consideration.

95. The correct answer is (D). This is a tricky question since the passage states the laws in the state and city of New York. The passage therefore does not apply to a case worker in Arkansas and the problem, therefore, should be researched consistent with laws existing in the locality given in the preamble of the question. Note that there is no indication that the person cannot find other work, and the inability to work is usually a primary factor in all localities to determine eligibility for public assistance.

96. The correct answer is (C). The passage states that eviction can never be considered discrimination when it is for nonpayment of rent. Therefore, you must verify and determine the real reason for the eviction before proper action can be taken.

97. The correct answer is (C). The passage clearly indicates discrimination because of sexual preferences is illegal in New York State. Given the poor work history of the client, the reason for dismissal given by the client should be verified in order to determine if an antidiscrimination suit is appropriate in this instance. Note that the facts given in the question warrant a frank discussion with the client regarding her work habits and attitudes before advising her to file suit.

98. The correct answer is (B). Refer to the first sentence in the passage.

99. The correct answer is (A). Refer to the second sentence of the first paragraph. The other choices contain facts not included in the passage and therefore should not be considered.

100. The correct answer is (D). This choice of action not only represents all that one can do concerning this problem, but it is also likely to reassure the woman.

ANSWER SHEET PRACTICE TEST 4

1. Ⓐ Ⓑ Ⓒ Ⓓ 21. Ⓐ Ⓑ Ⓒ Ⓓ 41. Ⓐ Ⓑ Ⓒ Ⓓ 61. Ⓐ Ⓑ Ⓒ Ⓓ 81. Ⓐ Ⓑ Ⓒ Ⓓ

2. Ⓐ Ⓑ Ⓒ Ⓓ 22. Ⓐ Ⓑ Ⓒ Ⓓ 42. Ⓐ Ⓑ Ⓒ Ⓓ 62. Ⓐ Ⓑ Ⓒ Ⓓ 82. Ⓐ Ⓑ Ⓒ Ⓓ

3. Ⓐ Ⓑ Ⓒ Ⓓ 23. Ⓐ Ⓑ Ⓒ Ⓓ 43. Ⓐ Ⓑ Ⓒ Ⓓ 63. Ⓐ Ⓑ Ⓒ Ⓓ 83. Ⓐ Ⓑ Ⓒ Ⓓ

4. Ⓐ Ⓑ Ⓒ Ⓓ 24. Ⓐ Ⓑ Ⓒ Ⓓ 44. Ⓐ Ⓑ Ⓒ Ⓓ 64. Ⓐ Ⓑ Ⓒ Ⓓ 84. Ⓐ Ⓑ Ⓒ Ⓓ

5. Ⓐ Ⓑ Ⓒ Ⓓ 25. Ⓐ Ⓑ Ⓒ Ⓓ 45. Ⓐ Ⓑ Ⓒ Ⓓ 65. Ⓐ Ⓑ Ⓒ Ⓓ 85. Ⓐ Ⓑ Ⓒ Ⓓ

6. Ⓐ Ⓑ Ⓒ Ⓓ 26. Ⓐ Ⓑ Ⓒ Ⓓ 46. Ⓐ Ⓑ Ⓒ Ⓓ 66. Ⓐ Ⓑ Ⓒ Ⓓ 86. Ⓐ Ⓑ Ⓒ Ⓓ

7. Ⓐ Ⓑ Ⓒ Ⓓ 27. Ⓐ Ⓑ Ⓒ Ⓓ 47. Ⓐ Ⓑ Ⓒ Ⓓ 67. Ⓐ Ⓑ Ⓒ Ⓓ 87. Ⓐ Ⓑ Ⓒ Ⓓ

8. Ⓐ Ⓑ Ⓒ Ⓓ 28. Ⓐ Ⓑ Ⓒ Ⓓ 48. Ⓐ Ⓑ Ⓒ Ⓓ 68. Ⓐ Ⓑ Ⓒ Ⓓ 88. Ⓐ Ⓑ Ⓒ Ⓓ

9. Ⓐ Ⓑ Ⓒ Ⓓ 29. Ⓐ Ⓑ Ⓒ Ⓓ 49. Ⓐ Ⓑ Ⓒ Ⓓ 69. Ⓐ Ⓑ Ⓒ Ⓓ 89. Ⓐ Ⓑ Ⓒ Ⓓ

10. Ⓐ Ⓑ Ⓒ Ⓓ 30. Ⓐ Ⓑ Ⓒ Ⓓ 50. Ⓐ Ⓑ Ⓒ Ⓓ 70. Ⓐ Ⓑ Ⓒ Ⓓ 90. Ⓐ Ⓑ Ⓒ Ⓓ

11. Ⓐ Ⓑ Ⓒ Ⓓ 31. Ⓐ Ⓑ Ⓒ Ⓓ 51. Ⓐ Ⓑ Ⓒ Ⓓ 71. Ⓐ Ⓑ Ⓒ Ⓓ 91. Ⓐ Ⓑ Ⓒ Ⓓ

12. Ⓐ Ⓑ Ⓒ Ⓓ 32. Ⓐ Ⓑ Ⓒ Ⓓ 52. Ⓐ Ⓑ Ⓒ Ⓓ 72. Ⓐ Ⓑ Ⓒ Ⓓ 92. Ⓐ Ⓑ Ⓒ Ⓓ

13. Ⓐ Ⓑ Ⓒ Ⓓ 33. Ⓐ Ⓑ Ⓒ Ⓓ 53. Ⓐ Ⓑ Ⓒ Ⓓ 73. Ⓐ Ⓑ Ⓒ Ⓓ 93. Ⓐ Ⓑ Ⓒ Ⓓ

14. Ⓐ Ⓑ Ⓒ Ⓓ 34. Ⓐ Ⓑ Ⓒ Ⓓ 54. Ⓐ Ⓑ Ⓒ Ⓓ 74. Ⓐ Ⓑ Ⓒ Ⓓ 94. Ⓐ Ⓑ Ⓒ Ⓓ

15. Ⓐ Ⓑ Ⓒ Ⓓ 35. Ⓐ Ⓑ Ⓒ Ⓓ 55. Ⓐ Ⓑ Ⓒ Ⓓ 75. Ⓐ Ⓑ Ⓒ Ⓓ 95. Ⓐ Ⓑ Ⓒ Ⓓ

16. Ⓐ Ⓑ Ⓒ Ⓓ 36. Ⓐ Ⓑ Ⓒ Ⓓ 56. Ⓐ Ⓑ Ⓒ Ⓓ 76. Ⓐ Ⓑ Ⓒ Ⓓ 96. Ⓐ Ⓑ Ⓒ Ⓓ

17. Ⓐ Ⓑ Ⓒ Ⓓ 37. Ⓐ Ⓑ Ⓒ Ⓓ 57. Ⓐ Ⓑ Ⓒ Ⓓ 77. Ⓐ Ⓑ Ⓒ Ⓓ 97. Ⓐ Ⓑ Ⓒ Ⓓ

18. Ⓐ Ⓑ Ⓒ Ⓓ 38. Ⓐ Ⓑ Ⓒ Ⓓ 58. Ⓐ Ⓑ Ⓒ Ⓓ 78. Ⓐ Ⓑ Ⓒ Ⓓ 98. Ⓐ Ⓑ Ⓒ Ⓓ

19. Ⓐ Ⓑ Ⓒ Ⓓ 39. Ⓐ Ⓑ Ⓒ Ⓓ 59. Ⓐ Ⓑ Ⓒ Ⓓ 79. Ⓐ Ⓑ Ⓒ Ⓓ 99. Ⓐ Ⓑ Ⓒ Ⓓ

20. Ⓐ Ⓑ Ⓒ Ⓓ 40. Ⓐ Ⓑ Ⓒ Ⓓ 60. Ⓐ Ⓑ Ⓒ Ⓓ 80. Ⓐ Ⓑ Ⓒ Ⓓ 100. Ⓐ Ⓑ Ⓒ Ⓓ

answer sheet

Practice Test 4

SOCIAL SERVICES

100 Questions • 3 hours, 30 Minutes

Directions: Each question has four possible answers. Choose the letter that best answers the question and mark your answer on the answer sheet.

1. The primary function of any department of social services is to
   (A) refer needy persons to legally responsible relatives for support.
   (B) enable needy persons to become self-supporting.
   (C) refer ineligible applicants to private agencies.
   (D) grant aid to needy eligible clients.

2. A public assistance program objective should be designed to
   (A) provide for eligible clients in accordance with their individual requirements and with consideration of the circumstances in which they live.
   (B) provide for eligible clients at a standard of living equal to that enjoyed while they were self-supporting.
   (C) make sure that assistance payments from public funds are not too liberal.
   (D) guard against providing a better living for clients receiving aid than is enjoyed by the most frugal independent families.

3. An individual would be denied assistance for TANF (Temporary Assistance for Needy Families) if they were which of the following?
   (A) A mother who is married with 3 children from different fathers
   (B) An individual convicted of a drug felony
   (C) A teen parent living in an adult-supervised setting
   (D) A person who is on assistance and is cooperative with child support officials

4. Which of the following types of public assistance is frequently described as a "special privilege"?
   (A) Veterans assistance
   (B) Emergency assistance
   (C) Aid to dependent children
   (D) Vocational rehabilitation of the handicapped

239

5. The Personal Responsibility and Work Opportunity Reconciliation Act of 1996 ends the federal entitlement of individuals to cash assistance under Title IV-A (AFDC), giving states complete flexibility to determine eligibility and benefits levels. Under the new law, Title IV-A funds are replaced with block grants for Temporary Assistance for Needy Families (TANF). State plans filed with the U.S. Department of Health and Human Services must explain the state's use of these funds. In the plans, a state must

   (A) establish criteria for delivering benefits.

   (B) deny services as they see fit to reduce budgetary constraints.

   (C) follow the same regulations as all other states; otherwise, there would not be equitable treatment to recipients.

   (D) explain how it will provide an administrative appeals process for recipients only when questioned in a public court hearing.

6. Census Bureau reports show certain definite social trends in the U.S. population. One of these trends, which was a major contributing factor in the establishment of the federal old-age insurance system, is the

   (A) increased rate of immigration to the United States.

   (B) rate at which the number of Americans living to 65 years of age and beyond is increasing.

   (C) increasing amounts spent for categorical relief in the country as a whole.

   (D) number of states that have failed to meet their obligations in the care of the elderly.

7. Which of the following lawful permanent residents (LPRs) can lose their green card status?

   (A) People on health-care programs

   (B) People receiving food program assistance

   (C) People who leave the country for more than six months at a time

   (D) People who avoid long-term care

8. The Women, Infants, and Children (WIC) program

   (A) denies support to mothers who are breastfeeding and their children.

   (B) provides supplemental food support to pregnant, postpartum, and nursing mothers and their infants and children aged 1 to 5 years old.

   (C) teaches mothers how to achieve balanced diets using fast foods and starches as those foods are available to the poor.

   (D) is a one-time service to be utilized during any one pregnancy that a preteen or older mother faces.

9. Casual unemployment, as distinguished from other types of unemployment, is traceable most readily to

   (A) a decrease in the demand for labor as a result of scientific progress.

   (B) haphazard changes in the demand for labor in certain industries.

   (C) periodic changes in the demand for labor in certain industries.

   (D) disturbances and disruptions in industry resulting from international trade barriers.

10. Labor legislation, although primarily intended for the benefit of the employee, may aid an employer by

   (A) increasing the employer's control over the immediate labor markets.

   (B) prohibiting government interference with operating policies.

   (C) protecting the employer, through equalization of labor costs, from being undercut by other employers.

   (D) transferring to the general taxpayer the principal costs of industrial hazards of accident and unemployment.

11. When employment and unemployment figures both decline, the most probable conclusion is that

   (A) the population has reached a condition of equilibrium.

   (B) seasonal employment has ended.

   (C) the labor force has decreased.

   (D) payments for unemployment insurance have been increased.

12. You are meeting with Ms. Smith, a 54-year-old single parent of three. In evaluating her income, you would focus on which of the following?

   (A) The purchasing power of her income

   (B) Where and how she obtains her income

   (C) Her income in comparison to her potential earning capacity

   (D) Her income value compared to the average

13. An individual with an IQ of 100 may be said to have demonstrated

   (A) superior intelligence.

   (B) absolute intelligence.

   (C) substandard intelligence.

   (D) approximately average intelligence.

14. If a state passed a law in a field under Congressional jurisdiction and if Congress subsequently passed contrary legislation, the state provision would be

   (A) regarded as never having existed.

   (B) valid until the next session of the state legislature, which would be obliged to repeal it.

   (C) superseded by the federal statute.

   (D) still operative in the state involved.

practice test

QUESTIONS 15–24 ARE BASED ON THE FOLLOWING TABLE.

WELFARE CENTER CASELOAD SUMMARY

June–September

	June	July	August	September
Total Cases Under Care at End of Month	13,790	11,445	13,191	12,209
Home relief	4,739	2,512	6,055	5,118
Old-age assistance	5,337	b	5,440	2,265
Aid to dependent children	3,487	1,621	1,520	4,594
Aid to the blind	227	251	176	232
Net Change During Month	−344	c	1,746	−982
Applications Made During Month	1,542	789	3,153	1,791
Total Cases Accepted During Month	534	534	2,879	982
Home relief	278	213	342	338
Old-age assistance	43	161	1,409	f
Aid to dependent children	195	153	1,115	307
Aid to the blind	18	7	13	14
Total Cases Closed During Month	878	d	1,133	1,964
To private employment	326	1,197	460	870
To unemployment insurance	96	421	126	205
Reclassified	176	326	178	399
All other reasons	280	935	e	490
Total Cases Carried Over to Next Month	a	11,455	13,191	12,209

15. What is the number that should be placed in the blank indicated by "a"?

   (A) 12,912

   (B) 13,466

   (C) 13,790

   (D) None of the above

16. What is the number that should be placed in the blank indicated by "b"?

   (A) 7,061

   (B) 7,601

   (C) 8,933

   (D) None of the above

17. What is the number that should be placed in the blank indicated by "c"?

   (A) −2,345

   (B) −344

   (C) 344

   (D) None of the above

18. What is the number that should be placed in the blank indicated by "d"?

   (A) 2,789

   (B) 2,345

   (C) 7,601

   (D) None of the above

19. Of the total number of cases closed during the month of August, what is the percentage closed for reasons other than reclassification or receipt of unemployment insurance?

    (A) 13.8%

    (B) 73.17%

    (C) 26.83%

    (D) 40.60%

20. In comparing June and July, the figures indicate that with respect to the total cases under care at the end of each month

    (A) the percentage of total cases accepted during the month was lower in June.

    (B) the percentage of total cases accepted during the month was higher in June.

    (C) the percentage of total cases accepted during both months was the same.

    (D) there is insufficient data for comparison of the total cases under care at the end of each month.

21. What is the total number of cases accepted during the entire period in the category in which most cases were accepted?

    (A) 1,409

    (B) 1,936

    (C) 1,770

    (D) 4,929

22. In comparing July and September, the figures indicate that

    (A) more cases were closed in September because of private employment.

    (B) the total number of cases accepted during the month consisted of a greater proportion of home relief cases in September.

    (C) in one of these months, there were more total cases under care at the end of the month than at the beginning of the month.

    (D) None of the above

23. The total number of applications made during the four-month period was

    (A) more than four times the number of cases closed because of private employment during the same period.

    (B) less than the combined totals of aid-to-dependent-children cases under care in June and July.

    (C) 4,376 more than the total number of cases accepted during August.

    (D) 5,916 less than the total number of cases carried over to September.

24. The ratio of old-age assistance cases accepted in August to the total number of such cases under care at the end of that month is expressed with the greatest degree of accuracy by the figures

    (A) 1:4

    (B) 1:25

    (C) 4:1

    (D) 10:39

25. The word *deviant* refers to

    (A) ordinary.

    (B) crafty.

    (C) insubordinate.

    (D) unacceptable.

26. Competence most directly represents

    (A) grandiosity.

    (B) responsiveness.

    (C) proficiency.

    (D) heedful.

27. The technical term used to express the ratio between mental and chronological age is called the

    (A) mentality rating.

    (B) intelligence quotient.

    (C) psychometric standard.

    (D) achievement index.

28. In social case work, the disorganizing factors in a personal or familial situation that prevent or hinder rehabilitation are called

(A) median deviations.

(B) transference situations.

(C) rank correlations.

(D) liabilities.

29. Dementia was once referred to as

(A) mental retardation.

(B) senility.

(C) stupidity.

(D) gerontology.

QUESTIONS 30–32 ARE BASED ON THE FOLLOWING PASSAGE.

Aid to dependent children shall be given to a parent or other relative as herein specified for the benefit of a child or children under 16 years of age or of a minor or minors between 16 and 18 years of age if in the judgment of the administrative agency: (1) the granting of an allowance will be in the interest of such child or minor; (2) the parent or other relative is a fit person to bring up such child or minor so that his physical, mental, and moral well-being will be safeguarded; (3) aid is necessary to enable such parent or other relative to do so; (4) such child or minor is a resident of the state on the date of application for aid; and (5) such minor between 16 and 18 years of age is regularly attending school in accordance with the regulations of the department. An allowance may be granted for the aid of such child or minor who has been deprived of parental support or care by reason of death, continued absence from the home, or physical or mental incapacity of parent, and who is living with his father, mother, grandfather, grandmother, brother, sister, stepfather, stepmother, stepbrother, stepsister, uncle, or aunt. In making such allowances, consideration shall be given to the ability of the relative making application and of any other relatives to support and care for or to contribute to the support and care of such child or minor. In making all such allowances, it shall be made certain that the religious faith of the child or minor shall be preserved and protected.

30. The passage is concerned primarily with

(A) the financial ability of people applying for public assistance.

(B) compliance on the part of applicants with the "settlement" provisions of the law.

(C) the fitness of parents or other relatives to bring up physically, mentally, or morally delinquent children between the ages of 16 and 18.

(D) eligibility for aid to families with dependent children.

31. On the basis of the passage, which of the following statements is the most accurate?

(A) Mary Doe, mother of John, age 18, is entitled to aid for her son if he is attending school regularly.

(B) Evelyn Stowe, mother of Eleanor, age 13, is not entitled to aid for Eleanor if she uses her home for immoral purposes.

(C) Ann Roe, cousin of Helen, age 14, is entitled to aid for Helen if the latter is living with her.

(D) Peter Moe, uncle of Henry, age 15, is not entitled to aid for Henry if the latter is living with him.

32. The passage is probably an excerpt from
    (A) a city's administrative code.
    (B) a state's social welfare law.
    (C) the Federal Security Act.
    (D) a city's charter.

33. The length of residence required to make a person eligible for the various forms of public assistance available in the United States
    (A) is the same in all states but different among various public assistance programs in a given state.
    (B) is the same in all states and among different public assistance programs in a given state.
    (C) is the same in all states for different categories.
    (D) varies among states and among different assistance programs in a given state.

34. Social Welfare Law often requires that whenever an applicant for aid to dependent children resides in a place where there is a central index or a social services exchange, the public welfare official shall register the case with such index or exchange. This requirement is for the purpose of
    (A) preventing duplication and coordinating the work of public and private agencies.
    (B) establishing prior claims on the amounts of assistance furnished when repayments are made.
    (C) having the social service exchange determine which agency should handle the case.
    (D) providing statistical data regarding the number of persons receiving grants for aid to dependent children.

35. A person who knowingly brings a needy person from one state into another state for the purpose of making him or her a public charge is generally guilty of
    (A) violation of the Displaced Persons Act.
    (B) violation of the Mann Act.
    (C) a felony.
    (D) a misdemeanor.

36. Clients sometimes lose motivation in terms of seeking out other alternatives for support. In general, a client can become dependent on public assistance as a means of living when
    (A) public assistance only covers bare necessities.
    (B) the client is earning a small salary within the general community.
    (C) the client has been receiving assistance for too long.
    (D) the client is having a difficult time finding work and feeding his family.

37. Adoption is the process through which
    (A) the natural parents' rights and obligations toward their child is always maintained.
    (B) the adoptive parents assume all rights and obligations once a child has been adopted.
    (C) the natural or birth parents are always legally responsible for their child.
    (D) the natural or birth parents maintain all the obligations, and rights between a parent and child are established between them.

38. The most successful adoptions are often a result of
    (A) a teen birth mother who has already had an abortion.
    (B) less expensive housing options for adoptive parents.
    (C) an investigation of the home prior to an adoption.
    (D) lower adoption fees.

39. Any person or organization soliciting donations in public places in New York City is required to have a license issued by the

(A) police department.

(B) Department of Sanitation.

(C) Division of Labor Relations.

(D) Department of Social Services.

40. A person who is in good health but harbors disease germs that may be passed on to others, is called a(n)

(A) instigator.

(B) carrier.

(C) incubator.

(D) inoculator.

41. In the population at large individuals who tend to be at the greatest risk for contracting HIV are

(A) single women from homes with household incomes over $90,000.

(B) African-American males over 30.

(C) Asian-American males.

(D) young disadvantaged women, particularly African-American women.

42. The term *psychopharmacology* implies that an individual is being treated by

(A) medication prescribed by a psychiatrist.

(B) meetings with other survivors in a group format.

(C) the process of taking prescription medication in addition to mandatory participation in a twelve-step program.

(D) one-on-one psychotherapy for a minimum of three years.

43. Proper utilization of the term *carious* would involve reference to

(A) teeth.

(B) curiosity.

(C) shipment of food packages to needy persons in Europe.

(D) hazardous situations.

44. Victims of domestic violence include

(A) females.

(B) same-sex partners.

(C) elders, children, and siblings.

(D) All of the above

45. The medical term for "hardening of the arteries" is

(A) carcinoma.

(B) arthritis.

(C) thrombosis.

(D) arteriosclerosis.

46. Children with growth retardation, abnormal facial features, central nervous system problems, and serious lifelong disabilities, including mental retardation, learning disabilities, and serious behavioral problems are most likely victims of

(A) domestic violence.

(B) ARC.

(C) CP.

(D) FAS.

47. If the characteristics of a person were being studied by competent observers, it would be expected that their observations would differ most markedly with respect to their evaluation of the person's

(A) intelligence.

(B) height.

(C) temperamental characteristics.

(D) weight.

48. If there is evidence of dietary deficiency in families where cereals make up a major portion of the diet, the most likely reason for this deficiency is that

(A) cereals cause absorption of excessive water.

(B) persons who concentrate their diet on cereals do not chew their food properly.

(C) carbohydrates are deleterious.

(D) other essential food elements are omitted.

49. Although malnutrition is generally associated with poverty, dietary studies of population groups in the United States reveal that

    (A) malnutrition is most often due to a deficiency of nutrients found chiefly in high-cost foods.

    (B) there has been overemphasis of the causal relationship between poverty and malnutrition.

    (C) malnutrition is found among people with sufficient money to be well fed.

    (D) a majority of the population in all income groups is undernourished.

50. The etiology of HIV would most likely discuss

    (A) ways to treat HIV.

    (B) new medications being developed.

    (C) the historical development of HIV in Africa.

    (D) the increased spread of HIV infections.

51. The organization that has as one of its primary functions the mitigation of suffering caused by famine, fire, floods, and other national calamities is the

    (A) National Safety Council.

    (B) Salvation Army.

    (C) Public Administration Service.

    (D) American Red Cross.

52. In the welfare system of any state, the broad policies and patterns of social services are laid down by

    (A) the people of each state through its legislature.

    (B) the state's board of Social Welfare.

    (C) the state's Department of Social Welfare.

    (D) each of the local city, county, or town public welfare districts for their respective jurisdictions.

53. A recipient of public assistance in New York City who is in need of the services of an attorney but is unable to pay the customary fees, should generally be referred to the

    (A) small-claims court.

    (B) Legal Aid Society.

    (C) New York County Lawyers Association.

    (D) New York City Corporation Counsel.

54. An injured worker should attempt to obtain compensation through the state's

    (A) Labor Relations Board.

    (B) Division of Placement and Unemployment Insurance.

    (C) Industrial Commission.

    (D) Workers' Compensation Board.

55. Which of the following increases the risks for infant morbidity and mortality?

    (A) Latex paint

    (B) Sociodemographic and behavioral characteristics

    (C) Perinatal exposure to cocaine

    (D) Lack of exposure to breast milk

56. Which of the following is a sexually transmitted disease?

    (A) Trichomoniasis

    (B) Hepatitis C

    (C) Toxic Shock Syndrome

    (D) Candidiasis

57. In rearing children, the problems of the widower are traditionally greater than those of the widow, largely because of the

    (A) tendency of widowers to impose excessively rigid moral standards.

    (B) increased economic hardship.

    (C) added difficulty of maintaining a desirable home.

    (D) possibility that a stepmother will be added to the household.

58. After interviewing a client who complains about the inadequate size of his living quarters, which of the following words would a case worker properly use in the record of the interview?

(A) Spaceal

(B) Spacial

(C) Spatial

(D) Spatiel

59. One of the most common characteristics of the chronic alcoholic is

(A) low intelligence level.

(B) wanderlust.

(C) psychosis.

(D) egocentricity.

60. Of the following factors leading toward the cure of the alcoholic, the most important is thought to be

(A) removal of all alcohol from the immediate environment.

(B) development of a sense of personal adequacy.

(C) social disapproval of drinking.

(D) segregation from former companions.

61. You are working with Ms. Smothers, a stroke victim who has two children and has suffered the demise of her 3-month-old baby after ignoring her doctor's orders not to get pregnant again. The clinic OB/GYN staff has told her that they consider her attempting to have another child to be a risk. Ms. Smothers insists on trying to have another child because this loss has been devastating for her 10-year-old daughter and 8-year-old son. You meet with the children and they show no signs of depression and seem well adjusted. You would recommend

(A) that this patient consider not having any more children as she is inflicting great pressure on her children and projecting her feelings of loss onto them.

(B) that this patient consider not having any more children as she has an increased risk of giving birth to a child with severe birth effects as a result of her health condition.

(C) that the patient be followed for ongoing counseling to help her deal with her loss and understand her reasons for wanting to go against her doctors orders in order to endure another high-risk pregnancy.

(D) that this patient consider not having any more children as she is inflicting great pressure on her body and that she is at a great risk for having another, possibly more severe, stroke.

62. An individual suffering from a mental disorder characterized by some eccentricity or emotional instability is frequently found to be

(A) psychopatic.

(B) psycopatic.

(C) psycopathic.

(D) psychopathic.

63. Because circumstances under which applications are made to a Department of Welfare are so often the result of financial conditions, the nature of home relief assistance is usually

(A) monetory.

(B) monetary.

(C) monitory.

(D) monitary.

64. Another way of expressing a financial relationship is by describing it as

(A) pecuniary.

(B) pecuniory.

(C) pecunary.

(D) picuniary.

65. An unfortunate occurrence that threatens to happen immediately is one that is
    (A) immanent.
    (B) immenent.
    (C) imminent.
    (D) omenent.

66. A case worker assigned to the child welfare program would occasionally mention in his reports the science that treats the hygiene and diseases of children. Which of the following words should be used to describe this medical science?
    (A) Pidiatrics
    (B) Pediatrics
    (C) Pideatrics
    (D) Pedeatrics

67. Strabismus is usually associated with
    (A) hearing.
    (B) sight.
    (C) blood pressure.
    (D) bone structure.

68. Which of the following is NOT one of Erikson's eight stages of psychological development?
    (A) Generativity vs. stagnation
    (B) Industry vs. inferiority
    (C) Initiative vs. guilt
    (D) Autonomy vs. rejection

69. Which of the following is the best example of recidivism?
    (A) John Smith is released on parole and begins to sell drugs, after which he is arrested and placed back into prison.
    (B) John Smith is released on parole and declines an opportunity to sell drugs from an old contact.
    (C) John Smith is released on parole and begins to sell drugs. He avoids getting arrested and becomes a high-profile drug dealer.
    (D) John Smith is released on parole and tries to get arrested and placed back into prison.

70. A client has a phobia about enclosed places like elevators. This is called
    (A) examphobia.
    (B) acrophobia.
    (C) agoraphobia.
    (D) claustrophobia.

71. A personality restraint imposed upon one psychical activity by another, which is harmful and may lead to mental illness, is known as
    (A) expression.
    (B) transference.
    (C) symbiosis.
    (D) inhibition.

72. The ophthalmic professions are concerned principally with problems affecting
    (A) eyesight.
    (B) drugs.
    (C) prognostication.
    (D) weather control.

73. When a public assistance agency assigns its most experienced interviewers to conduct initial interviews with applicants, the most important reason for its action is that
    (A) experienced workers are always older, and therefore command the respect of applicants.
    (B) the applicant may be given a complete understanding of the procedures to be followed and the time involved in obtaining assistance payments.
    (C) applicants with fraudulent intentions will be detected and prevented from obtaining further services from the agency.
    (D) the applicant may be given an understanding of the purpose of the assistance program and of the bases for granting assistance in addition to the routine information.

74. Responsibility for fully informing the public about the availability of public assistance can most successfully be discharged by

(A) local public assistance agencies.

(B) social service exchanges.

(C) community chest organizations.

(D) councils of social agencies.

75. The most significant and pervasive indicator of alcoholism is

(A) early morning drinking.

(B) blackouts.

(C) defensive behavior.

(D) withdrawal.

76. One of the major purposes of the federal Social Security insurance system for unemployment compensation and old-age and survivors insurance is to

(A) lessen the need for public assistance because it is degrading for the individual.

(B) provide maintenance of income for the people deprived of such, in order to keep the economy in balance.

(C) make certain that no one goes hungry in this land of abundance.

(D) bring order out of the chaos of fifty state laws.

77. The least likely symptom of depression is

(A) disturbances in orientation and thinking.

(B) sadness and hopelessness.

(C) insomnia.

(D) disturbances in food intake and elimination.

78. The use of token economies has been most successful in

(A) schools.

(B) homes.

(C) social service departments.

(D) mental hospitals.

79. An emotionally mature adult is a person who has

(A) no need to be dependent on others and who is proud of his or her independence and ability to help others who are dependent on him or her.

(B) little need for satisfaction from social relationships and who is able to live comfortably alone.

(C) insight into and understanding of his or her emotional needs and strengths.

(D) considerable need to depend on others and to be loved and cared for.

80. An essential part of the case worker's job is recording the facts of a client situation, the client's activity in self-help, and the worker's activity on the client's behalf. Of the several methods of recording a case history, the topical summary

(A) is best because it contains only pertinent information and saves time for both the writer and readers.

(B) has value only for certain types of interviews because it does not reflect, where necessary, the client's movement and the case worker's activity.

(C) is a good method because it is easiest for the new and inexperienced case worker to use.

(D) is not a good method because it tends to make the case worker follow the outline in the interviews as well as in the recording.

81. In making a social study of an application for service, a thorough review of the previous history of a family's contacts with the Department of Social Service contained in the department's case records is

(A) not important because current eligibility is based on contemporary facts and these will have to be secured and verified anew.

(B) important because the case worker can anticipate whether he or she will have trouble with the family in determining their eligibility by learning how they behaved in the past.

(C) important but should not be made until after the case worker has formed his or her own opinion in personal contact because previous workers' opinions may prejudice him or her.

(D) important so that current investigation can be focused on such additional information as is needed, with a minimum of time and effort and in a manner that will be of help to the family.

82. "It is recognized that many workers choosing public welfare as their field of professional activity have done so out of readiness to live beyond themselves, out of their liking and concern for people." This quotation suggests that these workers

(A) have no personal needs to be realized in their work.

(B) have readiness to understand and some capacity to deal with their own personal needs.

(C) have a neurotic basis for their choice of vocation.

(D) have a tendency to reform their clients.

83. "The fact that an individual receives his means of support from an assistance agency rather than from wages or other recognized income is a fact of difference from his neighbors that cannot be denied or dismissed lightly. There is a deeply rooted tradition in this country that the person who is 'anybody' supports himself by his own efforts, that there is something wrong about getting one's support from a source created by the whole. Thus, the individual who gets his support from a social agency is considered in a group apart and different from his neighbors." Relating this statement to practice, you should

(A) recognize the client as different and give such case work service as will enable him or her to become a member of the self-supporting community as soon as possible.

(B) explain to each client that you understand the difficulties of asking for and receiving help, and there is no need to be self-conscious with you.

(C) analyze your own feelings toward the particular client to secure some insight into how you personally relate to this cultural pattern and to the client, and what your own attitudes towards dependency are.

(D) make strenuous efforts to change the cultural pattern of the community, which is harmful to so large a part of it.

84. "No piece of social legislation, no matter how worthy its objectives, is any better than its administration. And yet, simultaneously, it must be recognized that administration is the servant of social objectives, never the master." The application of this principle to practice means that you should

(A) not help to have the law improved until administration catches up with the philosophy of the current law.

(B) not have to feel any responsibility toward the function you represent.

(C) handle each case on an individual basis, making such exceptions to general policy as indicated by the need of the client.

(D) always work within the existing limitations of agency function, however narrow and punitive it may seem to you in relation to a particular case.

85. Mr. Wilson comes to a Department of Social Services to request assistance. He matter-of-factly presents his situation; methodically submits bills, receipts, and other verification documents; and then asks how much help he will get and how soon he may expect it. This behavior should indicate to an alert case worker that Mr. Wilson

(A) is probably a relatively secure adult with considerable strength and capacity for independence.

(B) is probably a chronically dependent person who has been through this routine so often before that he has the procedure memorized.

(C) is a naturally aggressive individual accustomed to sweeping everything before him in the accomplishment of his purpose.

(D) has probably prepared a fictitious story in order to hide his real situation and "beat" the eligibility requirements.

86. Ms. Lewis, an unmarried mother, has applied for temporary placement of her 6-month-old baby until she "gets back on her feet." Her financial resources are almost exhausted. During the investigation, the case worker learns that the baby was born strong and well developed, but is now pale and thin. He is not taken regularly to a "well baby" clinic. He cries a great deal, particularly when his mother picks him up. She handles him roughly, complaining about her loss of sleep because the baby is spoiled and cranky. He has a feeding problem and, the case worker observes, if he refuses the first offer of food, it is withdrawn immediately. In this instance the case worker should

(A) refer Ms. Lewis for Aid to Families with Dependent Children, because regular income may make her more comfortable and more patient with the baby, and babies are better off with their own mothers.

(B) discuss the possibilities for and encourage a decision to place the baby for adoption, since there are indications of the mother's emotional rejection of the baby in his and her behavior.

(C) go along with the mother's plan since she knows her situation best.

(D) refer Ms. Lewis to a psychiatric clinic since her behavior is definitely pathological.

Questions 87–92 are based on the following table.

DISTRIBUTION OF WELFARE HOUSEHOLDS IN YAGGERSTOWN BY NUMBER OF PUBLIC ASSISTANCE RECIPIENTS

January 2003 and December 2005

Number of Recipients in Household	Thousands of Distribution*		Percentage Change 2003–2005	Percentage of Households	
	Jan. 2003	Dec. 2005		Jan. 2003	Dec. 2005
1	119.4	164.6	37.9	37.3	39.2
2	97.8	134.9	37.9	30.5	39.1
3	61.3	76.0	24.0	19.2	?
4	?	29.8	10.4	8.4	7.1
5	6.4	6.5	1.6	2.0	1.6
6	8.3	7.8	6.0	2.6	1.9
TOTAL	320.3	419.8	?	100.0	100.0

* Distributions may not add exactly to totals because of rounding.

87. What is the number of households with 4 or more recipients in the household in January 2003?

(A) 2,700

(B) 27,000

(C) 4,200

(D) 42,000

88. What is the total percentage change in the distribution of welfare households in 2003–2005?

(A) 186.5%

(B) 180.5%

(C) 24%

(D) 31.1%

89. What is the percent change during 2003–2005 for households with 6 or more recipients?

(A) 5%

(B) 6%

(C) .93%

(D) 1.17%

90. What is most nearly the average percentage change between January 2003 and December 2005?

(A) 37.9%

(B) 19.63%

(C) 23.56%

(D) 117.8%

91. What is most nearly the percentage distribution of households having 3 recipients in the household in December 2005?

(A) 13.7%

(B) 16.4%

(C) 18.1%

(D) 81.9%

92. In January 2003, the percentage of households that contain 6 recipients receiving public assistance was most nearly

(A) 26%.

(B) 2.5%.

(C) 4%.

(D) 6%.

QUESTIONS 93–95 ARE BASED ON THE FOLLOWING PASSAGE.

The Medicaid program is designed to help low-income people who cannot pay for their own medical care. In order to be eligible, an individual must meet certain income and assets limitations. The program is directly administered by local social services agencies throughout the United States, under the overall supervision of each state's Department of Social Services in accordance with both federal and state regulations. The eligibility rules may differ somewhat in each state but are similar and follow the same basic guidelines.

If you are found eligible for Medicaid, your medical bills will be paid in whole or in part. In New York State, you must be a resident of the state, a citizen of the United States, or an alien admitted for lawful permanent residence in the United States, or have resided in the state continuously for five years. In New York State, you meet the financial requirements for Medicaid eligibility if you receive public assistance or Supplementary Security Income (SSI). You may also be eligible for Medicaid depending on your income and assets (property and/or money), and on the extent of your medical expenses. You also may qualify for Medicaid if you meet the criteria for disability, which are given in the Federal Social Security Act and if your assets (money and property) and medical expenses warrant it. You also may be eligible if you received both Social Security and SSI but were later found ineligible for SSI.

93. Based on the passage, medical bills may be paid through the Medicaid program and administered by New York State if the individual meets the income and assets requirements and is a

- **(A)** citizen of France visiting New York City and becomes ill.
- **(B)** U.S. citizen and resident of New Jersey working in New York and becomes hospitalized in New York City.
- **(C)** naturalized American residing in New York State for five years.
- **(D)** Brazilian youth residing in New York on a student visa.

94. Assume that you are a case worker in the public assistance division of a social services center in Badgerville, New York. After investigation, you determine that you must deny an application for supplementary assistance of an obviously ill man and his family because he works on a part-time basis, which puts his funds just above the income level allowed for such assistance. He complains bitterly that just because he works, even though he is frequently ill, his family cannot get assistance and he cannot afford to visit the doctor to cure his chronic bronchitis. You should

- **(A)** make an exception in this case and approve the family's application for public assistance.
- **(B)** deny the application but suggest the man apply for Medicaid for himself and his family.
- **(C)** deny the application and explain the importance of finding full-time work so that he can take proper care of his health.
- **(D)** deny his application and inform him that he can probably get free medical assistance from a municipal health or hospital clinic.

95. A middle-aged, severely disabled woman living in New York City complains to you, the worker in a public assistance center, that she must have assistance in paying the medical bills she has been receiving from her private doctor. She formerly received SSI as well as Social Security, but due to a recent slight increase in the amount of her monthly Social Security check, she has been found ineligible for continued SSI. You should

(A) have her apply for supplementary public assistance.

(B) refer her to the state office handling SSI for reconsideration of her case.

(C) refer her to the nearest municipal hospital.

(D) refer her to possible acceptance on Medicaid.

QUESTIONS 96–100 ARE BASED ON THE FOLLOWING PASSAGE.

One of the problems involved in living to an older age is the increasing possibility of becoming homeless. Because both pensions and Social Security benefits have not kept up with rising inflation and with rent costs, many elderly persons find it impossible to pay their rent and upkeep of their apartments or homes. Many homeowners over age 65 have homes that predate the 1920s and, therefore, require higher costs for maintenance than most elderly couples or individuals can afford. In addition, the elimination of federally funded housing projects and the lack of transitional shelters have resulted in an urban-wide increase in homelessness in which the elderly are just one more group seeking places to live.

The problem is further exacerbated by the fact that many homeless elderly people are former mental patients who have recently been released from institutions. While an institution is not the best place for rehabilitation and healthy living, the decision to deinstitutionalize many of these people without first providing adequate alternate community mental health-care programs for them in our communities has resulted in increased numbers of homeless people and has broadened the scope of the problem of homelessness. Many of these individuals, both young and old, are disoriented and unable to cope with the decisions they must make in their daily lives. Since many of the elderly deinstitutionalized homeless have spent a large period of their lives in institutions, this unsupervised discharge into general community life has been particularly traumatic.

96. According to the passage, the elimination of federal funds for housing projects has resulted in

(A) the inability of a number of elderly homeless people to move into housing projects.

(B) an exacerbated conflict between the elderly and the young people seeking apartments in housing projects.

(C) severe trauma among elderly people who prefer the safety and security of living in housing projects to living in other types of living quarters.

(D) no special problem to elderly people who as a whole prefer to live in their own homes.

97. Based on the passage, in comparison with younger people returned to the community from mental institutions, elderly people in the same situation

(A) are more able to cope with homelessness since they have more life experience than do younger people.

(B) are more disadvantaged because many of them have spent a large part of their lives in a sheltered environment.

(C) frequently must be returned to the mental institution because they cannot find places to live.

(D) frequently are ill-treated or abused by the community at large because of their inability to cope with normal people.

98. In a few large cities, rent increases on certain apartments are controlled or stabilized if the tenants are elderly. It can be inferred from the passage that this practice

(A) makes the homeless problem for the elderly in such cities nonexistent.

(B) would not affect the mentally ill elderly since they are returned to the institution if they cannot pay their rent.

(C) would not affect most of the elderly since they own their own homes.

(D) would result in those elderly people being able to remain in the same apartments in which they have always lived.

99. Based on the passage, a major cause for homelessness among the elderly is the

(A) inability to properly manage their funds.

(B) ineligibility of many elderly persons for Social Security or pension funds.

(C) failure of the amount of monthly received Social Security funds to meet rising housing and general living costs.

(D) inability of elderly people to compete with younger, more aggressive people for vacant apartments.

100. According to the passage, the need for many elderly people to abandon their private homes is due to

(A) poor management on the part of these elderly people.

(B) preference of such elderly people to live in apartment houses when they can no longer cope with the management of a home.

(C) the rising costs of maintenance of their homes.

(D) their inability to continue to pay the high interest on the mortgages on their homes.

ANSWER KEY AND EXPLANATIONS

1. D	21. B	41. D	61. C	81. D
2. A	22. D	42. A	62. D	82. B
3. B	23. D	43. A	63. B	83. C
4. A	24. D	44. D	64. A	84. C
5. A	25. D	45. D	65. C	85. A
6. B	26. A	46. D	66. B	86. B
7. C	27. B	47. C	67. B	87. D
8. B	28. D	48. D	68. D	88. D
9. B	29. B	49. C	69. A	89. B
10. C	30. D	50. C	70. D	90. B
11. C	31. B	51. D	71. D	91. C
12. A	32. B	52. A	72. A	92. B
13. D	33. D	53. B	73. D	93. C
14. C	34. A	54. D	74. A	94. B
15. C	35. D	55. C	75. B	95. D
16. A	36. C	56. A	76. B	96. A
17. A	37. B	57. C	77. A	97. B
18. D	38. C	58. C	78. D	98. D
19. B	39. D	59. D	79. C	99. C
20. A	40. B	60. B	80. A	100. C

1. **The correct answer is (D).** The chief duty of a public welfare agency is to investigate the eligibility of a person or family applying for public assistance and to grant such assistance to those found eligible.

2. **The correct answer is (A).** The level of assistance granted an individual or family by a public agency should enable the recipients to have the standard of living established under the appropriate statutes of that community or state. The amount of actual money required depends on the individual circumstances. Thus, for example, if housing is available to the client, no rent is included in their budget. Standard amounts of money are provided for basic necessities, e.g., X amount of dollars for food for Y number of persons on assistance, but special individual needs may also be provided (e.g., for purchase of special food if the client has medical need, etc.).

3. **The correct answer is (B).** The federal law limits the provision of TANF and requires that a family's benefit be reduced if parents do not cooperate with child support officials, denies assistance to individuals convicted of a drug felony, denies assistance for ten years to any person convicted of fraud in the receipt of benefits in two or more states, and denies assistance to teen parents not living in an adult-supervised setting.

4. **The correct answer is (A).** Public assistance accorded to a group deemed to be worthy of special attention (like veterans of the armed forces) is generally referred to as a "special privilege" category.

5. **The correct answer is (A).** The Personal Responsibility and Work Opportunity Reconciliation Act of 1996 ends the federal entitlement of individuals to cash

assistance under Title IV-A (AFDC), giving states complete flexibility to determine eligibility and benefits levels. Under the new law, Title IV-A funds are replaced with block grants for Temporary Assistance for Needy Families (TANF). State plans filed with the U.S. Department of Health and Human Services must explain the states' use of these funds. In the plans, a state must establish criteria for delivering benefits and determining eligibility and for providing fair and equitable treatment to recipients. The state must also explain how it will provide an administrative appeals process for recipients.

6. **The correct answer is (B).** A major reason for the passage of the Federal Age Insurance System (Social Security) legislation was the increase in the number of people who live beyond the age of 65. It became evident that a method was needed to ensure that such people should continue to live in an acceptable manner after they could no longer successfully compete in the labor market. Personal savings from prior years of employment was often insufficient as people continued to live longer.

7. **The correct answer is (C).** LPRs who leave the country for more than six months at a time can be questioned about whether they are "public charges" when they return, and the use of cash welfare or long-term care may be considered. In very rare circumstances, LPRs who use cash welfare or long-term care within their first five years in the United States for reasons (such as an illness or disability) that existed before their entry to the United States could be considered deportable as a public charge.

8. **The correct answer is (B).** The WIC program provides supplemental foods for pregnant, postpartum, and nursing mothers and their infants and children from 1 to 5 years old, and teaches mothers how to achieve balanced diets.

9. **The correct answer is (B).** Casual unemployment—i.e., frequent periods of unemployment between the same type of job or the same job—results from the irregular demand for workers in a particular industry (e.g., a factory or industry where the demand for unskilled help fluctuates haphazardly).

10. **The correct answer is (C).** Labor legislation may be helpful to employers because it forces all employers in the same industry to pay at least the same minimum wages and provide the same workers' compensation and disability insurance. This equalizes much of the labor costs in an industry and lessens the ability of the company to cut labor costs and thus sell its products at a lower price than competitors.

11. **The correct answer is (C).** When there are both fewer employees and fewer unemployed, the labor force—i.e., the number of persons available for work—has decreased.

12. **The correct answer is (A).** The purchasing power of Ms. Smith's income represents the power of the dollar. This amount varies from place to place. The money she will receive in public assistance should be evaluated by the amount she will be able to purchase with it.

13. **The correct answer is (D).** An IQ of 100 is demonstrative of average intelligence. IQs below the 100 mark are demonstrative of varying degrees of substandard intelligence. IQs above 100 are demonstrative of varying degrees of superior intelligence.

14. **The correct answer is (C).** Basic constitutional law in the United States provides that a federal law supersedes a state law. Note: Choice (A) is wrong because the state law is in effect *until* federal law supersedes it.

15. The correct answer is (C). You are asked the number of cases carried over from June to July. This would be the same number appearing on the first line of the chart which is labeled "Total Cases Under Care at End of Month," i.e., 13,790.

16. The correct answer is (A). You are asked for the total number of OAA cases at the end of July. Total number of public assistance cases at the end of July = 11,445. Total number of public assistance cases *except* for OAA at the end of July = 4,384. Therefore, the number of OAA cases = 11,445 − 4,384 = 7,061.

17. The correct answer is (A). You are asked to give the net change in the number of cases between the end of June and the end of July. Total number of cases at the end of June = 13,790. Total number of cases at the end of July = 11,445. 13,790 − 11,445 = 2,345.

18. The correct answer is (D). You are asked for the total number of cases closed in July. You are given four categories comprising case closings and the numbers of cases closed in each category. The total of those numbers equals the total number of cases closed, i.e., 1,197 + 421 + 326 + 935 = 2,879. This number is *not* given as any of the possible answers.

19. The correct answer is (B). Find the number of cases closed in August for "all other reasons." Total number of cases closed in August = 1,113. Total number of cases closed in August except for other reasons = 829. 829 ÷ 1,113 = 73.17%

20. The correct answer is (A). Number of total cases accepted in June = 534. Total cases in June = 13,790. 534 ÷ 13,790 = .038%. Number of total cases accepted in July = 534. Total cases in July = 11,145. 534 ÷ 11,445 = .05%

21. The correct answer is (B). First you must determine what "f" is, i.e., the number of old-age assistance cases accepted in September. It is 323. Total number of cases accepted in September = 982. Total number of non-OAA cases accepted in September = 659. Total number of OAA cases accepted in September = 323. Inspection will show you that HR cases and AB cases can be eliminated. Total number of OAA cases accepted in four months = 43 + 161 + 1,409 + 323 = 1,936. Total number of AD cases accepted in four months = 195 + 153 + 1,115 + 307 = 1,770. Therefore, the 1,936 cases accepted in the OAA category is the correct answer.

22. The correct answer is (D). You must test possible answer choices (A), (B), and (C) to see which if any are correct. Choice (A) is incorrect. Private employment resulted in the closing of 870 cases in September and 1,197 cases in July. Choice (B) is also incorrect. In September, 338 HR cases were accepted out of a total of 982 cases accepted that month, or 34.42 percent. In July, 213 HR cases out of a total of 534 were accepted, or 39.89 percent. Choice (C) is also wrong. In July, the total number of cases under care at the end of the month was 13,790 − 11,445 = 2,345 *fewer* cases. In September, there were 13,191 − 12,209 = 1,981 *fewer* cases.

23. The correct answer is (D). Total number of applications made was 1,542 in June + 789 in July + 3,153 in August + 1,791 in September = 7,275 applications made in four months. Test each possible answer. In choice (A), the total number of cases closed by private employment was 326 + 1,197 + 460 + 870 = 2,853. The number of cases closed by employment, 7,275, is *not* four times 2,853. Thus, choice (A) is incorrect. In choice (B), ADC cases under care in June and July were 3,487 + 1,621 = 5,108; 7,275 is more than 5,108, so, choice (B) is also incorrect. In choice

(C), the total number of cases accepted in August was 2,879; 7,275 − 2,879 = 4,396 cases, so, choice (C) is incorrect as well. In choice (D), the total number of cases carried over to September was 13,191; 13,191 − 7,275 = 5,916. This is the correct answer.

24. **The correct answer is (D).** In ratio and proportion problems, you establish a relationship between the two variables: 1409:5440 = .259; 10:39 = .256

25. **The correct answer is (D).** Deviant behavior is one of the features of certain types of mental illness. In his speech, the politician criticized what he called "the deviant minorities" in society.

26. **The correct answer is (A).** Competence is the ability to do something to a level that is acceptable.

27. **The correct answer is (B).** An intelligence quotient is derived by dividing the mental age of the individual being tested by his/her chronological age. For example:

$$\frac{\text{level of intelligence per test}}{\text{chronological age of testee}} = \frac{1,500}{15} = 100 \text{ IQ}$$

28. **The correct answer is (D).** This is a factual question. Choices (A) and (C) are mathematical/statistical terms. Transference situations as presented in choice (B) refer to psychological situations.

29. **The correct answer is (B).** Dementia was once called senility. It is now defined as a gradual worsening in memory and other mental abilities as a result of brain damage, rather than as the natural result of aging. A common form of dementia is Alzheimer's disease.

30. **The correct answer is (D).** The passage discusses the facts that must be considered and the rules that apply in establishing eligibility in the category of public assistance called Aid to Families with Dependent Children.

31. **The correct answer is (B).** The passage clearly states that eligibility for AFDC is conditioned upon whether the parent of other relatives applying for the assistant is a "fit" person to bring up such a child so that his "physical, mental, or moral well-being will be safeguarded." Such a situation is not indicated in the situation described in the correct answer. Note that choice (A) is incorrect because the child is 18 years of age. Choices (C) and (D) are not true according to the passage.

32. **The correct answer is (B).** The passage concerns the legal requirements for eligibility for the Aid to Families with Dependent Children's category of public assistance. This program is a statewide program, and the statutes governing such a program would be found in the state's welfare laws.

33. **The correct answer is (D).** Public assistance is determined by individual states based on that state's particular residency requirements.

34. **The correct answer is (A).** A central index or a social service exchange will contain information about all families who have sought or are seeking social services and/or financial aid. Registration of all such cases and study of the cases listed by other agencies will prevent duplication of effort and will help coordinate activities concerned with the children and family.

35. **The correct answer is (D).** In most states, the action indicated in the sentence would make the person who committed such action guilty of a misdemeanor. None of the other answer choices are appropriate for the action described.

36. **The correct answer is (C).** Social welfare studies have determined that when people depend on assistance for too long they can lose their desire to become financially independent and strive to support themselves. It is important for individu-

als to be motivated and seek employment as long as they are emotionally and physically capable.

37. **The correct answer is (B).** Adoption is the process through which the natural parents' rights and obligations toward their child is terminated, and the adoptive parents assume these rights and obligations. Once a child has been adopted, the natural or birth parents are no longer responsible for their child; the obligations that they have toward their child, likewise, cease to exist. The adoptive parents become responsible for the child and all the obligations and rights between a parent and child are established between them.

38. **The correct answer is (C).** Experts in the industry have reported that advanced knowledge of the proposed adoptive parent's quality of life at home and style of living via home investigations lead to more successful adoptions.

39. **The correct answer is (D).** The social service agency in most localities is responsible for validating charities within its areas.

40. **The correct answer is (B).** A carrier is defined as "one who carries the causative agent of a disease systemically but is asymptomatic or immune to it."

41. **The correct answer is (D).** Young disadvantaged women, particularly African-American women, are being infected with HIV at younger ages and at higher rates than their male counterparts, according to a study.

42. **The correct answer is (A).** Patients managed through psychopharmacology are treated with psychiatric medication that is prescribed by a psychiatrist or medical doctor.

43. **The correct answer is (A).** Carious is defined as "affected with caries," which is another term for tooth decay.

44. **The correct answer is (D).** Many people think of it as the deliberate physical assault of a woman by an intimate partner such as a spouse, ex-spouse, boyfriend, or ex-boyfriend. But in recent years, the term "domestic violence" has begun to include other forms of violence including abuse of elders, children, and siblings. The term "domestic violence" also tends to overlook male victims and violence between same-sex partners.

45. **The correct answer is (D).** Arteriosclerosis is defined as "a chronic disease characterized by abnormal thickening or hardening of the arteries."

46. **The correct answer is (D).** Fetal alcohol syndrome (FAS) is a birth defect caused by a woman drinking heavily during pregnancy. FAS is characterized by growth retardation, abnormal facial features, and central nervous system problems. Children with FAS can have serious lifelong disabilities, including mental retardation, learning disabilities, and serious behavioral problems.

47. **The correct answer is (C).** Height and weight are easily and accurately measured. Standardized tests result in marks that measure intelligence with sufficient accuracy so that most experts utilizing such tests will come out with the same evaluation of a person's intelligence. Observances of temperamental characteristics are *not* scientifically measured, and experts frequently differ in their evaluations depending on the tests used, the expert's own biases, and the situation surrounding the observations.

48. **The correct answer is (D).** While cereals can provide many nutritional benefits, a diet composed largely of cereal will result in a deficiency of the essential food elements not found in cereal.

49. **The correct answer is (C).** Dietary studies, especially in the United States, show that many people, although affluent enough to feed themselves properly, suffer from malnutrition because they prefer to eat foods lacking in nutritional value (i.e., "junk food") rather than nutritive foods and/or diet-conscious but not diet-wise foods.

50. **The correct answer is (C).** Etiology is the science of the causes and origins of diseases.

51. **The correct answer is (D).** This is a factual question. Case workers should be aware of the functions and purposes of the American Red Cross as well as the other three answer choices in this question.

52. **The correct answer is (A).** The broad policies and patterns of social services in the United States are determined by each state legislature elected by the voters of that state. The individual state's Department of Social Services administers the social services programs and promulgates rules and regulations to implement the broad policies and may also administer/audit programs. Local, city, county, or town public welfare agencies actually carry out public welfare activities subject to review by the state authorities.

53. **The correct answer is (B).** The Legal Aid Society may also be known as the public defender in other localities.

54. **The correct answer is (D).** Compensation for work-related injuries is provided through a State Workers' Compensation Board. A state's Labor Relations Board is generally concerned with matters dealing with employer (industry)/worker (union) relations. A Department of Placement and Unemployment Insurance administers the granting of money and attempts to find employment for people who lose their jobs and are unable to find other employment on their own. A state's Industrial Commission is generally not concerned with individual workers.

55. **The correct answer is (C).** Maternal cocaine use during pregnancy is associated with adverse health effects for both the mother and the infant (e.g., intrauterine growth retardation, placental abruption, preterm delivery, congenital anomalies, and cerebral injury).

56. **The correct answer is (A).** Trichomoniasis is one of the most common sexually transmitted diseases, mainly affecting 16- to 35-year-old women. In the United States, it is estimated that 2 million women become infected each year.

57. **The correct answer is (C).** Traditionally, a widower has more trouble in raising children because he has been the breadwinner and must continue to be away from the home for a good part of the day, leaving the care of the house and children to relatives or paid helpers.

58. **The correct answer is (C).** The correct spelling of the word is *spatial*.

59. **The correct answer is (D).** Studies of chronic alcoholics show many such individuals to be concerned with and unwilling or unable to focus on problems outside of their own immediate concern.

60. **The correct answer is (B).** The other three answer choices are only temporary deterrents to continuance of alcoholism. The cure must be linked to a personality change. The alcoholic must be convinced of personal worth, the ability to resist alcohol, and the ability to resume a worthwhile place in society.

61. **The correct answer is (C).** This patient needs to be followed for ongoing counseling to help her deal with her loss and understand her reasons for wanting to go against her doctor's orders in order to

endure another high-risk pregnancy. As a result, she is causing her family, her future family, and herself great undue stress.

62. **The correct answer is (D).** The correct spelling is *psychopathic*, which refers to someone who suffers from antisocial personality disorder.

63. **The correct answer is (B).** The correct spelling is *monetary*, which means "of or relating to money or to the mechanisms by which it is supplied to and circulates in the economy."

64. **The correct answer is (A).** The correct spelling is *pecuniary,* which means "consisting of or measured in money."

65. **The correct answer is (C).** The correct spelling is *imminent*, which means "about to take place or hanging threateningly above one's head."

66. **The correct answer is (B).** The correct spelling is *pediatrics*, which refers to "a branch of medicine dealing with the development, care, and diseases of children."

67. **The correct answer is (B).** Strabismus is a disorder of vision due to the inability of one or both eyes to turn from the normal position. Therefore, both eyes cannot be directed at the same point or object at the same time (i.e., squint or cross-eye).

68. **The correct answer is (D).** Autonomy vs. shame and doubt is the second stage that occurs in toddlerhood. In this case, the child begins to explore the world, striving to be autonomous while being pulled by dependency needs.

69. **The correct answer is (A).** Recidivism is when an individual has a chronic relapse or a tendency to relapse into a criminal or antisocial behavior.

70. **The correct answer is (D).** Claustrophobia is the abnormal fear of enclosed places.

71. **The correct answer is (D).** Inhibition is the correct word for the mental process that restrains an action. Look up the meanings of the words given in the other answer choices to be sure you understand their psychological and scientific meanings.

72. **The correct answer is (A).** Ophthalmic professions are concerned with eye problems. Note: You should know the differences between optometrists, ophthalmologists, and opticians.

73. **The correct answer is (D).** At the initial interview with an applicant for public assistance, the purpose of the programs, the basic rules for eligibility, and the responsibilities in proving eligibility must be explained and understood. The ability to impart this data to a new applicant and to set the proper tone for future relations between the applicant and the agency requires skills that are best taught by experience. For further information about intake procedures, read "The Investigative Process" chapter in this book.

74. **The correct answer is (A).** Only a governmental agency may be assigned the responsibility under the law to inform the public at large of the availability of public assistance. This is ordinarily done by the local social service agency.

75. **The correct answer is (B).** The most significant and pervasive indicator of alcoholism is blackouts. Blackouts are periods where individuals lose conscious memory of their actions and behavior while in a highly intoxicated state.

76. **The correct answer is (B).** Choice (B) is correct because of the stated and implied purpose of the function. Choice (A) is incorrect because the process may be degrading to some, but it is not degrading to all its beneficiaries. This choice is too positive. If people have money, they will spend it and the businesses dependent on this spending will not suffer. Thus, the economy will stay in balance.

77. **The correct answer is (A).** The least likely symptom of depression is disturbances in orientation and thinking.

78. **The correct answer is (D).** The use of token economies has been most successful in mental hospital programs as a means to prepare the inpatients to function in society. In addition, token economies are used as a reward system.

79. **The correct answer is (C).** One who is emotionally mature knows himself or herself, including any emotional weaknesses and strengths and, to an extent, his or her reasons. The other answer choices may be true of some emotionally mature people, but these characteristics do not differentiate them from emotionally immature individuals.

80. **The correct answer is (A).** A topical summary of a case situation will give both the reader and the worker a quick, concise picture of the important elements in the case, including the problems and the steps being taken towards their solutions.

81. **The correct answer is (D).** A case worker should thoroughly examine case records concerning a family's past contacts with the agency under the circumstances described because it will avoid duplication of investigation verification. Furthermore, discussion that has been thoroughly investigated and verified can then lead to concentration on current problems and/or changes in the situations, e.g., the death of the father of a family need not be discussed if previously verified.

82. **The correct answer is (B).** The quotation states many public welfare workers do so "out of readiness to live beyond themselves, out of their liking and concern for people." Such persons are able to understand their own needs and then go beyond concentration on such personal needs to think about and have concern for others. None of the other answer choices are implied in the quotation.

83. **The correct answer is (C).** The quotation concerns the fact that society in general feels that people on public assistance are somehow set apart and are different from the rest of society. It is most important that a case worker in a public agency examines personal attitudes and prejudices toward public assistance in general and his or her own caseload in particular in order to be able to relate objectively to clients as individuals who are able to be understood and assisted.

84. **The correct answer is (C).** The case worker who follows the principle stated in the quotation will handle each client as an individual with individual problems and will try to obtain exceptions to general policy and rules if such exceptions are needed to realize the individual's social objectives.

85. **The correct answer is (A).** In this situation, Mr. Wilson displays ideal client behavior, and it can be deduced that he is a relatively secure individual with the strength of character needed to remain independent and possibly to become self-supporting again.

86. **The correct answer is (B).** The course of action indicated in choice (B) would at least serve to determine the mother's feelings toward the adoption of her child who is apparently causing her difficulties. After ascertaining the mother's feelings along these lines, appropriate action can then be taken. Money alone, as indicated in choice (A), is not likely to solve the problem. Choices (C) and (D) are also incorrect because obviously the mother is not doing what is best for the child at the present time, and the determination that the mother is pathological is not supported by the evidence given in the preamble of the question.

87. **The correct answer is (D).** Add all figures that are given in Column One—total 293.2. Subtract this figure, 293.2

answers

from 320.3 to obtain the missing number, 27.1. Then add 27.1 + 6.4 + 8.3 = 41.8. Multiply 41.8 × 1000 = 41,800 (most nearly).

88. **The correct answer is (D).** 419.8 − 320.3 = 99.5. 99.5 ÷ 320.3 = 31.1%

89. **The correct answer is (B).** This answer is a gift. Read it right from the table. The percentage change from 2003–2005 in a 6-recipient household is 6%.

90. **The correct answer is (B).** Add all of the changes in percents that are given for period 2003–2005. The total is 117.8. Obtain the average by dividing by 6. The answer is 19.63%.

91. **The correct answer is (C).** If you add all percent distributions given for December 2005, the total is 81.9%. Subtract 81.9% from 100% = 18.1%.

92. **The correct answer is (B).** Divide 8.3 by 320.3. The answer is .0259, which is closest to 2.5%.

93. **The correct answer is (C).** The passage clearly indicates that to be eligible, a person must be a citizen or legal alien residing in New York State.

94. **The correct answer is (B).** Regulations must he adhered to; however, the suggestion that Medicaid benefits might solve his problem is the only course you can take.

95. **The correct answer is (D).** The passage clearly indicates the strong possibility that this woman too might qualify for Medicaid benefits.

96. **The correct answer is (A).** The passage implies that because of the curb on the building housing projects, and the withholding of federal funds for that purpose, the elderly, among others, have a reduced opportunity to move into housing projects. The other answer choices contain statements that may or may not be true. However, they cannot by implied from the information contained in the passage.

97. **The correct answer is (B).** Refer to the last sentence of the passage.

98. **The correct answer is (D).** The passage indicates that the inability of the elderly to pay increased rents because they are on fixed incomes is alleviated in some large cities by rent-control laws.

99. **The correct answer is (C).** Refer to the second sentence of the first paragraph.

100. **The correct answer is (C).** Refer to the second sentence of the first paragraph.

ANSWER SHEET PRACTICE TEST 5

1. Ⓐ Ⓑ Ⓒ Ⓓ	21. Ⓐ Ⓑ Ⓒ Ⓓ	41. Ⓐ Ⓑ Ⓒ Ⓓ	61. Ⓐ Ⓑ Ⓒ Ⓓ	81. Ⓐ Ⓑ Ⓒ Ⓓ
2. Ⓐ Ⓑ Ⓒ Ⓓ	22. Ⓐ Ⓑ Ⓒ Ⓓ	42. Ⓐ Ⓑ Ⓒ Ⓓ	62. Ⓐ Ⓑ Ⓒ Ⓓ	82. Ⓐ Ⓑ Ⓒ Ⓓ
3. Ⓐ Ⓑ Ⓒ Ⓓ	23. Ⓐ Ⓑ Ⓒ Ⓓ	43. Ⓐ Ⓑ Ⓒ Ⓓ	63. Ⓐ Ⓑ Ⓒ Ⓓ	83. Ⓐ Ⓑ Ⓒ Ⓓ
4. Ⓐ Ⓑ Ⓒ Ⓓ	24. Ⓐ Ⓑ Ⓒ Ⓓ	44. Ⓐ Ⓑ Ⓒ Ⓓ	64. Ⓐ Ⓑ Ⓒ Ⓓ	84. Ⓐ Ⓑ Ⓒ Ⓓ
5. Ⓐ Ⓑ Ⓒ Ⓓ	25. Ⓐ Ⓑ Ⓒ Ⓓ	45. Ⓐ Ⓑ Ⓒ Ⓓ	65. Ⓐ Ⓑ Ⓒ Ⓓ	85. Ⓐ Ⓑ Ⓒ Ⓓ
6. Ⓐ Ⓑ Ⓒ Ⓓ	26. Ⓐ Ⓑ Ⓒ Ⓓ	46. Ⓐ Ⓑ Ⓒ Ⓓ	66. Ⓐ Ⓑ Ⓒ Ⓓ	86. Ⓐ Ⓑ Ⓒ Ⓓ
7. Ⓐ Ⓑ Ⓒ Ⓓ	27. Ⓐ Ⓑ Ⓒ Ⓓ	47. Ⓐ Ⓑ Ⓒ Ⓓ	67. Ⓐ Ⓑ Ⓒ Ⓓ	87. Ⓐ Ⓑ Ⓒ Ⓓ
8. Ⓐ Ⓑ Ⓒ Ⓓ	28. Ⓐ Ⓑ Ⓒ Ⓓ	48. Ⓐ Ⓑ Ⓒ Ⓓ	68. Ⓐ Ⓑ Ⓒ Ⓓ	88. Ⓐ Ⓑ Ⓒ Ⓓ
9. Ⓐ Ⓑ Ⓒ Ⓓ	29. Ⓐ Ⓑ Ⓒ Ⓓ	49. Ⓐ Ⓑ Ⓒ Ⓓ	69. Ⓐ Ⓑ Ⓒ Ⓓ	89. Ⓐ Ⓑ Ⓒ Ⓓ
10. Ⓐ Ⓑ Ⓒ Ⓓ	30. Ⓐ Ⓑ Ⓒ Ⓓ	50. Ⓐ Ⓑ Ⓒ Ⓓ	70. Ⓐ Ⓑ Ⓒ Ⓓ	90. Ⓐ Ⓑ Ⓒ Ⓓ
11. Ⓐ Ⓑ Ⓒ Ⓓ	31. Ⓐ Ⓑ Ⓒ Ⓓ	51. Ⓐ Ⓑ Ⓒ Ⓓ	71. Ⓐ Ⓑ Ⓒ Ⓓ	91. Ⓐ Ⓑ Ⓒ Ⓓ
12. Ⓐ Ⓑ Ⓒ Ⓓ	32. Ⓐ Ⓑ Ⓒ Ⓓ	52. Ⓐ Ⓑ Ⓒ Ⓓ	72. Ⓐ Ⓑ Ⓒ Ⓓ	92. Ⓐ Ⓑ Ⓒ Ⓓ
13. Ⓐ Ⓑ Ⓒ Ⓓ	33. Ⓐ Ⓑ Ⓒ Ⓓ	53. Ⓐ Ⓑ Ⓒ Ⓓ	73. Ⓐ Ⓑ Ⓒ Ⓓ	93. Ⓐ Ⓑ Ⓒ Ⓓ
14. Ⓐ Ⓑ Ⓒ Ⓓ	34. Ⓐ Ⓑ Ⓒ Ⓓ	54. Ⓐ Ⓑ Ⓒ Ⓓ	74. Ⓐ Ⓑ Ⓒ Ⓓ	94. Ⓐ Ⓑ Ⓒ Ⓓ
15. Ⓐ Ⓑ Ⓒ Ⓓ	35. Ⓐ Ⓑ Ⓒ Ⓓ	55. Ⓐ Ⓑ Ⓒ Ⓓ	75. Ⓐ Ⓑ Ⓒ Ⓓ	95. Ⓐ Ⓑ Ⓒ Ⓓ
16. Ⓐ Ⓑ Ⓒ Ⓓ	36. Ⓐ Ⓑ Ⓒ Ⓓ	56. Ⓐ Ⓑ Ⓒ Ⓓ	76. Ⓐ Ⓑ Ⓒ Ⓓ	96. Ⓐ Ⓑ Ⓒ Ⓓ
17. Ⓐ Ⓑ Ⓒ Ⓓ	37. Ⓐ Ⓑ Ⓒ Ⓓ	57. Ⓐ Ⓑ Ⓒ Ⓓ	77. Ⓐ Ⓑ Ⓒ Ⓓ	97. Ⓐ Ⓑ Ⓒ Ⓓ
18. Ⓐ Ⓑ Ⓒ Ⓓ	38. Ⓐ Ⓑ Ⓒ Ⓓ	58. Ⓐ Ⓑ Ⓒ Ⓓ	78. Ⓐ Ⓑ Ⓒ Ⓓ	98. Ⓐ Ⓑ Ⓒ Ⓓ
19. Ⓐ Ⓑ Ⓒ Ⓓ	39. Ⓐ Ⓑ Ⓒ Ⓓ	59. Ⓐ Ⓑ Ⓒ Ⓓ	79. Ⓐ Ⓑ Ⓒ Ⓓ	99. Ⓐ Ⓑ Ⓒ Ⓓ
20. Ⓐ Ⓑ Ⓒ Ⓓ	40. Ⓐ Ⓑ Ⓒ Ⓓ	60. Ⓐ Ⓑ Ⓒ Ⓓ	80. Ⓐ Ⓑ Ⓒ Ⓓ	100. Ⓐ Ⓑ Ⓒ Ⓓ

answer sheet

Practice Test 5

ELIGIBILITY SPECIALIST

100 Questions • 3 Hours, 30 Minutes

Directions: Each question has four possible answers. Choose the letter that best answers the question and mark your answer on the answer sheet.

When answering questions on this test, assume that you are an Eligibility Specialist. Your duties and responsibilities are to determine and verify initial eligibility of applicants applying for public assistance and to determine and verify continuing eligibility of clients for social services whenever necessary.

If a question describes policy that differs from that followed by the social services agency in your locality, answer the question based on the policy described in the question.

1. While meeting with an applicant to determine his eligibility, you find him to be tentative when you ask him to share some personal documents. As an eligibility specialist, you should

   (A) be firm with the applicant and assert your role. Very often, applicants do this to avoid confrontation and disclosure of personal documents that may hinder their application.

   (B) be understanding as this application process is stressful and anxiety provoking for many people. The applicant may have many reasons for his hesitancy.

   (C) report the applicant, as he is clearly putting himself under suspicion, but inform him that you will be doing so.

   (D) let the applicant get away with not disclosing this potentially significant material, as you must find the means to be compassionate with people.

2. During an interview with Mrs. Smith, you find that you do not understand her response to your question. Which of the following is the correct reaction to Mrs. Smith?

   (A) Repeat Mrs. Smith's answer, as she states it, and ask her what she means.

   (B) Ask her the question again later in your assessment so that you will be able to compare her responses.

   (C) Ask her if she understands what you are asking.

   (D) Tell Mrs. Smith that she has confused you with her answer.

3. During your interview with the Chow family, you find that there are periods of silence in between the family's answers that follow your questions. The best way to respond to these quiet moments would be to

(A) restate the question so they may understand it better.

(B) suggest answers to the family such as "yes" and "no."

(C) wait for the family to answer the question at their own comfort level.

(D) explain that this is a lengthy process and we should hurry it along.

4. As an eligibility specialist, you will come in contact with many different ethnic and religious groups. In your assessments, you should

(A) be careful not to provide services when you sense that the family is undeserving.

(B) provide extra services when you believe a family really is in need of extra services.

(C) consider providing extra services to some ethnic and religious groups that have strong political ties.

(D) provide services to individuals who are entitled to those services.

5. When you interview the Klein family, you notice that you have been rephrasing the questions repeatedly. You realize this is a problem because

(A) your grammar and accent should be correct and clear.

(B) you are not sure if you are clearly communicating the information that you want to the applicants.

(C) the applicants may follow your lead and not phrase their responses properly.

(D) you should state each question in the same manner to all applicants.

6. You are having a busy day, and as you complete an appointment your client, Mr. Martinez, stops you and asks you to fill out some forms for him. You explain that he should complete the forms. He asks you to do it for him stating that he is not sure what they want him to say and he is afraid of filling it out poorly. You should

(A) explain to him that this is a responsibility of his, and that you cannot help anyone fill out the applications.

(B) explain that he should try filling out the papers the best that he can, and that you can always help him read through it together.

(C) tell him that all of your applicants fill out their own applications.

(D) fill out the applications for him.

7. You are conducting an interview as an eligibility specialist and you are beginning to think that the applicant has been untruthful in some of the information that he has shared with you. At the point that you begin to question this client's honesty, you should

(A) tell the applicant that his statement is not truthful.

(B) confront the applicant by asking him if he is telling the truth or not.

(C) trust that he is being truthful.

(D) question the person in greater detail to gain more information about his response.

8. You are an eligibility specialist interviewing the Wright family for the first time for public assistance. Which is the best way to begin?

(A) Ask questions that the Wrights can and will answer.

(B) Ask questions that have nothing to do with the interview in order to relax the Wrights.

(C) Ask the Wrights that questions will most likely reveal hostility on their part.

(D) Ask the Wrights questions that will be answered with a brief series of statements.

9. You are meeting with Ms. Aleni for a public assistance assessment and she appears to be extremely nervous during your interview. The first thing you should do is

   (A) assure her that you will try to help her in any way so that she will be able to receive any assistance that she is entitled to.

   (B) make sure Ms. Aleni realizes that she must stop acting so nervous and cooperate so that you can finish her application.

   (C) make Ms. Aleni aware that she must back up all her statements with proof; otherwise, her application will be considered incomplete and void.

   (D) tell Ms. Aleni that as long as she is truthful, her application will definitely be approved.

10. Assume that, as an eligibility specialist, it is part of your job to prepare a monthly report for your unit head that eventually goes to the director of your welfare center. The report contains information on the number of applicants you have interviewed that have been approved for different types of public assistance and the number of applicants that have been turned down. Errors on such reports are serious because

    (A) you are expected to be able to prove how many applicants you have interviewed each month.

    (B) accurate statistics are needed for effective management of the department.

    (C) they may not be discovered before the report is transmitted to the welfare center director.

    (D) they may result in a loss of assistance to the applicants left out of the report.

11. There are many ways to obtain information in an interview. Which of the following would provide you with the least information?

    (A) The client tells his story and you gather information from his verbal responses to your questions.

    (B) The client changes his body position based on each question that you ask.

    (C) The client's facial expressions indicate that he is reacting to your questions in a different manner from what his answers might indicate.

    (D) The client speaks in varying tone. You notice that the tones of his voice change based on what questions you are asking him.

12. While interviewing Mr. Thompson and completing his public assistance application, you notice that his voice becomes elevated. In addition, he appears to become angered by your questioning and uses harsh and unrestrained language. How should you respond to him?

    (A) Lower your voice and slow your rate of speech, with the intention of having him mirror your behavior and calm down.

    (B) Respond to him in the same manner to show him that you have the upper hand.

    (C) Let him continue but speed up the pace of the interview, and do not feel badly if he does not get approved for public assistance since he is really not deserving based on his behavior.

    (D) Interrupt him and tell him you are going to close this assessment because he is becoming hostile and agitated.

13. You have been informed that no determination has been made yet regarding the eligibility of an applicant for public assistance. The decision depends on further investigation. Her situation, however, is similar to that of many other applicants whose eligibility has been approved. The applicant calls you, quite worried, and asks you whether her application has been accepted. What would be best for you to do under these circumstances?

(A) Tell her that her application is being checked and you will let her know the final result as soon as possible.

(B) Tell her that a written request addressed to your supervisor will probably get faster action for her case.

(C) Tell her not to worry since other applicants with similar backgrounds have already been accepted.

(D) Tell her since there is no definite information and you are very busy, you will call her back.

14. Suppose that you have been talking with an applicant for public assistance. You have the feeling from the latest information the applicant has provided that some of his answers to earlier questions were not true. You guess that he might have been afraid or confused earlier but that your conversation has now put him in a more comfortable frame of mind. In order to test the reliability of information received from the earlier questions, the best thing for you to do now is to ask new questions that

(A) allow the applicant to explain why he deliberately gave you false information.

(B) ask for the same information, although worded differently from the original questions.

(C) put pressure on the applicant to clear up the facts in the earlier answers.

(D) indicate to the applicant that you are aware of his deceptiveness.

15. You are an eligibility specialist interviewing Ms. Alfred, who is applying for public assistance. During the interview Ms. Alfred informs you that she does not know who the father of her child is. You should

(A) proceed to the next question.

(B) tell her that must be very difficult for her, and offer to come back another time for some counseling.

(C) discuss safe sex practices and suggest that she consider having an HIV test conducted.

(D) ask her to share her story with you, because this is significant to her application.

16. You are interviewing Mr. and Mrs. Lopez and their family. You want to know what Mr. and Mrs. Lopez's usual occupations are. You should ask

(A) "Did you ever work as a waiter?"

(B) "Do you know how to work on a computer?"

(C) "Where are you employed now?"

(D) "What type of work do you do now?"

17. Assume that as an eligibility specialist, a clerk from another office starts questioning you about one of the applicants you have just interviewed. The clerk says that she is a relative of the applicant. According to department policy, all matters discussed with applicants are to be kept confidential. Of the following, the best course of action for you to take in this situation would be to

(A) check to see whether the clerk is really a relative before you make any further decision.

(B) explain to the clerk why you cannot divulge the information.

(C) tell the clerk that you do not know the answers to her questions.

(D) tell the clerk that she can get from the applicant any information the applicant wishes to give.

18. During an eligibility assessment for public assistance, Mr. Bertolli goes off on a tangent. You should refocus him by

    (A) telling Mr. Bertolli that he needs to focus on the questions that you are asking him.

    (B) pointing out that this interview is time limited and that you must keep to a schedule to make your next appointment.

    (C) asking Mr. Bertolli a question that is related to the subject matter.

    (D) explaining to Mr. Bertolli that you would be glad to hear his stories at another time, but that you need to keep to the subject matter of today's meeting.

19. Assume that, as an eligibility specialist, you notice that your coworker has accidentally pulled the wrong form to give to her client. Of the following, the best way for you to handle this situation would be to tell

    (A) the other eligibility specialist about her error, and precisely describe the problems that will result.

    (B) the other eligibility specialist about her error in an understanding and friendly way.

    (C) the other eligibility specialist about her error in a humorous way and tell her that no real damage was done.

    (D) your supervisor that eligibility specialists need more training in the use and application of departmental forms.

20. You are meeting with Ms. Stein and she is very upset because she has just found out that she is receiving less public assistance money than she thought she was entitled to. In addition, her neighbor is receiving more than she in public assistance. You should respond to this by

    (A) telling her that life is unfair sometimes and to be glad she got any assistance at all.

    (B) telling her about other families who have had the same situation happen to them.

    (C) repeating the rules as they apply to Ms. Stein's situation.

    (D) being patient, empathetic, supportive, and understanding of Ms. Stein's situation.

21. Of the following, the most reasonable implication of the preceding question is that an eligibility specialist should, when speaking to a client, control and use his or her voice to

    (A) simulate a feeling of interest in the problems of the client.

    (B) express emotions directly and adequately.

    (C) help produce in the client a sense of comfort and security.

    (D) reflect his or her own true personality.

22. Mr. and Mrs. Stone appear to be very hostile during an interview. In preparing your report, how would you best capture this?

    (A) Report specific examples of their remarks, with a description of their actions and behavior.

    (B) Share the significant material that was revealed as a result of Mr. Stone's hostility.

    (C) Make a recommendation for their application to be rejected as a result of their behavior.

    (D) Provide a detailed explanation of what caused their hostility.

23. When making recommendations in a report to your supervisor, you should do all of the following EXCEPT

(A) leave the recommendations for your supervisor to complete after reading your evidence.

(B) present your recommendations in a logical manner in your report.

(C) if warranted, offer alternative courses of action for your recommendations.

(D) provide recommendations along with supporting evidence.

24. It is often necessary that the writer of a report present facts and sufficient arguments to gain acceptance of the points, conclusions, or recommendations set forth in the report. Of the following, the least advisable step to take in organizing a report, when such argumentation is the important factor, is a(n)

(A) elaborate expression of personal belief.

(B) businesslike discussion of the problem as a whole.

(C) orderly arrangement of convincing data.

(D) reasonable explanation of the primary issues.

QUESTIONS 25–33 ARE BASED ON THE FOLLOWING PASSAGE.

The establishment of a procedure whereby the client's rent is paid directly by the Social Service Agency has been suggested recently by many people in the social service field. It is believed that such a procedure would be advantageous to both the agency and client. Under the current system, clients often complain that their rent allowances are not for the correct amount. Agencies, in turn, have had to cope with irate landlords who complain that they are not receiving rent checks until much later than their due date.

The proposed new system would involve direct payment of the client's rent by the agency to the landlord. Clients would not receive a monthly rent allowance. Under one possible implementation of such a system, special rent payment offices would be set up in each of the five boroughs in Midvale City, and staffed by Social Service clerical personnel. Each office would handle all work involved in sending out monthly rent payments. Each client would receive monthly notification from the Social Service Agency that the rent has been paid. A rent office would be established for every three Social Service Centers in each borough. Only in cases where the rent exceeds $350 per month would payment be made and records kept by the Social Service Center rather than a special rent office. However, clients would continue to make all direct contacts through the Social Service Center.

Files in the rent offices would be organized on the basis of client rental. All cases involving monthly rents up to, but not exceeding, $150 would be placed in salmon-colored folders. Cases with rents ranging from $151 to $250 would be placed in buff folders, and those with rents exceeding from $251 but less than $350 would be filed in blue folders. If a client's rent changes, he or she would be required to notify the center as soon as possible so that this information could be updated in the folder and the color of the folder changed, if necessary. Included in the information needed, in addition to the amount of rent, are the size of the apartment, the type of heat, and the number of flights of stairs to climb if there is no elevator.

Discussion of whether the same information should be required of clients residing in city housing projects was resolved with the decision that the identical system of filing and updating of files should apply to such project tenants. The basic problem that could arise from the institution of such a program is that clients would resent being unable to pay their own rent. However, it is likely that such resentment would be only a temporary reaction to change and would disappear after the new system became standard procedure. It has been suggested that this program first be experimented with on a small scale to determine what problems may arise and how the program can be best implemented.

25. According to the passage, there are a number of complaints about the current system of rent payments. Which of the following is a complaint expressed in the passage?

(A) Landlords complain that clients sometimes pay the wrong amount for their rent.

(B) Landlords complain that clients sometimes do not pay their rent on time.

(C) Clients say that the Social Service Agency sometimes does not mail the rent out on time.

(D) Landlords say that they sometimes fail to receive a check for the rent.

26. Assume that there are fifteen Social Service Centers in one borough of Midvale City. According to the passage, what is the number of rent offices that should be established in that borough under the new system?

(A) 1

(B) 3

(C) 5

(D) 15

27. According to the passage, a client under the new system would receive

(A) a rent receipt from the landlord indicating that Social Services has paid the rent.

(B) nothing, since the rent has been paid by Social Services.

(C) verification from the landlord that the rent was paid.

(D) notices of rent payment from the Social Service Agency.

28. According to the passage, a case record involving a client whose rent has changed from $155 to $270 per month should be changed from a

(A) blue folder to a salmon-colored folder.

(B) buff folder to a blue folder.

(C) salmon-colored folder to a blue folder.

(D) yellow folder to a buff folder.

29. According to the passage, if a client's rent is lowered because of violations in his or her building, he or she would be required to notify the

(A) building department.

(B) landlord.

(C) rent payment office.

(D) Social Service Center.

30. Which of the following types of information about a rented apartment is NOT mentioned in the passage as being necessary to include in the client's folder?

(A) The floor number, if in an apartment house with an elevator

(B) The rent, if in a city housing project apartment

(C) The size of the apartment, if in a two-family house

(D) The type of heat, if in a city housing project apartment

31. Assume that the rent payment proposal discussed in the passage is approved and ready for implementation in Midvale City. Which of the following actions is most in accordance with the proposal described in the passage?

   (A) Change to the new system completely and quickly to avoid the confusion of having clients under both systems.

   (B) Establish rent payment offices in all of the existing Social Service Centers.

   (C) Establish one small rent payment office in one of the boroughs for about six months.

   (D) Set up an office in each borough and discontinue issuing rent allowances.

32. According to the passage, it can be inferred that the most important drawback of the new system would be that once a program is started, clients might feel

   (A) as if they have less independence than they had before.

   (B) unable to cope with problems that mature people should be able to handle.

   (C) too far removed from Social Service personnel to successfully adapt to the new requirements.

   (D) too independent to work with the system.

33. The passage suggests that the proposed rent program be started as a pilot program rather than be instituted immediately throughout Midvale City. Which of the following is stated in the passage as the most direct reason for a pilot program?

   (A) Any change made would be only on a temporary basis.

   (B) Difficulties should be determined from small-scale implementation.

   (C) Implementation on a wide scale is extremely difficult.

   (D) Many clients might resent the new systems.

34. A client meets with you for an assessment and tells you her name. When the assessment is complete, you realize that you do not how to spell her name. You should

   (A) ask her to spell her name so that her information is accurate.

   (B) ask her to spell her name because you are showing her that you will be working on her case and obtaining the information that she needs.

   (C) not ask her to spell her name because you will offend her.

   (D) not ask her to spell her name because she will think that you were not giving her application serious consideration.

35. As an eligibility specialist, you must prepare reports. These reports need to be revised several times before final preparation and distribution. In order to prepare your report, which of the following is the best way for you to address all the significant points?

   (A) Ask a subordinate to assess the viability of the report.

   (B) Have a coworker evaluate your report and provide you with feedback.

   (C) Review the bibliography in your report to see that it was truly comprehensive.

   (D) Use a checklist to measure the material in your report for its content.

36. Visual aids in a report may be placed either in the text material or in an appendix. Deciding where to put a chart, table, or any such aid should depend on the

   (A) title of the report.

   (B) purpose of the visual aid.

   (C) title of the visual aid.

   (D) length of the report.

37. In which of the following situations is an oral report preferable to a written report?

(A) When a recommendation is being made for a future plan of action

(B) When a department head requests immediate information

(C) When a long-standing policy change is made

(D) When an analysis of complicated statistical data is involved

38. When an applicant is approved for public assistance, the eligibility specialist must fill out standard forms with certain information. The greatest advantage of using standard forms rather than having the eligibility specialist write the report as he or she sees fit is that

(A) the report can be acted on quickly.

(B) the report can be written without directions from a supervisor.

(C) coded information is less likely to be left out of the report.

(D) information that is written up this way is more likely to be verified.

39. In some types of reports, visual aids add interest, meanings, and support. They also provide an essential means of effectively communicating the message of the report. Of the following, the selection of the suitable visual aids to use with a report is least dependent on the

(A) nature and scope of the report.

(B) way in which the aid is to be used.

(C) aids used in other reports.

(D) prospective readers of the report.

40. The eligibility specialist was quick to recognize the *imparity* in the treatment that was offered to his client. The word *imparity* means most nearly

(A) prejudice.

(B) inequality.

(C) impartiality.

(D) weakness.

41. The client's *devious* behavior made it difficult for the eligibility specialist to gather substantial information for his report. In this sentence, *devious* means most nearly

(A) crafty.

(B) prudent.

(C) logical.

(D) offensive.

42. During the assessment, the client appeared agreeable; however, she answered the questions with *trepidation*. In this sentence, *trepidation* most nearly means

(A) confusion.

(B) violence.

(C) apprehension.

(D) confidence.

43. The *vigilant* supervisor was always aware of her employees and their hard work. In this sentence, *vigilant* most nearly means

(A) religious.

(B) fervent.

(C) watchful.

(D) loving.

44. The case worker's *egocentric* behavior affected the quality of her client assessments. In this sentence, *egocentric* most nearly means

(A) confident.

(B) selfish.

(C) altruistic.

(D) connected.

45. The client's *antagonistic* style was portrayed in the responses that he gave to the case worker. In this sentence, *antagonistic* most nearly means

(A) affable.

(B) willful.

(C) forthcoming.

(D) oppositional.

46. When the client was *dispossessed,* she was unable to believe that anyone could help her. In this sentence, *dispossessed* most nearly means

(A) evicted.

(B) insulted.

(C) depressed.

(D) moody.

47. Employees may become bored unless they are assigned *diverse* duties. The word *diverse* means most nearly

(A) interesting.

(B) different.

(C) challenging.

(D) enjoyable.

48. During the probation period, the worker proved to be *inept.* The word *inept* means most nearly

(A) incompetent.

(B) insubordinate.

(C) satisfactory.

(D) uncooperative.

49. The *putative* father was not living with the family. The word *putative* means most nearly

(A) reputed.

(B) unemployed.

(C) concerned.

(D) indifferent.

QUESTIONS 50–53 ARE BASED ON THE FOLLOWING PASSAGE.

Some authorities have questioned whether the term "culture of poverty" should be used since "culture" means a design for living that is passed down from generation to generation. The culture of poverty is, however, a very useful concept if it is used with care, with recognition that poverty is a subculture, and with avoidance of the "cookie-cutter" approach. With regard to the individual, the cookie-cutter view assumes that all individuals in a culture turn out exactly alike. It overlooks the fact that, at least in our urban society, every individual is a member of more than one subculture; and which subculture most strongly influences his or her response in a given situation depends on the interaction of many factors, including his or her individual makeup and history, the specifics of the various subcultures to which he or she belongs, and the specifics of the given situation. It is always important to avoid the cookie-cutter view of culture with regard to the individual and to the culture or subculture involved.

With regard to the culture as a whole, the cookie-cutter concept again assumes homogeneity and consistency. It excludes the fact that within any one culture or subculture there are conflicts and contradictions, and that at any given moment an individual may have to choose, consciously or unconsciously, among conflicting values or patterns. Also, most individuals, in varying degrees, have a dual set of values—those by which they live and those they cherish as best. This point has been made and documented repeatedly about the culture of poverty.

50. The "cookie-cutter" approach assumes that

(A) members of the same culture are all alike.

(B) culture stays the same from generation to generation.

(C) the teen culture should not be applied to groups who are poor.

(D) there are value conflicts within most cultures.

51. According to the passage, every person in urban society

    (A) is involved in the conflicts of urban culture.

    (B) recognizes that poverty is a subculture.

    (C) lives by those values to which he or she is exposed.

    (D) belongs to more than one subculture.

52. The passage emphasizes that a culture is likely to contain within it

    (A) one dominant set of values.

    (B) a number of contradictions.

    (C) one subculture to which everyone belongs.

    (D) members who are exactly alike.

53. According to the passage, individuals are sometimes forced to choose

    (A) among cultures.

    (B) among subcultures.

    (C) among different sets of values.

    (D) between a new culture and an old culture.

QUESTIONS 54–57 ARE BASED ON THE FOLLOWING PASSAGE.

There are approximately 33 million poor people in the Unites States; 14.3 million of them are children, 5.3 million are old people, and the remainder is in other demographic categories. All together, 6.5 million families live in poverty because the heads of the households cannot work; they are either too old, too sick, or too severely handicapped; or they are widowed or deserted mothers of young children. There are the working poor—the low-paid workers and the workers in seasonal industries. There are the underemployed—those who would like full-time jobs but cannot find them, those who would like year-round work but lack the opportunity, and those who are employed below their level of training. There are the nonworking poor—the older men and women with small retirement incomes and those with no income, the disabled, the physically and mentally handicapped, and the chronically ill.

54. According to the passage, approximately what percentage of the poor people in the United States are children?

    (A) 33%

    (B) 16%

    (C) 20%

    (D) 44%

55. According to the passage, people who work in seasonal industries are likely to be classified as

    (A) working poor.

    (B) underemployed.

    (C) nonworking poor.

    (D) low-paid workers.

56. According to the passage, the category of nonworking poor includes people who

    (A) receive unemployment insurance.

    (B) cannot find full-time work.

    (C) are disabled or mentally handicapped.

    (D) are single mothers.

57. It can be inferred from the passage that among the underemployed are those who

(A) can find only part-time work.

(B) are looking for their first job.

(C) are inadequately trained.

(D) depend on insufficient retirement incomes.

QUESTIONS 58–67 ARE BASED ON THE FOLLOWING CHARTS.

CHILD CARE SERVICES 2000–2004

CHILDREN IN FOSTER HOMES AND VOLUNTARY INSTITUTIONS, BY TYPE OF CARE, IN BERGERSVILLE AND UPSTATE*

Foster Family Homes

Year End	Boarding Homes	Adoptive or Free	Wage, Work, or Self-Supporting	Total in Foster Homes	Total in Voluntary Institutions	Total in Other	Total Number of Children
Bergersville							
2000	12,389	1,773	33	14,195	7,187	1,128	22,510
2001	13,271	1,953	42	15,266	7,277	1,237	23,730
2002	14,012	2,134	32	16,178	7,087	1,372	24,637
2003	14,558	2,137	29	16,742	6,717	1,437	24,778
2004	14,759	2,241	37	17,037	6,777	1,455	25,264
Upstate							
2000	14,801	2,902	90	17,793	3,012	241	21,046
2001	15,227	2,943	175	18,345	3,067	291	21,703
2002	16,042	3,261	64	19,367	2,940	273	22,580
2003	16,166	3,445	60	19,671	2,986	362	23,121
2004	16,357	3,606	55	20,018	3,024	485	23,527

* "Upstate" is defined as all of the state, excluding Bergersville.

NUMBER OF CHILDREN BY AGE UNDER FOSTER CARE FAMILY IN BERGERSVILLE 2004

Children's Ages

Borough	One Year or Younger	Two Years	Three Years	Four Years	Over Four Years	Total All Ages
Manto	1,054	1,170	1,060	1,325	445	5,070
Johnston	842	1,196	1,156	1,220	484	4,882
Kiley	707	935	470	970	361	?
Appleton	460	555	305	793	305	2,418
Richardson	274	505	160	173	112	1,224
Total All Boroughs	3,337	4,361	3,151	4,481	?	17,037

58. According to the table of Child Care Services, 2000–2004, the number of children in Bergersville boarding homes was at least twice the number of children in Bergersville voluntary institutions in

    (A) only one of the five years.

    (B) only two of the five years.

    (C) only three of the five years.

    (D) all of the five years.

59. If the number of children cared for in voluntary institutions in the entire state increased from 2004–2005 by exactly the same number as from 2003–2004, then what would be the 2005 year-end total of children in voluntary institutions in the state?

    (A) 3,062

    (B) 6,837

    (C) 7,494

    (D) 9,899

60. If the total number of children under Child Care Services in Bergersville in 2000 was 25 percent more than in 1999, then what was most nearly the 1995 Bergersville total?

    (A) 11,356

    (B) 11,647

    (C) 16,883

    (D) 18,008

61. From 2000–2004, what is most nearly the average number per year of children in Child Care Services classified as "other"?

    (A) 330

    (B) 728

    (C) 1,326

    (D) 1,650

62. Of all the children under foster family care in Johnston in 2004, what is most nearly the percentage that was 1 year of age or younger?

    (A) 16%

    (B) 17%

    (C) 18%

    (D) 19%

63. Suppose that upstate, the "wage, work, or self-supporting" type of foster family care is given only to children between the ages of 14 and 18, and that, of the children in "adoptive or free home" foster care in each of the five years listed, only 1 percent each year are between the ages of 14 and 18. The total number of 14- to 18-year-olds under foster family care upstate exceeded 95 in

    (A) each of the five years.

    (B) four of the five years.

    (C) three of the five years.

    (D) two of the five years.

64. What is most nearly the average number of 2-year-olds under foster family care in each of Bergersville's five boroughs in 2004?

    (A) 872

    (B) 874

    (C) 875

    (D) 882

65. What is the difference between the total number of children of all ages under foster family care in Kiley in 2004, and the total number under foster care in Richardson that same year?

    (A) 1,224

    (B) 2,219

    (C) 3,443

    (D) 4,667

66. Suppose that by the end of 2005, the number of children 1 year or younger under foster family care in Appleton was twice the 2004 total, while the number of 2-year-olds was four fifths the 2004 total. In 2005, what was the total of children 2 years or younger under foster family care in Appleton?

(A) 2,418

(B) 1,624

(C) 1,364

(D) 1,015

67. What was the total number of children over 4 years of age under foster care in Bergersville in 2004?

(A) 1,607

(B) 1,697

(C) 1,707

(D) 1,797

68. At the start of a year, a family was receiving a public assistance grant of $191 twice a month, on the first and fifteenth of each month. On March 1, their rent allowance was decreased from $75 to $71 a month, since they had moved to a smaller apartment. On August 1 their semimonthly food allowance, which had been $40.20, was raised by 10 percent. In that year, what was the total amount of money disbursed to this family?

(A) $2,272.10

(B) $3,290.70

(C) $4,544.20

(D) $4,584.20

69. It is discovered that a client has received double public assistance for two months by having been enrolled at two service centers of the Department of Social Services. The client should have received $84 twice a month instead of the double amount. He now agrees to repay the money by equal deductions from his public assistance check over a period of twelve months. What will the amount of his next check be?

(A) $56

(B) $70

(C) $77

(D) $80

70. Suppose a study is being made of the composition of 3,550 families receiving public assistance. Of the first 1,050 families reviewed, 18 percent had 4 or more children. If, in the remaining number of families, the percentage with 4 or more children is half as high as the percentage in the group already reviewed, then what (most nearly) is the percentage of families with 4 or more children in the entire group of families?

(A) 12

(B) 14

(C) 16

(D) 27

71. Suppose that food prices have risen 13 percent, and an increase of the same amount has been granted in the food allotment given to people receiving public assistance. If a family has been receiving $406 a month, of which 35 percent is allotted for food, then what will the total amount of public assistance this family receives per month be changed to?

(A) $402.71

(B) $420.03

(C) $424.43

(D) $449.71

72. Assume that the food allowance is to be raised 5 percent in August but will be retroactive for four months to April. The retroactive allowance is to be divided into equal sections and added to the public assistance checks for August, September, October, November, and December. A family that has been receiving $420 monthly, 40 percent of which was allotted for food, will receive what size check in August?

(A) $426.72

(B) $428.40

(C) $430.50

(D) $435.12

73. A client who receives $105 public assistance twice a month inherits fourteen shares of stock worth $90 each. The client is required to sell the stock and spend his inheritance before receiving more monetary assistance. Using his public assistance allowance as a guide, how many months are his new assets expected to last?

(A) 6

(B) 7

(C) 8

(D) 12

74. The Department of Social Services has sixteen service centers in Yodersville. These centers may be divided into those that are downtown (south of Central Street) and those that are uptown. Two of the centers are special service centers and are downtown, while the remainder of the centers are general service centers. There is a total of seven service centers downtown. What is the percentage of the general service centers that are uptown (most nearly)?

(A) 56%

(B) 64%

(C) 69%

(D) 79%

75. On January 1, a family was receiving supplementary monthly public assistance of $56 for food, $48 for rent, and $28 for other necessities. In the spring, their rent rose by 10 percent, and their rent allotment was adjusted accordingly. In the summer, due to the death of a family member, their allotments for food and other necessities were reduced by one seventh. For how much should their monthly allowance check be in the fall?

(A) $124.80

(B) $128.80

(C) $132.80

(D) $136.80

76. Twice a month, a certain family receives a $170 general allowance for rent, food, and clothing expenses. In addition, the family receives a specific supplementary allotment for utilities of $192 a year, which is added to their semimonthly check. If the general allowance alone is reduced by 5 percent, what will be the total amount of their next semimonthly check?

(A) $161.50

(B) $169.50

(C) $170.00

(D) $177.50

77. If each eligibility specialist in a certain unit sees an average of 9 clients in a 7-hour day and there are 15 eligibility specialists in the unit, approximately how many clients will be seen in a 35-hour week?

(A) 315

(B) 405

(C) 675

(D) 945

78. Under public assistance programs in many communities, allocations for payment of a client's rent and security deposits are given in check form directly to the welfare recipient, and not to the landlord. This practice is used mainly as an effort to

(A) increase the client's responsibility for his or her own affairs.

(B) curb the rent overcharges made by most landlords.

(C) control the number of welfare recipients housed in public housing projects.

(D) limit the number of checks issued to each welfare family.

79. The crusade against environmental hazards in the United States is concentrated in urban areas mostly on the problems of

(A) air pollution, sewage treatment, and noise.

(B) garbage collection.

(C) automobile exhaust fumes and street cleanliness.

(D) recycling, reconstitution, and open space.

QUESTIONS 80–83 ARE BASED ON THE FOLLOWING PASSAGE.

City social work agencies and the police have been meeting at City Hall to coordinate efforts to defuse the tensions among teenage groups that they fear could turn into warfare once summer vacations begin. Police intelligence units, with the help of the district attorney's office, are gathering information to identify gangs and their territories. A list of 3,000 gang members has already been assembled, and 110 gangs have been identified. Social workers from various agencies like the Department of Social Services, Neighborhood Youth Corps, and the Youth Board, are out every day developing liaisons with groups of juveniles through meetings at schools and recreation centers. Many street workers spend their days seeking to ease the intergang hostility, tracing potentially incendiary rumors, and trying to channel willing gang members into participation in established summer programs. The City's Youth Services Agency plans to spend a million dollars for special summer programs in ten main city areas where gang activity is most firmly entrenched. Five of the "gang neighborhoods" are clustered in an area forming most of the southeastern part of the borough of the Bronx, and it is here that most of the 110 identified gangs have formed. Special Youth Services programs will also be directed toward the Rockaway section of the borough of Queens, Chinatown and Washington Heights in the borough of Manhattan, and two neighborhoods in the northern part of the borough of Staten Island noted for heavy motorcycle gang activity. Some of these programs will emphasize sports and recreation, others will emphasize vocational guidance or neighborhood improvement, but each program will be aimed at benefiting all youngsters in the area. Although none of the money will be spent specifically on gang members, the Youth Services Agency is consulting gang leaders, along with other teenagers, on the projects they would like developed in their area.

80. The passage states that one of the steps taken by street workers in trying to defuse the tensions among teenage gangs is

(A) conducting summer school sessions that will benefit all neighborhood youth.

(B) monitoring neighborhood sports competitions between rival gangs.

(C) developing liaisons with community school boards and parent associations.

(D) tracing rumors that could intensify intergang hostilities.

81. Based on the information given in this passage on gangs and gang members, it is correct to state that

    (A) there are no teenage gangs located in the borough of Brooklyn.

    (B) most of the gangs identified by the police are concentrated in one borough.

    (C) there is a total of 110 gangs.

    (D) only a small percentage of gangs in New York City is in the borough of Queens.

82. According to the passage, one important aspect of the program is that

    (A) youth gang leaders and other teenagers are involved in the planning.

    (B) money will be given directly to gang members for use on their projects.

    (C) only gang members will be allowed to participate in the programs.

    (D) the parents of gang members will act as youth leaders.

83. Various city agencies are cooperating in the attempt to keep the city's youth "cool" during the summer school vacation period. The passage does not specifically indicate participation in this project by the city's

    (A) police department.

    (B) district attorney's office.

    (C) board of education.

    (D) department of social services.

QUESTIONS 84–86 ARE BASED ON THE FOLLOWING PASSAGE.

It is important that interviewers understand to some degree the manner in which stereotyped thinking operates. Stereotypes are commonly held, but predominantly false, preconceptions about the appearance and traits of individuals of different racial, religious, ethnic, and subcultural groups. Distinct traits, physical and mental, are associated with each group, and membership in a particular group is enough, in the mind of a person holding the stereotype, to assure that these traits will be perceived in individuals who are members of that group. Conversely, possession of the particular stereotyped trait by an individual usually indicates to the holder of the stereotype that the individual is a group member. Linked to the formation of stereotypes is the fact that mental traits, either positive or negative, such as honesty, laziness, avarice, and other characteristics, are associated with particular stereotypes. Either kind of stereotype, if held by an interviewer, can seriously damage the results of an interview. In general, stereotypes can be particularly dangerous when they are part of the belief patterns of administrators, interviewers, and supervisors who are in a position to affect the lives of others and to stimulate or retard the development of human potential. The holding of a stereotype by an interviewer, for example, diverts his or her attention from significant essential facts and information upon which really valid assessments may be made. Unfortunately, it is the rare interviewer who is completely conscious of the real basis upon which he or she is making his or her evaluation of the people being interviewed. The specific reasons given by an interviewer for a negative evaluation, even though apparently logical and based upon what, in the mind of the interviewer, are very good reasons, may not be the truly motivating factors. This is why the careful selection and training of interviewers is such an important responsibility of an agency that is attempting to help a great diversity of human beings.

84. Of the following, the best title for the passage is
    (A) Positive and Negative Effects of Stereotyped Thinking.
    (B) The Relationship of Stereotypes to Interviewing.
    (C) An Agency's Responsibility in Interviewing.
    (D) The Impact of Stereotyped Thinking on Professional Functions.

85. According to the passage, most interviewers
    (A) compensate for stereotyped beliefs to avoid negatively affecting the results of their interviews.
    (B) are influenced by stereotypes they hold, but put greater stress on factual information developed during the interview.
    (C) are seldom aware of their real motives when evaluating interviewees.
    (D) give logical and good reasons for negative evaluations of interviewees.

86. According to the passage, which of the following is NOT a characteristic of stereotypes?
    (A) Stereotypes influence estimates of personality traits of people.
    (B) Positive stereotypes can damage the results of an interview.
    (C) Physical traits associated with stereotypes seldom exist.
    (D) Stereotypes sometimes are a basis upon which valid personality assessments can be made.

QUESTIONS 87–91 ARE BASED ON THE FOLLOWING PASSAGE.

The quality of the voice of eligibility specialists is an important factor in conveying to clients and coworkers their attitudes and, to some degree, their character. The human voice, when not consciously disguised, may reflect a person's mood, temper, and personality. It has been shown in several experiments that certain character traits can be assessed with accuracy through listening to the voice of an unknown person who cannot be seen.

Since one of the objectives of eligibility specialists is to put clients at ease and to present an encouraging and comfortable atmosphere, a harsh, shrill, or loud voice could have a negative effect. A client who displays emotions of anger or resentment would probably be provoked even further by a caustic tone. In a face-to-face situation, an unpleasant voice may be compensated for to some degree by a concerned and kind facial expression. However, when one speaks on the telephone, the listener cannot see the expression on the speaker's face. Eligibility specialists who wish to represent themselves effectively to clients should try to eliminate as many faults as possible in striving to develop desirable voice qualities.

87. If eligibility specialists use sarcastic tones while interviewing a resentful client, the client, according to the passage, would most likely
    (A) avoid the face-to-face situation.
    (B) be ashamed of his or her behavior.
    (C) become more resentful.
    (D) be provoked to violence.

88. According to the passage, experiments comparing voice and character traits have demonstrated that

   (A) prospects for improving an unpleasant voice through training are better than chance.

   (B) the voice can be altered to project many different psychological characteristics.

   (C) the quality of the human voice reveals more about the speaker than his or her words.

   (D) the speaker's voice tells the listener something about the speaker's personality.

89. Which of the following, according to the passage, is a person's voice most likely to reveal?

   (A) His or her prejudices

   (B) His or her intelligence

   (C) His or her social awareness

   (D) His or her temperament

90. It may be most reasonably concluded from the passage that an interested and sympathetic expression on the face of an eligibility specialist

   (A) may induce a client to feel certain that he or she will receive welfare benefits.

   (B) will eliminate the need for pleasant vocal qualities in the interviewer.

   (C) may help to make up for an unpleasant voice in the interviewer.

   (D) is desirable as the interviewer speaks on the telephone to a client.

91. It may be concluded from the passage that the particular reason for an eligibility specialist to pay special attention to modulating his or her voice when talking on the phone to a client is that during a telephone conversation,

   (A) there is a necessity to compensate for the way in which a telephone distorts the voice.

   (B) the voice of the eligibility specialist is a reflection of his or her mood and character.

   (C) the client can react only on the basis of the voice and words he or she hears.

   (D) the client may have difficulty getting a clear understanding over the telephone.

92. An applicant owns a three-family frame house, the income from which is barely adequate to meet taxes, interest, and mortgage amortization. He has no funds for other maintenance. He is willing to permit your bureau to place a lien on his property for aid. You would recommend that the agency

   (A) deny aid on the assumption that property owners are not entitled to assistance.

   (B) grant aid and take lien on the property as agreed upon.

   (C) force the applicant to sell the property regardless of present market value and use the small balance left after all payments for his own needs.

   (D) take over management of the property to get better returns.

93. A client refuses to permit insurance adjustment, insisting he has kept his insurance because ethnic custom demands an elaborate funeral. The premium of the policy is being paid by a married daughter, who is just able to manage herself. You would

    (A) cut off aid, after persuasion has failed and the client still refuses to adjust the policy.

    (B) continue aid on basis of need.

    (C) persuade the daughter to drop the policy.

    (D) induce the insurance company to surrender cash value to the city to reimburse for aid granted.

94. An applicant for aid is the recipient of a pension from the firm for which he has worked for thirty years. This is inadequate for the needs of his family. You should

    (A) refuse aid because of income from this source.

    (B) grant supplemental aid.

    (C) induce the firm to increase the applicant's pension.

    (D) insist upon the applicant's securing work.

95. A wife complains that her husband spends most of his assistance check on alcohol, denying the family their needs. You would recommend that the agency

    (A) discontinue aid because of the client's wastefulness.

    (B) arrest the husband for drunkenness.

    (C) arrange for the check to be given to the wife.

    (D) get the saloon keeper to refuse to sell him a drink.

96. A family consisting of a wife and 3 young children has been receiving aid for three years because of the husband's desertion. Persistent efforts have revealed no trace of the husband. You would

    (A) continue assistance on the basis of continuing need.

    (B) force the wife to obtain a divorce on the grounds of desertion.

    (C) place the children in a foster home and force the wife to support herself.

    (D) make application for Aid to Dependent Children.

97. You find that an applicant for aid has a bank account. He explains that this is not his own money, but that the account has been placed in his name for safekeeping for an old friend who has returned to his native country for a temporary visit. He cannot give the exact whereabouts of his friend. You would

    (A) accept this explanation and grant assistance.

    (B) deny aid on the assumption that the story is implausible.

    (C) insist that he close the account and utilize the money.

    (D) interview neighbors to find out whether the applicant has such an old friend.

98. A complaint is received that a client and his wife neglect their 2 young children and beat them cruelly. Investigation bears out the truth of these statements. You should

    (A) refer the matter to the agency responsible for the prevention of cruelty to children.

    (B) arrest the father and mother.

    (C) discontinue aid immediately.

    (D) continue aid on promise of the parents to reform.

99. A formerly well-to-do family applies for aid. Their son is in his last year at law school, his tuition for the year having been paid. The last of their savings, a small amount, has been set aside for the son's maintenance at school for the balance of the year, rendering the parents immediately destitute. You would recommend

(A) the parents be required to use the money for their own needs.

(B) insisting at once upon the son's leaving school and going to work.

(C) giving aid on the assumption that when the son completes his education, he will be equipped to maintain himself and parents.

(D) denying any aid on the basis that parents who are able to send their son to law school have other resources to draw upon.

100. When a landlord complains to you that a certain aid recipient has consistently neglected to pay his rent, present case work practice would indicate that you should first

(A) arrange to discontinue aid payments until you can verify the reason for the nonpayment of rent.

(B) tell the client to pay his rent within a certain period of time if he does not want his aid discontinued.

(C) tell the client about the landlord's complaint and inform him that the Department of Social Services assumes that rent is an obligation the client is expected to settle directly with his landlord.

(D) arrange for the landlord to collect his rent at the center in the future.

ANSWER KEY AND EXPLANATIONS

1. B	21. C	41. A	61. D	81. B
2. A	22. B	42. C	62. B	82. A
3. C	23. A	43. C	63. C	83. C
4. D	24. A	44. B	64. A	84. B
5. B	25. B	45. D	65. B	85. C
6. B	26. C	46. A	66. C	86. D
7. D	27. D	47. B	67. C	87. C
8. A	28. B	48. A	68. D	88. D
9. A	29. D	49. A	69. B	89. D
10. B	30. A	50. A	70. A	90. C
11. B	31. C	51. D	71. C	91. C
12. A	32. A	52. B	72. D	92. B
13. A	33. B	53. C	73. A	93. A
14. B	34. A	54. D	74. B	94. B
15. A	35. D	55. A	75. A	95. C
16. D	36. B	56. C	76. B	96. D
17. B	37. B	57. A	77. C	97. B
18. C	38. C	58. B	78. A	98. A
19. B	39. C	59. D	79. A	99. C
20. D	40. B	60. D	80. D	100. C

1. **The correct answer is (B).** In the role of an eligibility specialist you must be understanding, as the application process is stressful and anxiety provoking for many people. Applicants may have many reasons for their hesitancy. Many people are reluctant to share private information. You must explain the importance of this data and its role in making a case for their eligibility.

2. **The correct answer is (A).** By restating Mrs. Smith's response to your question as she states it and asking her what she means, you allow her to hear what she has just said. Communication problems occur often, and it is important to clarify any misunderstandings.

3. **The correct answer is (C).** By waiting for the Chow family, you demonstrate patience. It is important to wait for the family to answer the question at their own comfort level to elicit from them a well thought-out response. In addition, an eligibility specialist wants to retrieve the best answer from the applicant. In rushing a family, you could pressure them into a quick response that was not well thought out.

4. **The correct answer is (D).** As an eligibility specialist, you will come in contact with may different ethnic and religious groups. In your assessments, you should provide services to individuals who are entitled to those services. All applicants and clients must be treated without regard to sex, ethnicity, or religion.

5. **The correct answer is (B).** It is a problem to rephrase the questions to the family because you will not be sure that you are clearly communicating the information that you want to the applicant. A basic rule of being an eligibility specialist is to communicate the information that you are looking for in a clear manner to the applicant.

6. **The correct answer is (B).** As an eligibility specialist, you have a responsibility in maintaining and establishing if someone qualifies for services. By having Mr. Martinez try to fill out the papers the best that he can you are having him fulfill his responsibility.

7. **The correct answer is (D).** You should not assume that the applicant is intentionally lying. By asking meaningful questions, you will be able to learn more information about the response given.

8. **The correct answer is (A).** As an eligibility specialist interviewing the Wright family for public assistance, you should begin your initial interview by asking questions that they will be willing and able to answer. In this way, you develop a rapport that will help you in the later portion of the interview.

9. **The correct answer is (A).** Because Ms. Aleni is nervous during your interview, you should assure her that you will try to help her in any way so that she will be able to receive any assistance that she is entitled to. It is essential that you have accurate answers. Never assure a client that she will be approved for public assistance. You cannot guarantee this.

10. **The correct answer is (B).** Effective management requires that the agency have current, *accurate*, and easily available information on the number of applications processed, approved, and disapproved so that fiscal, budgetary, and personnel adjustments can be made expeditiously. Errors on these reports will affect correct adjustments and, thus, hinder effective management.

11. **The correct answer is (B).** People provide information in many ways. You can receive information based on what people say, the tones that they use, and their facial expressions. However, body language is not easily interpreted by the untrained eye.

12. **The correct answer is (A).** By lowering your voice and slowing your rate of speech, Mr. Thompson will most likely mirror your behavior and calm down. If he remains agitated, you can always terminate the interview.

13. **The correct answer is (A).** In the circumstances present, your best reply is indicated in choice (A). There is no indication that the case has been pending for an unusually long period of time, but your assurance that the application is being checked and that a decision will be forthcoming as soon as possible should ease the client's worry. *Never* assure a client of probable case acceptance simply because it resembles so many other cases, as in choice (C). Each case is unique. *Never* promise to call back unless you intend to do so as in choice (D). It is *not* good to suggest that a client write the worker's supervisor, as in choice (B). It is *your* responsibility to follow up on the matter.

14. **The correct answer is (B).** Under the circumstances described, it would be best to test the reliability of the information received by rephrasing the original question later in the interview. *Remember*, you are *not* questioning the reliability of the response or the overall veracity of the applicant. Note: Compare this question and explanation against Question 7 and its answer and explanation of this practice exam.

15. **The correct answer is (A).** As an eligibility specialist, you should proceed to the next question. Your focus should be on the material that will determine her eligibility.

16. **The correct answer is (D).** The best way to determine what Mr. and Mrs. Lopez's usual occupations are would be to ask what type of work do they do now. This is a leading question, and it will allow the applicants to share more information.

17. **The correct answer is (B).** Basic case work procedure requires that information about an applicant is never ordinarily divulged to any other person without the applicant's permission. In this instance, the worker should remind the clerk of the agency's policy.

18. **The correct answer is (C).** When Mr. Bertolli goes off on a tangent, you can refocus him by asking him a question that is related to the subject matter. You want to be careful not to offend Mr. Bertolli because this would disrupt the rapport between the two of you.

19. **The correct answer is (B).** Good co-worker practice calls for you to simply show your peer the error so that the proper form will be used, but you will not give offense. It is not your function to teach your coworker, as in choice (A) or to minimize the error as in choice (C). It is also bad for future relations with that worker and with the rest of the staff for you to report the worker to your supervisor, as in choice (D).

20. **The correct answer is (D).** You should respond to Ms. Stein with patience, empathy, support, and understanding, as Ms. Stein's situation is quite stressful. Do not alienate her.

21. **The correct answer is (C).** The tone of voice you use can be very helpful in making a client feel comfortable about discussing problems with you.

22. **The correct answer is (B).** As an eligibility specialist, you are required to report all significant material that was revealed as a result of an assessment. Mention of the hostility on the part of the client should only be included if it is relevant to this application.

23. **The correct answer is (A).** Your report to your supervisor should always include your recommendations. Leaving this section for your supervisor to complete after reading your evidence would be negligent on your part.

24. **The correct answer is (A).** The other three answer choices are all useful points to remember in organizing a report. Personal beliefs should be kept to a minimum or omitted entirely in the type of report referred to in the question.

25. **The correct answer is (B).** The last sentence of the first paragraph of the passage clearly refers to irate landlords complaining about receiving late rent checks. The other answer choices are not expressed in the passage.

26. **The correct answer is (C).** The passage clearly states there would be one rent office for every three Social Service Centers in each of the five boroughs. $15 \div 3 = 5$.

27. **The correct answer is (D).** The second paragraph states that clients would receive monthly notification from the Social Service Agency that rent had been paid.

28. **The correct answer is (B).** The third paragraph states that cases with rents from $151 to $250 would be placed in buff folders, while rents from $251 to $349 would be placed in blue folders. It also states the color of the folder should be changed if the rent changes into a new rental category.

29. **The correct answer is (D).** The first paragraph states that clients should con-

tinue to make direct contact on rent matters with their Social Service Centers.

30. **The correct answer is (A).** There is nothing in the passage regarding the need for the floor number of a client's apartment *if there is an elevator in the building* where the client resides. All other data, as noted in the other answer choices, should be in the folder, according to the passage.

31. **The correct answer is (C).** The passage indicates the suggestion that an experimental project be set up on a small scale.

32. **The correct answer is (A).** The fourth paragraph states the possible problem that clients would resist being unable to pay their own rent. It can be inferred that clients might feel a loss of independence from this statement. The other possible answer choices cannot be inferred from the passage.

33. **The correct answer is (B).** The last sentence of the passage clearly states the pilot program would determine what problems "may arise and how the program can be best implemented" by being started first as a pilot program.

34. **The correct answer is (A).** By asking this client to spell her name, you are ensuring that the information in your report is accurate. You will avoid mistakes and confusion in processing her application.

35. **The correct answer is (D).** The best way to evaluate the content of the reports is to use a checklist of required information. This way, you can be sure that the report has covered all the areas you have intended to cover.

36. **The correct answer is (B).** Visual aids can be very useful in explaining, emphasizing, and proving a point made in this report. With a table or chart in the main body of the text, the reader can under-

stand that point more easily. If the chart is complex and might disturb the reader's ability to follow the arguments being given, it is more appropriate to include it in the appendix. If the reader is a very busy executive interested primarily in the conclusions and recommendations, visual aids should be placed in the appendix. In sum, the purpose of the report and the visual aid must be considered in determining where to include the visual aids.

37. **The correct answer is (B).** Immediate information requested by a superior is best imparted by an oral report. The superior does not have the time to read a report if quick straightforward information or an answer to a simple question is needed in order to take immediate action. The other answer choices are situations in which more detailed data is needed or in which time is not of the essence and, therefore, written reports would be more suitable.

38. **The correct answer is (C).** While the other answer choices are also reasons why standardized forms are useful, the *most* important reason for using the forms is that missing data is less likely to occur.

39. **The correct answer is (C).** The other answer choices are all important considerations in determining the selection of which visual aids to use in a particular report. Each report is different, and visual aids useful in one report may be useless in another. Thus, for example, a detailed statistical tabulation may be needed in an annual activity report going to management but is of no value in a report on a case closing that only your supervisor will read.

40. **The correct answer is (B).** *Imparity* is defined as "inequality or disparity."

41. **The correct answer is (A).** *Devious* is defined as "not straightforward; cunning or deceiving."

42. **The correct answer is (C).** *Trepidation* is defined as "apprehension."

43. **The correct answer is (C).** *Vigilant* is defined as "alertly watchful."

44. **The correct answer is (B).** *Egocentric* is defined as "self-centered or selfish."

45. **The correct answer is (D).** *Antagonistic* characterizes a person who "acts in opposition; counteracts."

46. **The correct answer is (A).** *Dispossessed* is defined as "deprived of homes, possessions, and security."

47. **The correct answer is (B).** *Diverse* is defined as "differing from one another; unlike."

48. **The correct answer is (A).** *Inept* is defined as "lacking in fitness or aptitude; unfit."

49. **The correct answer is (A).** *Putative* is defined as "commonly accepted or supposed."

50. **The correct answer is (A).** The passage tells you that the "cookie-cutter" approach "assumes that all individuals in a culture turn out exactly alike." The statements in the other answer choices may be found in the reading, but they do *not* answer the question being asked. Thus, choice (C) could be thought to be the correct answer since the reading states that poverty is a subculture, but that does *not* answer the question posed.

51. **The correct answer is (D).** The passage clearly states that every person "in an urban society" is a member of more than one subculture. While one or more of the statements *may* be correct statements, the reading passage does not include these statements.

52. **The correct answer is (B).** The second paragraph of the passage clearly states that "within one culture . . . there are conflicts and contradictions." There is nothing in the passage to indicate that any of the other answer choices are correct.

53. **The correct answer is (C).** The last paragraph of the passage indicates that most individuals have a dual set of values and have to choose among "conflicting values." It also states that "at any given moment," a person may have to choose among "conflicting values" within a culture or subculture, but it is the *values*, not the cultures as in choice (A) or the subcultures as in choice (B), from which a person has to choose.

54. **The correct answer is (D).** The passage indicates that of the 33 million poor people in the United States, 14.3 million are children. 14.3 million ÷ 33 million = 43.3% of all poor people in the U.S. are children.

55. **The correct answer is (A).** The passage states that "these are the working poor . . . workers in seasonal industries."

56. **The correct answer is (C).** The passage states that "these are the nonworking poor . . . the disabled . . . mentally handicapped."

57. **The correct answer is (A).** The passage indicates that the "underemployed" include "those who would like full-time jobs but cannot find them." It can be inferred from the passage that such persons have part-time jobs.

58. The correct answer is (B).

Number of children in Bergersville boarding homes:

2000	2001	2002	2003	2004
12,389	13,271	14,012	14,558	4,759

Number of children in Bergersville in voluntary institutions:

2000	2001	2002	2003	2004
7,187	7,277	7,087	6,717	6,777

Inspection of the two sets of figures shows that only in 2002 and 2003 were the number of children in boarding homes at least twice the number in voluntary institutions.

59. The correct answer is (D).

Bergersville: Total number in voluntary institutions in 2004 = 6,777. Total number in voluntary institutions in 2003 = 6,717. 6,777 − 6,717 = increase of 60 in Bergersville.

Upstate: Total number in voluntary institutions in 2004 = 3,024. Total number in voluntary institutions in 2003 = 2,986. 3,024 − 2,986 = increase of 38 in Upstate.

Total increase in 2004 = 98 more (60 + 38). Total number in 2004 = 6,777 + 3,024 = 9,801. 9,801 + 98 = 9,899.

60. The correct answer is (D). Total number under care in Bergersville in 2000 = 22,510. 22,510 × (125%) = 22,510. 22,510 ÷ 1.25 = 18,008.

61. The correct answer is (D). Step 1: Add all figures under column called "Total in Other" = 8,281. Step 2: Divide by 5 (number of years 2000 through 2004) 8,281 ÷ 5 = 1,656.2.

62. The correct answer is (B). Step 1: Total number of children in foster family care in Johnston = 4,882. Step 2: Number of children one year of age or under in Johnston = 842. Step 3: 842 ÷ 4882 = .1724 = 17%.

63. The correct answer is (C). Step 1: All the children upstate who are in the "wage, work, or self-supporting" category:

2000 = 90

2001 = 175

2002 = 64

2003 = 60

2004 = 55

Step 2: All the children upstate who are in the "adoptive or free home" category, ages 14–18:

2,902 × .01 = 29

2,943 × .01 = 29

3,261 × .01 = 33

3,445 × .01 = 34

3,606 × .01 = 36

Step 3: 2000 = 90 + 29 = 119 children in foster families

2001 = 175 + 29 = 204 children in foster families

2002 = 64 + 33 = 97 children in foster families

2003 = 60 + 34 = 94 children in foster families

2004 = 55 + 36 = 91 children in foster families

In three of the five years (2000, 2001, and 2002), the number of children ages 14–15 in foster families upstate exceeded 95.

64. The correct answer is (A). Number of 2-year-olds in foster family care in all boroughs in 2000 = 4,361. 4,361 ÷ 5 = 872.2.

65. The correct answer is (B). Total number of children in foster family care in Kiley in 2004 = 3,443. Total number of children in foster family care in Richardson in 2004 = 1,224. 3,443 − 1,224 = 2,219 more in Kiley.

66. The correct answer is (C). Total number of children 1 year of age or younger in Appleton in 2004 = 460. Total number of children 1 year of age or younger in Appleton in 2005 = 460 × 2 = 920. Total number of 2-year-olds in Appleton in 2004 = 555. Total number of 2-year-olds in Appleton in 2005 = 555 × 4/5 = 444. 920 + 444 = 1,364 children.

67. The correct answer is (C). Add the number of children over 4 years of age in all five boroughs of Bergersville. 445 + 484 + 361 + 305 + 112 = 1,707.

68. The correct answer is (D). Family received $382.00 for two months (January and February) = $764.00. Family received $378.00 for five months (March through July) = $1,890.00. Family received $386.04 for five months (August through December) = $1,930.20. $764.00 + $1,890.00 + $1,930.20 = $4,584.20.

69. The correct answer is (B). Client received $168 a month extra for two months = $336. Over twelve months (twenty-four checks), client will pay back $14 per check ($336 ÷ 24 = $14). Semimonthly check = $84 − $14 = $70.

70. The correct answer is (A). 1,050 × 18% = 189 families had 4 or more children. 3,550 − 1,050 = 2,500 × .9% = 225 more had 4 or more children. 189 + 225 = 414 of the 3,500 families had 4 or more children. 414 ÷ 3,500 = .118 (12%).

71. The correct answer is (C). $406 × .35 = $142.10 for food before increase. $142.10 × .13 = $18.47 more per month. $406 + $18.47 = $424.43 per month.

72. The correct answer is (D). $420 × .40 = $168 per month for food before change. $168.00 × .05 = $8.40 more per check for food effective August 1. $8.40 for four months = $33.60 more owed for months September through December. $33.60 ÷ 5 = $6.72 retroactive money each month. August check = $420 + $8.40 = 428.40, including old allowance and new amount for food but without retroactivity. August check = $420 + $8.40 + $6.72 (retroactive money) = $435.12.

73. The correct answer is (A). $14 × 90 = $1,260 received from stock sale. $210 per month = monetary allowance. 1260 ÷ 210 = 6 months.

74. The correct answer is (B). 5 general service stations downtown (7 service stations − 2 special service centers = 5 general service stations). 9 general service stations are uptown (16 − 7 = 9). 14 general service stations of which 9 are uptown or 9 ÷ 14 = 64% uptown.

75. The correct answer is (A). Allowance in January = $132 a month (56 + 48 + 28). In spring, $48 (rent) × .10 = $4.80 more per month for rent = $52.80. In fall, $84 (56 + 28) was reduced by 1/7 = $72. $72 + $52.80 = $124.80 per month allowance in fall.

76. The correct answer is (B). $192 ÷ 24 = $8 semimonthly more for utilities. $170 × .05 = $8.50 per check less because of general decrease. Therefore, $170 per check − $0.50 per check = $169.50 per check.

77. The correct answer is (C). 9 × 5 = 45 cases seen per worker per week. 45 × 15 workers = 675 cases seen per week.

78. The correct answer is (A). In accepting public assistance, a client also accepts

certain responsibilities, including maintenance of personal affairs as much as
possible. The duty to pay rent is, in many
cities, one of those responsibilities.

79. **The correct answer is (A).** In most
urban areas, the crusade against environmental hazards is currently focused on
air pollution, sewage treatment, and noise.
Garbage collection is emphasized as a
major crusade only in those few cities
where it has become a major environmental hazard.

80. **The correct answer is (D).** The passage
clearly states that many street workers
spend their days "tracing potentially incendiary rumors." It does not refer to the
specific activities mentioned in the other
answer choices.

81. **The correct answer is (B).** The passage
mentions that five of the gang neighborhoods are in the southeastern part of the
borough of the Bronx—"and it is here that
most of the 110 gangs have formed."

82. **The correct answer is (A).** The last
sentence in the passage states that the
Youth Services Agency consults with gang
leaders and other teenagers in the projects
to be developed in their respective areas.

83. **The correct answer is (C).** There is *no*
specific mention of the board of education
anywhere in the passage. The roles of the
agencies in the other answer choices are
found in the passage.

84. **The correct answer is (B).** The main
thrust of the passage is the effect stereotyped thinking can have on an interviewer.
Choice (A) is not discussed in the passage,
nor is choice (C). The passage *does* discuss
the impact of stereotyped thinking on
"administrative interviewers and supervisors who are in a position to affect the
lives of others and to stimulate or retard
the development of human potential," but
it is not concerned with the impact of such

thinking on "professional functions" of
persons *not* involved in concerns other
than the development of human potential. Therefore, choice (D) is also incorrect.

85. **The correct answer is (C).** The passage
clearly notes that the specific reasons
given by an interviewer for a negative
evaluation of an interviewee "may not be
the truly motivating factors." The correct
answer can be inferred from that statement. The statements in the other answer
choices cannot be found or inferred from
the passage.

86. **The correct answer is (D).** You are
asked to choose the statement that is not
characteristic of stereotypes according to
the passage. The entire reading emphasizes that stereotypes are *not* a basis for
making valid personality assessments.

87. **The correct answer is (C).** The passage
clearly states that a client "who displays . . .
resentment would probably be further
provoked by a caustic tone." That the
client would "be provoked to violence," as
in choice (D), cannot be inferred from the
passage.

88. **The correct answer is (D).** The passage
states that the speaker's voice tells the
listener something about the speaker's
personality. While the other answer
choices may or may not be true statements, they are not discussed or implied
in the passage.

89. **The correct answer is (D).** A person's
voice can, according to the passage, reveal
temperament. The other answer choices
are concerned with what the speaker *says*,
not the tone or quality of his or her voice.

90. **The correct answer is (C).** The passage
states that in a face-to-face interview,
appropriate facial expressions can somewhat compensate for an unpleasant voice.
The correct answer can be inferred from

this statement. None of the other answers can be inferred from the passage.

91. **The correct answer is (C).** The passage clearly implies that the client on the phone can only react to the tone of the speaker's voice and to what the speaker is saying. While the other answer choices may be true, they cannot be concluded from the passage.

92. **The correct answer is (B).** In the situation described, the applicant has insufficient available funds to maintain himself. To force him to sell the property at less than its market value, and thus, stay off public assistance until the funds from the sales are exhausted, is counterproductive for two reasons: the value of the land may increase and he will ultimately have to go on public assistance for rent purposes. Choice (D) is contrary to public assistance policy. A welfare agency is not in the property management business. The best solution is to allow the applicant to keep the property, grant him public assistance, and place a lien on the property. If the property is ultimately sold, the agency will recoup part or all of the assistance moneys granted. (A lien is a legal claim on another person's property as security for a lawful debt.)

93. **The correct answer is (A).** Insurance adjustment means that the amount of the premium paid by or for the insured person is reduced. This affects the worth of the policy (amount paid) when it comes due. Public welfare policy would not permit the excessive premium rate that is indicated in this case because the extra money, if the policy is adjusted, could be used elsewhere.

94. **The correct answer is (B).** In this situation, each month the applicant receives money that is insufficient to meet all the family needs based on public assistance standards. Supplementary aid is, there-

fore, granted. The other answer choices are inappropriate under the circumstances presented. (See the glossary for definition of supplemention.)

95. **The correct answer is (C).** In this situation, the best procedure would be for the wife to receive the check rather than the husband.

96. **The correct answer is (D).** The futility of the search mandates this action so that the children will not be neglected and proper assistance will be assured.

97. **The correct answer is (B).** Correct public assistance procedure mandates verification of both the applicant's bank account and the utilization of money in that account under most circumstances. In this situation, the applicant's story about the account is highly implausible. It is the applicant's responsibility to prove the veracity of the story. Without such proof, financial aid should be denied.

98. **The correct answer is (A).** In this serious situation, prompt contact with the municipal or private social agency responsible for handling matters involving child abuse should be made. Public assistance checks should not be discontinued pending disposition of the matter by the proper authorities.

99. **The correct answer is (C).** In the situation presented, the eligibility specialist should recommend that the family receive aid. Requiring that the small amount of money previously set aside to maintain the son, as presented in choice (A), be utilized by the family, would keep the family off assistance for only a short time. Choice (B) may alienate the son and spoil his future. There is no basis in the facts given to justify choice (D). Allowing the son to finish law school may very likely result in his ability to support the family completely or in large part, so that, in the end, the agency will save money.

100. **The correct answer is (C).** It is the client's responsibility in this situation to pay the rent in a timely manner, and your first responsibility is to be sure that the client understands the complaint and his own responsibility, both to discuss the matter with the landlord and to pay his rent in a timely manner. As noted in the explanations for previous questions, good social case work practice requires that a client be helped to maintain and develop as much control of daily life requirements as possible so that the landlord continues to be paid directly by the client in this situation. Only if the rent is not paid at all, and after you have spoken to the client, should the solutions given in the other answer choices be considered.

answers

ANSWER SHEET PRACTICE TEST 6

1. Ⓐ Ⓑ Ⓒ Ⓓ   21. Ⓐ Ⓑ Ⓒ Ⓓ   41. Ⓐ Ⓑ Ⓒ Ⓓ   61. Ⓐ Ⓑ Ⓒ Ⓓ   81. Ⓐ Ⓑ Ⓒ Ⓓ

2. Ⓐ Ⓑ Ⓒ Ⓓ   22. Ⓐ Ⓑ Ⓒ Ⓓ   42. Ⓐ Ⓑ Ⓒ Ⓓ   62. Ⓐ Ⓑ Ⓒ Ⓓ   82. Ⓐ Ⓑ Ⓒ Ⓓ

3. Ⓐ Ⓑ Ⓒ Ⓓ   23. Ⓐ Ⓑ Ⓒ Ⓓ   43. Ⓐ Ⓑ Ⓒ Ⓓ   63. Ⓐ Ⓑ Ⓒ Ⓓ   83. Ⓐ Ⓑ Ⓒ Ⓓ

4. Ⓐ Ⓑ Ⓒ Ⓓ   24. Ⓐ Ⓑ Ⓒ Ⓓ   44. Ⓐ Ⓑ Ⓒ Ⓓ   64. Ⓐ Ⓑ Ⓒ Ⓓ   84. Ⓐ Ⓑ Ⓒ Ⓓ

5. Ⓐ Ⓑ Ⓒ Ⓓ   25. Ⓐ Ⓑ Ⓒ Ⓓ   45. Ⓐ Ⓑ Ⓒ Ⓓ   65. Ⓐ Ⓑ Ⓒ Ⓓ   85. Ⓐ Ⓑ Ⓒ Ⓓ

6. Ⓐ Ⓑ Ⓒ Ⓓ   26. Ⓐ Ⓑ Ⓒ Ⓓ   46. Ⓐ Ⓑ Ⓒ Ⓓ   66. Ⓐ Ⓑ Ⓒ Ⓓ   86. Ⓐ Ⓑ Ⓒ Ⓓ

7. Ⓐ Ⓑ Ⓒ Ⓓ   27. Ⓐ Ⓑ Ⓒ Ⓓ   47. Ⓐ Ⓑ Ⓒ Ⓓ   67. Ⓐ Ⓑ Ⓒ Ⓓ   87. Ⓐ Ⓑ Ⓒ Ⓓ

8. Ⓐ Ⓑ Ⓒ Ⓓ   28. Ⓐ Ⓑ Ⓒ Ⓓ   48. Ⓐ Ⓑ Ⓒ Ⓓ   68. Ⓐ Ⓑ Ⓒ Ⓓ   88. Ⓐ Ⓑ Ⓒ Ⓓ

9. Ⓐ Ⓑ Ⓒ Ⓓ   29. Ⓐ Ⓑ Ⓒ Ⓓ   49. Ⓐ Ⓑ Ⓒ Ⓓ   69. Ⓐ Ⓑ Ⓒ Ⓓ   89. Ⓐ Ⓑ Ⓒ Ⓓ

10. Ⓐ Ⓑ Ⓒ Ⓓ   30. Ⓐ Ⓑ Ⓒ Ⓓ   50. Ⓐ Ⓑ Ⓒ Ⓓ   70. Ⓐ Ⓑ Ⓒ Ⓓ   90. Ⓐ Ⓑ Ⓒ Ⓓ

11. Ⓐ Ⓑ Ⓒ Ⓓ   31. Ⓐ Ⓑ Ⓒ Ⓓ   51. Ⓐ Ⓑ Ⓒ Ⓓ   71. Ⓐ Ⓑ Ⓒ Ⓓ

12. Ⓐ Ⓑ Ⓒ Ⓓ   32. Ⓐ Ⓑ Ⓒ Ⓓ   52. Ⓐ Ⓑ Ⓒ Ⓓ   72. Ⓐ Ⓑ Ⓒ Ⓓ

13. Ⓐ Ⓑ Ⓒ Ⓓ   33. Ⓐ Ⓑ Ⓒ Ⓓ   53. Ⓐ Ⓑ Ⓒ Ⓓ   73. Ⓐ Ⓑ Ⓒ Ⓓ

14. Ⓐ Ⓑ Ⓒ Ⓓ   34. Ⓐ Ⓑ Ⓒ Ⓓ   54. Ⓐ Ⓑ Ⓒ Ⓓ   74. Ⓐ Ⓑ Ⓒ Ⓓ

15. Ⓐ Ⓑ Ⓒ Ⓓ   35. Ⓐ Ⓑ Ⓒ Ⓓ   55. Ⓐ Ⓑ Ⓒ Ⓓ   75. Ⓐ Ⓑ Ⓒ Ⓓ

16. Ⓐ Ⓑ Ⓒ Ⓓ   36. Ⓐ Ⓑ Ⓒ Ⓓ   56. Ⓐ Ⓑ Ⓒ Ⓓ   76. Ⓐ Ⓑ Ⓒ Ⓓ

17. Ⓐ Ⓑ Ⓒ Ⓓ   37. Ⓐ Ⓑ Ⓒ Ⓓ   57. Ⓐ Ⓑ Ⓒ Ⓓ   77. Ⓐ Ⓑ Ⓒ Ⓓ

18. Ⓐ Ⓑ Ⓒ Ⓓ   38. Ⓐ Ⓑ Ⓒ Ⓓ   58. Ⓐ Ⓑ Ⓒ Ⓓ   78. Ⓐ Ⓑ Ⓒ Ⓓ

19. Ⓐ Ⓑ Ⓒ Ⓓ   39. Ⓐ Ⓑ Ⓒ Ⓓ   59. Ⓐ Ⓑ Ⓒ Ⓓ   79. Ⓐ Ⓑ Ⓒ Ⓓ

20. Ⓐ Ⓑ Ⓒ Ⓓ   40. Ⓐ Ⓑ Ⓒ Ⓓ   60. Ⓐ Ⓑ Ⓒ Ⓓ   80. Ⓐ Ⓑ Ⓒ Ⓓ

answer sheet

Practice Test 6

ELIGIBILITY SPECIALIST

90 Questions • 3 Hours

> **Directions:** Each question has four possible answers. Choose the letter that best answers the question and mark your answer on the answer sheet.
>
> When answering questions on this test, assume that you are an eligibility specialist. Your duties and responsibilities are to determine and verify initial eligibility of applicants applying for public assistance and to determine and verify continuing eligibility of clients for social services whenever necessary.
>
> If a question describes policy that differs from that followed by the social services agency in your locality, answer the question based on the policy described in the question.

1. Ms. Torres comes to her interview in a manic state. She is rambling on and her conversation goes off in tangents. You are finding it difficult to get her to focus. It would be best for you to

    (A) tell Ms. Torres that her rambling is making this assessment difficult.

    (B) interrupt Ms. Torres and ask her specific questions.

    (C) ask Ms. Torres to finish her story so you can get to the interview.

    (D) allow Ms. Torres to keep talking because it is essential to establish a good rapport with a client.

2. You have spent your day listening to many different family stories and while interviewing Mr. Jackson, you find yourself drifting off and becoming disinterested. You realize this is a problem because

    (A) if you appear disinterested, you are likely to lose the professional respect of other colleagues as well as your supervisor.

    (B) if you appear disinterested, you will lose the client's respect for you on a professional basis.

    (C) if you appear disinterested, Mr. Jackson will not share as much information with you.

    (D) if you appear disinterested, Mr. Jackson is more likely to tell lies.

3. In an interview for public assistance, a client, Mrs. Young, appears to be very shaky. She is showing anxiety and fears about her eligibility status. During the interview, she keeps mishandling her papers and dropping them. You should

    (A) ask Mrs. Young if you can hold the documents, as she seems nervous. This way you can expedite the interview.

    (B) ask Mrs. Young to call a family member in to assist her and make her feel more secure.

    (C) ask Mrs. Young politely if she has sought out any treatment for anxiety, as she appears to be very nervous and you are deeply concerned.

    (D) try to help Mrs. Young relax and help her organize her papers so that you can obtain the information that you need.

303

4. In your meeting with Mrs. Allen, you observe her to be frazzled. She explains to you tearfully that her husband has abandoned her and her 3 children, and she is completely lost as to what she should do. She explains that she has no family or friends that she can call upon for help. You learn that she is in immediate need of food since she and her children have not eaten for two days. Standard process requires the client to wait several days before she can be given any money for this case. Agency policy prohibits you from making any exceptions. You should

(A) send her to another center that may offer her more possibilities, and possibly give her referrals to a food pantry.

(B) tell her that you cannot give her money now. In a few days, after processing her application, she will receive some financial assistance. In addition, you can make her aware that she can contact a food pantry for some help on her own.

(C) ask your colleagues to pull together an emergency collection.

(D) use your human instinct and purchase some food for her on your own so that she and her children can get by. In addition, you can make her aware that she can contact a food pantry for some help on her own.

5. During a public assistance interview, a client becomes frustrated by the lengthy application process. He begins to complain that the application process is taking too long and he needs the money right away. He states it is ridiculous that he has to answer all of these personal questions. You should respond to the client by

(A) helping him understand that the questions are important to determine his eligibility and that it is important for you to ask him these questions to get him the assistance that he wants.

(B) referring him to your supervisor and telling him that it is out of your control, but you understand his frustration.

(C) telling him that his complaints are of no use since he must answer these questions.

(D) telling him that you agree with him but you must complete this assessment because it is part of your job.

6. As an eligibility specialist, which of the following would describe your main objective?

(A) To help clients

(B) To process as many applications as possible to help clients receive the assistance they need

(C) To help clients to become more assertive

(D) To increase your level of compassion and understanding for others on a daily basis

7. During an interview, Mrs. Applebaum is slow to answer your question. You proceed to restate the question. After doing this, you realize that this was incorrect because

   (A) Mrs. Applebaum will think you are confused and unsure of yourself.

   (B) as the interviewer, you should know how to phrase the question.

   (C) it will reveal that you do not know your job.

   (D) you may confuse Mrs. Applebaum.

8. As a white eligibility specialist working with clients who are of color, the best way to improve your work with this client population is to

   (A) ignore that your clients are people of color.

   (B) socialize with peers at your workplace who are of color.

   (C) be sensitive to the problems that people of color face.

   (D) begin your assessment by stating that you are not prejudiced.

9. During the assessment process with Mr. Rodriguez, he warns you that he is not afraid to fight for his rights, and if he does not get a satisfactory decision on his application, he will report you to the mayor's office. You should

   (A) review the process involved in making a decision regarding eligibility with Mr. Rodriguez.

   (B) encourage him to make any complaints that he sees fit because he is entitled to. In this way you are empowering him.

   (C) be understanding because Mr. Rodriguez is frustrated, but tell him if he continues to threaten you that he must leave your office.

   (D) tell Mr. Rodriguez to feel free to report you to the mayor's office and let him know that you can get your supervisor now, if he wants to speak to her immediately.

10. Sometimes, clients become silent during interviews. Of the following, the most probable reason for such silence is that the client is

    (A) getting ready to tell a lie.

    (B) of low intelligence and does not know the answers to your questions.

    (C) thinking things over or has nothing more to say on the subject.

    (D) wishing he or she were not on welfare.

QUESTIONS 11–21 ARE BASED ON THE FOLLOWING SCHEDULE, TABLE INFORMATION, AND CASE SITUATIONS. QUESTIONS 11–15 ARE BASED ON CASE SITUATION 1.

Public assistance grants are computed on a semimonthly basis. This means that all figures are first broken down into semimonthly amounts and that when a client receives a check twice a month, each semimonthly check covers his or her requirements for a period of approximately $2\frac{1}{6}$ weeks. The grants are computed by means of the following procedures:

1. Determine the semimonthly allowance for the family from the Semimonthly Family Allowance Schedule.

2. Determine total semimonthly income by deducting from the semimonthly gross earnings (the wages or salary before payroll deductions) all semimonthly expenses for federal, state, and city income taxes, Social Security payments, state disability insurance payments, union dues, cost of transportation, and $1 per work day for lunch.

3. Add the semimonthly allowance and the semimonthly rent (monthly rent must be divided in half).

4. Subtract the semimonthly income (if there is any income).

5. The formula for computing the semimonthly grant is: Family Allowance + Rent (semi-monthly) – Total Income (semimonthly) = Amount of Grant

6. Refer to the Conversion Table in order to convert weekly amount into semimonthly amounts.

SEMIMONTHLY FAMILY ALLOWANCE SCHEDULE
(BASED ON NUMBER OF PERSONS IN HOUSEHOLD)

Number of People in Household

1	2	3	4	5	6	Each Additional Person
$47.00	$75.00	$100.00	$129.00	$159.00	$184.00	$25.00

CONVERSION TABLE—WEEKLY TO SEMIMONTHLY AMOUNTS

Weekly Amount	Semi-weekly Amount	Weekly Amount	Semi-weekly Amount	Weekly Amount	Semi-weekly Amount	Weekly Amount	Semi-weekly Amount
$1.00	$2.17	$51.00	$110.50	$.01	$.02	$.51	$1.11
2.00	4.33	52.00	112.67	.02	.04	.52	1.13
3.00	6.50	53.00	114.83	.03	.07	.53	1.15
4.00	8.67	54.00	117.00	.04	.09	.54	1.17
5.00	10.83	55.00	119.17	.05	.11	.55	1.19
6.00	13.00	56.00	121.33	.06	.13	.56	1.21
7.00	15.17	57.00	123.50	.07	.15	.57	1.24
8.00	17.33	58.00	125.67	.08	.17	.58	1.26
9.00	19.50	59.00	127.83	.09	.20	.59	1.28
10.00	21.67	60.00	130.00	.10	.22	.60	1.30
11.00	23.83	61.00	132.17	.11	.24	.61	1.32
12.00	26.00	62.00	134.33	.12	.26	.62	1.34
13.00	28.17	63.00	136.50	.13	.28	.63	1.37
14.00	30.33	64.00	138.67	.14	.30	.64	1.39
15.00	32.50	65.00	140.83	.15	.33	.65	1.41
16.00	34.67	66.00	143.00	.16	.35	.66	1.43
17.00	36.83	67.00	145.17	.17	.37	.67	1.45
18.00	39.00	68.00	147.17	.18	.39	.68	1.47
19.00	41.17	69.00	149.50	.19	.41	.69	1.50
20.00	43.33	70.00	151.67	.20	.43	.70	1.52
21.00	45.50	71.00	153.83	.21	.46	.71	1.54
22.00	47.67	72.00	156.00	.22	.48	.72	1.56
23.00	49.83	73.00	158.17	.23	.50	.73	1.58
24.00	52.00	74.00	160.33	.24	.52	.74	1.60
25.00	54.17	75.00	162.50	.25	.54	.75	1.63
26.00	56.33	76.00	164.67	.26	.56	.76	1.65
27.00	58.50	77.00	166.83	.27	.59	.77	1.67
28.00	60.67	78.00	169.00	.28	.61	.78	1.69
29.00	62.83	79.00	171.17	.29	.63	.79	1.71
30.00	65.00	80.00	173.33	.30	.65	.80	1.73
31.00	67.17	81.00	175.50	.31	.67	.81	1.76
32.00	69.33	82.00	177.67	.32	.69	.82	1.78
33.00	71.50	83.00	179.83	.33	.72	.83	1.80
34.00	73.67	84.00	182.00	.34	.74	.84	1.82
35.00	75.83	85.00	184.17	.35	.76	.85	1.84
36.00	78.00	86.00	186.33	.36	.78	.86	1.86
37.00	80.17	87.00	188.50	.37	.80	.87	1.89
38.00	82.33	88.00	190.67	.38	.82	.88	1.91
39.00	84.50	89.00	192.83	.39	.85	.89	1.93
40.00	86.67	90.00	195.00	.40	.87	.90	1.95
41.00	88.83	91.00	197.17	.41	.89	.91	1.97
42.00	91.00	92.00	199.33	.42	.91	.92	1.99
43.00	93.17	93.00	201.50	.43	.93	.93	2.02
44.00	95.33	94.00	203.67	.44	.95	.94	2.04
45.00	97.50	95.00	205.83	.45	.98	.95	2.06
46.00	99.67	96.00	208.00	.46	1.00	.96	2.08
47.00	101.83	97.00	210.17	.47	1.02	.97	2.10
48.00	104.00	98.00	212.33	.48	1.04	.98	2.12
49.00	106.17	99.00	214.50	.49	1.06	.99	2.15
50.00	108.33	100.00	216.67	.50	1.08		

CASE SITUATION 1

The Smiths receive public assistance. The family includes John Smith, his wife, Barbara, and their 4 children. They occupy a five-room apartment for which the rent is $105 per month. Mr. Smith is employed as a porter and his gross wages are $100 per week. He is employed five days a week and spends $.70 a day in carfare. He buys his lunches. The following weekly deductions are made from his salary:

Social Security	$6.00
Disability Benefits	.38
Federal Income Tax	4.30
State Income Tax	2.80
City Income Tax	1.00

11. What is the weekly amount that Mr. Smith contributes toward Social Security, disability benefits, and income taxes?

(A) $31.37

(B) $23.14

(C) $14.48

(D) $10.58

12. What is the semimonthly family allowance for the Smith family?

(A) $129.00

(B) $159.00

(C) $184.00

(D) $184.50

13. What is the total of semimonthly expenses related to Mr. Smith's employment that will be deducted from semimonthly gross earnings to compute semimonthly income?

(A) $49.78

(B) $42.20

(C) $38.95

(D) $22.98

14. Which of the following amounts is the total semimonthly income for the Smith family?

(A) $216.67

(B) $200.00

(C) $166.89

(D) $22.98

15. What semimonthly grant amount is the Smith family entitled to receive?

(A) $236.50

(B) $184.00

(C) $139.22

(D) $69.61

QUESTIONS 16–21 ARE BASED ON CASE SITUATION 2.

CASE SITUATION 2

The Jones family receives public assistance. The family includes Steven and Diane Jones and their 2 children. They occupy a four-room apartment for which the rent is $85 a month. Mr. Jones is employed as a handyman, and his gross wages are $90 per week. He is employed four days a week and spends $.70 a day in carfare. He buys his lunches. He has the following weekly deductions made from his salary:

Social Security	$4.00
Disability Benefits	.27
Federal Income Tax	3.89
State Income Tax	2.05
City Income Tax	.62

16. What is the weekly amount that Mr. Jones contributes toward Social Security, disability benefits, and income taxes?

(A) $10.83

(B) $17.63

(C) $23.43

(D) $23.74

17. What is the semimonthly allowance for the Jones family?

(A) $75

(B) $100

(C) $122

(D) $129

18. What is the total amount of semimonthly expenses related to Mr. Jones's employment that will be deducted from semimonthly gross earnings?

(A) $17.23

(B) $18.93

(C) $38.20

(D) $40.72

19. Which of the following amounts is the total semimonthly income for the Jones family?

(A) $128.20

(B) $155.32

(C) $156.80

(D) $212.23

20. How much will the Jones family receive in grant money?

(A) $14.70

(B) $29.40

(C) $129.00

(D) $171.50

21. If Mr. Jones's monthly rent were $105, what would the amount of the grant be?

(A) $24.70

(B) $49.40

(C) $77.20

(D) $182.20

QUESTIONS 22–26 CONSIST OF INFORMATION GIVEN IN OUTLINE FORM AND FOUR
SENTENCES LABELED A, B, C, AND D. FOR EACH QUESTION, CHOOSE THE SENTENCE THAT
CORRECTLY EXPRESSES THE INFORMATION GIVEN IN OUTLINE FORM AND ALSO DISPLAYS
PROPER ENGLISH USAGE.

22. **Client's Name:** Joanna Jones None
    Client's Income: None
    Number of Children: 3
    Client's Marital Status: Single

    (A) Joanna Jones is an unmarried client
    with 3 children who have no income.

    (B) Joanna Jones, who is single and has
    no income, a client she has 3 children.

    (C) Joanna Jones, whose 3 children are
    clients, is single and has no income.

    (D) Joanna Jones, who has 3 children, is
    an unmarried client with no income.

23. **Client's Name:** Bertha Smith
    Client's Rent: $105 per month
    Number of Children: 2
    Number of Rooms: 4

    (A) Bertha Smith, a client, pays $105 per
    month for her four rooms.

    (B) Client Bertha Smith has 2 children
    and pays $105 per month for four
    rooms.

    (C) Client Bertha Smith is paying $105
    per month for 2 children with four
    rooms.

    (D) For four rooms and 2 children client
    Bertha Smith pays $105 per month.

24. **Name of Employee:** Cynthia Dawes
    Date Cases Were Assigned: 12/16
    Number of Cases Assigned: 9
    **Number of Assigned Cases
    Completed:** 8

    (A) On December 16, employee Cynthia
    Dawes was assigned nine cases; she
    has completed eight of these cases.

    (B) Cynthia Dawes, employee on Decem-
    ber 16, assigned nine cases, she com-
    pleted eight.

    (C) Being employed on December 16,
    Cynthia Dawes completed eight of
    nine assigned cases.

    (D) Employee Cynthia Dawes, she was
    assigned nine cases and completed
    eight; on December 16.

25. **Place of Audit:** Broadway Center
    Names of Auditors: Paul Cahn,
    Raymond Perez
    Date of Audit: 11/20
    Number of Cases Audited: 41

    (A) On November 20, at the Broadway
    Center 41 cases was audited by audi-
    tors Paul Cahn and Raymond Perez.

    (B) Auditors Raymond Perez and Paul
    Cahn has audited 41 cases at the
    Broadway Center, on November 20.

    (C) At the Broadway Center on Novem-
    ber 20, Auditors Paul Cahn and
    Raymond Perez audited 41 cases.

    (D) Auditors Paul Cahn and Raymond
    Perez at the Broadway Center, on
    November 20, is auditing 41 cases.

26. **Name of Client:** Barbra Levine
    Client's Monthly Expenses: $452
    Client's Monthly Income: $210

    (A) Barbra Levine is a client, her monthly
    income is $210 and her monthly ex-
    penses is $452.

    (B) Barbra Levine's monthly income is
    $210 and she is a client, with whose
    monthly expenses are $452.

    (C) Barbra Levine is a client whose
    monthly income is $210 and whose
    monthly expenses are $452.

    (D) Barbra Levine, a client, is with a
    monthly income which is $210 and
    monthly expenses which are $452.

practice test

Any person who is living in New York City and is otherwise eligible may be granted public assistance whether or not he or she has established New York State residence. However, since New York City does not contribute to the cost of assistance granted to persons who are without state residence, the cases of all recipients must be identified formally as to whether or not each member of the household has state residence.

To acquire state residence, a person must have resided in New York State continuously for one year. Such residence is not lost unless the person is out of the state continuously for a period of one year or longer. Continuous residence does not include any period during which the individual is a patient in a hospital, an inmate of a public institution or of an incorporated private institution, a resident on a military base, or a minor residing in a boarding home while under the care of an authorized agency. Receipt of public assistance does not prevent a person from acquiring state residence. State residence, once acquired, is not lost because of absence from the state while a person is serving in the U.S. armed forces or the merchant marines; nor does a member of the family of such a person lose state residence while living with or near that person in these circumstances.

Each person, regardless of age, acquires or loses state residence as an individual. There is no derivative state residence except for an infant at the time of birth. He or she is deemed to have state residence if he or she is in the custody of both parents and either one of them has state residence, or if the parent having custody of him or her has state residence.

27. According to the passage, an infant is deemed to have New York State residence at the time of birth if

(A) he or she is born in New York State but neither of the parents is a resident.

(B) he or she is in the custody of only one parent, who is not a resident, but his or her other parent is a resident.

(C) his or her brother and sister are residents.

(D) he or she is in the custody of both parents but only one of them is a resident.

28. The Jones family consists of 5 members. Jack and Mary Jones have lived in New York State continuously for the past eighteen months after having lived in Ohio since they were born. Of their 3 children, 1 was born ten months ago and has been in the custody of his parents since birth. Their second child lived in Ohio until six months ago and then moved in with his parents. Their third child had never lived in New York until he moved with his parents to New York eighteen months ago. However, he entered the armed forces one month later and has not lived in New York since that time. Based on the passage, how many members of the Jones family are New York State residents?

(A) 2

(B) 3

(C) 4

(D) 5

29. Assuming that each of the following individuals has lived continuously in New York State for the past year, and has never previously lived in the state, which one of them is a New York State resident?

   (A) Jack Salinas, who has been an inmate in a state correctional facility for six months of the year

   (B) Fran Johnson, who has lived on an army base for the entire year

   (C) Arlene Snyder, who married a nonresident during the past year

   (D) Gary Phillips, who was a patient in a Veterans Administration hospital for the entire year

30. The passage implies that the reason for determining whether or not a recipient of public assistance is a state resident is that

   (A) the cost of assistance for nonresidents is not a New York City responsibility.

   (B) nonresidents living in New York City are not eligible for public assistance.

   (C) recipients of public assistance are barred from acquiring state residence.

   (D) New York City is responsible for the full cost of assistance to recipients who are residents.

31. Assume that the Rollins household in New York City consists of 6 members at the present time: Anne Rollins, her 3 children, her aunt, and her uncle. Anne Rollins and one of her children moved to New York City seven months ago. Neither of them had previously lived in New York State. Her other 2 children have lived in New York City continuously for the past two years, as has her aunt. Anne's uncle had lived in New York City continuously for many years until two years ago. He then entered the armed forces and has returned to New York City within the past month. Based on the passage, how many members of the Rollins household are New York State residents?

   (A) 2

   (B) 3

   (C) 4

   (D) 6

32. You are meeting with Mrs. Samson to review her case to continue her present level of assistance. When you review her financial statements, you find that the information that she has provided you with appears to be inaccurate. You should

   (A) discuss these differing financial statements with the client, and have her explain them.

   (B) give Mrs. Samson the benefit of the doubt; after all, she has been trustworthy up until now, and there might be a computer error. In addition, you do not want to offend Mrs. Samson.

   (C) show Mrs. Samson the records and warn her to tell you the truth or she will lose her benefits.

   (D) make a recommendation that her case be closed, and support your recommendation with Mrs. Samson's documents.

33. In an interview with Mr. Freed, you find that the tone of his voice is becoming elevated and hostile each time you ask him a question for your assessment. You proceed with your questions and he appears to become angry. The best way to handle this situation would be to

(A) omit the questions that are bothering Mr. Freed and continue with the rest of the interview.

(B) end the interview since he appears to be trying to hide something.

(C) tell him that he must answer the questions no matter how much they bother him, or else he should leave.

(D) explain to Mr. Freed that you must obtain all the answers to these questions in order to help him.

34. You are meeting with Mr. Brown to determine his eligibility for public assistance. The interview is going along well. Mr. Brown asks you to dinner that evening, since the interview went so long. Your dinner plans were just canceled. How should you respond to this invitation?

(A) Accept, but with the caveat that you should split the dinner bill. Then explain to him that this cannot influence your decision on his eligibility.

(B) Explain that it is against your work policy to accept this invitation; do not allow it to influence your decision on their eligibility.

(C) Explain that it is against your work policy to accept this invitation as his budget does not include money for such an expense, and do not allow it to influence your decision on their eligibility.

(D) Explain that it is against your work policy to accept this invitation. Explain that this would be considered a bribe and that you will have to report this to higher authorities.

QUESTIONS 35–39 ARE BASED ON THE FOLLOWING TABLE AND ASSUMPTIONS. EACH
QUESTION DESCRIBES AN APPLICANT FAMILY. YOU ARE TO DETERMINE INTO WHICH OF THE
FOUR CATEGORIES (A, B, C, OR D) EACH OF THE APPLICANT FAMILIES SHOULD BE PLACED.
IN ORDER TO DO THIS, YOU MUST MATCH THE DESCRIPTION OF THE APPLICANT FAMILY WITH
THE FACTORS DETERMINING ELIGIBILITY FOR EACH OF THE FOUR CATEGORIES. EACH
APPLICANT FAMILY MUST MEET ALL OF THE CRITERIA FOR THE CATEGORY.

Category of Applicant Family	Factors Determining Eligibility
(A)	• There is at least 1 dependent child in the home. • Children are deprived of parental support because the father is a. deceased. b. absent from the home. c. incapacitated due to medically verified illness. d. over age 65. e. not fully employed because of verified ill health. • One or more parent or guardian resides in the same home as the children. • Applicant family must have resided in New York State for a period of one year or more.
(B)	• There is at least one dependent child in the home. • Both parents are in the home and are not incapacitated. • Both parents are the children's natural parents. • Father is unemployed or works less than 70 hours per month. • Father is has recent work history. • Father is not currently receiving unemployment insurance benefits. • Father is available and willing to work. • Applicant family must have resided in New York State for a period of one year or more.
(C)	• There is a veteran of the Vietnam War in the home. • Applicant families do not meet the criteria for Category A or B.
(D)	• Applicant families do not meet the criteria for Category A, B, or C.

Assumptions

1. The information in the above table does not necessarily reflect actual practice in a municipal Department of Social Services.

2. The date of application is January 25, 2004.

3. Each applicant family that cannot be placed in categories A, B, or C must be placed in category D.

4. A "dependent child" is a child who is less than 18 years old, or less than 21 years old if attending school full-time, who depends upon its parents for support.

5. A mother in a family with 1 or more dependent children is not expected to work and her work status is not to be considered in establishing the category of the family.

35. A woman, age 52, has a 6-year-old child whom she states was left in her home at the age of 2. The woman states the child is her niece, and she has no knowledge of the whereabouts of parents or any other relatives. Both woman and child have resided in New York State since June 15, 2003.

36. A married couple has 2 dependent children at home. The family has resided in New York State for the last five years. The wife cannot work. The husband, a veteran of the Korean War, can work only 15 hours a week due to a kidney ailment (verified).

37. A married couple, both age 35, has 3 dependent children at home, 1 of whom is 17 years old. The wife is available for work and presently working two days a week, 7 hours each day. The husband, who was laid off two weeks ago, is not eligible for unemployment insurance benefits. The family has resided in New York State since January 1, 2003.

38. A married couple has 1 dependent child at home. They have resided in New York State since January 25, 2002. The wife must remain home to take care of the child. The husband is a veteran of the Gulf War. The husband is available for work on a limited basis because of a heart condition, which has been verified. A second child, a married 17-year-old son, lives in California.

39. A married couple has 2 children, ages 16 and 12, at home. The family has resided in New York State since June 12, 1991. The wife is not available for work. The husband, who served in the Vietnam War, was laid off three weeks ago and is receiving unemployment insurance benefits of $50 weekly.

40. During an interview with the Smith family, you refer the family for employment and training. You do this because it will

(A) give them improved quality of life.

(B) make them ineligible for public assistance.

(C) help them to be self-sufficient.

(D) help to maintain a very important program that the city is running.

41. Mrs. Alfred, a struggling woman who is in recovery for drug abuse and grew up in the foster-care system, is supporting an aging relative and 2 mentally challenged children. She is at her wit's end, as she desperately needs financial support. At the end of your interview, she asks you if you think she will get assistance. You should tell her that

(A) you are not certain whether or not her application will be approved.

(B) she is putting the cart before the horse and that you have no way of knowing what the status of her application will be.

(C) it will not help her application for her to ask such questions. She needs to respect the process.

(D) you believe that she should receive public assistance, but you are unsure how the department will review her application and it is out of your hands.

42. You are conducting an interview with Mr. Ray, an unemployed executive whose life has taken a turn for the worse. He is unable to see light at the end of the tunnel. You should never do which of the following?

(A) Try to understand Mr. Ray's situation, and the reasons for his views on life.

(B) Try to make Mr. Ray understand the agency's concern for him.

(C) Repeat Mr. Ray's statements back to him in his own accent and speech pattern.

(D) Let him know that your agency will do what it can for him.

QUESTIONS 43–46 ARE BASED ON THE FOLLOWING FOSTER CASE HISTORY.

FOSTER CASE HISTORY

Form W-341-C   **Date:** Jan 25, 2004
Rev. 3/1/88   **Case Name:** Foster
600M-804077-5-200 (73)-245   **Case #:** ADC-3415968
Family Composition: Ann Foster, b. 7.23.61
                          Gerry, b. 1.7.86
                          Susan, b. 4.1.88
                          John, b. 5.3.91
                          Joan, b. 10.14.94

Mrs. Foster was widowed in June 2001 when her husband was killed in a car accident. Since that time, the family has received public assistance. Mrs. Foster has been referred for housekeeping service by the Social Service Department of Lincoln Hospital where she is being treated in the neurology clinic. Her primary diagnosis is multiple sclerosis. The hospital reports that she is going through a period of deterioration characterized by an unsteady gait, and weakness and tremor in the limbs. At this time, her capacity to manage a household and 4 children is severely limited. She feels quite overwhelmed and is unable to function adequately in taking care of her home.

In addition to the medical reasons, it is advisable that a housekeeper be placed in the home as part of a total plan to avoid further family breakdown and deterioration. This deterioration is reflected by all family members. Mrs. Foster is severely depressed and is unable to meet the needs of her children who have a variety of problems. Joan, the youngest, is not speaking, hyperactive, and in general not developing normally for a child her age. John is showing learning problems in school and has poor articulation. Susan was not promoted last year and is a behavior problem at home. A fire left Gerry, the oldest, deformed at age 2. It is clear that Mrs. Foster cannot control or properly discipline her children, but even more important is the fact that she is unable to offer them the encouragement and guidance they require.

It is hoped that providing housekeeping service will relieve Mrs. Foster of the basic household chores so that she will be less frustrated and better able to provide the love and guidance needed by her children.

43. At the date of the report, how old was the child described as not developing normally, hyperactive, and not speaking?
    - **(A)** 3
    - **(B)** 7
    - **(C)** 10
    - **(D)** 13

44. Which of the following cannot be verified on the basis of the Foster case history?
    - **(A)** William Foster was Ann Foster's husband.
    - **(B)** Mrs. Foster has been seen in the neurology clinic at Lincoln Hospital.
    - **(C)** John Foster has trouble with his speech.
    - **(D)** The Foster family has received public assistance since June 2001.

45. The form on which the information about the Foster family is presented is known as

(A) Family Composition Form.

(B) Form Rev. 3/1/88.

(C) Form W-341-C.

(D) ADC-3415968.

46. According to the case history, housekeeping service is being requested primarily because

(A) no one in the family can perform the household chores.

(B) Mrs. Foster suffers from multiple sclerosis and requires assistance with the household chores.

(C) the children are exhibiting behavior problems resulting from the mother's illness.

(D) the children have no father.

47. When you go into work in the morning, you notice Mr. Small, a client that you rejected the day before, sitting at the desk of another eligibility specialist in your group. You should

(A) request for the specialist officer to remove this applicant from the building, without an explanation.

(B) inform the applicant that you have met with him and denied his application and if he remains in the building you will have to call security and have him escorted out of the building.

(C) not inform the eligibility specialist, and allow him to form his own opinion.

(D) inform the eligibility specialist that you had previously interviewed the client the day before.

48. As your interview with Ms. Marcus comes to an end, you notice that she is becoming very agitated and is displaying a great deal of hostility towards you. You find Ms. Marcus to be ineligible for public assistance. You have the ability to notify her in person or by mail, a day or more after their application is accepted or rejected. You should

(A) inform Ms. Marcus of her rejection but have a security staff person at your desk at the time.

(B) request for a colleague to inform Ms. Marcus of the decision.

(C) tell Ms. Marcus of her rejection at the end of the interview.

(D) have the applicant notified by mail only.

49. Mrs. Ettiene speaks English poorly as her native language is French. Since you have no knowledge of this language, you should

(A) provide information to her in writing.

(B) do the best you can with hand gestures.

(C) ask her to return with a translator.

(D) try to locate a staff member who speaks this language.

50. During an interview with a client of another race, she accuses you of racial prejudice and asks for an interviewer of her own race. Of the following, which is the best way to handle the situation?

(A) In a friendly manner, tell the client that eligibility is based on regulations and facts, not on prejudice, and ask her to continue with the interview.

(B) Explain to your supervisor that you cannot deal with someone who accuses you of prejudice, and ask your supervisor to assign the client to someone of her own race.

(C) Assure the client that you will bend over backwards to treat her application favorably.

(D) Tell the client that some of your friends are of her race and that you could therefore not possibly be prejudiced.

QUESTIONS 51–55 ARE BASED ON THE ASSUMPTION THAT YOU, AS AN ELIGIBILITY SPECIALIST, HAVE BEEN ASKED TO WRITE A SHORT REPORT ON THE BASIS OF THE INFORMATION CONTAINED IN THE FOLLOWING PASSAGE ABOUT THE GRANTING OF EMERGENCY FUNDS TO THE SMITH FAMILY.

Mr. and Mrs. Smith, who have been receiving public assistance for the last six months, arrive at the Center the morning of August 2 upset and anxious because they and their family were burned out of their apartment the night before. The fire was of suspicious origin because at the time it broke out witnesses spotted 2 neighborhood teenagers running away from the scene. The police officers arrived on the scene shortly after the firefighters and took down the pertinent information about the alleged arsonists.

The Smiths have spent the night with friends but now request emergency housing and emergency funds for themselves and their 4 children to purchase food and to replace the clothing that was destroyed by the fire. The burned-out apartment had consisted of five rooms and a bath, and the Smiths are now worried that they will be forced to accept smaller accommodations. Furthermore, since Mrs. Smith suffers from a heart murmur, she is worried that their new living quarters will require her to climb too many stairs. Her previous apartment was a one-flight walk-up, which was acceptable.

As an eligibility specialist, you have studied the case, determined the amount of the emergency grant, made temporary arrangements for the Smiths to stay at a hotel, and reassured Mrs. Smith that everything possible will be done to find them an apartment that will meet with their approval.

51. Which of the following statements would be best to include in the report as the reason for the emergency grant?

(A) The police have decided that the fire is of suspicious origin.

(B) Two neighborhood teenagers were seen leaving the scene of the fire.

(C) The apartment of the Smith family has been destroyed by fire.

(D) Mrs. Smith suffers from a heart murmur and cannot climb stairs.

52. Which of the following would be best to accept as verification of the fire?

(A) A letter from the friend with whom the Smiths stayed the previous night

(B) A photograph of the fire

(C) A dated newspaper clipping describing the fire

(D) A note from the Smiths' neighbors

53. A report of the Smith family's need for a new apartment must be sent to the Center's housing specialist. Which of the following recommendations for housing would be most appropriate?

(A) Two bedrooms, first floor walk-up

(B) Five rooms, ground floor

(C) Two-room suite, hotel with elevator

(D) Three rooms, building with elevator

54. For which of the following are the Smiths requesting emergency funds?

(A) Furniture

(B) Food

(C) A hotel room

(D) Repairs in their apartment

55. Which of the following statements provides the best summary of your action on the Smith case and is most important for inclusion in your report?

   (A) Mr. and Mrs. Smith arrived upset and anxious and were reassured.

   (B) It was verified that there was a fire.

   (C) Temporary living arrangements were made and the amount of the emergency grant was determined.

   (D) The case was studied and a new apartment was found for the Smiths, which met with their approval.

56. You are interviewing Mr. Wu. During the interview, you begin to worry that you are not remembering all the information and you begin to write down notes. This is not a good idea because

   (A) you may find that in an effort to record information, you are not really listening to what the applicant is saying.

   (B) the applicant may feel as though you are not listening.

   (C) the material the applicant is sharing with you is confidential and you cannot afford to lose the notes, as they are private documentation.

   (D) the applicant will think that you are not intelligent enough to remember the material.

57. Before an applicant seeking public assistance can be interviewed, he must fill out a complex application form that consists of eleven pages of questions requesting very detailed information. Of the following, the best time for the eligibility specialist to review the information on the application form is

   (A) before interviewing the applicant.

   (B) after asking the applicant a few questions to put him at ease.

   (C) toward the end of the interview to have a chance to think about the information received during the interview.

   (D) after the interview has been completed.

FOR QUESTIONS 58–60, CHOOSE THE WORD THAT MEANS MOST NEARLY THE SAME AS THE <u>UNDERLINED</u> WORD IN THE SENTENCES.

58. He needed monetary assistance because he was <u>incapacitated</u>. The word <u>incapacitated</u> means most nearly

   (A) uneducated.

   (B) disabled.

   (C) uncooperative.

   (D) discharged.

59. The case worker explained to the client that signing the document was <u>compulsory</u>. The word <u>compulsory</u> means most nearly

   (A) temporary.

   (B) required.

   (C) different.

   (D) discharged.

60. The woman's actions did not <u>jeopardize</u> her eligibility for benefits. The word <u>jeopardize</u> means most nearly

   (A) delay.

   (B) reinforce.

   (C) determine.

   (D) endanger.

QUESTIONS 61–64 ARE BASED ON THE SITUATION AND FORM BELOW.

On October 7, 2004, John Smith (case # ADC-U 1467912) applied and was accepted for public assistance for himself and his family. His family consists of his wife, Helen, and their children: William, age 9; John Jr., age 6; and Mary, age 2. The family has lived in a five-room apartment located at 142 Wales Street, Midvale City, since July 18, 2000. Mr. Smith signed a two-year lease for this apartment on July 18, 2004, with a rent of $250 per month. The maximum rental allowance for a family of this size is $210 a month. Utilities are included in this rent-controlled multiple dwelling.

Since the cost of renting this apartment exceeds the allowable amount, the eligibility specialist is required to fill out a "Request for Approval of Exception to Policy for Shelter Allowance/Rehousing Expenses." A sample of a section of this form appears below.

Sample Form

Request for Approval of Exception to Policy for Shelter Allowance/Rehousing Expenses

Case Name		Case Number or Pending		Acceptance Date		Group No.
Present Address Zip		Apt. No. or Location	No. of Rooms	Rent per Mo. $		Occupancy Date

HOUSEHOLD COMPOSITION (*List all persons living in the household*) Column 1		Column 2	Col. 3	Column 4	Column 5	Column 6
Surname	First	Birthdate	Sex	Relation to Case Head	Marital Status	P.A. Status

61. Based on the information given in the passage, which one of the following should be entered in the space for "Occupancy Date"?

(A) October 7, 2004

(B) July 18, 2004

(C) July 18, 2000

(D) Unknown

62. What amount should be entered in the space labeled "Rent per Mo."?

(A) $250

(B) $210

(C) $150

(D) $40

63. Based on the information given in the passage, it is impossible to fill in which one of the following blanks?

   (A) Case Number or Pending
   (B) Acceptable Date
   (C) Apt. No. or Location
   (D) No. of Rooms

64. Which of the following should be entered in Column 4 for Helen Smith?

   (A) Wife
   (B) Head
   (C) Mother
   (D) Unknown

65. Add $4.34, $3.50, $37.00, $101.76, and $90.67. From the result subtract $60.54 and $10.56. What is the answer?

   (A) $76.17
   (B) $156.37
   (C) $166.17
   (D) $300.37

66. Add 2,200; 2,600; 252; and 47.96. From the result subtract 202.70; 1,200; 2,150; and 434.43. What is the answer?

   (A) 1,112.83
   (B) 1,213.46
   (C) 1,341.51
   (D) 1,348.91

67. Multiply 1,850 by .05 and multiply 3,300 by .08 and then add both results. What is the answer?

   (A) 242.50
   (B) 264.00
   (C) 333.25
   (D) 356.50

68. Multiply 312.77 by .04. Round off the result to the nearest hundredth. What is the answer?

   (A) 12.52
   (B) 12.511
   (C) 12.518
   (D) 12.51

69. Add 362.05, 91.13, 347.81, and 17.46 and then divide the result by 6. What is the answer rounded off to the nearest hundredth?

   (A) 138.409
   (B) 137.409
   (C) 136.41
   (D) 136.40

70. Add 66.25 and 15.06 and then multiply the result by $2\frac{1}{6}$. What is the answer (most nearly)?

   (A) 176.18
   (B) 176.17
   (C) 162.66
   (D) 162.62

71. Each of the following options contains three decimals. In which case do all three decimals have the same value?

   (A) .3; .30; .03
   (B) .25; .250; .2500
   (C) 1.9; 1.90; 1.09
   (D) 3.5; 350; 035

72. Add half the sum of (539.84 and 479.26) to a third of the sum of (1,461.93 and 927.27). Round off the result to the nearest whole number. What is the answer?

   (A) 3,408
   (B) 2,899
   (C) 1,816
   (D) 1,306

73. Multiply $5906.09 by 15% and then divide the result by 3. What is the answer?

(A) $295.30

(B) $885.91

(C) $8859.14

(D) $29,530.45

QUESTIONS 74–78 ARE BASED ON THE FOLLOWING PASSAGE.

The ideal relationship for the interview is one of mutual confidence. To try to pretend to put on a front of cordiality and friendship is unwise for the interviewer because he or she will almost certainly convey, by subtle means, his or her real feelings. It is the interviewer's responsibility to take the lead in establishing a relationship of mutual confidence.

As the interviewer, you should help the interviewee feel at ease and ready to talk. One of the best ways to do this is to be at ease yourself. If you are, it will probably be evident; if you are not, it will almost certainly be apparent to the interviewee.

Begin the interview with topics for discussion that are easy to talk about and not menacing. This interchange can be like the conversation of people when they are waiting for a bus, at the ball game, or discussing the weather. However, do not prolong this warm-up too long, since the interviewee knows as well as you do that these are not the things he or she came to discuss. Delaying too long in getting down to business may suggest to him or her that you are reluctant to deal with the topic.

Once you get onto the main topics, do all you can to get the interviewee to talk freely with as little prodding from you as possible. Avoid prejudicing or coloring the interviewee's remarks by what you say. Do not in any way indicate that there are certain things you want to hear, and others that you do not want to hear. It is essential that the interviewee feel free to express himself or herself unhampered by your ideas, your values, and preconceptions.

Try not to dominate the interview or have a patronizing attitude. Ask questions that will enable the interviewee to take pride in his or her knowledge. Take the attitude that the interviewee sincerely wants the interview to achieve its purpose. This creates a warm, permissive atmosphere that is most important in all interviews.

74. Of the following, the best title for the passage is

(A) Permissiveness in Interviewing.

(B) Interviewing Techniques.

(C) The Factor of Pretense in the Interview.

(D) The Cordial Interview.

75. Which of the following recommendations on the conduct of an interview does the passage make?

(A) Conduct the interview as if it were an interchange between people discussing the weather.

(B) The interview should be conducted in a highly impersonal manner.

(C) Allow enough time for the interview so that the interviewee does not feel rushed.

(D) Start the interview with topics that are uncontroversial and not threatening to the interviewee.

76. The passage indicates that the interviewer should

(A) feel free to express his or her opinions.

(B) patronize the interviewee and display a permissive attitude.

(C) permit the interviewee to give the needed information in his or her own fashion.

(D) provide for privacy when conducting the interview.

77. The meaning of the word "unhampered" as it is used in the last sentence of the fourth paragraph of the passage is most nearly

    (A) unheeded.

    (B) unobstructed.

    (C) hindered.

    (D) aided.

78. It can be inferred from the passage that

    (A) interviewers, while generally mature, lack confidence.

    (B) certain methods of interviewing are more successful than others in obtaining information.

    (C) there is usually a reluctance on the part of interviewers to deal with unpleasant topics.

    (D) it is best for the interviewer not to waver from the use of hard and fast rules when dealing with clients.

79. In your interview with Mr. Gomez, you observe that his speech is slurred, he appears to lack rational thought, and he smells of alcohol. After a period of time, he admits to you that he had several drinks before the interview because he was so nervous. You should

    (A) cancel the interview and reschedule for another time.

    (B) have compassion for Mr. Gomez, because you know that this can be an anxiety-producing experience.

    (C) be patient and sympathetic and continue with the interview.

    (D) tell Mr. Gomez he can go get some coffee and then attempt to continue with the interview after he has sobered up.

80. You are interviewing Mr. Francis for public assistance. During your meeting, he becomes tearful and starts to tell you about his daughter who is sick with a terminal illness. He begins to cry. You should

    (A) tell Mr. Francis that you are confident that his application will be approved.

    (B) explain to Mr. Francis that you would be glad to refer him to a therapist but that you really need to complete his assessment or you will need to reschedule.

    (C) end the interview and reschedule another appointment.

    (D) be compassionate and proceed when Mr. Francis is ready to continue the interview.

81. A social service agency uses a family budget as a means of determining which of the following?

    (A) A comprehensive statistical quotient that is compared with other families as a means of reporting on demographics

    (B) Census statistics

    (C) The needs of the families and the amount of assistance that is required to address these needs

    (D) The city's public assistance budget for the following fiscal year

QUESTIONS 82–84 ARE BASED ON THE FOLLOWING PASSAGE.

A city's policy might well tackle the problem of homelessness by having the following two goals.

1. Prevent both individuals and families from becoming homeless. If we are to halt the growth of homelessness, we must help both single persons and families attain or maintain self-sufficiency. We must not only continue but also expand existing governmental programs that directly and indirectly help those who are potentially or actually threatened with eviction so that they will not be forced to abandon their place of residence.

2. Increase the number of permanent homes that are affordable and available to both the homeless and to those who are potentially homeless.

Both of these goals are based on the belief that aside from certain individual cases, people are better off if they live outside of municipal shelters. Although there is no doubt that the conditions under which many people live today are horrifying and include terrible and/or unstable housing and family situations, utilization of the shelter system on a long-term basis will solve neither these housing nor these familial problems. A municipal shelter cannot provide the physical space, privacy, or amenities an individual or family needs if they are to lead normal lives. It affords them no real chance to live in a viable community. Above all, long-term residence in a municipal shelter almost inevitably results in a disincentive to independence.

82. Assume that a family has been living in a municipal shelter set up for the temporary housing of the homeless for almost a year. Based on the passage and on good social case work practice, you should

(A) take steps immediately to have the family leave the shelter, since law and public policy do not permit long-term residence at a shelter.

(B) bring the matter of their long-term residence at the shelter to the immediate attention of those in charge of finding suitable housing outside the shelter for the family for possible priority consideration.

(C) allow the family to remain at the shelter since they have apparently adjusted well to that type of living arrangement.

(D) inquire whether the family desires to remain in the shelter or would prefer housing elsewhere and take action based on their response.

83. According to the passage, which of the following is the most important reason for NOT allowing a family or an individual to remain in a shelter for an extended period of time?

(A) It has been determined that it is more expensive to provide shelter care in a city-run shelter than in a privately owned hotel.

(B) Allowing an individual or family to remain in the city-owned shelter for a long time prevents placement of another newly homeless person or family in the facility, and there are only a limited number of accommodations available in the facility.

(C) Long-term reliance on housing in a public facility is detrimental to an individual's or family's ability to retain independence and interest in becoming self-supporting.

(D) Shelters are not usually attractive or well managed and are very crowded, which makes long-term residence at a municipal shelter depressing.

84. Assume that the landlord of a family on public assistance has stated that he is going to raise the family's rent above the amount currently being paid. Of the following, based on the passage, you should

    (A) refuse to allow the family to pay the increase even if they are going to be evicted because the rent is exorbitant.

    (B) threaten to bring the landlord to court for extortion.

    (C) remove the family from the apartment and send them to a municipal shelter since it will be less expensive for the agency than paying the increased rent.

    (D) recommend that the rent increase be allowed if it is still within the agency's maximum rental allowance.

QUESTIONS 85–87 ARE BASED ON THE FOLLOWING PASSAGE.

During the past few years, there has been increasing concern over the many thousands of children forced to reside with their parents or guardians in welfare shelters or in hotels catering to the welfare population. At the same time, it has been found that many of these children are not attending school and are not living under the normal family conditions thought to be proper for youngsters in the United States. Neighbors and other residents of the hotels in which these families are forced to reside often complain of the mischief and vandalism allegedly perpetrated by the youngsters.

There has also been increasing fear, however, that even if a family is ultimately placed in an apartment owned by the municipality, such dwelling is often substandard and in a dangerous environment. These apartments have been specifically rehabilitated and are rented at a lower cost primarily to homeless people. Although these dwellings may be an improvement over these families' prior housing accommodations and are in better condition than other houses in the neighborhood, it is *not* good economic, social, or humanitarian practice to *redevelop* housing, which, when completed, is still substandard. Many of the houses rehabilitated by a municipal agency soon become dilapidated and in need of significant repair. Recent studies have shown that, contrary to the belief of many neighbors, very often it is not the poor personal habits of the new tenants that cause deterioration, but rather the substandard nature of the rehabilitation work done on the accommodations that is the basis of the rapid decline of the building.

85. According to the passage, the neighbors of the formerly homeless families who have been accommodated in the municipally owned apartments frequently

    (A) believe their own rents should be lowered since the buildings in which they live are in similar or worse condition than the ones occupied by the formerly homeless families.

    (B) believe that the presence of poor families in their neighborhood decreases the value of their own homes or apartment houses.

    (C) are of the opinion that the deterioration of the municipally owned building is primarily the fault of the formerly homeless people who have been moved into them.

    (D) suspect that the children in these families have not been properly cared for or controlled by their parents.

86. According to the passage, it is poor economic practice to

(A) house the homeless in municipal shelters that are more costly than placing them in apartments or dwellings.

(B) place the homeless in city-owned dwellings because such people rapidly spoil the dwelling and diminish its worth.

(C) move people into substandard dwellings rather than into hotels that are less costly.

(D) rehabilitate a city-owned building in such a substandard manner that it quickly deteriorates.

87. Assume that a homeless AFDC family with 2 children, ages 9 and 12, has been moved into a single-room-occupancy (SRO) hotel six weeks previously. You are visiting the dwelling for the first time. Based solely on the passage, it would be good case work practice to

(A) arrange that the rent be paid by your agency directly to the hotel management to avoid possible thefts of same.

(B) ascertain from the hotel management whether the homeless family has actually paid the rent.

(C) find out whether the children have been registered for and are attending school.

(D) discuss with the family your plans to move them into a municipal shelter since living in a SRO hotel is not healthy for children.

QUESTIONS 88–90 ARE BASED ON THE FOLLOWING PASSAGE.

All scientific evidence indicates that HIV is *not* spread through casual contact with people who are HIV positive. It has been determined, for example, that a person cannot get HIV by any of the following activities.

1. Donating blood at the Red Cross
2. Being in a classroom with a person who is HIV positive
3. Sharing a room with a person who is HIV positive
4. Kissing on the cheeks a person who is HIV positive
5. Using the same towel as a person who is HIV positive
6. Eating food prepared by a person who is HIV positive
7. Using a toilet seat used by a person who is HIV positive
8. Being sneezed upon by a person who is HIV positive
9. Shaking hands with a person who is HIV positive

HIV, the virus causing AIDS, is *not* transmitted through the air as are illness such as colds or measles. Neither is it transmitted to humans through bites or through contact with insects or animals as is malaria or rabies. You cannot contract HIV by consuming contaminated food or water or by contact with inanimate objects like doorknobs or tissues or by touching unbroken skin of a person with the disease. In sum, while the dangers of HIV transmission are real and devastating, unwarranted fear about exposure in an individual's home and in public places, including schools, can be alleviated by knowledge and by prudent actions based on such knowledge.

88. The mother of an AFDC family that is temporarily living in a hotel comes to the welfare center in great distress. She tells you, her case worker, that the family must share the toilet with a person who is HIV positive and is afraid her family will contract the virus. Based on the passage and on good case work practice, you should

(A) arrange for immediate housing elsewhere.

(B) arrange for immediate notification of the proper authorities about the person who is HIV positive.

(C) explain that other housing is not easily available and that a great deal of trouble had been taken to find suitable housing for the family, so that nothing can be done about the matter.

(D) calmly explain that HIV cannot be contracted by use of the same toilet facility, and the family's health is not in danger.

89. You are visiting the Bank family, who is on public assistance, and you find out that one of the sisters, Cecile, has been diagnosed as HIV positive. Cecile is living in a bedroom that is separate from the rest of their family. You become aware that all of the family's things are kept separate from Cecile's things and that she is excluded from most family activities, including family meal times. The family appears to avoid all unnecessary contact with Cecile. During your interview you should

(A) tell the family nothing, and continue on with your interview.

(B) notify the Division of AIDS Services and have Cecile removed from the home.

(C) ask the family about how they are coping with Cecile's illness and inform the family that HIV is not contracted by casual contact with relatives, and that Cecile may need their support.

(D) tell them to be careful because the presence of someone who is HIV positive can be a danger to all involved.

90. This passage implies which of the following?

(A) The risk of HIV usually pertains to people who have a complex and dangerous lifestyle.

(B) Concrete information is beneficial in decreasing the spread of HIV.

(C) Fear of contracting HIV should be reconciled, as a cure for the virus will surely be found.

(D) If you are knowledgeable about HIV, you will not be at risk for contracting this illness.

ANSWER KEY AND EXPLANATIONS

1. B	19. C	37. B	55. C	73. A
2. C	20. A	38. A	56. B	74. B
3. D	21. A	39. C	57. A	75. D
4. B	22. D	40. C	58. B	76. C
5. A	23. B	41. A	59. B	77. B
6. A	24. A	42. C	60. D	78. B
7. D	25. C	43. A	61. C	79. A
8. C	26. C	44. A	62. A	80. D
9. A	27. D	45. C	63. C	81. C
10. C	28. B	46. B	64. A	82. B
11. C	29. C	47. D	65. C	83. C
12. C	30. A	48. D	66. A	84. D
13. A	31. C	49. D	67. D	85. C
14. C	32. A	50. A	68. D	86. D
15. D	33. D	51. C	69. C	87. C
16. A	34. B	52. C	70. B	88. D
17. D	35. D	53. B	71. B	89. C
18. C	36. A	54. B	72. D	90. B

1. **The correct answer is (B).** By interrupting Ms. Torres and asking her specific questions during the interview, you help her reduce her manic state and focus. As an eligibility specialist, you do not have the time to listen to all the stories that each client may have. You must prioritize your work and complete your assessment.

2. **The correct answer is (C).** It is important to maintain your interest and to encourage Mr. Jackson to disclose as much information as he feels comfortable sharing. If you appear disinterested, it is likely that he will not share as much information with you.

3. **The correct answer is (D).** Getting Mrs. Young to relax and helping her organize her papers will help you obtain the information that you need. You are decreasing her level of anxiety and achieving your goals of completing a thorough assessment.

4. **The correct answer is (B).** In a few days after processing Mrs. Allen's application, she will receive some financial assistance. By making her aware of her ability to contact a food pantry for some help, you are giving her a partial solution that may alleviate some of her anxiety. Because agency policy prohibits you from making any exceptions and because giving out money of your own goes against professional practice, you have no other choices.

5. **The correct answer is (A).** Helping the client understand that the questions are important to determine his eligibility and how important it is for you to ask him these questions will greatly reduce his frustration in filling out applications. In addition, make him aware that the personal information he provides is used only to determine his eligibility.

6. **The correct answer is (A).** As an eligibility specialist, the main objective is to help your clients. This is your primary function.

7. **The correct answer is (D).** You may confuse Mrs. Applebaum if you proceed to restate the question. Be patient and give her time to answer.

8. **The correct answer is (C).** In order to be objective, an eligibility specialist must be sensitive to the problems that people of color sometimes face.

9. **The correct answer is (A).** The best you can do is to review the decision-making process with Mr. Rodriguez. If that remains insufficient to him, consult your supervisor.

10. **The correct answer is (C).** Experienced interviewers know that when a client becomes silent during an interview, the client is probably either trying to frame an answer or question correctly, thinking over what has been said, or has no more to say on the subject.

11. **The correct answer is (C).** Add the weekly figures given for Social Security, disability benefits, and income taxes in Case Situation 1: $6.00 + $.38 + $4.30 + $2.80 + $1.00 = $14.48

12. **The correct answer is (C).** If you refer to the Semimonthly Family Allowance Schedule, you'll see that a family of six receives an allowance of $184.

13. **The correct answer is (A).** The expenses related to Mr. Smith's employment include the figures given in Question 11 concerning his semimonthly costs *plus* his semimonthly lunch expenses *plus* his semimonthly travel expenses. Social Security, disability, income taxes: $14.48 weekly = $31.37 semimonthly; Lunch: $5.00 weekly = $10.83 semimonthly; Travel: $3.50 weekly = $7.58 semimonthly;

Total: $31.37 + $10.83 + $7.58 = $49.78 semimonthly.

14. **The correct answer is (C).** Income: $100 a week = $216.67 semimonthly; Expenses (see Question 13): $49.78; Total: $216.67 − $49.78 = $166.89.

15. **The correct answer is (D).** Family allowance + rent − total income = grant: $184.00 + $52.50 − $166.89 = $69.61.

16. **The correct answer is (A).** Add the weekly deductions listed in Case Situation 2: $4.00 + $.27 + $3.89 + $2.05 + $.62 = $10.83.

17. **The correct answer is (D).** According to the Semimonthly Family Allowance Schedule, a family of four receives $129.

18. **The correct answer is (C).** Deductions: $10.83 weekly = $21.67 + $1.80 = $23.47 semimonthly; Travel: $2.80 weekly = $4.33 + $1.73 = $6.06 semimonthly; Lunch: $4.00 weekly = $8.67 semimonthly. $23.47 + $6.06 + $8.67 = $38.20.

19. **The correct answer is (C).** Total semimonthly income = gross semimonthly income − deductions − lunch − travel: $195.00 (from conversion table) − $38.20 (from Question 18) = $156.80.

20. **The correct answer is (A).** Family allowance + rent (semimonthly) − total income (semimonthly) = amount of grant (semimonthly): $129.00 + $42.50 = $171.50. $171.50 − $156.80 = $14.70.

21. **The correct answer is (A).** If rent were $105.00, semimonthly rent = $52.50. $129.00 + $52.50 = $181.50. $181.50 − $156.80 = $24.70.

22. **The correct answer is (D).** The correct answer is written in clear, grammatically correct English, and states all the pertinent facts. Choice (A) says the children have no income, not that both Mrs. Jones and the children have no income. Choice

(B) uses incorrect English and is unclear. While choice (C) says the three children are clients, it omits income information.

23. **The correct answer is (B).** Choice (B) is clear, accurate, shows proper English usage, and states all the pertinent facts. Choice (A) makes no reference to the 2 children in the case. Choice (C) states that Ms. Smith is paying for her 2 children who have four rooms. Choice (D) states that Ms. Smith is paying for four rooms and 2 children.

24. **The correct answer is (A).** Choice (A) is written in correct English and states all the pertinent facts. Choice (B) states Ms. Dawes was employed on December 16, not that she was assigned nine cases that day. Choice (C) does not tell you that the cases were assigned on December 16. It implies that the cases were assigned because she was employed on that date. It also implies that the cases were completed on that date, which is not a fact given to you. Choice (D) also implies that the cases were assigned and completed on December 16. The word *she* is improperly used and is not necessary in the sentence.

25. **The correct answer is (C).** The correct answer states *all* the pertinent facts clearly and shows proper English usage and grammar. Choice (A) demonstrates incorrect use of the singular verb *was*. The subject is plural (41 cases). Therefore, the plural verb *were* is needed. In choice (B), the correct verb *is audited* or *had audited* is required, not *has audited*. In choice (D), the verb should be in the past tense, i.e., *audited,* not *is auditing*.

26. **The correct answer is (C).** The correct answer uses proper English and grammar and contains all the facts. In choice (A), the plural word *expenses* requires the use of a plural verb *are,* not *is.* In addition, the sentence is really two sentences. The comma after the word *client* should be a

period, and the word *her* should be capitalized. Choice (B) exhibits poor English usage and is unclear. Choice (D) demonstrates poor English usage. *Is with* should be *has, which is* should be *of,* and *which are* should be *of.*

27. **The correct answer is (D).** The correct answer is found in the last sentence of the passage.

28. **The correct answer is (B).** Jack and Mary Jones have state residence, having lived in the state continuously for eighteen months. The infant born ten months previously has residence, having been born to and in the custody of parents who have state residence. The second and third children do *not* have state residence according to the passage. Residence is not derivative for them because the second child has been in the state only six months and the third child was not a resident when he entered the armed services.

29. **The correct answer is (C).** According to the passage, residence is *not* gained if the individual lived on a military base, in a hospital, or in a prison (a public institution) that is situated in the state. Hence, the only correct answer is choice (C).

30. **The correct answer is (A).** The passage clearly states that the city does *not* contribute to the cost of assistance of nonstate residents.

31. **The correct answer is (C).** Anne Rollins and the 1 child who moved to the state seven months ago do *not* have residence. The 2 children and the aunt with whom they lived have residence since they lived in the state for two years. The uncle also has residence, having lived in the state continuously. Residence was not lost by entrance into the armed forces. Thus, four persons have state residence.

32. The correct answer is (A). Discuss these differing financial statements with Mrs. Samson and have her explain the problems to you. She may be unaware of them herself, or she may have a meaningful explanation. It is important to maintain the client's confidence in your relationship and in you. Do not threaten her.

33. The correct answer is (D). If Mr. Freed appears hostile each time you ask him a question, explain to him in a calm manner that you must obtain all the answers to these questions so you can help him. It is a client's obligation to complete this interview in order to receive services.

34. The correct answer is (B). In a polite manner, explain that it is against your work policy to accept this invitation; do not allow it to influence your decision on his eligibility. Going on to say that his budget doesn't allow for such extravagance is unnecessary and may offend the applicant.

35. The correct answer is (D). The case does not fit Category A because the woman may not be the child's guardian, and they have not lived in the state for one year. It does not fit Category B because both parents are not in the home. It does not fit Category C since there is no Vietnam War veteran in the home. Therefore, the answer must be (D).

36. The correct answer is (A). The case fits all the factors for determining eligibility listed in Category A.

37. The correct answer is (B). The case does NOT fit Category A because the children are not deprived of parental support. It does fit Category B since all the factors in Category B are present.

38. The correct answer is (A). The case fits all the factors for determining eligibility in Category A.

39. The correct answer is (C). The case does not fit Category A (no child deprived of parental support because of factors *a* through *e*). It does not fit Category B because the father *is* receiving unemployment insurance. It does fit Category C because the father is a Vietnam War veteran.

40. The correct answer is (C). An important element of the public assistance program is to see that people are helped not only financially but also emotionally. You want them to be self-sufficient, and referring them for employment and training can do this.

41. The correct answer is (A). By telling Mrs. Alfred that you are not certain as to the status of her application, you are being truthful. The other responses would agitate her or leave her feeling puzzled.

42. The correct answer is (C). To repeat Mr. Ray's statements back to him in his own accent and speech pattern would be insulting and very unprofessional. You must always show concern and respect for a client's dignity.

43. The correct answer is (A). The Foster case history shows the date of the history to be January 25, 2004. It also states that Joan was hyperactive and not developing normally and that she was born on October 14, 2000, and, therefore, 3 years old.

44. The correct answer is (A). The data presented in choices (B), (C), and (D) all appear in the Foster case history.

45. The correct answer is (C). Choice (A) is incorrect since the form is not *just* about the family composition but is rather about the Foster case history. Choice (B) is incorrect since it only indicates the date the form was revised. Choice (D) tells you the family's case type and number (Aid to Dependent Children – 3415968). The correct answer is the form number, i.e., Form W-341-C.

answers

46. The correct answer is (B). The case history clearly states that the housekeeper's service will relieve Mrs. Foster of basic housekeeping chores since she has multiple sclerosis and her capacity to manage both a household and 4 children is "severely limited."

47. The correct answer is (D). Everyone has the right to reapply for services if their application was previously denied. But since you just interviewed the applicant the day before, you should inform your colleague.

48. The correct answer is (D). You have the ability to notify Ms. Marcus in person or by mail a day or more after her application is accepted or rejected. This may lessen the chances of having a disruptive scene at your center. The applicant may always come back, but notifying her by mail gives her an opportunity to calm down before she comes back.

49. The correct answer is (D). Try to locate a staff member who speaks French. Since you have no knowledge of this language, you cannot go forward without a translator. If there is no one on staff who can speak French, then you must ask her to return with a translator.

50. The correct answer is (A). The situation is a familiar one to seasoned eligibility specialists and you must be prepared to deal with it. As an eligibility specialist, you are bound to consider only the facts of the case and the rules concerning the initial granting and continuation of public assistance. You must relay this to the client in a manner that will convince her that you are treating her under the same rules and regulations as every other eligibility specialist in the agency would, and ask her to continue the interview.

51. The correct answer is (C). The only possible answer that will provide a good reason for the emergency grant is that the family has no place to live. Choices (A) and (B) are irrelevant, and choice (D) refers only to the type of dwelling that may be needed, not to the reason for the grant.

52. The correct answer is (C). Written communication from a friend or relative is not good verification of the fire, nor is a photograph that could be of another building or of a prior time, or shows only prior destruction. The best verification, of the choices given, is a dated newspaper that describes the extent of the fire.

53. The correct answer is (B). You know that there are 2 adults and 4 children in the family, so a five-room apartment would be the most suitable one. You also know that Mrs. Smith has a heart murmur, so a ground-floor apartment would be most appropriate. Choice (A) is not appropriate because although there might be a room suitable to be used for a third bedroom, Mrs. Smith would have to walk up a flight of stairs.

54. The correct answer is (B). The data given tells you that the Smiths are requesting emergency money for food and clothing.

55. The correct answer is (C). The best summary of your actions is the one that indicates the solutions you effectuated in response to the requests made. In this instance, these would be the temporary housing arrangement you made and the amount of the emergency grant you requested and for which you obtained approval.

56. The correct answer is (B). Mr. Wu may feel as though you are not listening to him. There are times in your interview that it is important for you to concentrate on what is being said, rather than just recording the interview. This is a challenging skill that is important to learn.

57. **The correct answer is (A).** It is most important that the eligibility specialist be aware of the situation and the problems in a case *before* interviewing the applicant so that the interview can focus on these problems. In addition, the worker can spot confusing contradictions and points needing further clarification that must be handled in order to establish eligibility.

58. **The correct answer is (B).** *Incapacitated* is defined as "to deprive of capacity or natural power; disable."

59. **The correct answer is (B).** *Compulsory* is defined as "mandatory; enforced."

60. **The correct answer is (D).** *Jeopardize* is defined as "to expose to danger or risk."

61. **The correct answer is (C).** The passage tells you that the Smith family has lived in the apartment since July 18, 2000, which is the occupancy date. Note: The passage also alerts you to a two-year lease on July 18, 2004, but that is *not* the information called for in the box "Occupancy Date" on the sample form.

62. **The correct answer is (A).** The form is a request for approval of exception to policy for shelter allowance. Therefore, the amount to be put in the box "Rent per Month" is $250, which is the desired rent.

63. **The correct answer is (C).** The form has space to indicate "Apartment No. or Location," but this information is not given to you in the passage.

64. **The correct answer is (A).** The passage tells you that Mr. Smith is the case head since he applied for "self and family." Helen Smith is the *wife* in the Smith case, and the word wife should be indicated in column 4, "Relationship to Case Head."

65. **The correct answer is (C).** Step 1: Add the first five numbers = 237.27. Step 2: Add 60.54 and 10.56 = 71.10. Step 3: 237.27 − 71.10 = 166.17.

66. **The correct answer is (A).** Step 1: Add the first four numbers = 5,099.96. Step 2: Add the second set of four numbers = 3,987.13. Step 3: 5,099.96 − 3,987.13 = 1,112.83.

67. **The correct answer is (D).** Step 1: Multiply $1,850 \times .05 = 92.50$. Step 2: Multiply $3,300 \times .08 = 264.00$. Step 3: $92.50 + 264.00 = 356.50$.

68. **The correct answer is (D).** Step 1: Multiply $312.77 \times .04 = 12.5108$. Step 2: Rule for rounding off numbers to the nearest hundredths (two places after the decimal point): If the third number after the decimal point is 5 or more, change the second number after the decimal point to the next-higher number. If the third number is less than 5, disregard it. Step 3: $12.5108 = 12.51$.

69. **The correct answer is (C).** Step 1: $362.05 + 91.13 + 347.81 + 17.46 = 818.45$. Step 2: $818.45 \div 6 = 136.408$. Step 3: $136.408 = 136.41$.

70. **The correct answer is (B).** Step 1: $66.25 + 15.06 = 81.31$. Step 2: $81.31 \times 2\frac{1}{6} = 81.31 \times \frac{13}{6} = \frac{1,057.03}{6} = 176.17$.

71. **The correct answer is (B).** $\frac{1}{4} = \frac{25}{100} = \frac{250}{1,000} = \frac{2,500}{10,000}$. A zero added at the end of a decimal number does not change the value of the number.

72. **The correct answer is (D).** Step 1: 539.84 + 479.26 = 1,019.10 ÷ 2 = 509.55. Step 2: 1,461.93 + 927.27 = 2,389.20 ÷ 3 = 796.40. Step 3: 509.55 + 796.40 = 1,305.95. Step 4: To round off a decimal to the nearest whole number: If the number after the decimal point is 5 or more, add 1 to the number just before the decimal point, e.g., 1,305.95 = 1,306.

73. **The correct answer is (A).** Step 1: $5906.09 × .15 = $885.90. Step 2: $885.90 ÷ 3 = $295.30.

74. **The correct answer is (B).** The passage covers various techniques involved in good interviewing procedures. The title should therefore indicate the overall nature of the passage, and choice (B) indicates this generalized nature. The other answer choices give only individual techniques.

75. **The correct answer is (D).** The passage clearly indicates that the interviewer should begin with a discussion about matters that are "easy to talk about and not threatening." The passage does not convey the advice given in any of the wrong answers.

76. **The correct answer is (C).** The passage clearly states that the interviewer should "get the interviewee to talk freely with as little prodding from you as possible." This is exactly what choice (C) states. The statements in the other answer choices cannot be found in or inferred from the passage.

77. **The correct answer is (B).** The word *unhampered* in the last sentence of the fourth paragraph of the passage can be replaced by the word *unobstructed*.

78. **The correct answer is (B).** None of the statements in the other answer choices can be inferred from the passage. The statement that some interview methods are better than others for obtaining information, as in choice (B), *can* be inferred because the entire passage is providing you with what the author considers to be the best methods of obtaining information.

79. **The correct answer is (A).** You must cancel the interview with Mr. Gomez and reschedule for another time because the information that he will be providing will not necessarily be accurate. In addition, he may not be coherent.

80. **The correct answer is (D).** Be compassionate and proceed when Mr. Francis is ready to continue the interview. As an eligibility specialist, your primary function is to help the client. You must maintain your awareness of the client's problems and assist with any help he may need from you. In addition, you can never guarantee a client's eligibility for being approved. Never say that you can get an application approved before you know all the facts in the matter.

81. **The correct answer is (C).** The family budget is used to determine the wants of the families and the amount of assistance that is required to address these needs. This is the budget for the family in concrete numbers, which provides that the basic needs of a family are met.

82. **The correct answer is (B).** The passage emphasizes that long-term residence in a shelter is detrimental to a family's well-being. Immediate steps should be taken to find more suitable permanent housing for the family. In the situation presented, the shelter is designed only as temporary housing and does not allow for permanent residence.

83. **The correct answer is (C).** The passage emphasizes that one tends to lose his or her ability to take independent action after being housed in a municipal shelter for a long period of time.

84. **The correct answer is (D).** Based on the facts presented in the preamble of the question and the reasoning contained in the passage, it would be good social work practice to allow the rent increase to be paid by the municipality.

85. **The correct answer is (C).** The passage indicates that this is a common belief. The information in the other choices may or may not be true. However, they cannot be given serious consideration because they are not contained in the passage.

86. **The correct answer is (D).** Refer to the final sentence of the passage.

87. **The correct answer is (C).** Remember that you must answer based only on the information contained in the passage. The problem of children not attending school regularly is a fact stated in the passage. The other choices contain information and facts that are not referred to in the passage.

88. **The correct answer is (D).** This fact is stated in the passage, and you should make every effort to convince the mother of it.

89. **The correct answer is (C).** By asking the family how they are coping with Cecile's illness and informing them that HIV is not contracted by casual contact with relatives, you are providing the family with much needed education.

90. **The correct answer is (B).** This statement implies that concrete information is beneficial in decreasing the spread of HIV.

APPENDIX

Glossary

Glossary

A

Abandoned child: A child under the age of 16 who is abandoned or deserted in any place by both parents, or by the parent having its custody, or by any other person or persons, lawfully charged with its care or custody, and left (a) in destitute circumstances; (b) without proper food, shelter, or clothing; or (c) without being visited or having payments made toward his or her support for a period of at least one year by his or her parent, guardian, or lawful custodian without good reason.

Active case: A case receiving public assistance.

Adoption: A legal proceeding in which an adult person takes another adult or a minor into the relationship of child and thereby acquires the rights and incurs the responsibilities of parent with respect to the adopted person. The adoption process is controlled by laws that protect the child, natural parents, and adoptive parents. Two types of adoption are recognized in the law: voluntary adoption and adoption through an authorized agency.

Ambivalence: A set of mixed feelings about a person, a problem, or an issue.

Applicant: A person who is applying for public assistance and care, either directly or through a representative.

Application form: A form required by the local and/or state and federal agencies responsible for providing public assistance to be filled in by applicants for such assistance. It is the applicant's statement of pertinent facts and is used in helping determine his or her potential eligibility for financial assistance.

Application rejected: A statistical definition used by many public assistance agencies denoting that an application for public assistance has been rejected at the time of the initial interview without further investigation.

Assignment: A transfer to another of any property, real or personal, in possession or in action; or of any estate or right therein.

Authorization form (regular): Used to authorize assistance for two or more issues of a recurring allowance, to a maximum of six monthly issues, for all types of assistance.

appendix

Authorized agency: Any agency, corporation, institution, or other organization that is incorporated or organized under the laws of the state with corporate power or empowered by law to care for, to place out, or to board out children; and that actually has its place of business in this state and is approved, visited, inspected, and supervised by the State Board of Social Welfare; or that submits and consents to the approval, visitation, inspection, and supervision of the Board as to any and all acts in relation to the welfare of children.

B

Basic case name and number: The name and case number of the eligible payee designated as the responsible head in either a single case or a composite case.

Basic case record: The case folder maintained either for a case consisting of one eligible payee (single case) or for a case consisting of two or more eligible payees (composite case) where members of the household are budgeted together as a family unit.

Board out: To arrange for the care of a child in a family other than that of a relative within the second degree of the parents of such child where payment is made or agreed to be made for care and maintenance.

Boarder: A person who receives and pays for meals in a client's home but does not reside with the client or pay rent.

Boarder-lodger: A person who lives in the home of a client and receives meals there and pays for rent and board.

Budget deficit: The difference between those items in the budget that are required by individuals or families and the income or other resources in cash or in kind available to such individuals or families to meet these needs. The amount of the regular recurring grant is the budget deficit.

C

Case closed: A statistical definition denoting that public assistance has been terminated.

Case number: The serial number assigned to a public assistance case. The case number includes a prefix, the abbreviation of the type of assistance; and the suffix, the abbreviation of the form of charge; e.g., AB 100001 LC; OAA 214032 PSC.

Case record: A folder containing application form, face sheet, verification sheet when applicable, recorded material, and other pertinent material, including required forms and correspondence (sometimes called "case folder").

Caseload: The total number of cases assigned to 1 worker.

Child welfare: A field of practice in case work where the concern is the protection and strengthening of families.

Client (recipient): A person in receipt of public assistance and care.

Collateral visits: Visits to relatives, friends, former employers, landlords, etc., for the purpose of verifying information given by the applicant or client for establishing initial or continuing eligibility for public assistance.

Composite case: The case of a family group in which there is more than 1 eligible payee.

Cooperative cases: Cases that are jointly carried by the department and private agencies.

Correctional institution: A prison or other institution for the confinement of persons legally committed because of violation of the penal law.

Cost containment: Efforts on the part of administration to reduce the cost of services.

Cross-reference case and number: The name and case number of a basic case whose record contains pertinent information and documentation concerning individuals included in another basic case.

D

Delinquent child: A child over 7 and under 16 years of age who violates any law or municipal ordinance; or who commits any act, which, if committed by an adult, would be a crime.

Dependent child: A child who is in the custody of, or wholly or partly maintained by, an authorized agency, institution, or other organization of charitable, correctional, or reformatory character.

Destitute child: A child under the age of 6 who, through no neglect on the part of its parent, guardian, or custodian, is needy or homeless, or in a state of want or suffering due to lack of sufficient food, clothing, shelter, or medical or surgical care.

Direct grant: An allowance given directly to a client either by cash or check.

E

Eligible payee: The person designated to receive a public assistance check.

F

Fair hearing: If requested by the applicant or client and considered necessary by the State Department, that department will conduct a fair hearing. The commissioner of social welfare designates a referee to conduct the hearing. This designee is empowered to subpoena witnesses, administer oaths, take testimony, and compel the production of all records relevant to the hearing. Hearings are private and open only to interested parties, witnesses, counsel, and representatives of the state department of social welfare and the department of welfare. The proceedings and testimony are recorded. The referee transmits his or her findings to the commissioner of social welfare who renders the decision on the case. This decision is binding upon the department of welfare and the public welfare officials involved must comply.

Family home (for adults): Home of a relative or close friend in which a client resides and where the arrangement for board and care is not a commercial one. Ordinarily, payment would not exceed cost of food and shelter—i.e., there would be no charge for service and no element of profit.

Federal participation: That part of the total grant on which the federal government reimburses the state.

Forms of charge: LC—Local Charge; PCS—Presumptive State Charge.

Foster care: Care of a destitute, neglected, or delinquent child in an institution or a home other than that of the child's parents designated by an agency.

Foundling: A deserted infant whose parents are unknown.

G

Geographic caseload: A caseload having fixed territorial boundaries.

Guardian: One who legally has the care and management of the person, the estate, or both, of a child during its minority.

I

Indirect grant: An allowance made payable to a third party for goods or services provided to a client.

Intake worker: A worker who usually makes the first contact with a client and conducts some form of assessment of suitability for services.

L

LIAB: An abbreviation for the Life Insurance Adjustment Bureau, which is a service organized by the Metropolitan, Prudential, and John Hancock life insurance companies for the purpose of advising all public and private social agencies in the United States in adjusting, serving, and liquidating insurance policies; and assisting in securing benefits from policies carried by clients.

Lien: A legal claim on property as security for a debt or charge.

Lodger: A person who occupies a room in a client's home and pays rent but prepares meals or eats elsewhere.

M

Mandatory clients: Involuntary clients who are required to engage in services, usually by an agency policy, a court, an employer, or a family member.

Master file: The card system maintained in welfare centers and other public assistance granting divisions where the names of applicants and clients with whom the particular welfare center or division has had any contact are recorded. Its purpose is the proper identification of applicants and clients and prevention of duplication of public assistance.

Model: A representation of reality.

Mortgage: A pledge or security of particular property for the payment of a debt or the performance of some other obligation.

N

Neglected child: A child under the age of 16 who is without proper guardianship; or whose parent, guardian, or person with whom the child lives, by reason of cruelty, mental incapacity, immorality, or depravity is unfit to care properly for such child; or who is under unlawful or improper supervision, care, custody, or restraint by any person, corporation, agency, or other organization; or who wanders about without lawful occupation or restraint; or who is unlawfully kept out of school, or whose parent, guardian, or custodian neglects or refuses, when able to do so, to provide necessary medical, surgical, institutional, or hospital care for such child; or who is found in any place that is in violation of the law; or who is in such condition of want or suffering, or is under such improper guardianship or control, as to injure or endanger the morals or health of the child or other.

Nongeographic caseload: A caseload without territorial boundaries within the territory covered by the case unit (partially nongeographic caseload); or within the territory covered by the welfare center (totally nongeographic caseload).

Nonrecurring expenditures or grant (special grant): A special allowance granted, when necessary, to meet a specific need as it arises.

Nonreimbursable: Used for any item for which the City of New York bears the total cost and does not receive reimbursement from the state department of social welfare.

Norms: The rules of behavior that are generally accepted by the dominant group in society.

Not accepted: A statistical definition denoting that, after field investigation of an application for public assistance, a determination has been made that the applicant is ineligible.

O

Other eligible payee (only in composite case): Eligible payees other than the responsible head.

P

Pending case: A statistical definition denoting that an application for public assistance is under field investigation but no decision to accept or reject has yet been reached.

Petitioner: A complainant in a legal action.

Physically handicapped child: A person under 21 years of age who, by reason of physical defect or infirmity, whether congenital or acquired by accident, injury, or disease, is or may be expected to be totally to partially incapacitated for education or for remunerative occupation. "Physically handicapped child" does not include the deaf and the blind.

Private home for the aged: A not-for-profit institution caring for the aged that is incorporated and approved and inspected by the state department of social welfare.

Private nursing home: A home that is privately owned and operated for profit and offers board, room, and bedside care for compensation to persons 16 years of age and over. All private nursing homes are inspected and licensed and, if approved, a certificate is issued stating the maximum bed capacity, such certification being valid for only one year.

Proration: The method used to calculate the amount of the recurring grant if it is to be issued for a period other than the regular payment period.

Public assistance roll: Used by the disbursing section of the division of accounting to record the public assistance checks prepared in accordance with the authorization of the welfare center or division.

R

Rapport: An element of the working relationship where the client senses that he or she gets along well with the worker.

Readjustment (of cases): The reallocation of individual caseloads within a case unit, where caseloads are maintained on a nongeographic basis, with no resultant change in the total number of caseloads in the case unit.

Realignment: A general reallocation of the cases of an office resulting in an increase or decrease in the total number of caseloads or case units. The change may involve all of the territory administered (total) or a portion thereof (partial).

Reapplicant: An applicant who has previously applied to the department for public assistance.

Reassignment (of cases): The temporary allocation of cases of an uncovered caseload, without statistical transfer, to other caseloads in the same unit in order to provide coverage for all cases administered. A caseload is considered uncovered when no investigator has been assigned to it, or when the investigator formerly assigned has been absent from the assignment for any reason for any period in excess of thirty days.

Rebudgeting: Recomputation of each item of the budget as required when there is a change in the family situation involving needs or income, or whenever the budget schedules of the department are revised.

Reclassification: The action taken when an active case receiving one type of assistance is found eligible for another type of public assistance, when it is necessary to change the form of charge, or a combination of the two. Portions of one case may be reclassified from one type of assistance to one or more types of public assistance. Pending cases may be reclassified, when necessary, at the point of acceptance.

Redelivery: The action taken when a public assistance check returned undelivered by the United States Postal Service is delivered to the client personally either in the welfare center or in his or her home.

Redistribution: The reallocation of cases of individual caseloads within a case unit, where the caseloads and case unit are maintained on a geographic basis, resulting in changes in the caseload boundaries but with no change in the total number of caseloads in the case unit.

Reimbursable: Used for any expenditure for which part or all of the amount is repaid to the city by the state, by the federal government through the state, or both.

Residence club and residence center: Congregate living arrangements providing private rooms and common dining room facilities for persons needing protective care and desiring social contacts.

Resistance: Behavior on the client's part that appears to oppose the worker's efforts to deal with the client's problems. This is usually a sign of the client's pain associated with the work.

Respondent: A person in a legal proceeding who occupies the position of a defendant.

Responsible head: In a single case, the responsible head is the eligible payee. When both the husband and the wife are designated as eligible payees, the husband is the responsible head. In a composite case, the responsible head is the eligible payee who takes primary responsibility for the family group.

Restricted payment: A payment made to a third party for goods or service provided to a client or a grant or allowance given to a client with instructions that it be used for a specific purpose.

S

Self-determination: Recognizing the rights and needs of clients to make their own choices.

Service interview: An interview with a client in the service section of the intake unit regarding information submitted by the client, requests for assistance or services, complaints, or inquiries.

Single case: The case of an individual or family group in which there is only 1 eligible payee.

Single issue authorization form: Form used to authorize assistance for only one issue, for any and all items included in the budget or any single item not part of the regular budget, for a new or reopened case; for any single item that is in addition to the items included in the previous authorization; or for the replacement of a lost, stolen, or destroyed public assistance check or the proceeds thereof; or when the duplication of an allowance is necessary; or for any or all items included in the budget for under-care cases when the current department policy prohibits the authorization of an allowance for two or more issues.

Skill: Specific behaviors on the part of the worker that are used in the implementation of the case work function.

SSE: An abbreviation for Social Service Exchange. The Social Service Exchange is operated by the Welfare Council of New York and serves as a central registration and clearance agency for public and private social agencies. Member agencies register their cases and agree to furnish information from their records to other member agencies. This system provides for exchange of information between agencies and reduces the possibility of duplication of assistance and services by different agencies. Member agencies pay for each clearance and registration.

Status: Statistical classification of a case; i.e., pending, active, closed.

Stop authorization form: Form used to stop the issuance of public assistance for a particular case as of the date indicated on the form.

Supplementation (supplementary assistance): Term used when the department contributes only part of the total needs if there is outside income or contributions from relatives or other persons or agencies.

T

Temporary care: Care of a destitute or neglected child in an institution for a period less than three months.

V

Values: The customs, standards of conduct, and principles considered desirable by a culture, a group of people, or an individual.

Vulnerable: A term that describes a client who is exposed to the impact of oppression and stressful life events because of personal or social factors.

NOTES

ResumeEdge.com™

1-888-GET-AN-EDGE

You only have one chance to make a good first impression. So why leave your resume to chance?

Get a Job-Winning Resume at ResumeEdge.com

Our hand-picked team of certified professional resume writers have helped thousands of satisfied clients create powerful, distinctive resumes and land jobs with the nation's top employers in more than 40 industries.

Let our experts help you get your foot in the door. Visit **ResumeEdge.com** today to put our expert resume writers to work for you.

"Specializing in High-Impact Resumes for Executives and Professionals"

—The *Wall Street Journal's* CareerJournal

RE2006